Greetings Dear Reader,

The Oneida people have passed down from generation to generation their crucial role in the American Revolution. They will always remember the devotion and bravery of Han Yerry, his wife, and his son in the midst of the Battle of Oriskany, the bloodiest battle of the Revolution; and the selflessness of Polly Cooper, who accompanied an Oneida contingent bringing desperately needed Indian corn to General Washington's starving troops at Valley Forge. She cooked and cared for those same soldiers while refusing payment offered to her. Imbued in our memory are the inspiring words of our Oneida sachem Ojistalak, who declared our Nation's "unalterable resolution . . . to hold fast the Covenant Chain of friendship and with you be buried in the same grave or share the fruits of victory and peace."

Our elders have tenderly passed down these memories to us, and, like the generations before them, were taught them from their grandmothers and grandfathers. Our oral history is replete with these tales of courage and sacrifice, determination and principle, from the time of the birth of this nation, which are unknown to most of America.

Within these pages, these stories begin to take their proper place in United States history and in the composition of the American identity. Professors Glatthaar and Martin have reached into the mists of time to reveal, in brilliant historical color and vibrant detail, what many historians had not written: that, in their time of greatest need, the champions of freedom on these shores found their first and staunchest allies in the Indian nation known as the People of the Standing Stone (Onyota'ak:a̱:)—the Oneida Indian Nation.

We hope that you will be inspired by and share the honor we have in the legacy of our Oneida people in the creation of these United States and thus ensure that their sacrifice for this nation is never forgotten.

Nʌ ki² wa,

Ray Halbritter
Nation Representative

Also by Joseph T. Glatthaar and James Kirby Martin

Joseph T. Glatthaar

Leaders of the Lost Cause: New Perspectives on the Confederate High Command (coeditor, 2004)

The American Civil War: This Mighty Scourge of War (coauthor, 2003)

The American Civil War: The War in the West, 1863–1865 (2001)

Partners in Command: The Relationships Between Leaders in the Civil War (1994)

Forged in Battle: The Civil War Alliance of Black Soldiers and White Officers (1990)

The March to the Sea and Beyond: Sherman's Troops in the Savannah and Carolinas Campaign (1985)

James Kirby Martin

A Respectable Army: The Military Origins of the Republic, 1763–1789 (coauthor, 1982, 2006)

America and Its Peoples: A Mosaic in the Making (coauthor, 1989, 2004)

Ordinary Courage: The Revolutionary War Adventures of Joseph Plumb Martin (editor, 1993, 1999)

Benedict Arnold, Revolutionary Hero: An American Warrior Reconsidered (1997)

Drinking in America: A History, 1620–1980 (coauthor, 1982; expanded edition, 1987)

Citizen Soldier: The Revolutionary War Journal of Joseph Bloomfield (coeditor, 1982)

The American Revolution: Whose Revolution? (coeditor, 1977, 1981)

In the Course of Human Events: An Interpretive Exploration of the American Revolution (1979)

Interpreting Colonial America: Selected Readings (editor, 1973, 1978)

The Human Dimensions of Nation Making: Essays on Colonial and Revolutionary America (editor, 1976)

Men in Rebellion: Higher Governmental Leaders and the Coming of the American Revolution (1973)

Forgotten Allies

Forgotten Allies

THE ONEIDA INDIANS AND

THE AMERICAN REVOLUTION

JOSEPH T. GLATTHAAR

and JAMES KIRBY MARTIN

Hill and Wang

A division of Farrar, Straus and Giroux

New York

Hill and Wang
A division of Farrar, Straus and Giroux
19 Union Square West, New York 10003

Distributed in Canada by Douglas & McIntyre Ltd.
Printed in the United States of America
First edition, 2006

Library of Congress Cataloging-in-Publication Data
Glatthaar, Joseph T., 1956–
    Forgotten allies : the Oneida Indians and the American revolution / Joseph T.
Glatthaar, James Kirby Martin.—1st ed.
        p. cm.
    Includes bibliographical references and index.
    ISBN-13: 978-0-8090-4601-0 (hardcover : alk. paper)
    ISBN-10: 0-8090-4601-6 (hardcover : alk. paper)
    1. Oneida Indians—History—18th century.   2. Oneida Indians—Wars.
3. Oneida Indians—Politics and government.   4. Indians of North America—
History—Revolution, 1775–1783.   5. United States—History—Revolution,
1775–1783.   I. Martin, James Kirby, 1943–   II. Title.

    E99.O45G54 2006
    973.3089′975543—dc22

                                                        2006002369

Designed by Jonathan D. Lippincott

www.fsgbooks.com

10 9 8 7 6 5 4 3 2 1

FRONTISPIECE: This spectacular bronze statue, bearing the description "Allies in War, Partners in Peace," depicts two Oneidas, Chief Skenandoah and Polly Cooper, standing with General George Washington, at the time of Valley Forge. Polly carries a basket full of corn for the hungry Continental soldiers, and Skenandoah represents all the Oneida warriors who fought as rebel allies during the Revolutionary War. The work of artist Edward Hlavka, the statue resides majestically at the Smithsonian Institution's National Museum of the American Indian in Washington, D.C. (Sculpture and photograph by Edward Hlavka)

For
Niels Holch and Wilson J. Hoffman

We have experienced your love, strong as the oak, and your fidelity, unchangeable as truth. . . . While the sun and moon continue to give light to the world, we shall love and respect you. As our trusty friends, we shall protect you; and shall at all times consider your welfare as our own.

> —Pledge by the patriot delegates of the Continental Congress to the Oneida Indians, December 3, 1777

Accept my best thanks for your friendly Care and attention to the Interest of the united States. . . . I have often told you that the conduct which you have held would always entitle you to our Love & Esteem, yet, I repeat it with pleasure and sooner should a fond mother forget her only Son than we shall forget you.

> —Philip Schuyler, Continental Army general and Indian commissioner, message to the Oneida Indians, May 11, 1778

CONTENTS

LIST OF MAPS

Forgotten Allies

PROLOGUE: THE REVOLUTION'S JUBILEE, THE MARQUIS DE LAFAYETTE, AND SELECTIVE HISTORICAL MEMORY

Not yet twenty years old, the Marquis de Lafayette, a starry-eyed member of the French nobility who had volunteered his services for the rebel cause, sailed to North America for the first time in 1777. For this young idealist, the American Revolution represented an opportunity to strike a blow for human liberty, fulfill his desire for personal glory, and secure a measure of revenge against his nation's archrival, Great Britain. The Continental Congress, after much wrangling, had commissioned him a major general, hoping this appointment would further strengthen ties with France and become another reason for that nation to join the rebellious American patriots in a formal military alliance.

George Washington took an instant liking to Lafayette, whose full name was Marie Joseph Paul Yves Roch Gilbert du Motier. Despite Lafayette's youth and inexperience, Washington came to respect his abilities and soon entrusted him with important command responsibilities. Some of these assignments brought Lafayette into contact with members of the Oneida Indian nation, who were also informally allied with and fighting on the side of the American rebels.

In January 1824, nearly forty-one years after the American Revolution officially ended, President James Monroe invited Lafayette to return to his second home, the nation he had helped forge. As part of a number of fiftieth anniversary–related activities, the president, an aging Revolutionary War veteran himself, believed that Lafayette and the peoples of the United States should have one last opportunity to see

each other before the ever-relentless sands of time completely swept
away the hallowed Revolutionary generation.[1]

Always garrulous and charming in his persona but with a tincture of
vanity thrown in, Lafayette gladly accepted Monroe's invitation. With a
small coterie of traveling companions, including his son, George Washington Motier de Lafayette, the marquis arrived in New York City in
mid-August 1824 and began a tour that took him through all twenty-
four states before he sailed home to France in September 1825.

Everywhere Lafayette went, large, enthusiastic crowds welcomed
him. On his first day in New York City, some thirty thousand people
turned out to see the aging hero. So it was at all his appearances.
Crowds cheered him, politicians coddled him, old friends hugged and
cried with him. Three former presidents whom he had known long
ago—John Adams, Thomas Jefferson, and James Madison—hosted
him. Congress voted him the lavish sum of two hundred thousand dollars to recognize his personal sacrifices in fighting to secure America's
liberty and independence.[2]

Once more, it seemed, Lafayette had arrived when the American
people needed him. Divisive politics, especially over slavery, were
pulling the young American nation apart. As the last living Continental
Army major general, Lafayette allowed citizens north and south to put
their differences aside, even if only for a few moments, and harken back
to what some viewed as more purposeful times. In that spirit of selective
nostalgia, the marquis's tour became a celebration of what the young
republic had managed to accomplish, of the sacrifices of Lafayette and
his comrades in arms.[3]

For the people of Utica, New York, and other towns in the western
Mohawk Valley, Lafayette's visit to their region was a great honor. Even
though the citizens of Utica would have only a few hours with him,
they were anxious to show off their vibrant young community. They appointed a blue-ribbon committee to plan a celebration, particularly to
ensure wide exposure to civic leaders, veterans, and private citizens.[4]

On the morning of June 10, 1825, a large contingent from Utica
greeted the French hero at the small hamlet of Oriskany, a short distance to the northwest and the site of an Oneida village destroyed during the Revolutionary War. Stepping into an open carriage, the smiling
Lafayette took his seat next to committee chairman Judge Nathan

Williams. Following them in a lengthy procession in carriages and on horseback were prominent guests, blue-ribbon committee members, militiamen, and private citizens. People lined the route to offer welcoming cheers and then joined the convoy. When the marquis reached Utica's boundary, the reverberating sounds of a twenty-four-gun salute echoed through the community. The cavalcade turned onto Lafayette Street, where an assemblage of soldiers, including Revolutionary War veterans, grandly saluted the marquis. On a bridge over the Erie Canal, the local populace had constructed an arch with a flag that read, LAFAYETTE, THE APOSTLE OF LIBERTY, WE HAIL THEE — WELCOME![5]

The column halted in front of the Shepard Hotel, where the mayor of Utica delivered some effusive remarks. Lafayette responded with his usual grace. Then he greeted "an immense number of gentlemen of the county of Oneida and the vicinity," and "in one of the most solemn and affecting scenes," some Revolutionary War veterans stepped forward to speak with him. A few the old general recognized. The men eventually yielded so that the women would have a chance to meet this legendary hero.[6]

While Lafayette mingled with the citizens of Utica, a thought kept bothering him. Some persons were missing. He had visited Rome, then Oriskany, and now Utica, but he had not seen any of his Oneida Indian comrades from the days of the conflict, even though these towns were in the locale of what had once been the Oneida homeland. Finally, Lafayette wondered aloud to his hosts. He wanted to know if any Oneidas still resided in the area and if he might have the opportunity to visit with them.

Lafayette's request caught his hosts by surprise. Many of them were too young to know the Revolution intimately, even if they had heard stories about the Oneidas fighting in conjunction with the rebels during the war. The aging veterans, however, knew better, but by virtue of their selective memories about events long since past, they had more or less divested their minds of Oneida involvement, let alone contributions. The marquis had not.[7]

Lafayette asked if someone among his large throng of Utica admirers could take action so that he might spend at least a few moments conversing with these forgotten allies . . .

1

THE PEOPLE OF
THE STANDING STONE

They called themselves Onyotaʼa:ká:. Early Dutch settlers referred to them as either *Maquas*, the same term settlers used for neighboring Mohawk Indians, or *Sinnekens*, a composite word for various Native Americans living west of the Mohawks and later applied to the largest of those tribes, the Senecas—all of them members of the Iroquois Confederacy. The French who penetrated up the St. Lawrence River and into the Great Lakes opted for the expression *Onneiouts*, a derivation of the Huron name for them. In time, English settlers tinkered with both and came up with the word *Oneidas*.[1]

The image of the name Onyotaʼa:ká:, or "People of the Standing Stone," conveyed the impression of endurance and permanence. Like the boulder that weathers nature's storms century after century, the Oneidas possessed a lasting character, even in seasons of hardship. They perceived themselves as a bastion of stability amid ever-swirling gusts of change, known for constancy and reliability.

The Oneidas drew from this stone insights into the flow of human existence. Because they believed beings from the spirit world imbued all objects, the concept of the standing stone provided a nexus between ancestors gone by and descendants to come, always reminding the Oneidas to draw from the past in order to confront the present and boldly envision the future. Generations came and went; the boulder defied the limitations of time.[2]

Along with the rock's symbolism, the tradition of storytelling served succeeding generations of Oneidas, becoming a vital link from the past to the present and into the future. After the first hard freeze each autumn, the Oneidas gathered night after night to listen to the retelling of their Creation Narrative and other sacred stories. A few specially selected individuals, identified in their youth for keen intelligence and sharp memories and then trained at great length by their elders, were keepers of this flame. The patriarchs emphasized the importance of accurate content and precise details, since the stories not only preserved the Oneidas' heritage but also offered guideposts for their way of life. Individual expression for these "historians" lay in the style of their presentation, their intonation of particular words or passages, and their ability to connect one saga component to the next.[3]

The Creation Narrative, which all Iroquois nations shared, represents a richly nuanced saga about the struggle between good and evil. The story begins with a village in the Sky World consisting of single-family bark houses and focuses on a female known as Sky Woman. Through magical means, she becomes pregnant. Her jealous husband fumes with suspicion, and in a rage he shoves her down a hole in the ground. As Sky Woman plummets through the air, some birds catch her. Other animals plaster mud on the back of a turtle, and the birds place Sky Woman there. As she walks about, soil grows on the turtle's back, creating Earth.[4]

Sky Woman gives birth to a daughter. In the fullness of time, the daughter comes of age and begins entertaining suitors. None interests her except for one, whom she marries. Her husband turns out to be the turtle in disguise. She soon becomes pregnant with twins. In their mother's womb, the twins argue over how to enter the world. One child, the Good Twin, called Skyholder, comes into the world in the conventional manner, but the Evil Twin bursts through his mother's side, killing her. The Evil Twin then convinces his grandmother, Sky Woman, that his brother was responsible for their mother's death. In her grief, Sky Woman banishes her good grandson, Skyholder.

Fortunately for Skyholder, his father rescues him. As a dutiful parent, Turtle instructs him in how to use his magical powers for good and to create wonderful things, including human beings. His brother and grandmother, however, undo this work by inventing dangerous animals, virulent diseases, killing frosts, and treacherous waterfalls to impede travel.

Ultimately, the terrible struggle between good and evil takes place, a titanic contest for supremacy between the twins. Skyholder wins the battle, and as his brother sinks into the earth, he becomes the Evil Spirit. Because Skyholder cannot undo the harmful activities of his brother and grandmother, he instead teaches human beings various ceremonies designed to honor the spirit world and ward off evil.

Before Skyholder finishes his work and enters the spirit world, he completes two more deeds. He joins forces with the animals to pilfer his mother's head from Sky Woman and place it in the sky as the sun. Then, while inspecting his creations, he encounters Hadu?i?, a grotesque hunchback who is the master of the winds and the sponsor of disease. In a contest of power, Skyholder shifts a mountain while holding his breath, which Hadu?i? bet him he could not do. Since Skyholder wins, Hadu?i? must help rid the world of the Evil Twin's monsters and cure disease. Hadu?i? creates the Falseface Society to train individuals to wear a mask and impersonate him to heal illness. In return for his commitment to share his knowledge, tobacco must be continuously offered to Hadu?i?. With Skyholder's work done for the time being, he and Sky Woman ascend into the Sky World, vowing to return at the end of time.[5]

The Creation Narrative offers hints of the world in earlier times. As the Wisconsin glacier receded northward from New York some twelve thousand to fourteen thousand years ago, it left behind a massive sea, Lake Iroquoia, perhaps twice the size of Lake Ontario. Tundra surrounded this lake, and small groups of migratory peoples hunted roaming herds of caribou. Over thousands of years, as the glacier continued to retreat, the water supply to Lake Iroquoia diminished, and its banks contracted. Fresh ground had indeed sprung from the turtle's back. As the weather warmed and the growing season lengthened, the frozen ground melted, and pine forests began to sprout everywhere. Caribou followed the tundra, as did their hunters, who, around nine thousand years ago, left the region in pursuit of their game.[6]

The invasion of the hardwoods commenced around the same time. By about 1000 B.C.E., deciduous timber dominated much of the landscape, with oaks, chestnuts, and poplars taking hold in selected areas. Huge sycamore, walnut, and butternut trees sprouted on islands and some bottomland; hickories, elms, and maples staked claim to many of the more fertile areas; and pines and hemlocks secured sandy, barren spots.

With the hardwoods came an assortment of wild animals, both herbivores and omnivores. Among other species, deer, elk, moose, black bears, and turkeys began to flourish. Human beings in search of game as a stable source of food pressed into the region as well. An abundance of meat, supplemented by fish, berries, fruits, and other plant life, supported the proliferation of a flourishing indigenous human population.[7]

Because much of the available game did not follow substantial migratory patterns, hunters no longer had to travel long distances to obtain meat. Also, by learning to preserve quantities of food underground, the populace could now remain in the same location for longer periods of time. Agricultural techniques relating to the cultivation of corn, beans, and squash developed by around A.D. 1000 and likewise supported the establishment of semipermanent settlements. Known as the "Three Sisters," these crops became a mainstay of life in Iroquoia.

With reliable sources of food, villages started to expand in size and consolidate for defense against unfriendly neighbors. By around A.D. 1100, the various bands inhabiting the region at the time of European contact began to take shape. Tribes formed, and subtle language differences became more pronounced but not so extensive as to prevent verbal communication outside the group. To the east were the Maquas, or Mohawks, the "People of the Flint." Their immediate western neighbors were the Oneidas. Next resided the Onondagas, the "People of the Mountain," then the Cayugas, the "People at the Landing," and finally the Senecas, the "People of the Great Hill."[8]

The Five Nations most likely banded together to form a league sometime during the latter half of the fifteenth century. Initially, their goal was to guarantee peace among themselves by resolving disputes through discussion rather than violent acts. In time, this pact blossomed into an alliance, which enabled them to draw warriors from all five nations during selective crises, thereby harnessing unparalleled strength to conquer their enemies. By confederating, the Five Nations became a powerful and influential indigenous force east of the Mississippi River. Their war parties sometimes ranged as far away as Canada, the Carolinas, and the Great Lakes region.[9]

Iroquois storytellers described the formation of the league as the work of a Mohawk named Deganawi:dah, assisted by an Oneida named Odatshehdeh (Quiver Bearer). During precarious times, Deganawi:dah worked to end strife. First securing the cooperation of his own people, he then traveled to Oneida territory, where he convinced Odatshehdeh to assist him. Odatshehdeh then persuaded his fellow Oneidas to join in the league of peace. In subsequent years, he and Deganawi:dah visited the Onondagas, Cayugas, and Senecas, gaining their consent as well.[10]

The Five Nations assumed the name Hodinonhsyo:ni, translated as "People of the Long House." The term referred to Iroquois dwellings, which provided living quarters for an extended family. Aptly, the phrase imparted an image of the Five Nations as components of a single family of Iroquois peoples combined under an extended roof. English settlers called the Five Nations "Confederates." Thus, the combination of terms resulted in the title Iroquois Confederacy.[11]

With their combined strength, the Five Nations expanded their landholdings over the next couple of centuries. After many wars, they vanquished their neighbors and dominated an area from the Hudson River in the East to Lake Erie in the West, and from the St. Lawrence River and Lake Ontario in Canada southward into modern-day Pennsylvania. In time, the Iroquois also claimed lands out into the Ohio Valley–Great Lakes region and down toward the Chesapeake and Delaware bays.

Each nation had a magnetic attachment with its own territory. As an Oneida sachem named Kanaghwaes explained in the early 1770s, "[t]he Great Spirit gave us our lands." Tribal domains represented the home of passing generations, a region now filled with not only deities but also the spirits of these ancestors. They imbued the trees, the water-

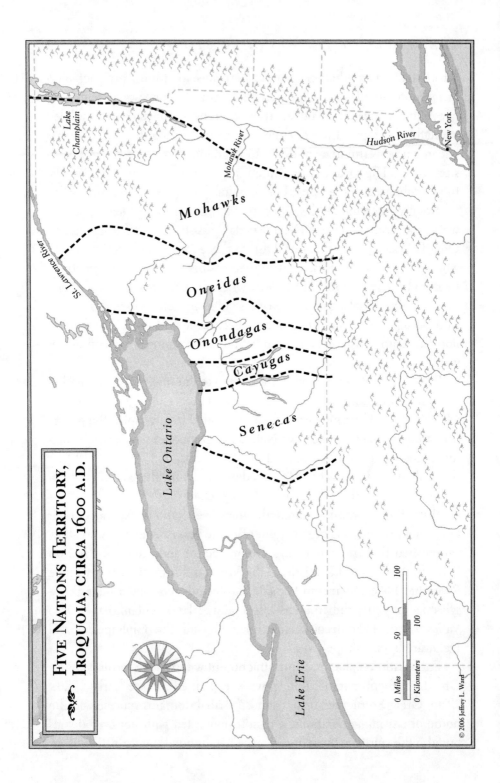

FIVE NATIONS TERRITORY,
IROQUOIA, CIRCA 1600 A.D.

Mohawks

Oneidas

Onondagas

Cayugas

Senecas

Lake Ontario

Lake Erie

Lake Champlain

St. Lawrence River

Mohawk River

Hudson River

New York

0 Miles   50   100

0 Kilometers   100

© 2006 Jeffrey L. Ward

ways, the animals, the sky—all objects, animate and inanimate—with their essence. For the living Oneidas, their homeland served as a kind of longhouse stretching into the past, a spiritual haven for those who had come before and whose flesh was forever gone.[12]

The Oneidas constructed villages and homes for the comfort and security of their people. A Dutch colonist named Harmen Meyndertsz van den Bogaert offered the first recorded description of an Oneida village in December 1634. Van den Bogaert and two comrades trudged from Fort Orange (Albany) through various Mohawk hamlets to the Oneida town. This settlement lived up to the Dutch depiction of Iroquois villages as "castles." (The English employed the same term, which reflected the fortress-like appearance of Iroquois towns.) Communal fields cleared for spring cultivation lay outside a high wooden fence, or palisade, that protected the village. A three-and-a-half-foot opening offered one of only two entries through the two rows of palisades. Above the gateway dangled three scalps, trophies from a recent raid. On the opposite side, another opening through the palisade was about half as wide. In crises, the residents could seal off these gaps quickly.

The village rested on a commanding hill. Van den Bogaert marched 767 paces around the palisade, which meant that nearly 37,000 square yards of land contained the 66 longhouses the Dutch visitor counted. The longhouses, decorated with paintings of animals, consisted of birch and elm bark covering a frame of saplings. They measured up to one hundred feet long and twenty-five feet wide, with high ceilings and removable roof panels to permit smoke to escape and sunlight to illuminate the interior. Inside the longhouses, the Oneidas divided the space into compartments, one for each nuclear family. Family living quarters consisted of platform beds, shelves for storage, and a fireplace.[13]

Every couple of decades, soil depletion, sanitary problems, and insect infestation compelled Oneida villagers to relocate. In 1677, an English observer visited a community of Oneidas and commented that they had recently resettled at a new site, apparently not far from the one van den Bogaert had described four decades earlier. As at the former location, the Oneidas lived in one community containing about one hundred longhouses and a double stockade for defense, "but little ground cleared, so thatt they are forced to send to the Onondagoes to buy corne." During relocation, men selected and designed the site and cut and hauled heavy timber, while women took responsibility for the children and for moving household goods. Both sexes labored at the dismantling of buildings and their reconstruction at the new village.[14]

The longhouse represented much more than a functional shelter. Each one provided living quarters for a family lineage, called an *ohwachira*, the basic unit in the Oneida and Iroquois social structure. An elderly matron almost always headed each family lineage, which consisted of all her direct female descendants and their families. When a man married a woman, he usually moved into a compartment in her longhouse. His wife, her sisters and brothers, and her mother's sisters assumed virtually all the burden of raising his children, which secured strong ties with the lineage. The importance of the mother-daughter relationship remained intact, and powerful bonds also formed between sons and mother's brothers. Usually, the father functioned as an uncle might in most European societies.[15]

Like Skyholder's experience when his grandmother cast him out and Turtle cared for him, the blood father assumed responsibility for the well-being of his sons. A son, likewise, had to fulfill obligations to his father's family. When his father's mother called on him to join a raiding party to alleviate grief over the death of her offspring, Oneida society expected him to participate.

The family lineage established bonds and obligations that lasted for lifetimes. The *ohwachira* offered a communal training ground for the development of such essential skills as hunting and fishing or basket making and cooking, and also socialized individuals in the customs and beliefs of the Iroquois. The lineage resolved feuds and aided the grieving process by seeking various forms of compensation for the loss of loved ones. Within a mother's extended household, a child mastered the art of gift giving and the practice of honoring and respecting other people. The lineage also tutored young people in cross obligations, called reciprocity, such as those duties that sons had in relation to their father's family and that a father's family had in relation to sons.[16]

Lineages served as a fundamental building block for affiliations with clans. According to Iroquois legend, Deganawi:dah explained to Odat-shehdeh that his people had been segmented into three clans—Turtle, Wolf, and Bear—and that each clan consisted of three extended family lineages. Each lineage held a sachem title, making nine in the Mohawk Nation. The Oneidas adopted the same structure. They established three clans—Turtle, Wolf, and Bear—with three extended family lineages composing each clan. As their Mohawk neighbors had done, the Oneidas designated nine hereditary sachemships as civil leaders in tribal affairs.[17]

As with families, clans were matrilineal in organization. At one time, these lineages likely came from the same female ancestor, but after hundreds of years, the Iroquois could no longer track that common connection. Yet clan members still acted as if they were related, when in reality their bloodlines had at best become very diluted.[18]

Clans had several responsibilities. They sponsored all sorts of ceremonial events, from harvest and fishing feasts to funeral rites. They also helped individuals interpret and act out their dreams. Each individual possessed a set of personal names that the clan matron, or head female, controlled. A child would receive an initial name at birth and then a second name at puberty, the latter of which remained with that person for a lifetime.[19]

Even though individuals established powerful ties with their specific clan, most had deep and binding relationships with persons from other clans as well. One of the clan's most important functions was to ensure exogamy—the custom of marrying outside the clan—thereby cementing one clan and lineage with another. In the Oneida Nation, a person from a large family could have a spouse and in-laws from all three clans.[20]

Beyond significant cultural and social functions, clans performed an essential role in the Iroquois political system. The nine hereditary sachems, three from each clan, comprised the Oneida Council, and they also represented the nation in Iroquois League gatherings. The matron of each lineage determined which well-connected male should become a sachem. She then nominated him for a lifetime appointment, subject to recall in rare instances should the matrons disapprove of his performance in office. Once a male was nominated, the other two clans had an opportunity to approve or reject the matron's choice. A successful candidate then required the endorsement of the league.[21]

Family matrons were also central to the process of selecting counselors. They nominated senior males of demonstrated good judgment to help them manage the clan, with all clan members having an opportunity to ratify the choices. Matrons, sachems, counselors, and selected elders met together at the clan council, a deliberative body that handled clan affairs. Usually, they chose one male among the group to serve as head counselor.[22]

Clan warriors, by comparison, designated several persons from their own numbers to serve as chief warriors and represent their interests in tribal deliberations and decision making. Those selected were invariably hunters and fighters of great renown. As time passed, chief warriors started having differences with the sachems and matrons over the handling of tribal affairs, especially in relation to matters involving external enemies and warfare.[23]

Clan councils comprised most of the village council, which addressed community issues. The group gathered frequently to thrash out solutions to all sorts of problems. Since no coercive force punished Oneidas for disobeying the directives, the acceptance of council decisions rested on the strength of the council's ideas and the influence of individual leaders. Each Oneida had the right to form personal opinions. Leaders could win an individual over only by persuasion or by commanding universal respect through other accomplishments, such as military prowess or beneficence in gift giving. Thus, council decisions could be enforced only by the popular support of the community.[24]

Once the Oneidas established more than one village, the nine sachems convened national councils, consisting of the various village councils. These gatherings also lacked coercive force. Just as with local councils, Oneida governmental and social systems succeeded because of popular participation. The national council certainly spoke with some authority out of respect for the sachems, but villages could adopt an independent course when circumstances required.[25]

When village or national councils assembled for treaties, women actively participated. Because the duty of diplomacy rested with males, women could not deliver speeches, but a speaker would convey their opinions for them. Since the Oneidas tried to function by consensus, they forged agreements behind the scenes, where the thoughts of respected matrons weighed heavily. The latter's sentiments, as expressed in debates or occasional signatures on treaties, testified to their power and influence.[26]

The Grand Council of the Iroquois League convened at Onondaga, usually during the autumn season but, when necessary, also at other times of the year. This body's purpose was not governance but rather the resolution of differences among the member nations. Because each nation could act independently, just as villages and individuals had the right to do, the goal was to sustain peace and harmony among the Five Nations based on common cultural values, customs, and traditions.

Based on league tradition, fifty sachems participated in the Grand Council. The Oneidas and Mohawks each held nine seats; the Onondagas fourteen; the Cayugas ten; and the Senecas eight. Despite the disparity in numbers, each nation had only one vote. The intention was to build consensus for united actions; majority rule would not have forged that unanimity. Later, in the early decades of the eighteenth century, colonists drove the Tuscarora Indians from their lands in North Carolina, and the Oneidas invited them to use some of their landholdings. The Tuscaroras then became one of the Six Nations of the Iroquois Confederacy, but they received no League sachemships.

The structure and seating in council reflected the parallel relationships and reciprocal duties that existed at each level, beginning with the nuclear family. The Oneidas and their brother nation, the Cayugas, sat together, forming one moiety, or "side." The Mohawks, Senecas, and Onondagas comprised a second moiety. As the league's administrative head, the Onondagas occupied a position north of the fire, with the Mohawks and Senecas seated across from the Oneidas and Cayugas. In accordance with the Deganawi:dah epic, the Mohawks, Senecas, and Onondagas were the Father's clan, and the Oneidas and Cayugas called them uncles. They, in turn, viewed the Oneidas and Cayugas as off-spring and referred to them as nephews. Only when the Oneidas and Cayugas performed a reciprocal function, such as a condolence cere-mony or the installation of a sachem, did they refer to those of the other moiety as brothers. The Tuscaroras and subordinate nations sat on the Oneida and Cayuga side.[27]

Within the confederacy, all accepted important responsibilities. The two largest nations, the Mohawks and Senecas, controlled the outer extremities of Iroquoia. Mohawks were the keepers of the eastern "door," while Senecas maintained the western "door." The Onondagas, the nation most centrally located, preserved the council fire. Wampum belts created of shells strung together served as the records of various councils. Individuals presented such belts during the course of their speeches to remind others of their words and agreements. The "trea-sury," or league archive, consisted of belts deposited at Onondaga by member nations.[28]

The Oneidas took great pride in their contributions to the league. As one of their leaders stated, he was sure they were "esteemed as hon-orable and important in the confederacy." Although they drew from the smallest population base of the Five Nations, they never shirked their military obligations. The French Jesuit Jacques Bruyas, a missionary during the 1660s and a stern critic of Oneida ways, considered them "the most cruel of all the Iroquois" and an extremely determined foe.[29]

The Oneidas earned respect among their fellow Iroquois for more than martial prowess. Skilled negotiators of good judgment, Oneida leaders were often called on by confederacy members and other peo-ples to mediate disputes. One observer described the Oneidas as "a peo-ple remarkably deliberate in all their proceedings, having no extensive schemes in view, their wants confined within a narrow compass."[30]

In Oneida villages, men and women worked together to sustain life, but with clear divisions of labor. In the Creation Narrative, Sky Woman prepared and hauled the food; her husband furnished the venison. Guided by this example, men hunted, fished, fought wars, and attended councils while women cultivated crops, foraged for fruits and nuts, cooked, collected firewood, and reared children. Females also maintained longhouses and other village buildings, drawing on males only for essential labor. Because of their more demanding workloads and their roles as the bearers of children, the standard rule for taking a woman's life specified that "the atonement should be double that of a man."[31]

Women's agricultural labor produced a variety of dietary mainstays. After clearing acreage by girdling trees and harvesting or burning the dead timber, women ingeniously sowed bean, squash, and pumpkin seeds in the same fields with their corn. The practice maximized the use of space and labor and ensured a more appetizing and healthy mixture of food in the dinner bowl. The bean plants provided protein to complement corn's carbohydrates and also restored nitrogen to the soil, thereby extending the life of any field. Squash and pumpkins offered unique flavor and nutrition.[32]

To supplement food crops, women also harvested apples from groves of trees they had raised from saplings. In early spring, they trapped the oozing sap from maple trees and converted it into a tasty syrup for flavoring. From the forest floor they collected chestnuts, which they roasted over fires or ground down to recover the oil. A variety of berries abounded in the region, especially wild strawberries. Women served these fresh or dried and blended them into their corn porridge. They even gathered selected herbaceous plants and roots, which they boiled for beverages and medicinal concoctions.[33]

Within the fields, women also devoted space to tobacco plants. For the Oneidas, tobacco held a highly valued place. The nation offered tobacco to win favor with Hadu?i? and other supernatural beings, and the narcotic effects of nicotine allowed its users to get in touch more easily with the spirit world.[34]

Fields could remain productive for several years. With seemingly limitless acreage, the Oneidas and fellow Iroquois did little to revive depleted soil. When harvests became too thin, they abandoned old sites and designated fresh ground for cultivation. Nature then launched its own lengthy reclamation process. Shrubs, baby trees, and other undergrowth began to sprout in old fields. This greenery fed deer, elk, and moose, and thereby provided excellent hunting grounds.[35]

Men furnished the fish and animal flesh for family meals. In the spring and fall, migratory salmon packed the creeks and rivers that poured into Oneida Lake. Fishing these same areas year after year, Oneida males developed expertise with nets and spears. An impressed eyewitness commented that "one Oneyda Indian took by aid of his spear 45 within one hour—an other in one night 65—and another 80."[36]

Semi-annual fishing excursions culminated in salmon feasts to celebrate the trips' success and to give thanks to the spirit world for so bounteous a catch. Since the Oneidas lacked an understanding of salting fish for long-term preservation, they ate a portion of their salmon fresh and dried the rest for later consumption, particularly during the cold months before their hunting season.[37]

Late in autumn, the men went into the woods to hunt for meat. Their excursions lasted until the full onset of winter and commenced again in the spring. Armed with bows and arrows, hatchets and knives, and eventually muskets, small parties stalked deer, elk, bears, beavers, and other game, including fowl.

Throughout their youth, Oneida males honed their hunting skills with a variety of weapons. By the time they reached adulthood, most Oneida men were excellent marksmen. If they killed their prey near the village, the men returned home and sent the women out to haul back the carcasses. Social taboos derived from the Creation Narrative discouraged men from carrying dead game when women were available to do so. If the hunters traveled considerable distances from villages, they reluctantly brought the game back themselves.[38]

Once the men returned from their sojourns with the bounty, the women took charge, preparing the meat for consumption and storage and dressing the hides for clothing or trade. Sometimes individuals even wore the hide temporarily to break it in and increase its market value. When European traders appeared across the landscape, the Oneida men assumed responsibility for bartering the hides, usually during late spring and the summer.[39]

Oneidas did not devote all their time to the production of food, shelter, and other essentials. They worked to live, rather than lived to work. "*Time,* the most precious thing in the World," commented a European observer, "is held with them in little estimation." Men loved to engage in sports or just relax around the fire, discussing various issues, or reposing with pipe in hand. Women, too, appreciated leisure moments, despite their disproportionate labor burdens. They enjoyed socializing around the home and attending athletic events.[40]

Food existed for everyone's use. Skyholder had created meats, grains, vegetables, and fruits for all humans to consume, not just favored persons. The fortunate shared with the less fortunate. As such, successful hunters regularly gave meat to less fortunate comrades. The same concept applied to any form of property. So long as individuals were using an item, it belonged to them. When set aside or discarded, anyone could claim it. Stealing, then, was theoretically never necessary.[41]

In traditional Oneida society, the accumulation of material goods was not a personal goal. The obverse was the case. An Oneida male aspired to bring home more meat, fish, and furs so that he could provide for the needs of other persons. From early childhood, all Iroquois learned the art of sharing. The more someone gave, the more the community admired that person. Successful hunters who generated the most meat and goods, and retained the least, gained the community's highest esteem.[42]

Besides hunting and fishing, the task of engaging in combat fell to the men. Warfare was a central element of Oneida history and culture. Like other nations, the Oneidas fought to ward off encroachments on their land, to expand their holdings, and to seize booty (especially valuable furs). Moreover, as with other nations in the Iroquois Confederacy, they adhered to the practice of retaliatory military strikes to help bring closure to the loss of human life and to the grieving process.[43]

The death of individuals did more than reduce the strength of the Oneidas. Because spirits were believed to be present in all things, any fatality caused a disruption in the forces of life and lessened the spiritual might, called *orenda*, of affected maternal lineages, clans, and villages. To restore the lost spiritual power, the Iroquois replaced these people through requickening ceremonies, in which they transferred the name, social duties, and spirit of the deceased person to someone else. Such actions ensured the continuity of life in the community.[44]

The Oneidas practiced a lengthy and complex grieving period, up to a year and sometimes longer. For ten days a family entered into deep mourning, its members disregarding their physical appearance and societal responsibilities. For the rest of the year, they grieved with less intensity. Meanwhile, members of another lineage in an unaffected clan held funeral ceremonies and feasts and offered condolence gifts. A requickening ceremony then completed the grieving process.[45]

Requickening ceremonies served a dual purpose: to bring closure and to restore the damaged *orenda* by reviving the spirit of the deceased in another being. The ceremony also rescued the dead person from the clutches of the Evil Twin by relocating the spirit of the deceased in a living human. A newly selected sachem, if requickened with the spirit of the deceased sachem, could serve with greatly enhanced wisdom at council fires.[46]

In some situations, the Iroquois employed warfare to fulfill the needs of requickening and to conclude the mourning process. Whenever the steps of grieving failed to console the female members of a lineage, they had the right to demand a raid on peoples outside the confederacy to seize captives who could help ease their emotional pain. As a form of atonement for deeply felt grief, the captive might even be killed rather than adopted or requickened into the lineage. However, if a family had no one to become a replacement for the deceased, then its only choice was to kidnap someone from another tribe to serve as the substitute.[47]

Customarily, males from the lineage that had suffered the loss did not participate in the raid. Warriors from other families with ties to the grieving women organized and led the attack. They usually targeted a traditional enemy or people with whom they had recently experienced difficulties. In some instances, Oneidas raised large war parties, with the intention of securing a significant number of captives.

Long-held tribal custom required that eligible males take part in these raids. Oneida boys spent their childhood days in unstructured apprenticeships, preparing themselves for two critical tasks in adulthood: hunting and war making. Since Oneidas defined masculinity according to a man's prowess as a skilled hunter and warrior, adolescent males proved their manhood through their performance in hunting for game or in combat situations. And throughout adulthood, they knew they had to keep renewing their credentials by participating successfully in raiding ventures.

When young men approached fifteen years of age, they underwent a ceremonial rite of passage that admitted them into the warrior brotherhood. Using communal scissors, elders sliced the adolescent's ears into strips and ornamented them with rings of silver, trinkets, and stones. A European observer believed that the rite "originated to demonstrate an indifference to the loss of blood and to suffering." The cutting inflicted so much pain that the boy's "cries were heard at more than a mile's distance." Social influences and communal necessity demanded that virtually all males become warriors.[48]

Even more than expert hunters, great fighters commanded respect and acquired renowned reputations. To preserve their standing in the community, many notable Oneida warriors participated in combat well into their dotage. By contrast, those who performed poorly in martial engagements or who refused to join raiding parties carried the stigma of cowardice, which brought shame to their families.

Before war parties left on missions, villagers celebrated the expeditions by throwing feasts and performing all sorts of rituals. Grief-stricken members from the lineage reminded the warriors of their pain and urged them to bring back captives to ease their suffering. Such communal events helped to bond the village in a collective statement of condolence and reinforced the community's unity in support of the warriors.

Unlike Europeans, Oneidas and their Iroquois brethren rarely fought large-scale battles. In a nation whose total population hovered around 1,200 but dipped as low as 500, and whose number of warriors ranged from approximately 300 to less than 100, the Oneidas could ill afford military disasters. Such losses would expose the People of the Standing Stone to the prospect of tribal extinction. For this reason, among others, including the limited objectives of their raids, they opted for hit-and-run tactics—quick strikes that captured prisoners, seized goods, and perhaps burned down enemy villages.[49]

Early in the seventeenth century, Oneida warriors entered battle with war paint and a form of body armor composed of hemp woven tightly together, a material that could repel stone-headed arrows. The introduction of muskets and metal-tipped arrows rendered such protective gear superfluous. During summers, warriors donned loincloths, moccasins, and feathers. Their weapons included bows and arrows, hatchets, knives, and eventually muskets. Winter campaigns necessitated much heavier clothing and snowshoes.

In most combat situations, the ultimate objective was to seize prisoners. Surprise strikes offered the best opportunity to grab and carry off unsuspecting victims. In larger set-piece battles, warriors advanced and fell back more as a show of force; they were probing enemy weaknesses. Tactically, a warring party much preferred to maneuver its warriors in hopes of isolating a portion of the enemy and compelling them to surrender. Scalps served as a record of those whom they could not bring back, those they injured and killed. Warriors who returned with prisoners won the greatest acclaim for their military performance; scalps rated second best. Village leaders apportioned captives either for execution or for incorporation through requickening, as the clan council and aggrieved family matrons saw fit.[50]

Throughout the seventeenth and eighteenth centuries, pressing population needs convinced the Oneidas to adopt larger and larger numbers of captives. European diseases, to which they, like other Native American peoples, had built up no immunity, took a terrible human toll on the nation. Those deaths, combined with casualties from various wars, compelled the Oneidas not only to replace their extensive losses through requickened captives but also to seek males to live with them from neighboring Iroquois nations.[51]

By the late eighteenth century, full-blooded Oneidas comprised less than a quarter of the nation's population, perhaps no more than 15 to 20 percent. Taking in and adopting strangers from alien cultures and different language groups, they assigned them places in their families, lineages, clans, and communities. Over time, these foreigners by birth learned the new language and accepted Oneida customs. In return, villagers embraced them as members of the Oneida nation. The adoptees might not receive hereditary sachem titles, but they certainly could rise to positions of prominence, particularly as chief warriors and counselors.[52]

What took place among the Oneidas was an extraordinary achievement. Certainly other nations of the Iroquois Confederacy suffered horrible losses from disease and war. As the least populous of the Five Nations, however, the Oneidas struggled with particular difficulty to maintain their identity in the face of so many casualties. The absorption of considerable numbers of outsiders, while also perpetuating tribal customs, beliefs, and practices, demonstrated the resilient texture of the Oneida cultural, social, and political fabric, which stretched but refused to be torn to shreds.[53]

The Oneidas were a people who drew strength from the past to live successfully in the present. Like the standing stone that endured through the centuries, the institutions of the Oneidas promoted continuity and stability of purpose. Still, the Oneida Nation could not magically sidestep the forces of change emanating from European explorers, traders, and, ultimately, colonial settlers. The Europeans brought with them not only killer diseases but also a host of trade goods and an insatiable desire for land. Like other Indian nations, the Oneidas now had to reckon with these ever-aggrandizing strangers from across the ocean—and in ways that would forever alter their lives.

2

EUROPEAN INTRUDERS
AND CONSEQUENCES

On December 11, 1634, a party of three dauntless Dutch adventurers, including the chronicler Harmen Meyndertsz van den Bogaert, departed from Fort Orange, later called Albany. A few Mohawks served as their guides. Buoyed by hopes of establishing trade relations with Indian peoples to the west, van den Bogaert and company plowed through deep snows, waded across icy streams, and endured pounding winter winds. After nearly twenty days of exposure, they approached their destination, a large Oneida village. The inhabitants rushed out to greet these strangers, shouting, *"Saru:'tat! A:'re saru:'tat!"* (Fire! Fire again!). The Europeans pointed their muskets toward the sky and discharged them. A flash of fire anticipated a thunderous boom, and a huge cloud of black smoke belched out of the weapons. The Oneidas continued their chorus while the Europeans reloaded, and then entered through the castle gateway.[1]

Muskets fascinated the Oneidas, who kept asking their Dutch visitors to fire them. The Dutch did so when a chief returned to the community. Late in their stay, after they had received a gift of beaver pelts, they reciprocated by lofting a volley of shots skyward in thanks. And as they left the castle to return to Fort Orange, crowds of Oneidas lined the pathway, once again chanting the familiar phrase, *"A:'re saru:'tat!"* The Dutchmen delivered three rounds as a parting salute, and off they went.[2]

Like Native Americans elsewhere, the Oneidas regarded the European musket as a weapon well worth adding to their arsenal. They watched as Europeans poured gunpowder down the barrel, followed by a rounded lead ball, and packed both down tightly with a ramrod. In a small pan jutting off from the firing mechanism, the user placed some priming powder. When the user pulled the trigger, the hammer pressed a smoldering wick into the powder pan and, with a flash, ignited the powder that caused the explosion. The blast hurled a lead ball through the air, too quickly for the eye to follow. Then, suddenly, an animal some distance away might fall wounded or dead.

From the Oneida perspective, the musket could be used to supplement the bow and arrow in the hunt for game and in warfare with human enemies as well. The lead's penetrating power exceeded that of the stone-headed arrow and could crash through the tightly woven vests that warriors donned for battle. The high velocity of the lead projectile prevented a potential victim from dodging it, as might happen with arrows. The lethal range of muskets, too, might exceed that of the arrow.

The benefits, however, ceased at this point. European matchlocks weighed ten to fifteen pounds, and ammunition was heavy. Many of these weapons were so unwieldy that they required a stand to be fired. Both the accuracy of muskets and their rate of fire were suspect. By the time a musket-wielding individual reloaded, an Indian could aim and shoot a handful of arrows with superior accuracy at several dozen yards. Hasty attempts to reload muskets often resulted in spilled gunpowder, which reduced the speed and penetrating power of the ball. Bows and arrows likewise outperformed muskets in inclement weather. Once dampened, gunpowder lost its combustibility, and strong winds could blow priming powder from the pan.[3]

Still, the musket clearly represented an instrument of potential power in the minds of the Oneidas and their Iroquois brethren. Beyond its capacity for killing, the weapon provided a kind of spectacle. The booming report and the billow of gunpowder had the potential to intimidate enemies. The kick after firing, or recoil, indicated the weapon's sheer strength.

The musket sensation caused almost instantaneous demand. Indians soon began acquiring these weapons, and gunpowder and ammunition, from European traders, although the guns' popularity never

squeezed into obsolescence such traditional Oneida weapons as the
bow and arrow. The high price of firearms, the costliness and uncertain
supply of ammunition, and the weapon's erratic performance all imposed their own checks. Oneidas owned muskets, but these drawbacks
compelled them to maintain their skills with the bow and arrow.[4]

Alcohol, another commodity unfamiliar to the Oneidas and other Native Americans, sparked additional interest in European trade. As with
tobacco, Indians savored the mind-altering sensation that liquor offered, which enabled them to communicate better with the spirits. Frequently, Oneidas imbibed alcohol in groups, a sort of drinking feast
akin to passing the pipe. Potentially ruinous behavior, such as binge
drinking, produced acts of violence, illness, and general mayhem. For
several decades, however, supply shortages placed a check on alcohol's
damaging effects. In time, as supplies became more abundant, tribal
leaders did what they could to limit or cut off consumption, but liquor
became a source of problems among Native Americans almost everywhere.[5]

As they became more heavily involved with European traders, the
Oneidas found various goods that were of better quality than their own.
Europeans forged iron and brass blades that made for sharper, more
durable hand-held weapons and chopping tools than the stone, wood,
and flint versions of the Oneidas. Ceramics and brass kettles and pots
started to replace soapstone vessels and clay pottery. Oneida women
and men began wearing European-made clothing instead of finished
animal hides, and they turned to using European-made needles and
scissors to fashion and maintain the garments.

Virtually everyone among the Oneidas appeared to benefit from
these European products. Supplies never seemed to meet demand,
though; nor did the Indians always have enough trade goods to fulfill
their side of the bartering process.[6]

Initially, despite all the new European commodities, old habits and
patterns persisted. Moreover, Oneida culture was able to absorb the improved technology without suffering serious social or political disloca-
tion. The products made tasks easier, saving time and labor for males

and females, old and young alike. Even alcohol found its place in traditional functions.

Over time, however, as the Oneidas opted for more and more European goods, they lost interest in continuing to produce many items
themselves. Traditional skills fell into disuse, as adults declined to pass
them on to succeeding generations. By the mid-eighteenth century,
other than elm-bark canoes, moccasins, snowshoes, toboggans, and bas-
kets (all superior to their European counterparts), the Oneidas and
their fellow Iroquois had become reliant on trade with Europeans for
all sorts of material goods. The loss of some of their independence left
the Oneidas vulnerable to bad deals. Either they could accept the
traders' prices and related demands, or they would have to do without.[7]

Like native peoples elsewhere, the Oneidas had to find the means to
pay for European products, as they crafted few items the Europeans
wanted. Occasionally, when provisions were short, they traded corn or
other foodstuffs, although the Indians had their own challenges in consistently sustaining their food supplies. What the Oneidas could provide
was what the Dutch (and later English) traders coveted most—beaver
skins. Throughout the seventeenth century, demand soared in Europe
for animal pelts. Although the market slipped somewhat in the eighteenth century, diminishing supplies never exceeded demand. The relentless pursuit of these skins wrought dramatic changes in Oneida
society and politics, especially with regard to traditional hunting patterns and the influence of the sachems and matrons in comparison
with the emerging warrior class, both within and beyond the Oneida
Nation.[8]

Before contact with European traders, the Oneidas and other Iroquois had hunted beavers only during the late autumn and spring
months, when the animals' hides had thickened. They pursued
beavers, along with bears, deer, and elk, because these animals served
as a source of both hides and meat. But, weighing forty to sixty pounds
when fully grown, beavers brought only slight returns to native tribes in
comparison with other animals. Iroquois hunters preferred to stalk
bears and deer, whose meat they preferred, and whose hides proved

more serviceable for clothing. Indians seldom ate any portion of the beaver other than the tail, and it would take a few dozen beavers to equal the amount of meat an Oneida could obtain from a single deer, and even more to equal that from a bear.[9]

European consumers, likewise, had little interest in beaver meat, but they found lush beaver fur coats more appealing than garments made from bear or deer hides. Hats made from beaver fur also became all the rage. The French in Canada and the Dutch at Fort Orange sought all the pelts the Indians could provide, thereby undergirding the lucrative exchange of commodities.[10]

To meet the demand and obtain the goods that their own people desired, Oneida hunters and their Iroquois brethren devoted more and more time to tracking down beavers. Mostly, the Oneidas journeyed north, to areas around Oneida Lake and beyond, where the more fertile, untapped beaver regions lay. Expeditions to these more distant locations often lasted two months or more, and successful hunters returned with forty to eighty hides apiece. In the late 1650s, traders at Fort Orange sent more than forty-five thousand pelts down the Hudson River in a single year.[11]

Most certainly, Iroquois hunters did not seek beavers exclusively during these trips. They also encountered deer, elk, and bears as they scouted creek bottoms and pond- and lakeshores in search of beavers. Still, hunting and trapping beavers was not nearly as labor efficient as tracking bears, deer, and elk when their primary objective had been to obtain meat for their families.[12]

Wintertime beaver forays also placed greater burdens on the late-autumn hunt. Adult males, each one responsible for placing meat on the table for an average of four other people, would have to bring back more meat to sustain the village through the winter. These hunters would not be able to help villagers during the winter months, should food shortages arise, since they would be off searching for beavers up to hundreds of miles away.[13]

Still, by community acclaim, beaver hunts were worth the effort. With the pelts, the men were able to obtain clothing and blankets for everyone as well as firearms, ammunition, knives, and hatchets for themselves and pots, pans, knives, beads, and ceramics for the women.

However, although the male hunters were procuring many wares that the women had previously crafted, the shift toward beaver hunting did not reduce work responsibilities for women, since they had to devote increased time and labor to preparing beaver skins for market. Still, the labor-saving items these pelts brought in trade helped offset this expanded duty.[14]

The quest for beavers likewise broadened the role of hunters in providing for the community's well-being. As devoted Oneidas, they willingly shared goods obtained in trade with their fellow villagers. Also, the cultural components of gift giving allowed hunters to accrue greater prestige within their villages and the nation.

Traditionally, the Iroquois kinship system placed limits on the amount of decision-making authority any one person could wield. In most instances, birth connections alone, such as those possessed by matrons and hereditary sachems, enabled such individuals to enjoy tribal standing and influence. By gaining access to regular supplies of European goods, warriors started to breach the long-established lines of power. As major producers for the community, they began clamoring for more influence in village and nation affairs as befitting persons of their elevated status.[15]

Some degree of tension had existed between the traditional leaders and hunter/warriors for decades, perhaps even centuries. Various family lineages controlled the hereditary sachem positions. Selection by the matrons for these posts removed the favored males from the hunter/warrior class and assigned them to oversight responsibilities in the village, nation, and league. Since sachems owed their appointments to the matrons, they worked to preserve the matrons' power and influence in clan and village affairs.

The warriors, in turn, designated their own leaders, known as chief warriors. Chief warrior positions were anything but honorific. Tradition did not sustain them; achievements did. Holders felt a sense of duty to represent warrior-class interests as they lived up to their reputations as fearless fighters, even to the point of continuing to prove their combat worthiness into old age.[16]

The mere existence of chief warrior positions suggested a divergence in priorities and responsibilities regarding tribal decision making. Warriors not only called for more chieftaincies but also showed their designated chiefs greater respect than they did the sachems, because their own leaders had accomplished so much more directly for their class. Warriors listened more attentively to the opinions of their chiefs and responded more readily to their words.

Certainly the prestige of the sachems' office aided the traditional leaders in offering guidance to the nation. Most sachems executed their duties well and earned universal acclaim, but some lacked ability and floundered, losing their reputations. By comparison, force of character based on noteworthy achievements often gave the chief warriors the advantage in critical tribal decision making.

As the sachems started to slip in power, so too did the matrons who selected them. Along with the authority to instigate war, and the right to nominate counselors and sit on the village and nation councils, matrons traditionally could stifle warriors' designs by declining to endorse raids as part of condolence and requickening ceremonies or by recalling war parties. Although warriors might challenge the matrons, they rarely did so directly. Rather than demanding a redistribution of traditional authority, the warriors put considerable pressure on the matrons by encouraging them to nominate chief warriors as counselors and urging them to side with their own preferences in village and nation discussions and decisions.[17]

Contact with Europeans not only resulted in new trading patterns and altered tribal responsibilities but also triggered devastating cycles of disease and death that further strengthened warrior claims for more influence in the nation's affairs. Throughout the mid- to late seventeenth century, illness and the struggle for control of the beaver trade took a heavy toll on Oneida lives. Such losses demanded constant condolence activities. In many cases only the warriors, by delivering captives for requickening, could bring closure to the grieving process.

The Oneidas, like other natives of North and South America, had lived in a sealed hemisphere for thousands of years. People in Europe, by contrast, had interacted with Africans and Asians and been exposed to a host of bacteria and viruses. Diseases such as the bubonic plague proved to be monstrous killers, but over time Europeans built up antibodies to help them fight off these horrible illnesses. The Oneidas and other Indians lacked such antibodies. As more and more European traders and colonists made contact with the Iroquois, a biological time bomb exploded.[18]

In the late 1630s and early 1640s, smallpox, the first of the great European scourges, struck the Iroquois and neighboring peoples with unmerciful fury. Most likely, these Indians emerged from the initial epidemic with less than half their original numbers. Over the next four or five decades, succeeding outbreaks of smallpox and other European maladies reduced the population even more. Dysentery, diphtheria, and typhoid fever joined a bevy of such notorious illnesses as the mumps, measles, and chicken pox to strike down Oneidas and fellow Iroquois in staggering numbers.

During periodic epidemics, native adults suffered so badly that they could not hunt, fish, or cultivate the fields. Bodies further weakened from depleted nutrition sources had to struggle that much more to fight off these killer maladies. By the time the Oneidas and other Iroquois peoples built up antibodies, the unremitting onslaught of disease had left them with a population between one-fifth and one-tenth of their previous numbers.[19]

Meanwhile, the finite beaver supply began to disappear. The demand for European goods, and furs to pay for them, was so great that even before 1650, the Five Nations had trapped out the furs in their established territory.[20]

So the Iroquois began to look covetously beyond the geographic boundaries of Iroquoia for additional furs. During the late 1620s, the Mohawks had demonstrated the value of warfare in achieving their commercial objectives. To obtain reliable access to European goods, they attacked the neighboring Mahicans and drove them back from the western bank of the Hudson River. Once in full control of the upper Hudson River, the Mohawks dominated trade with the Europeans in the area, forbidding New England tribes from bringing their superior pelts directly to Dutch traders at Fort Orange.

The other Iroquois in New York learned this military lesson. Standing together or sometimes taking action independently, hunter/warrior bands from the Five Nations began striking at the Iroquoian-speaking Huron Confederacy in Canada. Initial attacks targeted Huron hunting parties, confiscating their furs. Later, Iroquois warriors shifted tactics and concentrated on hitting clusters of Indians returning home with their bounty from French trading posts. The object was to capture Hurons and their loot. Prisoners would haul the plunder under guard back to Iroquois villages, where requickening ceremonies would incorporate captives not killed.

During the mid-1640s, Oneida and Mohawk warriors abandoned their piracy raids in favor of a new operational approach. Transit along the St. Lawrence River included European goods destined for Montreal and other locations and Indians returning with their exchanges. Rather than pursuing enemy Indian parties on land, the Oneidas and Mohawks blockaded the St. Lawrence River, laying claim to everything that coursed its waters.

Before 1650, the Iroquois shifted operational tactics once again. Combining into larger war parties, they launched systematic assaults on Huron villages. Iroquois hunter/warriors killed Huron leaders, seized prisoners, confiscated goods, and destroyed villages. "So far as I can divine," observed a French missionary, "it is the design of the Iroquois to capture all the Hurons, if it is possible; to put the chiefs and a great part of the nation to death, and with the rest to form one nation and one country."[21]

Unity of purpose among the Five Nations was the key to success. Despite their heavy losses from disease, they could still mount much larger war parties than their rivals, who also suffered terribly from European sicknesses. This relentless demonstration of Iroquois power marked the beginning of militant expansionism known as the Beaver Wars, which extended for about fifty years to the very end of the seventeenth century. In a commanding display of martial might, Iroquois bands plundered booty and snatched, killed, and absorbed captives. In the process, they all but extinguished independent tribes and such nations as the Hurons.

From their advantageous geographic location stretching across New York, the Iroquois affected lives literally hundreds of miles away. Anyone traveling far north along the Hudson or west along the Mohawk rivers had to reckon with their strength. New England Indians lived in fear of Iroquois raiding parties. In time of war, the Five Nations were "so great a terrour to all our Indians," commented a New Englander, that "the appearance of four or five Maquas in the woods would frighten them from their habitations." Easy access to branches of the Susquehanna River enabled the Iroquois to influence backcountry Pennsylvania and permitted them to paddle their canoes to the Chesapeake Bay; other water routes took them to Delaware Bay. Travel over the Chautauqua portage in western New York and onto Lake Erie brought them into contact with native peoples in the Ohio Valley country and beyond. Hunter/warriors of the longhouse, led by their chiefs, crushed the Hurons, Petuns, Algonquins, Neutrals, and Eries in succession, and they forced the Susquehannocks to relocate. The Iroquois emerged from all this martial activity as the most powerful and feared Indians in eastern North America.[22]

The quest for furs, the ravages of disease, losses in warfare, and demands for requickening played on one another in synergistic fashion. The cultural obligations of condolence dictated future expeditions to restore lost lives for those who had perished from disease. Constant hunting and military raids magnified the problem, since these forays netted pelts but also resulted in additional tribal casualties. Sometimes, unwittingly, raiding parties would spread disease as they came and went from villages, further escalating the demand for captives to replace deceased family members. By the 1660s, an observer estimated that "two-thirds" of an Oneida village consisted of captured Hurons and Algonquins, "who have become Iroquois in temper and Inclination."[23]

The warriors kept track of their combat records on their tomahawks. As with notches on a gun, "they mark the Handle of their Tomahawks with human figures to signify prisoners, bodies without heads to express scalps." As these warriors increasingly provided the nation with new people and European products, everyone depended more and more on them, thus continuing to augment their stature and respect among fellow Oneidas.[24]

No doubt, the endless raids had other important effects. For adoles-

cent males, the forays enabled them to bond with adults of military accomplishment and fostered the development of leadership skills. At the
same time, young fighters paid tribute by calling on veterans to lead
them in additional raids, thereby acknowledging the attainments of
their seniors while elevating them to instructional and leadership roles.
Experienced warriors benefited from the campaigns by expanding their
martial honors and achieving newfound prestige. The nation, in turn,
relied increasingly on war parties to meet their special and vital needs,
which traditional leaders, the sachems and matrons, could not fulfill.[25]

As the warriors rose in esteem and power at each social level (family,
clan, village, and nation), their voices became louder, carrying greater
weight in councils than did sachems and matrons. While the sachems
convened to handle league affairs, the chief warriors met in parallel
gatherings to plan and coordinate allied campaigns. Eventually, the
chief warriors took a more active role in Iroquois councils and in artic-
ulating general diplomacy. They often spoke for their own class, representing their distinct interests and reflecting their power within each
nation. In time, the influence of the warriors and their military agenda
transformed the league from an association to preserve peace among
the Iroquois into a confederacy that allied and unified the Five Nations
for war and diplomacy, especially in relation to their dealings with
Europeans.[26]

In time, though, the warriors overstepped their bounds, allowing
their martial designs to exceed their capacity to wage war and control
events. Individual warriors began to confuse their desire for personal attainments with the needs of the nation. "They are so eager to commit
some murder in the enemy's country," noted a Jesuit, "that sometimes
even a single man will go and execute a stroke of prowess." Ultimately,
such presumptuous boldness in the never-ending search for greater personal glory would cause grave problems for everyone else in Iroquois
society.[27]

A warning sign regarding how individual and group warrior aggressiveness might produce unnecessary problems came in 1685. In negotiations with Maryland and Virginia officials concerning Iroquois attacks
in the backcountry, traditional sachems promised to stop these raids.
"We agree to observe that which you have told us," they pledged, "and

not only we, the old men, but our young warriors will obey us by following this punctually and not coming within the mountains." These
sachems thought they could still control the warriors, when peaceful
coexistence with neighbors was in everyone's best interest. Time proved
them wrong.[28]

Although the Five Nations may have initially prevailed in the Beaver
Wars and gained dominance of the fur trade, they did so only temporarily. In reality, they stirred up a hornet's nest of trouble among Indians
farther west, ultimately ensnaring themselves in a transcontinental contest for power.

Part of the problem related to the geographic location of Iroquoia,
which proved to be both a boon and a burden. According to Governor
Thomas Dongan of New York, writing in 1687, the Five Nations stood
as "a bulwark between us & the French & all other Indians." They lived
in a buffer zone between the French in Canada and the Dutch and
later the English in New York, New England, and Pennsylvania. These
long-standing European rivals recognized the Iroquois Confederacy's
strength and geographic value and courted their friendship, furs, and
military aid.[29]

Internally, too, the Beaver Wars had disunifying effects over and
above factionalism between warriors and traditional leaders. With traditional kinship bonds disrupted by an abundance of death and requickening, individuals and groups felt more inclined to pursue their own
interests, and many did so by attaching themselves to different European traders. In time, these relationships helped divide the Iroquois
into pro-English and pro-French camps, with a substantial portion of
the population caught in the neutralist center. The fortunes of these
two factions waxed and waned in accordance with the power and influence of their respective European champions.

In the process of eliminating much of the fur trade competition, the
Iroquois roused the ire of the French. Attacks on the Hurons occasionally resulted in French subjects falling into Iroquois hands, some of
whom were Jesuit missionaries. In 1663, the French monarchy took
complete control of Canada, and a force of one thousand royal troops

soon provided the martial backbone for stronger leadership by new French governors. The Oneidas quickly put aside their hatred of French traders, settlers, and spiritual leaders in Canada and, in the face of overwhelming strength, joined the Onondagas, Cayugas, and Senecas in striking peace with the new French regime. The Mohawks resisted and suffered the consequences. In 1666, a French command plundered and torched four Mohawk villages, sending a clear message to all New York Iroquois.[30]

Peace with French Canada presented novel opportunities for the Iroquois. With greatly reduced numbers of native peoples occupying the region north of Lake Ontario, French officials welcomed Iroquois hunters into what were once Huron lands. Hamlets and hunting camps popped up, and a town called Kahnawake (also known as Caughnawaga), a polyglot community composed predominantly of Oneidas and Mohawks, sprang into being near Montreal. In return, the Iroquois yielded to the French desire for Jesuit missionaries to take up residence in their villages.[31]

In 1664, the year after the French monarchy interceded in Canada, the English seized the Dutch colony of New Netherland and renamed it New York. The new rulers expressed great friendship for the Iroquois through a pact called the Covenant Chain. They offered higher prices for pelts at Albany—anywhere from two to four times what the Iroquois could obtain from Montreal. The English also provided a more reliable source of trade goods.[32]

To aid efforts in bringing furs to market, the English settled disputes between the Iroquois and various Indian tribes in New England and the Chesapeake. With relations shored up to the east and the south, Iroquois hunter/warriors could range well to the North and West in the search for pelts. Inevitably, they clashed with western Indians and the French. The combined Iroquois strength seemed to guarantee success—but only to a point.

Having staked their claim to the Great Lakes region, French trappers and local tribes brought their pelts to French trading posts. Iroquois raiders ambushed these parties, killing or capturing their competitors and taking their furs. Even more galling to the French, the Iroquois exchanged the confiscated pelts at Albany. The steady decline in trade compelled the French to bolster their Indian allies in the West by providing them with weapons and ammunition. From their perch in Canada, the French threatened the Five Nations with military retaliation.

The Iroquois, continuing to form pro-English and pro-French as well as neutralist factions, fell to bickering among themselves about how to respond to such external pressures. During the last three decades of the seventeenth century, no person or faction could achieve a consensus. At the same time, the threat of a French invasion, military disasters on the western frontier against Indians allied with the French, and indecisive English actions adversely affected each of the Five Nations. Sandwiched geographically between two rival European powers, the Iroquois found themselves exposed on all fronts, and their own internal divisions thwarted their efforts to protect themselves.

Like other members of the Five Nations, the Oneidas began suffering major reverses. The loss of even a few warriors on a raid translated into a staggering defeat for the disease-riddled people. In a single engagement in December 1691, Canadian Indians ambushed a party of Oneidas and Mohawks and killed all their pro-English war chiefs. These particular Oneida fatalities reduced the Oneidas' warrior strength by nearly 10 percent.[33]

Raids by western Indians penetrated into Iroquoia, and the threat of a massive invasion from Canada boded ill for the enfeebled Oneidas. In a desperate effort to stave off disaster, the Oneidas elevated a French Jesuit missionary to a hereditary sachemship and called on leaders in their pro-French faction to restore peace. Neither gesture helped.[34]

In the summer of 1696, well-armed French troops, augmented by Indian allies, marched into Iroquoia and first devastated the Onondagas. Next, they turned on a principal Oneida village. Incapable of resisting, the pro-French Oneidas begged for mercy. They received none. Completely outnumbered, the Oneidas fled their castle. From safe distances, these People of the Standing Stone observed the intermingled streams of black and gray smoke wafting up toward the sky. The French and Indians torched everything they could find and completely destroyed the Oneidas' crops. Lost were homes and stored food. Gone, too, were the pots, the pans, the knives, the scissors, the extra clothing, and all the other European goods their warriors had fought and labored to obtain. The Oneidas escaped with their lives but little more. Some had talked about establishing a new Oneida community in Canada, and about thirty of them fled northward to Kahnawake. With little food and the bare necessities of life, the remaining Oneidas and their Iroquois kin suffered woefully that winter.[35]

The pro-English warriors called for revenge, but they could only talk. The French and their allies had ravaged the Iroquois. Only the Cayugas had avoided the destruction of their towns, and the threat of future devastation lurked. With the Five Nations reeling, western tribes continued their devastating raids. The Iroquois could muster little resistance.

The other great European power in eastern North America, the English, proved to be all but useless in this crisis. Focused more on warfare in Europe (the War of the League of Augsburg was taking place, and England's potential military support was feeble in that conflict's American phase, known as King William's War), English officials in the colonies proposed no plans to assist the Five Nations.

Not sure where to turn, the neutralists joined forces with the pro-French Iroquois and called for a negotiated settlement with the French. The members of the pro-English faction could muster scant opposition. Without direct military assistance from the English, they knew their position was hopeless.

Even though the Iroquois sachems bargained from weakness, in 1701 they managed to broker a respectable agreement, often referred to as the Grand Settlement. The Five Nations declared peace with French Canada and the western tribes, and both sides exchanged captives. While blocking French overtures to restore Jesuits to their villages, the Iroquois even received permission to hunt again in Canada and the West. They could also trade at French posts. The French viewed their assault on Iroquoia as a severe spanking of undisciplined children, with no lasting or deep-seated hostility, so long as the Five Nations behaved in a manner that appeared supportive of French interests.[36]

Despite the welcome peace, the neutralist faction realized that to protect Iroquois interests, the Five Nations had to resolve their internal divisions. Only a unified confederacy could counterbalance the strengths of the European powers. For too many years, the cycle of external raids and internal bickering had signaled a failure of both traditional tribal and warrior-dominated leadership. As sanctioned representatives to the league, the hereditary sachems and matrons now stepped forward to lead the Iroquois toward the safer course of consensus.

The neutralists had to devise a plan that appealed to both the pro-French and pro-English factions, that advocated and preserved peace with the European powers, that restored some confidence in traditional leaders, and that buoyed the flagging reputation of the Five Nations. They did so by proposing a general strategy that encouraged the united Iroquois peoples to maintain in public a neutral posture toward the competing European powers. They would walk a fine line between the English and the French, assuring both sides of their friendship, while at the same time conveying the message that any objectionable action on the part of either power with regard to confederacy interests could result in an alliance with the other.[37]

The neutralist platform represented a truly independent course for the Iroquois. Its extraordinary strength depended upon full acceptance by both the pro-French and pro-English groups. The plan also brought those factions back into the fold and restored some of the internal unity that the Iroquois had lost in recent decades.

To complete the process of establishing their neutrality, the Iroquois donated the Great Lakes region, an area over which they had failed to establish control, to the English Crown. This action placed England in the center of a dispute with France over this territory and withdrew the Five Nations from the fight. At the same time, the Iroquois retained the right to hunt and trap in the region.[38]

From the early 1700s to the 1740s, the Five Nations generally remained at peace with both the European powers. When necessary, they tilted toward one or the other side, mostly favoring the English. Still, terrible memories of their experiences during the 1690s kept reminding them of the consequences of engaging in warfare with France or England. Despite continuing armed conflict in North America between the European archrivals as the eighteenth century progressed, chief warriors, sachems, and matrons mostly adhered to the preferred posture of neutrality.[39]

The migration of Iroquois peoples into fresh regions also helped preserve neutrality. Resettlement defused internal tensions while at the same time expanding the power and influence of the Five, later Six, Nations. (The Iroquoian-speaking Tuscaroras migrated northward from North Carolina after suffering severe losses in local warfare and officially became a part of the confederacy in 1722.) Individuals and groups who felt frustrated because their voices did not carry enough weight in village or tribal affairs could settle elsewhere, avoiding direct contact that might have threatened the nations' neutral stance. The Oneidas and their Iroquois kin moved into the Susquehanna River Basin, pushed into the Ohio country, or traveled to Canada for resettlement.[40]

The warriors, meanwhile, were not willing to relinquish their leadership gains of the previous century. Despite the terrible events of the 1690s, they nevertheless intended to remain major decision makers in Iroquois society. Warrior voices still carried great weight in councils, and war parties continued to fulfill their own agendas, seeking out adversaries far distant from the New York–Canadian theater.

With peace secured to the west, the Iroquois, especially the Oneidas, turned their attention to opponents in the South. Since the mid-seventeenth century, Iroquois raiders had struck as far away as South Carolina. In the early eighteenth century, they resumed their attacks, seizing prisoners and confiscating goods, all the while trying to build reputations as magnificent fighters. They traveled up to seven hundred miles or more searching out foes and disrupting life along the frontier in Pennsylvania, Virginia, and the Carolinas.

In the Catawbas, the Iroquois encountered a long-standing worthy adversary. The Catawbas rose in importance after they helped drive the Tuscaroras from North Carolina. When the Iroquois struck, the Catawbas resisted furiously, sometimes retaliating by sending their own war parties northward against the People of the Longhouse. Decade after decade, the Catawbas continued to fight.[41]

As the Oneidas learned once again, the quest for military recognition sometimes had dire consequences. In 1729, they suffered the worst disaster among the Five Nations in many, many years. About one hundred Oneida warriors ventured into the Carolina region, where they attacked an undefended Catawba village and seized a contingent of captives. The Catawba men, some two hundred in number, gave chase. After two days of fighting, the Catawbas proposed peace. "Recollecting the Govrs [Governor's] Admonition to them to make Peace with all their enemies," an indignant Oneida delegation complained to officials in Albany, they "agreed to their Enemies proposals wch they no sooner did, than the Virginia Indians [Catawbas] fell upon & Massacred several of their people," including their renowned chief warrior Currundawawnah. The Oneidas suffered fifty-nine warriors killed and wounded. The remainder had no alternative but to surrender. Having overextended themselves, the warriors paid a horrendous price for virtually no glory.[42]

For decades thereafter, the Oneidas and other New York Iroquois seethed at what they considered to be Catawba treachery. In 1743, when colonial officials approached the Iroquois about stopping their southern raids, which invariably affected English colonists as well, the warriors refused. The sachems confessed that they had tried to dissuade the warriors from raiding southward but that they lacked the power to corral them. "We the sachims do acknowledge that our men ought not to have gone there," they admitted, "and do declare that we used all our skill and authority that none should go a fighting and that those that went did go without our knowledge or consent which is all that we can say or do." Such words seemed to smack of duplicity in the minds of uninformed provincial leaders. In actuality, the hereditary sachems had little influence over their warriors. Despite colonial efforts to negotiate a peace, Iroquois war parties continued to harass the Catawbas up until the American Revolution.[43]

Even with ongoing differences between the traditional leaders and the warriors, the Oneidas and their Iroquois kin adhered to their strategy of outward neutrality toward the Europeans. They successfully played the English and the French against one another. Continuing warfare between the two European rivals, however, would eventually disrupt that delicate balance.

Neither the British nor the French showed much respect for the neutralist Iroquois policy. The Treaty of Utrecht, which ended the War of the Spanish Succession in 1713, designated the Iroquois as British subjects, but France retained its right to trade with them. Because so much commerce in furs now focused on Albany, the French squeezed the Senecas in western Iroquoia into acquiescing to the construction of a trading post and fort at Niagara, located at the vital waterway junction between Lakes Erie and Ontario. The British countered by demanding equal treatment and extracted consent to build a fort at Oswego, where the waters of the Oswego River emptied into the southeastern corner of Lake Ontario. These concessions placed the rival powers at vital strategic locations, on traditional Iroquois soil, and exposed the Oneidas to regular movement by colonists traveling through their territory to reach Fort Oswego.

During the 1740s, war broke out again between Great Britain and France. Known as the War of the Austrian Succession, this struggle spread into numerous European countries, with fighting (called King George's War, 1744–1748) also taking place in the American colonies. Traditional Iroquois leaders, fearful their homeland would become a primary battleground, hoped to maintain their neutral posture. The Senecas, with Fort Niagara strengthening the economic and social bonds between them and the French, expressed a preference for their Canadian neighbors. To the east, the British coaxed some Mohawks into aiding them. The other four Iroquois nations leaned toward one side and then the other, each time pulling back before they became too involved.

The Iroquois Confederacy failed to maintain a consensus, as did the Oneidas. Without official sanction, small parties of warriors from the four nations entered the conflict on behalf of the British or the French. Two rising Oneida warriors, Good Peter and Skenandoah, carved impressive martial reputations for themselves.

In 1754, fighting erupted again, this time in the Ohio River Valley. Over time the conflict, known as the Seven Years' War (1756–1763) and later called the French and Indian War, became worldwide. The

French in Canada sought to extend their influence into the Ohio Valley region, including western Pennsylvania. British leaders fought to block French expansionism. As usual, both powers attempted to draw the Six Nations into the conflict. With nearby Fort Niagara supplying the Senecas with all sorts of goods, that nation stood by their French associates. The British again convinced the Mohawks to assist them.[44]

For the second time in a decade, the outbreak of a European war compromised Iroquois unity and neutrality. Decision making again reverted to the local level, where warriors and their chiefs were most influential. Despite the actions of a few persons who rushed off to war, the chief warriors of the Oneidas, Onondagas, Cayugas, and Tuscaroras shrewdly held to an independent course early in the hostilities, thereby preventing Iroquoia from becoming a major combat zone.[45]

Late in the conflict, as the pendulum of victory swung decisively toward the British, warriors from the Oneidas, Onondagas, Cayugas, and Tuscaroras linked up with their Mohawk brothers against the French and their allies. They conducted various raids and joined in a successful British assault on Fort Niagara. In 1760, several hundred Iroquois fighters assisted in the capture of Montreal. Nearly fifty Oneidas, led by Skenandoah and Jimmy Tayaheure, participated in the invasion of Canada.[46]

During the campaign against Fort Niagara, the pro-British Iroquois exhibited extreme reluctance to do battle with Seneca warriors supporting the French enemy. Although the confederacy had failed to uphold Iroquois unity, strong cultural and political connections among the Five (now Six) Nations deterred the warriors from deliberately engaging with and slaughtering fellow Iroquois in battle.[47]

In the treaty—the Peace of Paris of 1763—that concluded the Seven Years' War, France ceded Canada to Great Britain. No longer were the Six Nations caught, by virtue of their geographic location and trading ties, in the international struggle for power between France and England.

Because of the breakdown of confederacy solidarity during these last two imperial wars, the hereditary sachems and the matrons suffered yet another blow to their leadership authority. Twice in the space of two decades, they had failed to preserve the ideal of internal harmony. Even worse, the stripping of Canada from France had deprived them of their diplomatic trump card, the balancing off of ever-meddling European powers on behalf of confederacy unity and peace.[48]

The Iroquois had been on a military footing for most of two decades. For nearly an entire generation, chief warriors had dominated village and nation councils, and the halo of honors, prestige, and power would continue to be theirs in the postwar years after 1763.

To a lesser extent, Iroquois involvement in these wars represented a failure by the chief warriors to control their fighters. As new crises developed, young men kept pushing for opportunities to prove themselves and to accrue concrete rewards, as previous generations had done. Warfare proved a kind of self-perpetuating activity, advancing the standing of some, maintaining widespread respect for others, and recasting warriors into freshly minted chieftaincies. The position of chief warrior, then, did not suffer the same sort of status blow that the sachems and matrons experienced.[49]

European contact and trade had acted as a springboard for the rise of the Iroquois warrior class; the War of the Austrian Succession and the Seven Years' War served to reify this ascendancy. With the elimination of France from the North American mainland, British policy makers hoped to achieve long-term peace on the continent that would help them avoid the financial burdens of warfare—and the consequent alarming growth of Britain's national debt. This new reality removed a main avenue of personal achievement for Iroquois warriors. Still, the demand for European commodities remained unaffected, and the warrior class could preserve its power and status by bringing in pelts and trading for these goods. At the same time, they, like all peoples of the Six Nations, had to reckon with the spread of colonial settlements, as well as European-based ideals and values, into Iroquoia.

3

CHANGES IN
THE ONEIDA LANDSCAPE

John Jost Hercheimer, later Anglicized to Herkimer, was representative of many other inhabitants in Lower Palatinate, one of the German states along the Rhine River. He sought a better life in North America, migrating to the colonies in the early 1720s. After securing a land grant in 1725, Herkimer prospered in agriculture in the area then known as the German Flatts, today running westward along the Mohawk River from the vicinity of Little Falls to Frankfort, New York.

As the years passed, Herkimer sired several children. When his eldest son, Nicholas, came of age, John Jost conveyed five hundred acres to him near Little Falls. On this tract Nicholas took up farming and built a large home. He also became involved in trade with local Indians, swapping goods at his father's fortified house, known as Fort Herkimer, all the way up to Fort Oswego, on Lake Ontario. Nicholas served as a colonial lieutenant in the French and Indian War. Like his father before him, he commanded respect among his neighbors and stood high in the ranks of well-to-do colonists in frontier New York.[1]

Not many colonists achieved the wealth of the Herkimers, but most shared their dream of greater prosperity in America. European settlers crossed the ocean in throngs. In 1771, a census determined that the region around Albany had a population of almost forty-three thousand colonists. Literally by the hundreds, European Americans kept moving into the Mohawk Valley and encroaching on Indian lands, to the extent that in 1773 some Mohawks petitioned the Oneidas, asking if they could relocate to their territory.[2]

By the end of the Seven Years' War, the Oneida Nation little resembled the one of six decades earlier. As Europeans poured into the region, each day trimming the Iroquois range, the frequent interaction helped effect more changes for the Oneidas. In addition, the threat of enemy attacks had disappeared, so that living in concentrated, fortified communities was no longer necessary. Even before the outcome of the Seven Years' War, the Oneidas had abandoned the palisades that had offered limited protection against European-style weapons.[3]

The sense of tribal communalism and collectivism that had stood unchallenged for centuries was now yielding to personal acquisition and private ownership of property. The Oneidas still shared generously among themselves during difficult times and cared for their infirm and elderly. Longhouses, however, were giving way to smaller residences designed for nuclear family units rather than extended family lineages. The Oneidas also began to acquire domesticated animals for themselves and their families, to ease the burden of securing food throughout the year. Personal goods became more plentiful. Even traditional taboos against men cultivating the land were showing signs of decay.[4]

With greater flexibility and enhanced security, the Oneidas established communities at diverse locations, as they had long ago. They claimed principal castles at Oriska, Oquaga, Old Oneida, and Kanonwalohale, with a few persons scattered elsewhere in Iroquoia and even into the Ohio River Valley. Oneidas lived with Onondagas; Mohawks and Oneidas dwelled in Oriska; Tuscaroras resided near Oneidas at Kanonwalohale; and Oneidas, Mohawks, Tuscaroras, and numerous other Indian peoples occupied villages at Oquaga.

Oriska, a small hamlet, straddled the strategic portage between the Mohawk River and Wood Creek called the Oneida Carrying Place. Because of the area's vital location, along a small strip of land that interrupted a direct water route from the Hudson River to Lake Ontario, the British had constructed Fort Stanwix there at the time of the Seven Years' War. Oriska popped up near the fort, probably in the early 1760s, to support the troops by selling food and other items and to benefit from the commercial activity at the portage. After the war, British officials reduced the garrison to a skeleton force. Still, the Oneida Carrying Place retained its value, as trading traffic continued to flow between Albany and the Great Lakes. Residents of Oriska serviced these passers-by, selling foodstuffs, hauling goods over the portage, and even trading a bit to supplement their income. The village consisted of "Seven Indian Huts," according to a visitor in 1765. "The Soil to judge from the Timber," he noted with some exaggeration, "is as excellent as any in the World." Perhaps ninety people resided in Oriska at that time, a little more than half of them Oneidas.[5]

No doubt, the most ethnically diverse Oneida community was *Oquaga*, a name translated roughly to mean "corn soup place." It was located near the Pennsylvania border, and the Oneidas originally established a village there around 1730 to oversee their valuable interests in the Susquehanna River Basin, which provided them with a water route to the Chesapeake Bay. During the 1750s, the population began to grow significantly. Oquaga offered a more secure location for those whose homes lay near the front lines during the two recent wars between the French and the British. Others apparently wanted to get away from internal tribal factionalism. Stated a contemporary, Oquaga became a haven for those "who are disgusted with the ruling Politics of their people." Over the years, others migrated to the area to get away from encroaching white settlers, so that not only Oneidas but Tuscaroras, Delawares, Mohawks, and a smattering of other tribespeople made Oquaga their home. (This diverse group of inhabitants came to be called Oquagas.) A colonial visitor in 1769 guessed that Oneidas comprised half the population of three hundred, although most likely the Tuscaroras had the largest numbers in this melting-pot community. Primary leadership at Oquaga, however, rested with the Oneidas.[6]

Oquaga actually consisted of four separate towns, with sundry ham-

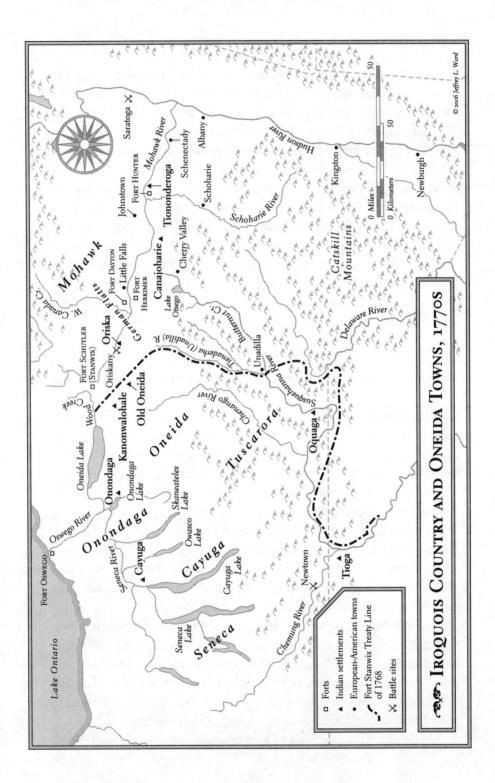

IROQUOIS COUNTRY AND ONEIDA TOWNS, 1770S

Lake Ontario

FORT OSWEGO

Oswego River

Seneca River

Onondaga

Onondaga

Onondaga Lake

Cayuga

Skaneateles Lake

Owasco Lake

Cayuga

Cayuga Lake

Seneca Lake

Seneca

Chemung River

Newtown

Tioga

Chenango River

Tuscarora

Oquaga

Susquehanna River

Oneida

Old Oneida

Kanonwalohale

Oneida Lake

Wood Creek

W. Canada C.

Mohawk

FORT SCHUYLER
(STANWIX)

Oriskany

Oriska

German Flatts

FORT HERKIMER

FORT DAYTON
Little Falls

Canajoharie

Cherry Valley

Lake Otsego

Butternut Cr.

Tienaderha (Unadilla) R.

Unadilla

Susquehanna River

Delaware River

Catskill Mountains

Johnstown

FORT HUNTER

Tiononderoga

Mohawk River

Saratoga

Schenectady

Albany

Schoharie

Schoharie River

Hudson River

Kingston

Newburgh

0 Miles   50

0 Kilometers   50

© 2006 Jeffrey L. Ward

□   Forts
▲   Indian settlements
•   European-American towns
━·━ Fort Stanwix Treaty Line
     of 1768
✕   Battle sites

lets scattered about the neighborhood. Farthest to the north, beyond Oquaga Mountain, the Tuscaroras established a village. Several miles to the south, the Oneida community, with a small contingent of Mohawks, straddled the Susquehanna River. About three more miles farther south, the Tuscaroras anchored the settlement, with a Delaware town about halfway between, on the west bank of the river.[7]

In the Oneida village, approximately fifteen large houses stood on the eastern bank, and a handful of homes lay to the west of the river. There was an occasional structure or two on islands in the waterway. Oquaga retained a communal feeling, with homes differing in look from the longhouses but preserving the same effect. Buildings consisted of "clumsy hewn Timbers & hewn Boards of Planks," with a shed at the entryway for firewood, and a kitchen. In size, they resembled truncated versions of longhouses.[8]

The Oneidas at Oquaga, on their own initiative, sought the aid of colonists to improve the quality of their lives and gain a surer supply of foodstuffs. In 1765, Isaac Tekayenenscis and Adam Wavonwanoren, two Oneida chiefs there, requested that Christian missionaries "assist us in setting up husbandry" by sending out knowledgeable persons to "build us mills, teach us husbandry, and furnish us with tools for husbandry." The Oneidas expected these consultants to live among them for a while, but they warned that "we should have you understand, brothers, that we have no thoughts of selling our lands to any that come to live among us. For if we should sell a little to-day," they stated, "by and by they would want to buy a little more and so our land would go by inches till we should have none to live upon." Years later, they still had no sawmill, although the Oneidas did combine European cultivation techniques and domestic livestock raising with their traditional farming methods to help ensure reliable food supplies.[9]

The presence of domesticated farm animals, some originally from Europe, required only the modification of traditional practices. For centuries, the Oneidas had penned up wild animals, particularly bear cubs. Tribespeople threw food scraps and other means of nourishment into the "pit" until the cub grew and fattened enough for slaughter. Such ancient habits thus facilitated a smooth adaptation to domesticated animals.[10]

Amid a diversity of tribes, the Oneidas at Oquaga had established a relatively comfortable and stable community, one that addressed not only the physical but the spiritual needs of its residents. For two decades, Christian beliefs had taken root among the villagers of Oquaga, so that a colonial traveler remarked in the late 1760s, "[w]e found the Inhabitants civil and sober." In 1748, the first in a rotating number of missionaries appeared in Oquaga. They all preached about God's saving grace and eternal life for those who accepted Jesus Christ as their Lord and Savior.[11]

Among those they converted were two eminent Oneidas who practiced and preserved the tenets of "new birth" Protestantism at Oquaga in the absence of consistent clerical presence. Isaac Tekayenenscis, known as Old Isaac, became a Christian in 1748 at the behest of the first missionary, the Rev. Elihu Spenser, a Presbyterian divine. An Oneida chief, Old Isaac "made it my Business, as soon as I had the opportunity, to learn letters, and as much of the Christian religion as I possibly could, and have endeavored all in my power to spread it amongst our people."[12]

The other prominent Oneida convert, Peter Agwelentongwas, was born in the mid-1720s and grew up in the Susquehanna Valley. Nicknamed Good Peter because of his piety, he accepted Christ as his Savior in the mid-1750s. Seized with religious fervor, he taught himself to read the Bible in Mohawk.[13]

With their Christian faith radiating outward, Old Isaac and Good Peter regularly witnessed to fellow Indians at Oquaga. They helped convert quite a few residents—Oneidas, Tuscaroras, and anyone else who would listen—to faith in the eternal saving grace of Jesus. One observer described them as an Oneida version of "Moses and Aaron," with Old Isaac "the chief here in religious affairs." In those years when ordained clergy were not present, Old Isaac and Good Peter ensured the continuation and even expansion of Christian religious practices. They preached sermons, taught Indians how to sing Psalms, and in every way looked after the souls of those at Oquaga who had become followers of Christ.[14]

When a colonist visited Oquaga in 1769, he observed a Sunday service with "near 100 Indians, Men, Women and Children including the chief of the Tuscarora Town 3 miles below with some of his People" in attendance. A horn sounded three times to announce the gathering. Men sat on one side of the meeting house, women on the other. Old Isaac was close to the pulpit, with Good Peter very near him. The Rev. Eleazer Moseley conducted the meeting in English. Good Peter translated the Psalms into Oneida "and the people joined in the Melody with exactness and Skill, the Tunes very lively & agreeable." James Dean, whose pious Connecticut parents had sent him to live at Oquaga at age eleven to prepare him for a missionary's life, rendered the sermon into Oneida. Overall, wrote the observer, "regularity and Solemnity" characterized the service.[15]

That afternoon, the Oneidas held another church meeting, this time in their native language, with Old Isaac as the "Indian Priest" and Good Peter as his deputy. They alternated between prayers and singing Psalms. Old Isaac drew on Moseley's morning sermon to deliver his own lecture. He elaborated on what Moseley had said and read various passages from religious books translated into Oneida. Then Old Isaac closed the service with a benediction. The witness claimed that Good Peter fell asleep during the sermon, but at the proper moment, he vigorously sang the Psalms in a "loud and hoarse voice."[16]

The longest standing of the principal Oneida communities bore the name Old Oneida. The Oneidas selected this strong defensive site, constructed on a lofty hill a few miles southeast of present-day Oneida, New York, shortly after the destructive French raid of 1696. Protected by a twelve-foot-high timber wall, this fortress-like community probably housed one thousand or more people at its peak. Around the year 1750 and thereafter, the population of Old Oneida started declining as other settlements such as Oquaga rose in prominence.[17]

Part of the reason for the exodus from Old Oneida related to better economic opportunities elsewhere. Also of consequence was ongoing political dissension within the Oneida Nation. Beginning in the 1750s, numbers of warriors and their families moved away from Old Oneida.

Their secession reflected the long-standing fissure between warriors and sachems and matrons, which was particularly pronounced during the Seven Years' War.[18]

Through their trading activities and warfare, the warriors had interacted more frequently with British leaders, merchants, and other European colonists. On the battlefield, they had witnessed English regulars stumble, but they had also observed their prowess in combat when effective leadership was at hand. When the British threw their hearts and minds into battle, as they had done in the latter phases of the Seven Years' War, they had proved themselves a formidable foe. Their martial capacities had impressed the Oneida warriors.

After 1763 and the demise of New France, the warriors relied on British officials and colonists to help sustain their status and power. The British doled out gifts to the warriors, including ample supplies of ammunition, in return for promises of friendship and peace. Other British gifts, which the warriors would then distribute throughout their villages, kept them in great favor with the Oneida people.[19]

The hereditary sachems, by comparison, looked askance at closer ties with British officials and European settlers. From their perspective, too many Oneida difficulties had stemmed from the ever-intruding colonists, who over time were nibbling away at Iroquois lands. Sometimes they devoured large chunks, as had recently happened to the Mohawks. White settlers regularly violated Oneida hunting grounds, and travelers to Oswego and beyond cut directly through Oneida lands, feeding themselves on Oneida game. Likewise, Iroquois to the west who went to Albany or other colonial settlements traversed through the Oneida homeland. Famines seemed to be occurring with greater frequency; the nation simply could not supplement its diet with wild game as it had several decades earlier. In addition, the sachems, with their keen sense of Oneida history, traced their own decline in power and influence to contact with the Europeans. They sought a return to traditional ways, including a rejection of the Christian faith and an end to all dealings with the colonists.[20]

This resounding anti-European sentiment served to make the warrior class look more like enemies than worthy contributors to the Oneida Nation. As a result, the hunter/warriors increasingly felt frustrated with life in Old Oneida. Some migrated to Oquaga during the 1750s; and around 1760 others linked up with natives living closer to Oneida Lake and founded a new village, Kanonwalohale. Old Oneida retained a disproportionate share of hereditary sachems and continued to keep the nation's symbol, the Oneida Stone, but real tribal power now was gravitating toward Kanonwalohale.

Translated from the Oneida language, *Kanonwalohale* means "Enemy's Head on a Pole." The village's organization and design closely resembled its founders' links to Europeans. No longer did these Oneidas reside in longhouses with fellow members of their lineage. Family lineages continued to exist, but better sanitation, greater privacy, and more material comforts persuaded the Kanonwalohale Oneidas that dispersing themselves into single- and double-family homes was a benefit to everyone.[21]

Kanonwalohale consisted of more than sixty dwellings, some constructed with traditional bark and others with European-style wood frames. A half dozen or so were log cabins. Because these smaller, freestanding dwellings had the effect of spreading out the population, health problems were less prevalent, whether in relation to sewage or to the transmission of various kinds of diseases and vermin. These Oneidas could remain in their dispersed property sites for much longer periods than they could when residing in longhouses.[22]

Residents of Kanonwalohale had little interest in European-style furniture, but they accumulated copper and brass pots. European knickknacks and niceties for the wealthiest among them included teapots, cups and saucers, and pewter plates and utensils. Among personal items, these Oneidas acquired a fair assortment of clothing and jewelry. Nearly every family had at least one trunk for storing prized goods.[23]

Agriculture at Kanonwalohale also integrated European and Oneida practices, including widespread efforts to raise a variety of European farm animals. Many households kept a dairy cow or two as a source of milk. They also raised hogs, turkeys, and chickens as surer sources of meat, and even an occasional sheep could be found for wool.

More than half the families had one or more horses for transportation and heavy work. With the horse came all the trappings—saddles, harnesses, wagons, and even sleighs for winter travel.[24]

Private ownership was often at odds with the traditional Oneida ideals of communalism and sharing of goods. Previously, the most esteemed members of a village possessed little; by 1770 striking evidence of material disparity among the Kanonwalohale Oneidas was beginning to surface. Some residents were living in larger, better-built houses besides owning more livestock and having higher-quality personal possessions. Instead of a community in which all shared or went without, Kanonwalohale had started to represent a world of haves and have lesses. In times of crisis the wealthier still shared, but the disparities were nonetheless evident.[25]

The warrior founders of Kanonwalohale had begun to drift away from their traditional moorings in other key ways, particularly with regard to time-honored Iroquois religious beliefs. Then, in 1766, they welcomed a sweet-faced young man into their midst. His consuming purpose was to spread the Gospel of Jesus Christ and preach reformed, "new birth" Christian faith among all Oneidas.

Samuel Kirkland was a native of Connecticut, born in 1741 to Daniel and Mary Kirkland. His father was a Congregational minister deeply moved by a massive, widespread religious revival sweeping through the colonies known as the Great Awakening. Like his father, Samuel counted himself among the "New Lights," those who held that a true conversion experience in which individuals accepted the Lord Jesus Christ as their Savior was the only pathway to personal salvation and eternal life. Being able to profess such an experience, literally a new birth through Christ's saving grace, was the essential requirement for full church membership.[26]

In 1760, Daniel entrusted Samuel's continued education to an old friend, the Rev. Eleazar Wheelock. Carrying over from the enthusiasm of the Great Awakening, Wheelock had founded a school in Connecticut to educate both Indian and colonial boys, and to train them to become Christian missionaries to the Native American population.

There, Samuel lived and labored alongside young Indian scholars, learning some Mohawk from his soon-to-be-famous schoolmate, Joseph Brant. Two years later, Wheelock financed Samuel's enrollment at the College of New Jersey. Founded in 1746 by conversion-oriented, "New Side" Presbyterians, the College of New Jersey (later to become Princeton University) drew students from all over the colonies. Its professors and curriculum also taught Whig political concepts that emphasized the importance of preserving at all costs fundamental political liberties.[27]

Even before completing his studies, Kirkland accepted his first assignment, doing missionary work among the Senecas. After eighteen difficult months, during which he faced starvation, he gave up and returned to Connecticut. Wheelock managed to convince college authorities to graduate Kirkland, and in June 1766, the Society in Scotland for the Propagation of Christian Knowledge ordained him a Presbyterian minister. Now Kirkland would focus on missionary service to the Oneidas.[28]

Tribal teachings relating to the Creation Narrative and the founding of the Iroquois League had served for centuries to justify the authority of the sachems and matrons. In denying or disregarding these traditional leaders, warriors such as those who left Old Oneida for Kanonwalohale opened a gateway for the introduction of various European concepts that had the potential to reshape basic societal assumptions among the Oneidas. Samuel Kirkland offered the warriors an alternative set of religious beliefs that also functioned to uphold many essential Oneida cultural constructions without sanctioning broader authority for the sachems. In Kirkland and his new-birth, biblically based Christian faith, the Kanonwalohale Oneidas found a messenger whose message resonated with them.[29]

During his first months with the Oneidas, Kirkland faced many difficulties. He built a small dwelling at Kanonwalohale, planted a garden for vegetables, and subsisted on roasted squash or a bit of corn—two meals a day. "Thus I lived, starved and laboured with my Hands till last Summer 1767," Kirkland recounted. "By my mean, starving, beggarly

Method of Life I had greatly dishonoured the Gospel Profession, and instead of Serving injured the cause. The Indians had now begun to conceive in general a very low Opinion of the English religion—I need not to say of me also." Some grew "very insolent" and treated Kirkland with "Contempt" because he labored at work predominantly performed by women and because of his unkempt appearance. The Oneidas could not envision this man as a credible guide to eternal salvation.[30]

By the autumn of 1767, Kirkland had realized that any hope of success demanded a change, and he called his followers together and explained his errors. He "told them I should no more labour with the Hands as I had done while I pretended to preach the Gospel of Christ, but should labour and watch for their Souls." Two days later, church-goers approached him to apologize for their inadvertent error. They had no idea they should support their minister physically while he cared for them spiritually. From that point on, they attended to his personal comforts while he nursed their souls.

Looking back a year later, Kirkland rated this moment as the key turning point. "Soon after," he assessed, "a general and unusual Attention to divine Truths appeared among them," and "my Influence and Character soon rose higher than ever." Word spread to other tribes that "[he] was a Man of God" and that all should accord him due respect.[31]

Kirkland had formulated a recipe for missionary success. He now appreciated that he could win converts only by elevating himself to a position of respect while ministering continually to his people. Once he had manifested in his own person a truly prospering, godly appearance, he made great headway with these Oneidas.[32]

Kirkland considered the Oneidas a disadvantaged people because they had been deprived of the Word of God. "We pity you in your pagan ignorance, & dark[ness]," he told them. "We view you as ignorant [of the] true God, & the way to happi[ness], by Jesus Christ." He maintained the righteousness of Christian beliefs, and he showed no reluctance to emphasize their superiority in relation to traditional Oneida religion.[33]

A strict New Side Presbyterian, Kirkland conveyed the idea that becoming a Christian was not for equivocators. God demanded a combination of complete devotion and unwavering faith. Kirkland described how Abraham had agreed to sacrifice his only son, whom he loved more than anything on earth, because God had wished it. In return, God's only Son laid down His life for the sins of humankind. "I thought my heart would have broken & fell in pieces," an Oneida confessed, "when I thought of God's giving his only Son, Jesus Christ, for us, & even us *poor Indians*. I could not comprehend it. I could not think halfways round this great love."[34]

To gain salvation and join God's true church, Kirkland insisted that potential converts had to profess the power of God, accept Jesus Christ as their personal Savior, and follow the teachings of God and Jesus. By studying the Bible, the Oneidas would learn about God's will for them. "I am the resurrection and the life," Kirkland quoted Jesus and then instructed them: "He that believeth in Me, though he were dead, yet shall he live; And whosoever liveth and believeth in Me, shall never die."[35]

Kirkland's conversion-oriented Christian faith resonated with the Iroquois tradition of individual freedom and independence within the context of communal service. Belief in Christ and His redeeming power and grace was voluntary and made separately by each individual, representing a conscious decision to turn over one's life to God and, in the process, become a worthier servant to all others in the community.

Doctrine alone, however, could not have ensured converts. In the process of separating from Old Oneida, the Indians at Kanonwalohale had disregarded portions of their traditional values. Still, they would not have embraced just any new set of beliefs. The villagers willingly accepted a religious faith that overlapped—and even sustained—some core Oneida beliefs, customs, and practices. Kirkland's New Side Christian tenets fused well with Oneida religion and culture.[36]

Similarities between the Oneida and Christian deities and Creation Narratives enabled the Oneidas to grasp the Christian version comfortably. Like other Native Americans, the Oneidas believed that spirits existed in all objects, animate and inanimate. Kirkland's God was not only all knowing and all loving but also omnipresent. God's spirit touched all people, animals, and objects. The Book of Genesis and the

Oneida Creation Narrative both reinforced that common theme. Both spoke of the rapid establishment of the Earth, with animals, plants, and other objects placed there to serve humankind. A power struggle between good and evil was central to each narrative. In both, the actions of the sinister forces could not be undone. People had to live in a world in which good and evil were constantly in conflict.[37]

The concept of sharing, which played such a central function in Oneida life, stood in high regard among Christians. Both doctrines urged practitioners to love their fellow humans and to give generously to those in need. Similar to the Oneida experience, Christians who performed charitable works gained favor with other human beings as well as with God.

Kirkland came to appreciate the obvious connection between the concepts of sharing and charity. He wanted to order his own life according to these values, which he did not find difficult since his missionary calling emphasized duty and service toward his fellow human beings. Had Kirkland not regularly acted with generous compassion while helping those in need, the Oneidas would have dismissed him as hypocritical.[38]

Rituals, too, transferred well from Oneida customs to Christianity. The Oneidas traditionally held commemoration ceremonies that began with thanksgiving for the bounties their creator had bestowed on them. Kirkland's weekly worship services were an offering to God, a celebration in thanksgiving for everything mighty Jehovah had given them and for Jesus Christ's complete sacrifice for humankind. As one Oneida described Sunday church meetings, they were "a feast, a feast of love."[39]

These weekly services also celebrated the Last Supper, the final "feast" before Christ sacrificed His life for human sins. Before anyone could participate fully at the Lord's table, Kirkland demanded that they undergo "the strictest examination into the State of the Soul." For those who wanted to take God completely into their hearts, the gathering was a celebration for hungry souls. "You are sent here by the Ministers of Christ & good people of God," spoke several Oneidas to Kirkland, "to teach us the way to heaven, to feed our souls with spiritual food." Those who truly believed and could demonstrate God's saving grace thereby gained full church membership and access to these weekly communion services. They ate the bread of life and drank from the cup of eternal salvation. As with requickening ceremonies, those who truly communed with God, who consumed the bread and wine, felt the spirit of Christ. "I have reason to believe the blessed Sacrament of the Lord's supper was this day made a feast . . . to many hungry souls," Kirkland wrote excitedly after this service. "They were fed with the Bread of Life!"[40]

The missionary also appreciated that commentary about Christianity lent itself to military expressions and martial imagery. He employed such language to reach his audience, especially the warriors who could identify with these concepts. Converts were "soldiers of Christ" who must crush evil wherever they encountered it. Unsuspecting victims were "attacked & overcome by Sin & the Devil." Nor did Kirkland hesitate to present stories from the Old Testament, many of them lessons in military history. For the warriors, these accounts captured their imagination and demonstrated as nothing else could the awesome power of God for those who believed.[41]

What Kirkland offered thus fit especially well with the needs of the Oneida warrior class. Over the decades, clashes with the sachems had driven the warriors farther and farther away from tribal customs and beliefs that supported the traditional leadership. The tenets of Christianity helped fill the resulting vacuum while offering the warriors alternate but familiar-sounding precepts on which to construct their lives. Furthermore, a rejection of Christianity would have made villagers more susceptible to traditionalist tribal revivals. This possibility in turn would have threatened the status and influence of the warriors by offering openings for a resurgence of power by the sachems. From their point of view, the warriors had an abundance of reasons to support Kirkland's Christian ministry.[42]

Kirkland was quick to master the Oneida language. He could preach in the native tongue and even translated portions of the Bible into Oneida. He set up a school to teach villagers how to read their language. With education, Kirkland believed, they could not only develop basic skills but also strengthen their souls by reading the Bible for themselves.[43]

Kirkland's employment of Oneidas as religious assistants and teachers further enhanced his ability to communicate God's message. In the cases of Good Peter, Old Isaac, an Oneida assistant at Kanonwalohale named Deacon Thomas (Adionghhonras), and others, Kirkland worked with allies who could conceive and relate Christian precepts in Oneida terms to aid nation members in grasping basic concepts. Whenever they spoke to friends and relatives, these Oneidas were especially effective in transferring biblical teachings and images into established Oneida constructions of reality. While depicting the wonder of Jesus taking the form of a man, Good Peter, for instance, described him in recognizable ways for his listeners. "He was the great God, who created all things," Good Peter sermonized one day in Kirkland's stead. "He walked on earth with men, and had the form of a man, but He was all the while the same Great Spirit; He had only thrown his blanket around Him." Good Peter thus expressed his own vision of his Savior's appearance, but in Oneida garb.[44]

Kirkland's strength within the Oneida community also developed from his living like the Oneidas, thereby according their culture a degree of dignity that few colonists had ever extended. Through everyday acts of kindness, continuing efforts to offer sage advice, and an exemplary lifestyle, he thus won their high regard and affection.[45]

In moments of seeming crisis, the Oneidas often turned to their missionary, who aided them to the best of his ability. From the mid- to late 1760s, famines afflicted the Oneidas and fellow Iroquois nations. Nature wreaked havoc on agriculture, with successive seasons of insect infestations and early frosts. Land encroachments by European colonists kept decreasing Oneida hunting grounds, with the effect of woefully reducing the available game population. "Seldom a wild fowl or Beast is killd under 70 miles" and "good fishing not under 70 or 80," Kirkland recorded. Failed crops and bad hunting combined to push many Oneidas to the brink of starvation.[46]

Many villagers in desperate need of food asked Kirkland for assistance. Alerting him of their plight, they pleaded, "We know not where to go for subsistence tomorrow unless you can relieve us." "The fishing season is not yet come on," they stated, "& good hunting is no more known amongst us, since the encroachments of the white people." Down to their last bushels of corn, families "begged my assistance for Christ's sake," Kirkland reported.

Kirkland opened his larder and shared all he had, providing for the needy when he had little of his own, and enduring hunger pangs alongside the Oneida villagers. He collected clothing, household items, and farming and carpentry tools for all to use. And in times of hardship, he dipped into his own shallow pockets to buy clothing and blankets for desperate people.

Having preached Christian charity, he could not behave contrarily toward his parishioners. "In such an Extremity, I apprehend no Christian spectator could stand unaffected," he explained to his sponsors back in New England. "It must move the most sturdy relentless heart to benevolence & charity, . . . even when I am destitute & in want myself. I have often borrowed, yea sometimes hired money to relieve Persons in such distressing circumstances." He concluded: "Now if some little Charities are not communicated in such cases of necessity, I don't know how the credit of the Gospel can be maintained among them."[47]

Kirkland aspired to live as an exemplar of Christian benevolence, and he succeeded. He accumulated almost nothing and spent his salary on food and goods for himself and the Oneidas. In days when communal responsibility and the concept of reciprocation seemed to be declining, and the European emphasis on individual acquisition increasing, the missionary's daily actions constantly reminded his Indian friends of those critical cultural and religious values deeply embedded in their traditional belief systems.[48]

Kirkland also exhibited the sort of personal courage necessary to tackle the serious problem of alcohol abuse. For more than a century, the Oneida Nation had suffered from the debilitations of excessive alcohol consumption and binge drinking. The Dutch had gladly sold the Iroquois kegs of brandy, and as waves of English colonists swept into the region, no one had the conviction to stem the flow of liquor. For his part, Kirkland refused to tolerate the drunken stupors and wanton destruction that excessive consumption entailed. When he threatened to abandon the mission if the Oneidas did not act and requested that eight chiefs at Kanonwalohale aid him in banning alcohol from the community, the village unanimously endorsed his proposal.[49]

As the missionary soon learned, gaining support for abstemious behavior was one thing, implementing it another. In October 1767, he responded to a report that several women were drinking heavily just outside the village. He reproached them for their misconduct and destroyed their rum supply. The next day, Jau-na-whau-na-gea, the husband of one of the women, confronted Kirkland and demanded repayment for the alcohol. The minister not only refused but also lectured Jau-na-whau-na-gea on the evils of drunkenness. Furious over his loss and Kirkland's intrusion into his personal affairs, Jua-na-whau-na-gea would not let the dispute go. The next day, he accosted Kirkland once more, this time drunk. He grabbed the missionary by the throat, but Kirkland managed to wrestle the fellow to the ground, and with some assistance, bound and gagged him. Later, Jau-na-whau-na-gea's wife assailed Kirkland, and he tied her up as well.[50]

After Kirkland released Jau-na-whau-na-gea, the warrior acted apologetically in the minister's presence; privately, he announced to friends that he planned to kill Kirkland. "The Minister," he proclaimed, "should never see another rising sun." Friends immediately conveyed the threat to Kirkland and pleaded with him to leave the village. And that first night, the missionary did; but after long hours in prayer, he returned the next morning. Again, various Oneidas begged Kirkland to leave. Jau-na-whau-na-gea was a very dangerous person, they reiterated. "We cant overcome the subtlety & malace of the Devil" in him when he was drunk, they stressed, but Kirkland would not budge. If the Oneidas were serious about their religion, then they had to oppose the mindless consumption of alcohol. "As for myself," he continued, "I told them I was wholly at God's disposal & willing to live or die." He quoted scripture in which Jesus prepares his Apostles for the difficulties of their charge: "And you will be hated by all for my name's sake; but he who has persevered to the end will be saved." The passage concluded with the words, "Therefore do not be afraid of them."[51]

The Oneidas, in demonstrating their concern, related to their minister the bold acts of Deacon Thomas the previous night. Thomas, widely recognized as "a man of Religion & Integrity," had become outraged by the drunken comportment of some of his fellow Oneidas. He seized a keg of rum by force from them and smashed it to pieces, at no small risk to himself. Reassured by this act, Kirkland persisted in his resolve to stop alcohol abuse. Several months later, he gladly reported that Jau-na-whau-na-gea had undergone "deep Convictions; and has made a public Confession in a most humble manner with Tears."[52]

Kirkland did not confine his missionary work to Kanonwalohale. Oneidas and Tuscaroras at Oquaga delighted in his presence among them. Regardless of the weather, Kirkland journeyed periodically to Oquaga, a distance of about ninety miles. These trips across rugged mountainous terrain were so enervating that he would often have to rest a day or two before continuing his activities.

The residents of Kanadesko, a small Tuscarora village near Kanonwalohale, coaxed Kirkland into frequent visits, and they in turn attended services at Kanonwalohale. The Oneidas ultimately invited Tuscaroras and Onondagas to move to Kanonwalohale, so that the latter could regularly hear the Gospel. As time passed, tales of Kirkland's work circulated so widely that the Senecas inquired if he might visit them. Kirkland wanted to establish a mission among the Senecas with Deacon Thomas as the preacher, but the plan never materialized.[53]

Although many Oneidas embraced Christianity, religious enthusiasm fluctuated. Kirkland never made much headway at Old Oneida. Conversions at the traditionalist village were few. In 1771, by comparison, Kirkland claimed attendance of three hundred to four hundred for his church services at Kanonwalohale. The conversions, he declared, represented a glorious sight. "How distinguishing the power of sovereign Grace!" he exclaimed. Seventeen months later, he grumbled that "[t]hings appear very dark & discouraging among my people." He lamented that only "a few here . . . appear on the Lords side & bear testimony for Jesus—But the love of many waxes cold & iniquity abounds."

Two years later, attendance had reversed itself again, and almost four hundred were now packing his services.[54]

Short-term fluctuations may have frustrated Kirkland, but over the long haul he achieved extraordinary results as a Christian missionary. Not only his devoted converts but even those Oneidas who were ambivalent or hostile toward his religious views accorded him respect. By the early 1770s, Kirkland had become a powerful and persuasive force among the Oneidas, a person with the potential to rival the region's most influential British official, Indian Superintendent Sir William Johnson.

Sir William possessed a commanding presence. Born in 1715 and reared in Ireland, he abandoned his inherited Catholic faith as a young man and joined the Church of England. He moved to the colonies to manage some estates in New York for his distinguished and extremely wealthy uncle, Peter Warren. Possessing an enterprising mind, Johnson acquired massive tracts of land for himself and entered the ranks of the colony's elite. By the 1760s, he was among the largest landholders in New York.

Over time, his activities brought him into contact with the Six Nations, especially the Mohawks. He treated the Indians fairly, learned to speak their language, and gained their trust. After the death of his first wife, Johnson took Mohawk chief Hendrick's niece as his mistress, and she bore him three children. Molly Brant (Koñwatsi'tsiaiéñni), the sister of Mohawk chief Joseph Brant, succeeded her as his "housekeeper." They had eight children.

During the Seven Years' War, Johnson earned accolades that enhanced his personal career as well as his standing with the Iroquois in the northern region. In 1755 he commanded a force of militiamen and Indians that won the Battle of Lake George, where he suffered a hip wound. A grateful King George II awarded him a baronetcy and appointed him Superintendent of Indian Affairs. Later, as the ranking officer present, he accepted the surrender of Fort Niagara by the French in 1759. In the years after the French defeat, as an acknowledged friend of the Iroquois and spokesperson and dispenser of gifts for the British

Crown, Johnson kept securing his position with the Six Nations. The Iroquois called him Warraghiyagey, which translated to "he who undertakes great things."[55]

According to a female contemporary, Johnson was "an uncommonly tall, well made man" who bore "an expression of dignified sedateness, approaching to melancholy." A military officer who served under Johnson described him as "a gentleman of uncommon smart sense and even temper." A person of few words, he was nonetheless "highly eloquent when the occasion called forth his powers."[56]

At the conclusion of the Seven Years' War in 1763, Great Britain became more assertive about its authority over the American colonies. The Crown had accumulated an enormous debt during the long series of imperial wars with France, Spain, and other nations. Officials in England did not expect the Americans to help pay off this debt, but they wanted to tax them to cover more completely the actual costs of administering the provinces. In this fashion, the colonies would not keep adding to the imperial debt.

Over the generations, settlers from Massachusetts down to Georgia had grown accustomed to managing their own internal affairs. They viewed their provincial assemblies as "little parliaments," their true representative bodies. They were in no mood to accept taxes levied on them by the British imperial government, especially since they lacked direct representation in Parliament. They therefore perceived any attempt by King and Parliament to tax them as a violation of their basic political liberties.[57]

Johnson was a devoted royal official. In the context of mounting differences between imperial leaders and the American colonists, he became increasingly apprehensive about Kirkland's influence with the Oneidas. The Anglican Church, formally known as the Church of England, represented the state-approved body of faith, and Presbyterians such as Kirkland were dissenters from that authority. The missionary's close ties to sponsors in New England, the center of provincial agitation, and to dissenting Presbyterians in Scotland, cast him in a suspicious light. For Johnson, a committed Anglican, the linkage was clear. Dissenting religion was a source of potential turmoil that could also have a direct impact on the allegiance of some Native American groups, should all the political unrest result in a full-scale colonial rebellion.[58]

Johnson did not care for the impact of Kirkland's theology on the Indians. He grumbled that those who converted to the dissenting faith "have imbibed an air of the most Enthusiastical cant, [*and are in short intermixed with the greatest Distortion of the features & zealous Belchings of the Spirit . . . Their whole time being spent in Singing psalms amongst the Country people, where by they neglect their Hunting & most Worldly affairs*]." From the superintendent's perspective, those natives who inclined toward Presbyterianism "[*become the most troublesome & discontented Exchanging their Morality for a Sett of Gloomy Ideas, which always renders them worse Subjects but never better men*]." How much better—and safer for Crown interests—would everything be, Johnson thought, if all natives just learned from the Book of Common Prayer and the rituals of the Anglican Church and performed good works as contented worshipers.[59]

Unfortunately for the superintendent, he could find no alternative to Kirkland and his New Side dissenting beliefs. Without an Anglican bishop in America, prospective clergy had to return to England for ordination, a costly, time-consuming practice that limited the number of credentialed Anglican clerics in the colonies. Nor could Anglican officials justify sending missionaries to the Oneidas when the Church of England was struggling to meet state church obligations among the colonial populace.[60]

A festering controversy over land and its use deepened this religious split. Since the early 1760s, Eleazar Wheelock had sought a large tract of land to build his Indian school near Iroquois homelands. Johnson squashed the idea, explaining to Wheelock that the Iroquois "are greatly disgusted at the great thirst which we all seem to shew for their Lands." The words failed to dissuade Wheelock, who kept pressing his request.[61]

As Wheelock's disciple, Kirkland shared his mentor's faith that the forces of white "civilization" would ultimately extinguish Indian "savagery." Someday, European colonists would conquer the forests and carve them up into family farms, perhaps with Indians as their neighbors. Kirkland's purpose, however, was not to bring about these changes. His grand design lay in the spiritual world—he hoped to convert as many Indians as possible to Christianity.

Johnson agreed with Wheelock and Kirkland that in time the Indians would be "civilized," admitting that "one day it must take place." Still, he mistrusted these missionaries, claiming they were "more intent on Extirpating the Indians to make room for themselves & wanted More to plant themselves than religion in the Country." As an official of the British Crown, the superintendent believed in the tenets of mercantilism. By placing the Indian populace on European-style family farms, the empire would "lose the benefit of the Furr Trade wch is a Material Consideration." For now, he much preferred to see the Indians become Anglican Christians and leave them in control of their lands and traditional communal lifestyles.[62]

Hoping to protect the Indians from colonial intrusions and, thereby, avoid the costs of frontier warfare, the home government decreed the Proclamation Line of 1763. Colonists could settle on land to the east of a decided-upon demarcation; all territory beyond the line belonged to the Indians. To fix the specific location of the boundary, Johnson held a huge conference at Fort Stanwix in 1768. During the negotiations, the superintendent placed enormous pressure on the Oneidas to cede a large parcel of land, including the Oneida Carrying Place. Worried about the decline in hunting grounds and unwilling to give up territory where their spirits resided, the Oneidas resisted these overtures as best they could. In the end, however, they yielded. During these years of famine, the Oneidas had to maintain good relations with British officials such as Sir William because they provided valuable gifts of clothing, ammunition, and even food on occasion. The Oneidas thus sacrificed traditional holdings, where generations of ancestors had walked and hunted, to survive in the present. Their only consolation was the pledge they extracted from Johnson, who staked his reputation on settlers abiding by the treaty line and not pressing farther into Oneida territory.[63]

Kirkland was not present at the Fort Stanwix conference. He had returned to New England for a visit with his sponsors. Through some emissaries, however, Eleazar Wheelock attempted to gain title to some land in the Susquehanna Valley. These actions outraged Johnson, who did not need outside intrusions during such delicate negotiations. In the superintendent's mind, Kirkland was guilty of interference by virtue of his connections with Wheelock. Sir William tarred all dissenting ministers with the same brush, even though years earlier Kirkland had pledged his solemn oath to the Oneidas that he would not take any land from them.[64]

Further disintegration of relations took place when Johnson and Kirkland tussled over hiring a blacksmith for the Oneidas and over the construction of a church at Kanonwalohale. With the widespread use of pots, pans, axes, hoes, muskets, and other European goods, the Oneidas had ever-greater need for a skilled metalworker. Once Kirkland introduced more sophisticated farming equipment (including the iron plow) and techniques to increase crop yields, the Oneidas urged their minister to intercede with Johnson on their behalf.

For some time, Sir William had known these wishes but had done nothing to grant them, claiming financial exigency and preferring that the Indians bring their damaged tools to his elaborate homestead at Johnstown for repair. He told Kirkland he could finance a blacksmith and necessary equipment for one year, but no funds would then be left to provide clothing and ammunition for the tribes. Nor did he have the authority to supply a blacksmith. "The King, has put that into ye hands of ye several Govern[or]s," he explained.

Evidently on Kirkland's recommendation, eight Oneida chiefs pursued the matter by petitioning New York's royal governor for assistance. They described the extraordinary burden of having to travel nearly a hundred miles to Johnson's blacksmith. "We stand in great need of a *Blacksmith* to work for us here at our *own* place if it be for a short while perhaps six months or a year in which time, some of our Young Men might acquire a small degree of skill in ye trade." They also requested all the necessary smithing tools.[65]

When the governor questioned Johnson about the petition, the embarrassed superintendent lied. He blamed Kirkland, stating that "the Missionary mistaking this matter, Instead of laying it before me, as he ought to have done, has Conceived that It became a Provincial Concern to Supply the Indn. Villages." Johnson also charged the petitioners with spreading "untruths." What he did not know was that in their petition, the Oneidas had quoted from his rejection letter to them, in which he claimed that only the provincial governor could help them.

The affair bruised the superintendent's image with the Oneidas. From Johnson's perspective, his actions made sense. If he had provided the Oneidas with a blacksmith, he would have reduced their dependence on him and the British government during a time when tensions between the colonies and the parent nation were increasing. From the Oneidas' point of view, Johnson had prevented them from procuring a blacksmith, thus conveying the misleading impression that both he and the British government did not care about their needs. As for Kirkland, because he had served as an advocate for the Oneidas, he gained yet more stature as the person committed to working for their well-being.[66]

Not long thereafter, the superintendent and the missionary clashed again. Johnson learned through Oneida sources that Kirkland hoped to build a church for his flock, and the former launched a preemptive strike. Seeing an opportunity to plant Anglican seeds among the Oneidas and thus enhance his own prestige at Kirkland's expense, the superintendent offered to construct a house of God for the Oneidas with the king's money—if they would accept a missionary from the Church of England. The Oneidas declined, but Johnson extracted a concession: the Oneidas would not have any religious facilities constructed for them "when they had refused to have a church built by Episcopalians."[67]

Kirkland, meanwhile, had discussed the subject with his sponsors in Boston. He presented them with an Oneida petition requesting funds to underwrite the construction of their own church. Impressed with the earnestness of this solicitation, the sponsors vowed to build a sawmill, which would facilitate cutting boards for a higher-quality but less costly structure.[68]

Word of the Oneida petition infuriated Sir William. He called in the Oneida Nation's leadership and lectured them on proper procedures. They were to bring all such requests to him, their Superintendent of Indian Affairs. Sir William also intimated that the king would find their conduct displeasing, and that "these Boston people are a seditious & Rebellious people, great enemies to government." He counseled those present to withdraw the petition to the Boston board and to file one through him to the king, which he assured them "would be granted you at once without any advice."[69]

Meeting among themselves to consider how to respond to Johnson, the warriors controlled the discussion. Pledging loyalty to Kirkland, they insisted that they would go with Kirkland to prison or death. "Where I followed Christ," Kirkland recorded their words, "they would follow me." They then criticized the Anglicans for their laxness in seeking God's redeeming grace as well as their looseness in personal conduct. They declared they wanted no part of Anglicanism.

In moderate tones, the warriors at Kanonwalohale dictated a reply for their counselors and sachems to deliver to Johnson. "Our petitioning to our Fathers, the Ministers in Boston, to build us a house for the Lord, was the Result of long Consideration & *much prayer* to God," they stated. The warriors went on to distance themselves from Johnson in religious matters: "We fully agree with you that all our affairs respecting Government shou'd be laid out before *Sir William*. But in church affairs, & even all that immediately respects the Kingdom & Government of Jesus Christ, we must go directly to God, by his word & ministers." They concluded by declaring their support for Kirkland: "We are content with the Man, the Minister, whom God hath sent to us, & we believe that . . . he teaches the *true way of salvation*." The Kanonwalohale village council unanimously ratified the warriors' statement.[70]

Another two years passed before the Oneidas finally built their own church. Kirkland happened to be absent from Kanonwalohale when they began construction of a substantial structure, thirty-six feet in length and twenty-eight feet in width, with an eighteen-foot-high ceiling and room for a gallery at one end. Unfortunately, the boards available to them fell short in size and length. When Kirkland returned, he recruited a master carpenter and two assistants from the provincial village of Cherry Valley to help complete the house of worship. In a strange twist of irony, Johnson donated the church bell.[71]

Johnson had enormous influence in British governmental circles, but Kirkland clearly had established greater credibility with most Oneidas. Johnson was a huge landowner, most of his land gained at Indian expense. Kirkland had promised he would not take any land, and after a number of years, he had not swayed from that pledge. Johnson offered ammunition and clothing as gifts, which helped him maintain tolerable relations with the Oneidas. Yet, as differences intensified between Great Britain and the colonies, provincial merchants called for trade boycotts. As a result, Johnson had difficulty procuring goods for distribution to the Indians. When the superintendent insisted on being the intermediary in obtaining valuable items and materials for the Oneidas, he also assumed the responsibility for failure to fulfill those requests. Kirkland, meanwhile, lived with the Oneidas. Unlike Johnson, he did not reside in an elegant mansion but in a modest dwelling. From his sponsors in Boston he received money to buy food for the hungry, clothing for the destitute, and support for various projects that the Oneidas needed. While Johnson provided for them only on special occasions, Kirkland addressed their needs with many acts of charity on a daily basis.[72]

Just as bad for Johnson, the Oneidas very much resented losing part of their homeland through the provisions of the Treaty of Fort Stanwix. Their financial compensation helped them survive the famine of 1769; on the other hand, Johnson had vowed he would defend their remaining lands from outside intruders. Colonists, however, continued to press around the edges of those lands and trudge across Oneida territory, killing and consuming what little game could still be found. Occasionally, they even clashed with various Oneidas. The message to the People of the Standing Stone was clear: although Sir William had pledged his word, he could not contain the transgressions of ever-expansive colonists.[73]

The ongoing friction between Kirkland and Johnson, and ever-increasing contact with European settlers, caused serious differences among the Oneidas. Some supported their superintendent; others, certainly the largest number, allied with their missionary; and a third group, the traditionalists, concentrated at Old Oneida, continued to want nothing to do with the Europeans.[74]

Traditionalists were critical of Oneidas who embraced any European influences, whether from Johnson or Kirkland. "You are now going to become praying people, like those in the East—," they taunted, "by this you will lose your warrior spirit and become like silly women and children." An attempt to resolve differences between tribal leaders at Kanonwalohale and Old Oneida failed. Warrior chief Tegawaron approached Kanaghwaes, a powerful sachem at Old Oneida whose name translated to "Erect Corn Cobs," and suggested a reconciliation. Kanaghwaes rejected the overture, insisting that he "would have nothing more to do with Sir Wm. or ye. English but look entirely to the Six Nat[ion]s." Tegawaron felt that most residents at Old Oneida actually favored the agreement, but Kanaghwaes's vigorous opposition swayed them to block any discussion.[75]

With no hope of restoring unity, Tegawaron called upon Johnson to appoint new sachems, persons not bound to the traditionalists, for Kanonwalohale. He asked Sir William to select from among "the best & Wisest Men amongst them, w'h [which] would enable them to transact business with more Spirit & Judgment." Tegawaron then recommended Skenandoah, a superb warrior, as an ideal choice.[76]

Tegawaron's bold move represented a direct swipe at the prerogatives of the matrons, who by tradition had the authority to remove sachems who failed to perform their duties satisfactorily. In this case, the matrons had refused to replace current sachems with men more sympathetic to the warriors at Kanonwalohale. Realizing he would alienate some portion of the Oneidas by acting for or against Tegawaron's request, Johnson promised to look into the matter, but he did nothing.[77]

As differences between the parent nation and the American colonists pointed toward rebellion, and as fissures among the Oneidas widened, the strain on Johnson mounted. Fighting in 1774 between the Shawnees and Virginia frontiersmen, known as Lord Dunmore's War, worsened his woes. Fearing that the Iroquois, who were Shawnee allies, might throw themselves into the conflict, Sir William called for a conference to gather at his imposing residence, Johnson Hall, with the hope of securing a commitment of neutrality from the Six Nations.

Johnson's health was declining. He did not feel up to the conference, but necessity demanded his appearance. On July 11, 1774, in the warm summer sun, he addressed the Iroquois. Despite a "compression and tightness across the stomach," he hammered at them to act prudently and explained the actions he had taken to restore peace. He called on the Iroquois to restrain themselves and others, asking that they not let the momentary upheaval sway their reasoned judgment. With his energy all but expended, Johnson announced a distribution of tobacco and liquor, then returned, with assistance, to his room. There he drank some water and wine, leaned back in his chair, and died.[78]

The passing of Warraghiyagey threw the gathering into chaos. Guy Johnson, Sir William's son-in-law and his designated successor as superintendent, stepped forward to oversee the condolence ceremonies and to convince the Iroquois that they should abide by Sir William's last wish. Officially, the Six Nations promised to remain neutral.[79]

News of Sir William's passing reached Kanonwalohale four days later. Two days after that, toward evening, Kirkland delivered an oration "on the solemn occasion [of] Sr. Wm['s] Death." Drawing from the Old Testament, he said, "Let not the wise *man* glory in his wisdom, neither let the mighty *man* glory in his might, and let not the rich *man* glory in his riches; but let him that glorieth, glory in this, that he understandeth and knoweth Me, for I *am* the Lord which exercise loving-kindness, and judgment, and righteousness in the earth: for in these *things* I delight, saith the Lord." His words were both a memorial to Johnson and a homily for the Oneidas as they faced an uncertain future in light of the colonists' continuing opposition to British imperial policies and the prospect of a shooting rebellion.[80]

4

INTO THE VORTEX
OF REBELLION

Bewilderment had seized Good Peter. He could not understand how Anglican religious beliefs had taken such quick hold in his village. For years, Oquaga had been a model of salvation-oriented Christianity among the Oneidas, a place where the New Side Presbyterian faith had fared well, even during the prolonged absences of missionary Samuel Kirkland. Now, in the year 1773, Good Peter felt alone, since nearly all his friends and neighbors, or so it seemed, had started professing the Anglican faith. Even his closest religious ally over the years, Old Isaac, had become a proponent of good works–oriented Anglicanism.[1]

Indian superintendent Sir William Johnson was prominent among those who had turned a cold shoulder to Good Peter. Just a few years before, Johnson had described him as "a very faithfully and Pious Indian" who "has been of much Service for some years past amongst his countrymen and others, gieving them all ye insight he could in the Principles of Religion." By 1773, amid ever-deepening tensions between England and thirteen of its North American colonies, the superintendent had lost his tolerance for the kind of dissenting religious faith Good Peter still espoused.[2]

In the face of such strong opposition, most persons would have wilted into conformity. Good Peter, however, was no ordinary practitioner of his faith. A "stout" fellow, probably in his sixth decade of life, he was "an understanding, sensible prudent man." By all accounts, he was a brilliant orator, and he counted himself among those Oneidas who spoke English reasonably well. These talents, combined with many martial achievements, had convinced his people to name him a chief warrior.[3]

Over the years, Good Peter had formed powerful bonds with his Savior. He took Christ deep into his heart and joined the legion of Christian believers who were ready and willing to suffer a martyr's fate, should circumstances require. From this spiritual depth, the Oneida chief found within himself the surety of conviction to stand with the local Presbyterian missionary, Aaron Crosby, in confronting the Oquagas' apostasy in favor of Anglicanism. He and Crosby were anxious to have Kirkland travel from Kanonwalohale and help them restore vital faith.

Both Oquaga and the political atmosphere had changed dramatically since the negotiations at Fort Stanwix in 1768. The final treaty had stripped the Mohawks of nearly all their territory, leaving them with little more than upper and lower settlements—Canajoharie, up or to the west along the Mohawk River, and Tiononderoga, frequently called Fort Hunter, along the waterway to the east. Many Mohawks found living among grasping, land-hungry colonists distasteful, so they migrated southwestward, where they joined other Iroquois kin at Oquaga along the Susquehanna River.[4]

The influx of Mohawks, mostly Anglican in their faith, had altered tribal numbers and the distribution of power at Oquaga. The community remained a melting pot, with Oneidas dominating the region politically and Tuscaroras numerically. Even after five decades of residency in the area, the Tuscaroras still felt beholden to the Oneidas for allowing them to relocate in Iroquoia. The Mohawk population surge, in contrast, undercut the Oneidas' dominance. As members of the opposite moiety and viewed as fathers to the Oneidas for three centuries, the Mohawks were not about to acquiesce so readily in political or religious matters to the People of the Standing Stone.[5]

Unlike the Oneidas, who fostered a relatively amicable rapport with the colonists while trying to maintain agreeable relations with Sir William Johnson, the Mohawks adored the superintendent but bitterly resented European settlers for gobbling up their land. As the easternmost of the Iroquois peoples, the Mohawks had experienced the most extensive contact with European colonists. Daniel Claus, one of Sir

William's sons-in-law and a member of his intimate circle, commented that the Mohawks "become every day more . . . obliged to follow agriculture as being surrounded by white people & their hunting grounds chiefly taken up & void of game." The loss of so much of their ancient tribal lands and forced changes in their lifestyle left the Mohawks with wrathful feelings. As the dispute between the colonies and the mother country continued to percolate, the Mohawks sided more openly with the superintendent and the Crown.[6]

When these embittered Mohawks moved to Oquaga, they brought their Anglican religious preferences with them. Under Johnson's auspices, missionaries had converted nearly all of the Mohawks to the less-exacting Anglican faith. The Church of England accepted everyone as full members, regardless of whether they had ever sought God's saving grace. For new birth–oriented Presbyterians such as Good Peter, mere church attendance and reciting words from the Book of Common Prayer would never serve to ensure righteous behavior, let alone eternal salvation. A doctrinal dispute thus could not be avoided at Oquaga.[7]

A well-connected young Mohawk named Thayendanegea, better known as Joseph Brant, was one source of the religious split at Oquaga. Born around 1743, Brant was the brother of Molly Brant, who became Sir William's common-law wife back in the late 1750s. Sir William saw great promise in Joseph and assumed responsibility for him as both patron and mentor. He even sent him to Eleazar Wheelock's Indian school in Connecticut, where the young lad learned English and Calvinist-oriented new-birth Christianity.[8]

As the handsome Brant came of age, he impressed people from both Iroquois and colonial society. Martial activity in Pontiac's War—an uprising in 1763–1764 of several Indian nations in the Old Northwest against the new British authority—earned him respect as a warrior. Through his personal rapport with the superintendent, his skills and knowledge of the English language, and his battlefield feats, Brant assumed a position among the Mohawks and all Iroquois peoples well beyond his years. His personal and familial relationship with Sir William also provided Joseph with access to the most powerful leaders in colonial America, something no other Indian could boast. Under Johnson's tutelage, Brant rejected the demanding religious training from his days at Wheelock's school and converted to Anglicanism. Like his patron, Brant assumed an aggressive pro-British posture in the dispute between the colonies and their parent nation.[9]

In the summer of 1765, Brant married Old Isaac's daughter Peggie. They lived mostly at Canajoharie, but Joseph acquired property in Oquaga, including "a farm with a comfortable house of squared logs, a flourishing orchard," fifty acres of cleared land and his own island, and "fifteen to twenty head of livestock." When Peggie died in 1771, Brant mourned her loss for a year and a half and then took her half sister as his new wife. Not only did these marriages bind Old Isaac with one of the most influential Mohawk families, they cemented the Oneida chief's ties with Sir William Johnson. In addition, the charismatic Brant convinced Old Isaac that Anglican forms of worship and beliefs should supplant Presbyterianism among all Oquagas.[10]

Brant was not the only sower of dissatisfaction with Presbyterian doctrine. Through infrequent ministrations by ordained preachers, poor interpreting, and the influence of more flexible clergymen in nearby colonial communities, the Christians at Oquaga were already lapsing into a state of laxness in faith that was appalling to Good Peter. The new Presbyterian missionary, Aaron Crosby, lacked the language fluency and established credibility to stand up against the Anglican tidal wave. The only hope for Good Peter and Crosby was for Kirkland to come to Oquaga to assist them.

In early March 1773, Kirkland journeyed from Kanonwalohale to Oquaga with his Oneida assistant Deacon Thomas and a young Oneida catechist named Wirom. For four and a half days, the party trudged through deep, soft snow, battling rain, flurries, and falling temperatures. On their third night out, Kirkland's legs and feet began to ache and swell. Only through the greatest exertion did he plod onward the next day. That evening, the three men rested in a small town fifteen miles shy of their destination, devouring their few remaining provisions of parched corn and Indian bread. Despite pain and hunger, Kirkland

and his companions resumed their journey the next morning and reached Oquaga shortly after noontime.[11]

Delighted to see Kirkland, Good Peter and Aaron Crosby met with him and others over the next few days. Virtually everyone except Good Peter thought that salvation and the prospect of eternal life required nothing more than knowledge of the Ten Commandments and "external good behavior." Further, most Oquagas were subscribing to the notion that baptized infants would have eternal life, and that if they did not hold a feast after the baptism, the ceremony "would avail nothing."[12]

Kirkland stated privately that he "was astonished, and grieved to the heart to find such inexcusable ignorance . . . among them." He chose to blame not individuals but rather the lack of a full-time missionary who could preach in Iroquois dialects rather than being misunderstood by inaccurate translations of English words. Both he and Deacon Thomas expounded on misinterpreted doctrines, and Good Peter noted his pleasure with these clarifications. "Time was when we could instruct you Onoide's," he explained, "but now the scale is turned, and we are glad to open our ears to your instructions."[13]

Kirkland had to deal with much more than differing interpretations of the Bible. The religious turmoil at Oquaga had produced a rupture in good relations between Good Peter and Old Isaac. For two decades, they had headed the church in Oquaga, with Isaac as first religious citizen and Peter as his second. Kirkland regarded Good Peter as an "Indian who hath long been distinguished for his Piety & good sense," while he viewed Old Isaac as "a speaker among the Indians who frequently officiates in their religious meetings but vain and conceited." Kirkland now proposed that Good Peter take a more prominent part in Oquaga's religious affairs by preaching publicly and interpreting for Aaron Crosby. This solution would cut deeply into Old Isaac's role as first religious citizen—a necessary action, Kirkland thought, because of Isaac's newfound penchant for Anglican doctrine.

Over the course of several days, Kirkland met repeatedly with Old Isaac. The chief remained intransigent, until a late-night conversation led to a breakthrough. Kirkland immediately woke Good Peter to notify him of an "unexpected revolution," Isaac's change of heart. An exuberant Good Peter exclaimed with delight, "*Rasatse ne Raweneiyoh*" (God is mighty).[14]

Kirkland had brokered a solution, temporarily. The root cause of the problem, however, stretched beyond religious differences. The dispute between England and its North American provinces had begun to dominate nearly every aspect of colonial life. Political quakes created shock waves that reverberated on both sides of the Atlantic and ultimately affected numerous nations and territories across the globe. In Iroquoia, the Mohawks and Oneidas were among the first persons to feel the vibrations, soon followed by the other Six Nations and native tribes elsewhere. The Oneidas experienced the initial tremors of rebellion in the form of contention between Anglicans and Presbyterians over proper Christian doctrine.

In early 1775, more religious turmoil broke out in Oquaga. Aaron Crosby initiated the controversy when he refused to baptize children unless their parents promised to raise them according to strict biblical dictates. When he would not baptize the child of a prominent resident named Captain Jacob, Old Isaac and Jacob himself publicly ordered Crosby to leave Oquaga. Isaac later admitted he had done so because John Butler, a close associate of the Johnson family who became a renowned loyalist, had urged them to "drive away their Minister, if he would not Baptize Capn. Jacob's child in that manner in which he desires." Various Oneidas and Tuscaroras intervened on behalf of Crosby; the community had reached an impasse.[15]

Tribal leaders in Oquaga decided to ask their new Indian superintendent, Guy Johnson, to provide a solution. Johnson favored Old Isaac's position, but he chose not to support the banishment of Crosby. He told the leaders that Sir William, shortly before his death, had written, "they had hitherto lived happily under the direction of Old Isaac, a pious Chief who had read the service to them, and gave them many wise exhortations." As such, the new superintendent thought Kirkland, by his earlier actions back in 1773, and Crosby, by his unwillingness to conform to Anglican doctrine, were a source of needless problems. "If the Missionary was disagreeable to them, or, endeavoured to force the consciences of those educated in a different persuasion," Guy Johnson advised that "he should certainly be prevented" from preaching. Oquaga's leaders decided to permit Crosby to remain, so long as he agreed "to abide by the [Anglican] Lithurgy printed in the Indian language." Crosby thus found himself gagged as a spiritual mentor in the community.[16]

The controversy became even more complex when various leaders at Oquaga concluded that tribal members could make doctrinal choices for themselves drawn from either Anglican or Presbyterian practices. Joseph Brant disagreed, insisting that only Anglican liturgy was acceptable and that "the Minister [Crosby] must leave his manner of worship entirely & follow all ye forms in ye [Anglican] Book." Old Isaac, for his part, felt fully vindicated and refused to compromise with regard to the shackling of Crosby and his Presbyterian teachings.[17]

Meanwhile, four Oneida leaders—Good Peter, Adam Wavonwanoren, Hendrick, and Beech Tree—decided they should reassure Guy Johnson of their respect for the king, despite their dissenting New Side faith. Like Jesus, "we thought also that ye King equally loved all those who were obedient & peaceable subjects." The four Oneidas pointed out that since 1773 they had grappled with the Presbyterian-Anglican split at Oquaga. "We have kept these troubles as secrets, hoping we should be able to settle them among ourselves without making them public." Now, however, with the latest flare-up, "we have no hope left of making peace among ourselves while we live together." Nor could they accept the Anglican takeover of their community. They had decided to move closer to Kanonwalohale. "Next summer, those of us who are united together with our Brethren the tuscaroras," they explained, "[plan] to remove towards Oneida, the place from which we sprang, & join our Bre[thre]n. there who have embraced Christianity."[18]

The continuing religious rift at Oquaga reflected the tribal loyalties that were emerging as the provincial resistance movement was about to become a civil war. Guy Johnson, Joseph Brant, and even Old Isaac, for that matter, wanted to thwart any influence that dissenting missionaries might wield in convincing various Iroquois to align themselves in some way with the patriot American cause.

In January 1775, Kanaghwaes, the sachem from Old Oneida who represented a group of disgruntled traditionalists, asked Guy Johnson to remove Kirkland from Kanonwalohale. Kanaghwaes had served as an Oneida spokesperson for two decades. He had gained Sir William Johnson's respect when he urged the superintendent to prohibit the selling of alcohol to the Oneidas, which "disturbs us in our Meetings & Consultations" and instigated "quarrelling." Johnson and his family perceived the Oneida sachem as a reliable ally, having called on him to sign the controversial Treaty of Fort Stanwix in 1768 for the Oneida Nation. Although Kanaghwaes preferred as little contact as possible with the Europeans, he maintained close ties with the Johnsons and used his connections whenever he thought he could make gains for the traditionalists.[19]

By the mid-1770s, Kanaghwaes viewed Kirkland as a disruptive influence and wanted to get rid of him. He complained to Guy Johnson that the missionary not only "refused to Baptise some of our people, who were not agreeable to him," but he also operated a store in the village (a charge that likely implied that the minister was selling alcohol), which was totally false. Just as damaging among his various allegations was Kanaghwaes's accusation that Kirkland was minding "public affairs more than Religion." Johnson called on the missionary to answer Kanaghwaes's charges. While pledging that "I never condemn any person unheard so," the superintendent insisted that "from a train they appear but too well founded."[20]

Friendly Oneidas, determined to help Kirkland, quickly mobilized supporters at Kanonwalohale to discredit Kanaghwaes's accusations. Three prominent chiefs—Thomas, Hendrick, and Lodwick (Gahsaweda)—visited Johnson as a delegation and challenged Kanaghwaes's veracity. The Oneida sachem had not visited Kanonwalohale in eight months, they reported, and therefore had no authorization to speak for anyone except himself. Residents at Kanonwalohale "love & esteem our Father" Kirkland, the chiefs declared, and "should we do such a thing as drive him off, we consider it as no other than saying to God, depart from us." They concluded by saying, "We therefore beg you will desist from any farther attempts to drive him off."[21]

With the Kanonwalohale Oneidas vigorously supporting Kirkland and Kanaghwaes's truthfulness under assault, the dissenting missionary was able to sidestep the matter of political interference, mostly because of the three chiefs' avowal that "he meddles not with State affairs." Their pledges of deep admiration for Kirkland and his labors testified to his popularity as a spiritual leader. The Presbyterian missionary wrote in his own defense that his purpose was to gain *"real Converts to Jesus Christ"* among Indian peoples. His doctrines were hardly strange; after all, he derived them directly from the Bible. Kirkland further stated that Joseph Brant, a key fomenter of religious conflict at Oquaga, had recently admitted to convincing the sachem Kanaghwaes to make the charges because that " 'would be agreeable to Col. Johnson.' "[22]

Kirkland knew the real source of Guy Johnson's misgivings. The Iroquois were questioning the superintendent about the meaning of the mounting troubles between the Crown and its American colonists. Hoping to ease their concerns, Johnson downplayed the quarrel as nothing more than "little differences between England and some people in America," which he expected "will soon be over." He explained that "this dispute was solely occasioned by some people, who notwithstanding a law of the King and his wise Men, would not let some Tea land, but destroyed it." King George had reacted angrily by sending royal troops "to see the Laws executed and bring the people to their sences."[23]

In reality, Kirkland had dabbled in political affairs, openly sympathizing with the disaffected colonists. His New England upbringing; his training at the College of New Jersey, a hotbed of thinking about protecting basic liberties; his adherence to a faith that dissented from the Church of England; and the financial support from his sponsors in Boston—all these strengthened his personal bond with colonists in Massachusetts and the resistance movement. He did not attempt to proselytize the Oneidas about joining the patriot cause. Instead, he waited until curious and concerned Oneidas questioned him, and then he offered his interpretation of events. As a missionary who strived in his personal and professional behavior to epitomize Christian faith and charity, his explanations carried great weight.

At the urging of various Oneidas, Kirkland had interpreted "parts of the doings of the grand Continental Congress," which had concluded its deliberations at the end of October 1774, as uniting the aggrieved colonists in a common course of action. By translating portions of Congress's minutes for them, the minister articulated the true reasons for the conflict from the rebel standpoint, thereby undercutting Guy Johnson's simplistic assessment. The Oneidas learned that tea was only an object, not the cause of contention. In the minds of the Whigs, or patriot rebels, the real dispute revolved around the nature and extent of their political liberties as British subjects living in America.[24]

Kirkland suspected that his days with the Oneidas were dwindling. Amid the rising tension, his predisposition toward the patriot cause would not allow him to work for neutrality. As a missionary to the Oneidas, he served with the sanction of the superintendent, and he realized that Johnson would not permit him to stay in Iroquoia as an open rebel partisan. To ensure a continued patriot voice among the Six Nations in his absence, Kirkland decided he would encourage the new Continental Congress, assuming such a body gathered in Philadelphia, to open direct channels of communication with the Iroquois.[25]

Kirkland, Johnson, and other European American inhabitants of central New York appreciated how powerful a unified Six Nations Confederacy could be, especially in time of war. Back in November 1774, Guy Johnson had estimated that the Six Nations could muster two thousand warriors alone, and their allies could augment that number substantially. At this point, neither side wanted to get the people of Iroquoia agitated. When the Six Nations declared their neutrality in late 1774, viewing the quarrel as a father-son matter and asserting that "it was contrary to their custom to interfere between parents and children," both Whig and loyalist partisans let out a sigh of relief.[26]

With each passing day, as the winter of 1774 gave way to the spring of 1775, rebel and Tory colonists became more identifiable. Many who remained loyal to the Crown had ties to the Johnson family as friends, tenants, and business associates. Others simply saw no good reason to shift their allegiance from the British government.

Local rebel committees, including the Tryon County Committee of Safety in the Mohawk Valley region, sprang up everywhere to challenge and intimidate persons who would not acknowledge support for the patriot cause. One test was the willingness to sign the comprehensive trade boycott known as the Continental Association, which the First Continental Congress had adopted back in October 1774. Those who refused to endorse the association could expect to face social ostracism and even physical violence. Demanding conformity in the name of liberty, these local committees caused thousands upon thousands of colonists to reckon with the crucial issue of their personal allegiance regarding British authority in America.[27]

Then, on April 19, 1775, in the hazy dawn, an assemblage of seventy armed Minutemen attempted to protest the passage of seven hundred British regulars at Lexington Green, in Massachusetts, on their way to Concord. Taut nerves snapped, and shots rang out. When the billowing smoke from spent gunpowder cleared, eighteen colonists lay wounded or dead. The War for American Independence had begun.[28]

With the onset of hostilities, Guy Johnson felt that his authority was slipping away and that his personal safety was in jeopardy. Pro-rebel forces started to choke the flow of supplies to him, including gunpowder, which cost the superintendent both his basic items for defense and his primary method of securing the loyalty of the Indians through gift giving. As rebel grumbling against King and Parliament grew louder, Johnson knew how critical it was to maintain Iroquois support for England. Among other considerations, he would no longer tolerate Kirkland's meddling. In mid-May 1775, on the advice of General Thomas Gage, he blocked Kirkland from returning to the Oneidas after the missionary had made a short trip to New England, and he banned all dissenting clergy from Iroquoia.[29]

Later that month, as organized patriot defiance of the imperial will gained momentum among Mohawk Valley colonists, Johnson hunkered down for protection. Receiving faulty intelligence that New Englanders had raised a force to capture him, he constructed fortifications around his home and caused alarm among the Mohawks with talk that the rebels would seize and imprison or execute him. Finally, in July, he fled with 220 Indians and loyalists to Fort Oswego, on Lake Ontario, and then on to Montreal. En route, he visited some Oneidas near Fort Stanwix, hoping to convince them to join him in Canada. On the recommendation of Chief Warrior Skenandoah, the Oneidas rejected Johnson's overture as well as his proffered gifts.[30]

Full-scale rebellion pulled the Oneidas in various directions. Most felt at least a pragmatic attachment to the position of the superintendent, who distributed goods to them, advised them, and communicated for them with the powerful king of England. As a counterweight of major proportions, Kirkland had won the hearts of many Oneidas during his nine years among them. Everyone knew he favored the patriot cause.

Traditionalists, meanwhile, concentrated at Old Oneida with a few adherents in other communities, encouraged their brethren to return to long-held customs and to reject all things European—Kirkland and the superintendent included. Unlike the Mohawks, whose territory was then being overrun, the Oneidas at Kanonwalohale, Old Oneida, and, to a lesser extent, Oriska and Oquaga, still lived far enough away from the colonists to avoid perpetual contact but near enough for occasional visits and business transactions. They had developed solid commercial and personal ties with these European Americans, a majority of whom embraced the rebellion.

Emotionally, then, most Oneidas leaned toward Kirkland and his patriot associates; from all other perspectives, however, they viewed neutrality as their best course of conduct. No one could predict the conflict's duration or severity, nor could the Oneidas anticipate how well the patriot rebels would fare against the mighty British king whose armed forces had crushed the French in Canada a decade before. Watchfulness and neutrality were the prudent choices.[31]

In June 1775, the Oneida Nation gathered in council at Kanonwalohale to discuss their alternatives. Representing the patriot cause, the Massachusetts Provincial Congress had written the Mohawks and other Iroquois peoples, urging them to stand with the rebel side in the event of war. The Oneidas now felt pressured to build a consensus among themselves and announce their position publicly.[32]

According to Jacob Reed, the Oneida who prepared an official statement by the "Chiefs, headmen, Councilers, warriors, & youngmen of the Onoida nation," they concurred that "we are together for Peace" and "will Exert our uttmost Endeavours to keep our Brethren the Six nations and others further back from disturbing you." Kirkland later drafted a reply to the New Englanders, which a dozen Oneida leaders signed, elaborating on the arguments that Reed recorded. "We cannot intermeddle in this dispute between two brothers," the Oneidas declared, feeling equal affection for all parties involved in the conflict.[33]

The two documents revealed the depth of support for neutrality. After many discussions, every major Oneida constituency endorsed the policy. Reed's summary represented the males, while the one Kirkland prepared came from "the Sachems, warriors, and female governesses of Oneida." Those who signed the latter document represented all four Oneida castles and included such prominent sachems as Kanaghwaes, Shononhse:s, and Jimmy Tayaheure and such respected chief warriors as Skenandoah and Good Peter.[34]

The two documents also revealed the Oneidas' dismay about the imperial dispute. For outsiders, "[t]he quarrel seems to be unnatural" for "two brothers of one blood," the Oneidas wrote. "The present situation of you two brothers is new and strange to us," they stated. "We *Indians* cannot find nor recollect in the traditions of our ancestors the like case or a similar instance." In their world, family members would never act toward one another in such potentially destructive ways.[35]

Even at the confederacy level, the Six Nations remained extremely reluctant to engage in combat with one another. The Iroquois had initially banded together first and foremost to resolve disputes and ensure peace among themselves and, then, to combine their strength for use against external enemies. In combat, however, Iroquois warriors shied away from fighting one another out of concern for injuring any of their distant kin. To strike a blow against a fellow Iroquois was an almost unthinkable act. The neutral course, then, was more than just sensible policy; it suggested the Oneidas' discomfort about supporting in any way violent clashes between British brothers.

During the challenging days ahead, the Oneidas labored diligently to maintain neutrality. Repeatedly, they proclaimed their peaceful intentions. Rumors of an imminent raid by the Six Nations, for example, triggered bolts of panic among colonists at German Flatts, causing them to toss up defensive works and scout for hostile war parties. Two Oneida messengers, Beech Tree and Thuegweyndack, tried to allay these fears. The Oneidas pledged their friendship and advised these settlers that "they should not give ear to any false reports, for they [the Oneidas] would always give notice of any bad news." When someone murdered a settler near Cherry Valley, and locals murmured about Oneida involvement, the nation launched its own inquiry, which concluded that none of its people had hunted or traveled in those woods that day. "We don't think you would have suspected any of us *Oneidas* to have done such a thing," the tribal investigators surmised, "were it not for the troubles and confusions that prevail" between British and rebel partisans. They urged the colonists to "quiet your minds, and by no means indulge any fears respecting us; and whenever we meet again, let it be in great friendship and brotherly love."[36]

The Oneida Nation's declaration of neutrality did not preclude individual tribal members from supporting or opposing the colonists' rebellion. That May, in Cherry Valley, local settlers crammed into a small church to discuss the momentous events of the day. In the crowd was a magnetic spokesperson whose words on behalf of the cause of liberty cast a seeming spell over those in attendance. His name was Thomas Spencer, an Oneida Indian.[37]

Spencer had learned to live in both the Indian and European worlds. Since his mother was an Oneida, her people accepted him as a full-fledged member of the nation. His father, a devout Anglo-American Presbyterian, had settled on a hill two miles east of Cherry Valley sometime around 1750. In his youth, Spencer spent enough time in each world to have warm feelings for both, and residents at Kanonwalohale and Cherry Valley enjoyed his company.

Like many Oneida males, young Spencer rejected farming, preferring instead to roam the forests and hone his hunting skills. By adult-

hood, he had learned the trade of blacksmithing and offered his services variously at Cherry Valley and Kanonwalohale. His skills, which
addressed a great need in Oneida villages, and his extensive exposure to
Presbyterianism ensured him high standing among the Oneidas.
Within his bifurcated universe, he mastered both the Oneida and English languages so thoroughly that he often acted as an interpreter,
which further enhanced his reputation in both communities.

Even though unschooled in political discourse, that May day in the
Cherry Valley church, Spencer rose from the pew to deliver a heartfelt
statement on American liberties and the justness of patriot complaints.
His forceful eloquence buoyed supporters and swayed some doubters.
In overwhelming numbers, the European American settlers of Cherry
Valley embraced the rebel cause. They resolved "never to become
slaves" and, within a few weeks, formed a militia company to fight, if
necessary, in defending "our Constitutional Rights and Priviledges"
against the "several arbitrary and oppressive Acts of the British Parliament."[38]

Even as settlers in Cherry Valley rallied behind the words of Thomas
Spencer, patriot leaders were gathering in Philadelphia to launch the
Second Continental Congress. In July 1775, the delegates listened
carefully to Samuel Kirkland, who had traveled from New England to
encourage the establishment of official patriot channels of communication with the native populace in such vital zones as the Mohawk River
region. Congress agreed to set up Indian departments that would seek
to preserve peace and to oversee the allocation of essential provisions,
such as clothing, weapons, and ammunition. Congress's Northern Indian Department would deal primarily with the Six Nations.

Before Kirkland left Philadelphia, Congress handed him a lengthy
message to deliver to the Iroquois. The delegates accused the Crown of
violating a long-standing covenant with their colonists by depriving
them of their property and political rights. "If our people labour on the
field, they will not know who shall enjoy the crop," they stated. "If they
hunt in the woods, it will be uncertain who shall taste of the meat, or
have the skins." Congress, at this juncture, sought no help from the In-

dians. This is a "family quarrel," and "[w]e desire you to remain at home, and not join on either side, but keep the hatchet buried deep." To promote neutrality, the delegates promised to have a council fire kindled at a conference in Albany, as some Oneidas had suggested, so that rebel leaders and the Six Nations could discuss their various concerns.[39]

Meanwhile, Guy Johnson, once in Montreal, was asking for much more than neutrality. With assistance from Joseph Brant and other associates, the refugee superintendent in late July 1775 gathered together nearly 1,700 Indians, mostly from Canadian tribes but a few hundred from the Six Nations, to induce them to fight for the Crown. After distributing presents to promote goodwill, Johnson "delivered each Nation a War Belt to be held ready for service." The Indians accepted the belts but warned Johnson that they must strike with the war hatchet soon or it "would cut them if they kept it long without using it." As a seal to their agreement, the participants feasted on oxen and wine, symbolizing the consumption of the body and blood of the rebels.[40]

The ideal of a unified Iroquois policy toward confederacy outsiders was suddenly in trouble. Many Mohawks, such as those with Johnson in Canada, now championed the British side, although many others in New York preferred neutrality. By comparison, the Oneidas mostly favored the Whigs, even though the tribe had declared itself neutral. The Tuscaroras had followed the Oneida lead and endorsed neutrality, despite strong ties to the rebels through Kirkland, Crosby, and Presbyterianism. Detached from the situation by distance, religion, and contact with colonists, the remaining Iroquois—Onondagas, Cayugas, and Senecas—generally preferred noninvolvement. Most of their interaction with persons of European descent had occurred when they dealt with Crown officials or post traders at such British forts as Niagara and during pilgrimages to the superintendent's home for consultation and presents. If their leaders had leanings, they were toward the Crown.[41]

Word quickly filtered back to New York regarding what had transpired with Guy Johnson in Montreal, even as Congress's commissioners made final preparations for the promised conference in the Mohawk Valley. Beginning in mid-August 1775, first at German Flatts and then in Albany, some four hundred Iroquois tribespeople and colonial patriots gathered to talk about their concerns and intentions. Oneidas and Mohawks comprised most of the Indians in attendance. A four-person delegation, headed by the wealthy local grandee Major General Philip Schuyler, spoke for the Continental Congress.[42]

The solemnity and dignity that the Iroquois brought to such gatherings amazed those unacquainted with their protocol. "The Behaviour of the poor Savages at a public Meeting ought to put us civilized people to Blush," the delegation secretary recorded. He did not then understand that for centuries the Six Nations had regularly met in councils among themselves, with other tribes, and with Europeans, and had thus long since developed a keen sense of how to conduct important negotiations with other parties.

At the conference, only designated leaders spoke. "The most profound silence is observed, [with] no interruption of a speaker," commented one witness, who also noted that "[w]hen anyone speaks all the rest are attentive." The audience never disputed the message or argued heatedly with the presenter. After listening to the speech, they would adjourn to deliberate and formulate their reply. Each speaker addressed the group in short sentences, which translators then converted into other languages. In this way, attendees from all Six Nations could comprehend the presentations. "It is amazing with what exactness these people recollect all that has been said to them," the conference's secretary noted.[43]

For one evening's entertainment, the Iroquois invited the representatives to a social dance, a two-hour extravaganza. Dressed in loin cloths, the Indians clustered around two large fires, while beating drums and striking sticks in rhythmic precision. The men sang songs that recounted the great deeds and martial achievements of their ancestors. "They would strike out into a Dance around the Fires with the most savage Contortions of Body & limbs," recorded one observer. Then, on a chief's signal, they would stop dancing and continue their singing. The tunes varied—sometimes slow and mournful, sometimes "more brisk & lively."[44]

During the two weeks of talks, the patriot commissioners compared the struggle between England and the colonies to a dispute between a father and a son over the weight of the son's backpack. The father kept putting more items in the son's pack, despite the boy's complaints, until the son's only alternative was to cast off the burden and refuse to carry the pack, because "such a weight will crush him down and kill him." The British government, the commissioners pronounced, had placed too many burdens on the shoulders of the colonists. "We do not take up the hatchet and struggle for honor or conquest," they explained, "but to maintain our civil constitution and religious privileges."[45]

In response, the Oneida sachem White Skin (Sughagearat) encouraged everyone present to preserve open channels of communication. Do not listen to scoundrels, he counseled, "as they would only mean to sow dissension between us and our brothers of the Twelve United Colonies." As with European American settlers, "there are liars and mischief-makers among the Indians." White Skin's advice was to disregard what any one person might say or do, but "attend to what you may hear from the mouth of the great council."[46]

The commissioners responded by stressing that although King George III had shattered the Covenant Chain with the colonies, the commissioners hoped to maintain peaceful relations with the Iroquois. Despite what had happened so recently with pledges to Guy Johnson and the British, a Mohawk sachem proclaimed that the Six Nations had decided "not to take any part" in the dispute between England and some of its American colonies. "It is a family affair," he elaborated, and the Mohawks preferred "to sit still and see you fight it out." They had delivered the same message to Guy Johnson, this sachem claimed. "We told him we should take no part in the quarrel, and hoped neither side would desire it. Whoever applies first, we shall think in the wrong."[47]

Once they had assented to the commissioners' primary request— that they remain neutral—the Iroquois then filed complaints about land encroachment, trade, and repairs. "They are thorough bred politicians," avowed a patriot participant. "They know the proper time of making demands." Early in the conference, the Indians turned in kettles, hoes, and axes for repair. That way, even if the meeting broke up on a sour note, they would not return home empty-handed. With the major issues resolved, "[t]hey reaped up several old Grievances and de-

manded Redress, well imagining that nothing would be denied them at
this time."[48]

Having assured Congress of Iroquois neutrality, the Six Nations believed the commissioners could now afford to act generously. They
were right. On the final day, the commissioners agreed to reopen trade,
ask Congress to investigate disputed land claims, and recommend that
Congress pay for two blacksmiths to work in Iroquoia. The Iroquois negotiators thus adroitly extracted benefits and concessions from the commissioners by carefully flashing their trump card, the possibility of their
supporting the British.

As the conference participants began their trek homeward, the Oneida
chief warrior Skenandoah agreed to accompany Samuel Kirkland to
the vicinity of Boston. The former wanted to evaluate the size and
strength of rebel forces so that he could "satisfy his Curiosity" and also
report back to his fellow Iroquois. After all, even if neutrality was the
prudent course, the Oneidas had no reason to remain overly cautious
and possibly alienate the British if the rebel military force amounted to
little more than a few bedraggled soldiers.[49]

Born in 1706 a Conestoga Indian, Skenandoah was requickened as
an Oneida in his youth. Tall and muscular, he had long since earned a
reputation as a ferocious fighter, so much so that the Oneidas had
named him a chief warrior. In 1755, after a night of binge drinking, he
awoke on a street in Albany stripped of his ornaments and clothing.
Disgusted by his own self-degradation, Skenandoah forswore alcohol
forever, a vow that he kept for the rest of his life. As he grew older, he
built a reputation for wisdom and good judgment. One person stated
that Skenandoah "possessed a vigorous mind, and was alike sagacious,
active and persevering."[50]

Skenandoah had developed a close personal friendship with Kirkland. He may have first met the missionary in 1765, but their relationship blossomed when Kirkland settled at Kanonwalohale. Soon the
chief warrior was seeking God's grace and embracing New Side Presbyterianism. Skenandoah regularly stood by his minister when Kirkland
had differences with Sir William and Guy Johnson. His vast prestige

within the nation and the Iroquois Confederacy served as a source of protection for the clergyman.[51]

The area surrounding Boston that Skenandoah and Kirkland visited had changed significantly in the weeks following the battles of Lexington and Concord. As many as fifteen thousand patriots under arms had poured into the vicinity and had the British regulars under General Thomas Gage trapped in Boston itself. On June 17, a bloodbath took place in what came to be called the Battle of Bunker Hill across the bay north of Boston, with nearly fifteen hundred troops killed or wounded, 60 percent of them British. Three weeks later, George Washington, the Continental Army commander in chief recently commissioned by Congress, arrived outside of Boston to direct future operations by patriot military forces.

Like Skenandoah, George Washington was a tall, powerful-looking person with a commanding presence. He possessed many talents, including sound judgment and the capacity to learn from his mistakes. Despite his oppressive workload, Washington appreciated the importance of preserving Iroquois neutrality and took time to meet with Skenandoah and Kirkland. He was also cognizant of the central role the Oneidas and their Presbyterian missionary had played in securing that stance. According to the general, "I have Studiously endeavoured to make his Visit agreeable," certainly by allowing a tour of the army and by hosting them at his Cambridge headquarters. When Skenandoah "express'd an Inclination to pay his Respects" to the Massachusetts Provincial Congress, then managing political matters for the patriot cause in that colony, Washington wrote an enthusiastic letter of introduction. "The Indian who accompanies Mr. Kirtland [sic] is an Oneida Chief of considerable Rank in his own Country," he pointed out. "He has come on a Visit to the Camp principally to satisfy his Curiosity." The commanding general also stressed that "his Tribe has been very friendly to the Cause of the United Colonies" and that the report Skenandoah planned to present when he returned home would "have important Consequences to the publick Interest."[52]

After meeting with the Provincial Congress, Skenandoah and Kirkland returned to Washington's headquarters, where the general penned a letter on behalf of Kirkland to John Hancock, recently named presi-

dent of the Continental Congress. Lauding the missionary's contributions to the cause, Washington hoped the delegates would secure
Kirkland's services with the Indians. He also indicated that the minister would be accompanied by an important Oneida chief. "I have endeavoured to make agreeable to him both by Civility & some small
Presents," Washington stated in hinting that Congress should treat
Skenandoah similarly.[53]

Skenandoah did not make it to Philadelphia that year. He and Kirkland traveled along an indirect route to Pennsylvania by way of Stockbridge, Massachusetts, where the missionary's family was then residing.
Skenandoah fell ill along the way. He was so sick that he stayed with
Kirkland and his family for several weeks, receiving constant medical
care. When the Oneida chief felt strong enough to travel, Kirkland purchased a horse for him, so that he could ride back to Kanonwalohale.
Belatedly, Skenandoah returned home with eyewitness confirmation of
the strength of rebel forces. Kirkland proceeded to Philadelphia, where
Congress reimbursed him for various expenses and promised to cover
other debts he might accrue while working with the Iroquois to ensure
their neutrality.[54]

Noncombatant status for the Oneidas did not mean that they withdrew
into isolation. They perceived the maintenance of neutrality as an activist responsibility. In the autumn of 1775, along with many fellow Iroquois, they intervened to discourage Canadian tribes from entering the
fray. In September, a sizable patriot detachment under General
Schuyler moved north across Lake Champlain with the purpose of capturing Montreal and Quebec and having Quebec Province become the
fourteenth colony in rebellion. During this campaign, some Kahnawakes and Mohawks fought alongside the British resisters, and a few
lost their lives.

Meanwhile, the Six Nations sent a delegation of four Oneidas—
Henry Cornelius of Oriska, Jacob Reed, Quedon, and Hanyost
T,hanaghghanegeaghu—to urge their brothers in Canada to embrace
the posture of neutrality. The Kahnawakes were Oneidas and Mohawks
who had adopted Catholicism and migrated to Canada a century ear-

lier. Like the peoples of the Six Nations, they had been divided by the rebellion. Some rallied to the standard of Johnson and Brant; others traveled to Cambridge to pledge their aid to General Washington.[55]

The Oneida visitors arrived at an opportune time. Intercepting a Kahnawake war party that was en route to aid British and Indians blocking the way of the invading rebel force, the Oneidas convinced them to return to their village for additional discussions. There, the Oneidas explained what had transpired at the recent German Flatts–Albany conference and that the Six Nations intended to remain neutral.

About that time, Brant, Claus, and a group of their Indian supporters arrived at the Kahnawake village and proposed that the Oneida envoys meet with Guy Johnson in Montreal. Sensing a trap, the Oneidas declined this overture. They had come to treat with the Kahnawakes, they replied, not with Johnson. They then presented a message from Schuyler, who hoped the Kahnawakes would stand aside in the conflict so that no more of their blood would be spilled and that a delegation of their leaders would meet with him. An incensed Brant stood up and declared, "It is over with Johnson; all the Indians will quit him." He and Claus returned to Montreal empty-handed.[56]

After some debate, the Kahnawakes adopted the Oneidas' proposition and sent a party to visit with Schuyler. At rebel headquarters, they met with his ranking assistant, Brigadier General Richard Montgomery, who had temporarily assumed command for the feverish Schuyler, and he sealed the agreement. At this juncture, they and others of the Seven Nations of Canada would not take sides in this family altercation between English brothers.[57]

Late that autumn, the Six Nations gathered in a Grand Council at Onondaga. There, Mohawk, Cayuga, and Seneca chiefs presented the war belt they had accepted from Guy Johnson in Montreal, who had called on them to fight on behalf of the British. Those Iroquois who had returned from the German Flatts–Albany conference "were much displeased." They insisted that the war belt be delivered to the rebel commissioners. Others argued that protocol demanded that it be returned to Johnson. After much consideration, a majority supported carrying the belt to the rebel commissioners in Albany. The Iroquois council then delivered a "severe and publick reprimand" to the Mohawks for permitting some of their warriors to engage in fighting against the rebels.[58]

In December 1775, sixty or more Iroquois chiefs arrived in Albany to surrender the belt and explain what had transpired, all the while reaffirming their neutral stance toward the patriot rebellion. The chiefs spoke sincerely and reassured their listeners, but their words camouflaged deep fissures in the ranks of the Six Nations. By then, most of the warriors who had rushed off to Canada in support of Johnson had returned to their villages. They spoke positively of their experiences with the British and expressed disillusionment that their brothers had not followed them. Those who had engaged in combat related tales of glory, tempting fellow warriors to join them when campaigning started anew in the spring of 1776. For the first time in years, eager young warriors had the opportunity to make names for themselves in battle—on the British side.[59]

Inevitably, boasting by the Mohawk warriors reached the ears of concerned local rebels. The Tryon County Committee of Safety demanded an explanation from the Mohawks living at Canajoharie. In November, their sachems traveled to Albany, where they attempted to smooth over differences. The blame, insisted the hereditary leaders, lay with their young warriors, who had been "debauched to go away" and fight. No doubt, they had embraced warfare too quickly, but the same could be said for the colonists, the sachems stated. "We have made a very strong agreement of friendship together," they concluded, "and we beg you will not break it for sake of some wrong done by some, who have been debauched. You will drop it, we hope, for the present." The committee members replied that those warriors who had taken up the hatchet should repent before them, which never happened.[60]

As biting winter temperatures replaced the autumn chill in late 1775, the Oneidas could sense the awkwardness of their position, knowing the Iroquois neutralist posture might easily unravel. They had labored actively for neutrality, but only the Tuscaroras had consistently stood alongside them. The Mohawks, especially their young warriors, felt they had good reasons for making war against the European American rebels. Crown officials in Canada carried substantial weight with the Senecas and correctly viewed the Oneidas as the primary obstacle to unified Iroquois involvement on behalf of Great Britain. How much longer the Oneidas could help maintain the Iroquois Confederacy's neutralist posture remained to be determined.

5

STRUGGLING TO
PRESERVE NEUTRALITY

In 1775, John Johnson could no longer shirk responsibility. For more than a third of a century, he had bounded through life carefree, basking in his father's riches and reputation. Too undisciplined to study seriously, he found distractions in almost everything around him. By adolescence, these allurements included members of the opposite sex. With an unusual burst of devotion, John put aside schoolbooks to chase after young Indian and white women, at least until his father packed him off to Philadelphia for further schooling. Then, in 1765, Sir William Johnson sent his dissolute son off to England, where John acquired a bit of polish and some valuable contacts during two years abroad, which helped cement his ties to imperial Britain.

Once back in America, John assumed control of one of his father's estates and planted himself in Sir William's old house overlooking the Mohawk River. John agreed to manage the estate and married into a prominent family, but when his ailing father proposed that he step into his place as the next Superintendent of Indian Affairs, he balked. Such service was too much of a nuisance, and the prize office went to John's brother-in-law, Guy Johnson. A baronetcy was enough for John, but when Guy Johnson and Daniel Claus fled to Canada in July 1775, the burden of Tory leadership in the Mohawk River Valley devolved on Sir John. This time he accepted the duty that befell him.

The principal inheritor of Sir William's extensive holdings, Sir John was the focus of much local speculation as to where he stood on the great issues of the day. The Tryon County Committee of Safety, the local bastion of rebel authority, pressed Sir John about his allegiance. Unabashedly, he proclaimed his unwavering attachment to the Crown. Before he would join any patriot association or "lift his hand up against his King," he declared, he would "rather suffer his head to be cut off." Regarding his many tenants, he would not forbid them to participate in insurgent activities, but he was certain they had no interest in joining the rebel cause.[1]

With his declaration of fealty to the Crown, Sir John assumed the mantle of chief Tory in the Mohawk Valley. His every movement fell under the watchful eye of local rebels. Soon rumors were circulating among Whig partisans that Sir John was organizing loyalist forces in the region and had secured the assistance of nearby Indians, mostly Mohawks, for an impending attack.

The hearsay had some merit. Sir John had taken action to consolidate the king's friends in the region, particularly his Scottish tenants. Unfortunately, he could hide his secret activities for only so long, especially among suspicious neighbors. When the Continental Congress learned of Sir John's actions in January 1776, that body ordered General Philip Schuyler, the head of the Continental Army's Northern Department, to place Johnson under arrest and disarm his Tory followers.[2]

Lacking regular troops, Schuyler asked the Tryon County Committee of Safety for militia support. Instead of the two hundred or three hundred citizen soldiers he sought, nearly three thousand patriots got word of this enterprise and assembled to march on Sir John's estate. Schuyler feared the worst from these largely untrained, undisciplined, but enthusiastic militiamen, especially since they would have to pass through Mohawk country to reach Johnson.

Schuyler appreciated the delicate nature of his assignment. As Warraghiyagey's eldest son, Sir John possessed a kinship network that stretched into the Mohawk Nation and included numerous half brothers and sisters. To prevent any unnecessary clashes with Mohawk warriors, Schuyler sent advance messengers, advising them of his operation and offering a peace belt to be passed throughout the Six Nations.[3]

Despite these gestures, Schuyler's approach ignited a furor among Mohawk warriors. The previous autumn in Canada, dozens of them had tasted combat, and their tales had stirred up passion among others to join British forces in the spring, so that they, too, could earn more prestige among their fellow Mohawks. Others wanted revenge for casualties or closure for the grieving process. Needing little additional motivation, they reached a near war pitch because of Schuyler's invasion of their homeland.

With the region about to explode in violence, Mohawk elders intervened to calm the warriors. If they attacked or resisted with force of arms, the sachems warned, both Mohawk villages could become bloody battlegrounds, with untold losses to women, children, and the elderly. In their pleas, the hereditary sachems urged their brothers to give them time to arrange a meeting with Schuyler, with the hope of brokering a solution to the crisis. Begrudgingly, the warriors yielded to diplomacy.[4]

At Schenectady, a Mohawk delegation intercepted Schuyler and his command. In what the general described as "a very haughty tone," the Mohawks demanded to know why Schuyler needed an army to speak to Sir John, when a half dozen men would do. The size of the rebel force appeared to violate the neutrality agreement of the previous summer. Schuyler replied that his orders required him to disarm Johnson, but in an effort to avoid bloodshed, he promised to employ the Mohawks as mediators.[5]

During the next few days, Schuyler and Sir John met under tense conditions and hammered out terms. Both sides hurled veiled threats, but give-and-take on their differences prevailed. Johnson surrendered all his weapons, powder, and ammunition, except for a few family heirlooms. He further consented to restrict his travel to New York but stopped short of giving Schuyler the names of Tories, claiming his lack of knowledge regarding who they were.

With this accord in place, Schuyler dispatched the translator and emissary James Dean through Iroquoia with a belt and a speech that explained what had transpired. The patriot general wanted no misunderstanding of his intentions among the Six Nations. He desired their neutrality. Schuyler also ordered his militia force to search for weapons in the hands of suspected loyalists. All told, his troops confiscated muskets from about five hundred suspected Crown supporters.[6]

Although the plan to squelch Sir John's activities may have succeeded temporarily, the heated Mohawk reaction represented a major signal that Oneida efforts to preserve Iroquois neutrality were decomposing. The negotiated solution seemed like a victory for the Mohawk sachems, but it also exposed fissures in the Mohawk ranks and deep-seated hostility among the warrior element toward the patriots. Some warriors stood "ready to take to their arms," a sachem confessed to Schuyler. "There are some among us of different minds, as there are among you," the Indian leader stated, and "it is not in our powers to rule them as we please."[7]

Attempts to turn the Iroquois toward the British cause accelerated as well. Some three hundred miles to the west at the major British base of Fort Niagara, portly John Butler, a wealthy Mohawk Valley loyalist who had fled to Canada with Guy Johnson and then assumed the duty of a deputy Indian agent for the Crown in far western New York, cajoled clusters of natives to be leery of patriot calls for neutrality. If the rebels gained their independence, Butler warned, the British shield that protected the Six Nations would vanish. The Iroquois would have to ward off the land-hungry colonists alone. As proof of the rebels' bad intentions, Butler pointed out how trade had slowed to a trickle, despite patriot pledges to keep goods flowing. Using such arguments, Butler convinced hundreds of Indians to doubt rebel motives, all the while luring pockets of warriors to renounce neutrality in favor of aligning themselves with Crown forces.[8]

About the same time Butler was laboring to entice the Iroquois into taking up the hatchet, a loyalist group, headed by Guy Johnson, arrived in London. They began lobbying for more resources to secure and sustain Iroquois assistance. Guy Johnson assured Lord George Germain, the Secretary for American Affairs and principal war planner, that with sufficient resources and proper leadership (referring to himself), "these people may be secured to the Crown and rendered serviceable now or on any future emergency." The Indians, Johnson asserted, had no affection for the rebels. Instead, they had legitimate complaints against them for ceaseless land encroachments in Mohawk territory and the Susquehanna River Basin. The Crown could easily exploit the land-grabbing issue and gain reliable allies among the Six Nations.[9]

Like Guy Johnson, Joseph Brant and his friend John Oteronyente had the opportunity to present their case to Lord Germain. "The Mohocks our particular Nation, have on all occasions shewn their zeal and loyalty to the Great King," the two asserted. The Crown, however, repeatedly failed to intervene on their behalf when the colonists treated them shabbily. Over the years, European Americans had stripped them of their tribal lands around Albany and were now encroaching on territory near Oquaga. "We are tired out in making complaints & getting no redress," the Mohawks declared, and they implored Germain to "give us such answers as will make our hearts light and glad before we go."[10]

Germain did just that. He pledged to investigate the land incursions once His Majesty's troops had quelled the rebellion, and he provided Guy Johnson with the authority and resources to coax the Six Nations onto the British side. In letters to his senior commanders in America — Generals William Howe, Guy Carleton, and John Burgoyne — Germain expressed his opinion that the Indians would serve as valuable allies, and he encouraged these commanders to secure their support.[11]

While British officials worked to gain the allegiance of the Six Nations, the Oneidas dangled in the middle. Basic geography alone convinced them of the wisdom of advocating a neutral stance for all Iroquois. In 1776 the British base of power extended eastward from Fort Niagara, and the patriot stronghold stretched westward from Albany; Oneida territory lay in between. Probable routes for forays by either combatant would lead directly through their homeland. However, should the Six Nations remain neutral, neither British nor American forces would likely traverse their territory, for fear of driving the Iroquois into the enemy's camp.

At the same time, the Oneidas could not actively oppose the rebellion, had they had notions of doing so, because of their close proximity to colonial settlements. Once Guy Johnson had fled to Canada and the local Whigs disarmed Sir John, the balance of power in the Mohawk Valley shifted markedly toward the rebels, whose numbers were much greater than those of local loyalists. If they wanted to aid the British, the Oneidas would have to abandon their traditional homeland and move west or north for protection, something they had no interest in doing.

Over the years, trade, religion, and other forms of contact with nearby colonists served to fix the rebels more firmly in the hearts and minds of the Oneida people. On the whole, the Oneidas, unlike the Mohawks, perceived these associations in positive terms, as exemplified by their deep respect for Kirkland. In addition, the patriots spoke of freedom and the liberties of individuals in ways the Oneidas easily grasped. Power-hungry Crown officials, the colonists claimed, were depriving them of their fundamental rights and turning them into political slaves. This perception resonated with the Oneidas, who referred to themselves as "a free people" with "absolute Notions of Liberty." The concept of fundamental rights reflected the Oneidas' long-held imperative to control their own destiny, both as individuals and as a nation.[12]

Throughout the colonial period, none of the Six Nations acknowledged the sovereignty of the British Crown. Certainly they referred to the king as their father, a truly great person to be treated with respect because of his power and wisdom. The Six Nations regarded the king's words as sage advice from an elder, but they were subjects to no one. They were their own masters, a free people.[13]

The critical component of freedom, as both Oneidas and the American rebels discerned, lay in the notion of choice. Skenandoah, Good Peter, and seven other Oneidas once explained: "We choose to regulate our Affairs and to conduct our Concerns by the Rules and Maxims of our Ancestors, without being governed by the Laws of our Brothers, the white People." Their political and social customs, traditions, and practices generated ample amounts of personal liberty, while at the same time providing for stability and continuity of purpose for the Oneida people. The idea of freedom enabled the Oneidas to think clearly and act properly. "We use freedom, brother, to open our minds to you." A person whose mind was full of prejudicial baggage or tainted ideas and corrupting influences no longer possessed freedom. Such distorting factors limited choices and clouded thinking.[14]

Like Europeans, the Oneidas defined slavery as the opposite of free-dom. Slavery signified the domination of one nation over another and the capacity to compel a weaker people to act against their collective will and interest. With the Oneidas' high regard for liberty, observed a colonial witness, "they allow of no kind of Superiority, and banish all servitude from their Territories."[15]

The Oneidas' recent turn toward ownership of property helped them appreciate rebel accusations against King and Parliament, espe-cially charges of England depriving the colonists of their property with-out their consent—what they called taxation without representation. The shift toward ownership sensitized the Oneidas to the injustice of forfeiting possessions without a voice in the process. Sharing one's bounty with others was one matter, but having property taken without one's concurrence was quite another.

Like the Oneidas, other Iroquois nations held basic ideas about free-dom in common with the rebels. What they lacked was regular expo-sure to patriot commentary. The Mohawks had the most frequent encounters with European Americans, but they had become embit-tered toward the land-grabbing colonists, having lost nearly all their tribal territory. As such, the patriots appeared as hypocrites in their cries about the Crown unfairly seizing their property. Had Sir William John-son and his family not acted as their protector, as most Mohawks viewed matters, they would have lost everything. Their most logical op-tion, then, was to support the British over the ever-aggrandizing Ameri-can rebels.

Other Iroquois peoples continued to grapple with their own set of concerns. As guests of the Oneidas, the Tuscaroras felt an obligation to follow the Oneida lead, although they were very hesitant about oppos-ing the other Iroquois nations. The Onondagas and Cayugas, buffered from colonials by the Oneidas, communicated far less often with Europeans. New-birth Christianity, such as that espoused by Samuel Kirkland, had not reached their villages; evidence of the Crown's gen-erosity, however, was present among them. Farthest to the west and closest to Fort Niagara, the Senecas interacted extensively with the

British and rarely with American colonists. Although they showed signs of favoritism toward the Crown and some wanted to fight the rebels, the Seneca Nation hesitated to involve itself.[16]

To discuss further the question of neutrality, the Six Nations agreed to meet in a Grand Council at Onondaga. In late February 1776, the Onondagas established a rough timetable, agenda, and ground rules. Among those invited to attend was James Dean, who had lived at Oquaga for many years and spoke the Oneida language fluently. He was to provide the council with any necessary information or interpretation of the Iroquois agreement about neutrality reached the summer before at Albany. Although the Six Nations did not offer John Butler a seat at the council, they had no intention of snubbing him. By agreement, two or three leaders from each nation were to travel to Niagara after the meeting and explain their discussions to him.[17]

Even before the council gathered, trouble started brewing. Wary of the close relationship between the Oneidas and the American patriots, some of the Iroquois nations did not provide the Oneidas with a full accounting of Butler's recent speeches and overtures. The Oneidas apparently heard only about Butler's advocation of peace, nothing more. From Kanonwalohale, Dean, an advocate of the rebellion, suspected that "the information which the people of this place received respecting that interview, was not to be depended on; and that the *Oneidas*, on account of their well-known attachment to the Colonists, are not at present very likely to be rightly informed."[18]

A visit to Kanonwalohale by Onondaga and Cayuga sachems unwittingly confirmed Dean's suspicions. A Cayuga sachem, in a "long and very spirited speech," rebuked the Oneidas for their friendship with the rebels. The Oneidas devoted more attention to Albany than to the ancient Iroquois fire at Onondaga, the sachem charged, implying that rebel interests were more important to the People of the Standing Stone than were those of fellow Iroquois. "White people, particularly the *Americans*, are in nature treacherous and deceitful," the sachem insisted. They never were friends of Indians and were unreliable for aid and protection. "Should they conquer in the present contest," the speaker declared, they would "no sooner . . . turn about and fall on the *Indians*." In cautioning the Oneidas to remain loyal to the confederacy, the sachem mentioned that the Indians to the west of New York were planning to stand alongside the Iroquois against the rebels. Since the Oneidas had never heard about talks with the western Indians, this slip of the tongue suggested that their Iroquois brethren were conducting negotiations behind their backs.[19]

The Cayuga sachem also fumed that some Oneidas had surrendered to Schuyler the war belt that Guy Johnson had given Iroquois warriors in Canada the previous summer. The Oneidas had dishonored Johnson, the sachem stated. In so doing, they had acted without the unanimous consent of the confederacy and in violation of an agreement to return the belt to Johnson. Their only recourse, he decreed, was to retrieve and return the war belt to Johnson or his representative, John Butler.[20]

The Oneidas replied that they had not lost sight of their loyalties to the other nations of the confederacy. They had aided specific rebel friends in minor ways, but now they would act with strict neutrality, and they hoped that other confederacy nations would follow their example. Concerning Johnson's war belt, the Oneidas contended that they had acted properly and by direction of a majority of the Iroquois Council. They refused to send a delegation in company with the Cayugas and Onondagas to Albany. They warned that attempting to retrieve the belt would provoke needless "suspicions and jealousies" among local colonists, who would view this action as tantamount to a declaration of war. With European American settlers so close to their borders, the Oneidas did not want to raise doubts about their neutral posture.

For three days "[t]he disputes between the parties ran very high," Dean reported. Numerous Indians remarked that "they never knew debates so warm, and contention so fierce, to have happened between these two brothers (the *Oneidas* and *Cayugas*) since the commencement of their union." The Oneida position ultimately prevailed, but not without lingering ill will. When the Cayugas and Onondagas finally left Kanonwalohale, they did so "with evident symptoms of disaffection and disgust."[21]

———

Rather than diminish, pockets of Iroquois resistance to the Oneida policy of neutrality multiplied. As the numbers of British supporters increased, they challenged the Oneidas more boldly. Some Mohawk, Seneca, and Onondaga warriors—from the senior moiety of the confederacy—hoped to strike a blow against the rebels and humiliate the Oneidas by hatching a plot to assassinate James Dean if he attended the Grand Council. In a drunken stupor, several Mohawks at Onondaga boasted of their plan. The next day, some sachems quizzed the hungover warriors. When they refused to abandon their design, the hereditary leaders sent a messenger to warn the Oneidas and urged Dean to stay away.

Dean and the Oneida party first learned of the plot at the Tuscarora and Onondaga village of Kanaghsaraga, where they had joined in condolence rites for a deceased Tuscarora sachem. The Oneidas sent repeated dispatches to Onondaga, inquiring what steps the council was taking to ensure Dean's safety. Certainly Dean could have returned to Kanonwalohale, but he refused to do so. He held to his conviction that the council was too important to leave. Finally, a messenger from Onondaga arrived with assurances that council leaders had convinced the plotters to drop the plan. For added comfort, Dean wrote, the Oneidas, Kahnawakes, and Tuscaroras vowed to "defend me to the utmost of their power should any violence be offered me." To protect him during the Grand Council, the Oneidas and others kept a detail of warriors with him at all times and maintained a camp separate from that of the other Iroquois nations.[22]

On March 28, 1776, the Grand Council formally inaugurated its deliberations. Introductory remarks called for everyone to wipe tears from one another's eyes so that they could see clearly; to "cleanse each other's seats from blood" so as to rid their minds of retaliation and violence; and to "remove that load of grief which obstructed their utterance, that they might freely disclose their minds to each other."[23]

During the substantive discussions the next day, the other nations put the Oneidas on the defensive, where they remained throughout the council. A Seneca sachem reported that the Oneidas had proposed to seize John Butler and turn him over to Schuyler for a reward. In reply, the Oneidas insisted the tale was false. They did admit to aiding a few rebels who had befriended them for years, but they vowed not to do so again. They would "let white people conduct their own affairs as they pleased."[24]

Over the next few days, the Iroquois ambassadors debated the earlier speeches by Butler and discussed how to respond to them. A skilled master at beguiling argumentation, Butler had proposed that the Six Nations preserve peace. Then he proceeded to undermine this position by suggesting issues he hoped would cause the Iroquois to align with the British. Butler had artfully reminded them of Sir William Johnson's advice, that the Six Nations retain their unity, knowing that a plurality and, perhaps, the majority leaned toward the British. Within a few months, he cautioned, more of the king's warriors would arrive to chastise the rebels.

Mostly, though, Butler had urged the Six Nations to demand that the colonists reestablish trade with them at Fort Stanwix, Fort Niagara, and posts in Canada. At the time, rebel forces were in control of Montreal and the St. Lawrence River and had Quebec City under siege. Any proposal to reopen trade through Canada would have compelled rebel forces to relinquish their stranglehold on Quebec Province, besides enabling British officials on the New York frontier to obtain supplies for themselves and trade goods for the Indians. With basic supplies once again available, the Iroquois would have another compelling reason to link their interests with the Crown.[25]

Even though the Six Nations did "declare a strict neutrality in the present quarrel," the senior moiety pressed hard on the trade issue. They wanted a formal address, explaining their distressed condition and requesting the restoration of trade as usual. The Oneidas, Tuscaroras, and Canadian Indians balked at this proposal. Any attempt to reopen trade through the St. Lawrence River would interfere with military operations. As the Oneidas explained to their Cayuga brothers, they much preferred to wait until the upcoming summer conference at Albany to raise the issue of trade. The Cayugas, "much dissatisfied with this reply," lined up with the senior moiety against them.[26]

On April 2, an Onondaga speaker, representing the senior moiety, rose to speak. All the Six Nations should prepare an address to the rebel commissioners, he stated. If they did not honor the trade request, then the Iroquois should reverse their stand on neutrality. To this, White Skin, an influential sachem from Kanonwalohale who favored the rebel cause, hammered back, deriding his opponents for so transparent an effort to provoke trouble. Later, before the entire assembly, White Skin pronounced the Oneidas and Tuscaroras "unalterably fixed in their determination not to interfere in the present quarrel." The two nations refused to "obstruct or hinder, by words of otherwise, any of the military operations of the contending parties, while they themselves were uninjured." A chief warrior from the Oneida and Tuscarora nations then confirmed White Skin's declaration. Any request to the rebels for reopening trade through Canada would not carry their endorsement.[27]

Even before the Onondaga keepers extinguished the council fire, the Oneidas fully appreciated the depth of hostility toward the American rebels. Four of the original Five Nations now leaned in varying degrees toward the British. So piercing was the sound level of anti-rebel sentiment that the senior moiety, along with the Cayugas, had urged the council to issue to patriot leaders what was tantamount to an ultimatum: either alter your military operations and reopen trade, or the Six Nations will support the British. In the end, the gathering did send a belt to the rebel Indian commissioners in Albany promising to remain at peace with both sides. In reality, the belt represented a desperate attempt to maintain a semblance of harmony in the confederacy when neutrality was in the final stages of collapse.[28]

Before the council ended, a report from Schuyler arrived announcing the British evacuation of Boston. When Dean read the letter to the Iroquois, "[a] variety of passions appeared in the faces of the assembly. . . . Some seemed much elated with joy, and others as much depressed with vexation and disappointment." The mixed reaction provided yet another example of deepening divisions within the Iroquois community.[29]

With support from longtime brethren and allies collapsing, the Oneidas were at a loss for ways to reestablish harmony. They did not worry much about the maneuverings of Sir John Johnson, who was covertly rallying loyalist support while keeping in contact with John Butler through Mohawk intermediaries. Rebel tolerance for his actions was wearing thin, and he would soon be in flight to Canada. The most dangerous source of British influence stemmed from Fort Niagara. As Dean explained to Schuyler, "[t]he *Oneidas* look upon *Niagara* as the place from whence proceeds the cause of this sudden and unexpected change in the minds of their brethren." Butler seemed to know exactly how to entice the Iroquois onto the British side. With hopes of unity and peace vanishing before their eyes, the Oneidas began warning Dean and Kirkland that only the capture of Niagara would "unite the minds of the *Indians* in their friendship to the Colonies."[30]

What bothered the Oneidas about the recent Grand Council was the level of contention that fellow Iroquois had directed at them. In their acts, words, and tone, the Mohawks, Senecas, Onondagas, and Cayugas had exhibited outright hostility. Perhaps they were attempting to scold and shame the Oneidas into abandoning neutrality. Regardless, the other Iroquois nations' behavior had offended the Oneidas. Worse yet, the venom directed at them had communicated a potentially lethal message. The Oneidas now felt that they could not fully trust or depend on their Iroquois brothers and sisters. At worst, their enemies at some future date might be these very same persons.[31]

Within weeks of the council, the Oneidas adopted a dramatic measure to protect themselves. They secretly formed a defensive league with the Tuscaroras, Kahnawakes, and Oquagas "to support each other against other nations." No longer confident that the protective cloak of the Six Nations Confederacy would shield them from attack, or that membership would protect them from violence perpetrated by other Iroquois, the Oneidas sought security against their closest traditional allies.[32]

As the Iroquois had earlier agreed, representatives from each of the nations, accompanied by some warriors, visited John Butler in May 1776 to discuss the Grand Council proceedings. Henry Cornelius of Oriska was one of two Oneidas who traveled to Niagara. The delegation announced the Iroquois determination to remain united and neutral and to "receive no Ax from either." With his usual deftness, Butler lauded their decision, coyly noting that the king would have punished them if he had discovered they had aided the rebels. Butler felt that he should also mention the disastrous territorial losses facing the Iroquois if the revolutionaries won. The rebels lacked resources, he declared, but the Crown had unlimited supplies of weapons and trade goods, a remark that suggested that victory was inevitable and implied that those who aided the British would receive great rewards.[33]

For several days, the Iroquois resisted Butler's baiting. One Seneca wondered why a king who possessed such overwhelming resources would need their assistance. In concurrence, a Seneca chief warrior said he would not budge from neutrality. "When they hurt us," he explained, "it is time enough to strike them."[34]

Struggling to gain support, Butler altered his tack. He employed a Mohawk warrior, who declared that the king "has taken Pity on us & promises to assist us in driving the Americans out of the Country they have cheated us of." The speaker then asked, "What then shall we not be able to accomplish, if we unite in this good work?" Not until Butler plied his visitors with rum, however, did he make significant headway with the intransigents. Soon several chiefs proclaimed their desire to participate in a Canadian expedition. In no time, fifty warriors from the Six Nations had volunteered to go along, as did a few dozen fighters from western tribes.[35]

Butler thus kept chipping away at Iroquois neutrality. According to a trader at Niagara, the deputy agent kept a number of key Indian representatives in a constant state of drunkenness, filling them with not just alcohol but also tales of future combat glory. Butler was sure that once he coaxed some warriors into actual service, their actions would generate a momentum on their own. Stories of combat would serve as a lure to others, especially young males seeking to win reputations for themselves. Combat losses, in turn, would result in condolence ceremonies and demands for retribution. As one Seneca chief predicted, "Some of them will get killed—the Death Hollow will go through our towns—Resentment will be uppermost & the Relations & Friends of the deceased must go to revenge his death until we all get to blows."[36]

As Butler continued to work his charm, substantial numbers of Senecas, Cayugas, and Onondagas renounced their neutrality just weeks after their sachems had reconfirmed it in the Grand Council. As for the Mohawks, they would fight against the rebels retreating from

Canada, transport messages for loyalists, and openly challenge and even threaten patriot settlers and military forces in the Mohawk Valley. Iroquois neutrality was slipping into its death throes.

In early May 1776, British reinforcements reached Quebec City and started driving patriot forces out of Canada. The Oneidas feared that enthusiasm for the king's troops, which military success often inspired, might sway the Kahnawakes from their neutral stance. To bolster Kahnawake resolve, the Oneidas sent north a party of thirteen, led by Henry Cornelius, the sachem designate Thomas Sinavis, and a young, newly appointed sachem who had adopted the name of his deceased predecessor, Kanaghwaes. Along the way, the Oneidas met with General Schuyler and reported to him about Butler's activities. In turn, Schuyler conveyed disturbing news that the Kahnawakes had suffered heavy losses, perhaps sixty warriors, in combat. With the general's blessing and a letter directing rebel military leaders to assist them when possible, the party of Oneida delegates pressed on to Canada.[37]

The Oneida mission yielded mixed results. Much to their delight, the story about major Kahnawake losses proved false. The group visited other Canadian tribes and convinced them to bury the hatchet that Guy Johnson had handed them the year before. The Oneida mission's problem lay in the poor treatment they received from rebel officers. An officer assigned to accompany them near St. Johns abandoned them. Then Brigadier General Benedict Arnold, pressed from all sides as the patriot campaign was collapsing, said he had too much urgent military business to spend much time with the Oneidas. "Besides," Henry Cornelius complained to Schuyler, "it appeared that he was suspicious of our designs, especially when an officer came into the room who told him in *English* that we would cut their throats as soon as an opportunity offered, and that we were not to be trusted." Arnold had no idea that one of his guests spoke English.[38]

Although Arnold assigned an officer to work with the visiting Oneidas, the party never received the amount of clothing that Schuyler had pledged. They had traveled great distances over the course of a month on a mission that would clearly benefit the patriots. They felt they deserved better treatment.

Determined to preserve good relations with his best native ally, Schuyler made amends immediately. He apologized for the conduct of Arnold and other officers, explaining that they had to focus all their energy on the British forces descending on them. General Arnold had not given them gifts for their services, Schuyler likewise stated, because he did not have such items on hand. Nevertheless, they would not return to their homes empty-handed. Schuyler donated a wagonload of gunpowder and shot for the Oneidas to take with them.[39]

What appeared to the Oneidas and other Iroquois peoples as insensitive rebel behavior did little to support their neutrality. In one instance, a rebel commissioner attempted to pressure some Iroquois into selling him land. This act lent credence to the image cultivated by John Butler that if the revolutionaries defeated the British, they would soon target the Indians for their territory. When the rebel invasion of Quebec Province undercut the British ability to use the St. Lawrence River to import trade goods for the Indians, the rebels failed to step into the breach. Plagued themselves by shortages of all kinds, including financial resources, Congress did not authorize funds to purchase Indian trade items until the end of January 1776. Many local merchants declined to make deals, and others demanded exorbitant prices. Without ammunition, the Iroquois could not hunt, and with no hides, they could not procure many necessary goods.[40]

The British seemed to have the resources to lure the Iroquois out of a neutral posture, especially after the former started regaining control of Canada and the St. Lawrence trade route. In an effort to retain good rapport with the Six Nations, the patriots had not acted boldly or taken advantage of circumstances. As the rebels kept calling for nothing more than neutrality, Butler and others promised the Six Nations an abundance of supplies, military glory, and freedom from future rebel encroachments onto tribal lands. Many Iroquois found these promises too enticing to resist.

Even before Oneida complaints reached rebel ears, Whig leaders had decided to act more decisively. By mid-April 1776, Commander in Chief Washington had concluded that the Six Nations ultimately would not remain neutral. He urged Congress to get as many Iroquois as possible to join the patriot side. Early the next month, when some 225 Iroquois went to Albany to hand over the peace belt from the Onondaga Grand Council, the rebels began to implement that more aggressive posture.[41]

One way to do so was to demonstrate patriot martial strength. On May 9 the Iroquois attended a review of Brigadier General John Sullivan's brigade. One witness observed that the soldiers "made a most brilliant & warlike appearance." The Iroquois, commented Schuyler, were "greatly pleased with the Order & Regularity of the Troops, & surprised at the numbers." "I am exceedingly Glad that so large a Number of Indians was present at the Review of General Sullivan's Brigade," Washington stated when he learned about the event. "They, probably from the Appearance of so many armed Men, . . . may have received some favorable Impressions of our Strength, sufficient to Counter operate all the Ingenuous & Insidious Arts of Toryism."[42]

Building on this martial display, Schuyler invited the Iroquois representatives to explore the size and power of rebeldom and meet its leaders. An interpreter would accompany them first to New York, and from there they could visit Boston or Philadelphia. The Cayugas declined. Only a few of them had traveled to Albany, and no Senecas were present. Eight Mohawks volunteered to make the journey, as did four Onondagas and nine Oneidas and Tuscaroras. Among the Oneida contingent were Jacob Reed, who had attended Eleazar Wheelock's Indian school, and the young sachem Kanaghwaes.[43]

Before they left Albany, the Iroquois discussed travel plans with their host. Amid requests for fresh meat, ample water, and adequate transportation, the delegation wanted to travel to Philadelphia and visit the Continental Congress. By late May, they had reached the grid-patterned streets of the rebel capital, where they met with George Washington and members of Congress. Schuyler had suggested that the tour be stretched out. As long as the delegation remained with the patriots, they were "a Kind of hostage for [the] peaceable Demeanor of the others." At Washington's urging, the rebel leaders had no difficulty keeping the Indians occupied with sightseeing tours, various meetings, and social gatherings.[44]

On June 11, just before their departure, officials formally presented the Iroquois delegation to Congress. At the Pennsylvania Statehouse, later known as Independence Hall, John Hancock expressed hope that the Iroquois and the colonists "may be as one people, and have but one heart." He promised that rebel soldiers would not attack the Iroquois, and he called on them to prevent their young warriors from aligning with the enemy. Congress then offered a variety of gifts, and the Iroquois saluted Hancock by granting him a name, Kerantawa:neh, meaning Great Tree.[45]

The tour generated goodwill on both sides, and the Iroquois delegation left for home at just the right time. Dissension was once again stirring among the Six Nations because John Butler had called another council. The Iroquois travelers dispersed to their villages and spoke well of the patriot cause, spreading information about the rebels' strength and resources. "A lucky circumstance," Washington commented, "if it will gain either their friendship, or secure their Neutrality." Congress evidently had similar feelings. The delegates adopted a resolution directing Schuyler to hold a conference with the Six Nations "to engage them in our interest upon the best terms that can be procured."[46]

Following an Oneida recommendation, rebel authorities also adopted a tougher stance with their loyalist opponents in the Mohawk Valley. Despite Sir John Johnson's pledge to remain neutral, evidence mounted that he was acting as the major instigator of Tory activity in the region, besides keeping up communication links with Crown officials at Niagara and in Canada. Rebel leaders decided to arrest him again, and they sent out Colonel Elias Dayton with three hundred soldiers to execute the order. Tipped off by friends, Sir John left his pregnant wife behind and fled with 170 loyalists through the woods to Montreal, living at times on wild onions, roots, and beech tree leaves.[47]

As before, the Mohawks confronted the rebel forces. When Dayton's column entered Mohawk territory, rebel commissioner Volkert P. Douw went forward to explain their purpose. Several warriors ridiculed Douw and his translator. Dayton, too, received a venomous reception and had to halt his march and negotiate. According to an Onondaga witness, "[t]he Mohawks were impudent—insulting to a very great degree."

Only when Dayton said he would make war, destroy their villages, and kill their warriors if they kept blocking him, did the Mohawks back off.[48]

The Oneidas expressed "surprise" to the rebel leaders for what seemed like their "want of resolution" in dealing with the Mohawks. They explained that the "the lenity and forbearance shown in the *Mohawks,* after repeated breaches of promise," would only serve to convince pro-British and uncommitted Indians of the "cowardice" or "want of a manly spirit" among the European American patriots.[49]

The time had come to distinguish friends from foes. In their advice, the Oneidas were not sure that the Six Nations would continue much longer in a state of neutrality; too many powerful factors were at work to undermine Iroquois unity. They urged the rebel commissioners to hold a council and "demand who are our friends and who are not." When Schuyler learned from some Oneidas that John Butler had circulated an invitation for another council, he immediately issued his own call for a major gathering, to begin on July 1, 1776. The general announced that he had matters of "great importance" to communicate from leaders in Philadelphia. The Indians should assemble at German Flatts, "where you will be in no danger of taking the small-pox," which had broken out in Albany. Both Washington and the Congress lauded Schuyler's resoluteness, encouraging him to "form an Alliance on Such Terms and Conditions, as shall seem most likely to secure their Interest and Friendship."[50]

After much consideration, Schuyler also decided in early June to re-occupy Fort Stanwix, near the Oneida village of Oriska. Once in proper repair and adequately garrisoned, Fort Stanwix would provide a valuable shield for colonial settlements in the Mohawk Valley. Further, Schuyler was acknowledging the Oneida prediction that unless the rebels demonstrated greater resolve, the Six Nations would not stay neutral. They would have to declare themselves for or against Whig forces soon, so the assertive act of restoring Fort Stanwix might improve rebel standing among the Iroquois. A rejuvenated fort could also serve as a convenient trading post for friendly Oneidas and Tuscaroras nearby and, perhaps, for more distant Iroquois. With the blessing of Washington and Congress, Schuyler ordered troops into the bastion at the beginning of July.[51]

The Oneidas lauded these initiatives. They perceived the Mohawks as provocateurs and, after repeated warnings from their Oneida brothers, welcomed and encouraged a stronger rebel stance as the only hope for preserving neutrality. A firm patriot backbone would send the right signal to all Iroquois that they should not trifle with the revolutionaries.[52]

The binding linkages between trade and peace were also on the minds of the People of the Standing Stone. The Oneidas recognized the value of trading ties to Fort Stanwix at a time when the Iroquois were struggling to procure essentials. They had founded their Oriska settlement to take advantage of commercial traffic at the Oneida Carrying Place and at the fort. This post would once more become a focal point of trade, attracting merchants, goods, and money. As the Iroquois came to rely on the Fort Stanwix exchange, the policy of neutrality would be strengthened out of economic necessity.[53]

What the Oneidas needed was enough time for the post to commence operations without competition from British trading outlets. Unfortunately, time was in short supply. By the early summer of 1776, rebel forces had succumbed to the British counterthrust into Quebec Province and had retreated in disarray from Canada. In the process, the British restored their control of the St. Lawrence River and with it the flow of critical trade goods. Before Fort Stanwix could attempt to reorient trade away from such outposts as Niagara, the British had replenished their shelves with a host of necessities sought by the Iroquois.[54]

Obvious setbacks did not shake the Oneidas from their course. Too seasoned at politics and diplomacy to depend solely on rebel actions, the Oneidas kept working through traditional channels trying to keep their Iroquois brethren neutral. The Oneidas were among those who pressed for a new council to address the behavior of pro-British warriors. In mid-June, sachems, matrons, and some chief warriors from the Six Nations assembled on short notice at Onondaga to discuss these flagrant violations of Iroquois neutrality. Only the Mohawks stayed away. During the week-long gathering, the aged and revered Seneca chief warrior Old Smoke (Sayenqueraghta) and the Oneida sachem White Skin spoke most forcefully. Old Smoke warned the assemblage of Butler's scheme to induce the Iroquois into doing the fighting "they cannot do

themselves." The British feared the rebels would cut them off at Niagara and wanted the Six Nations to provide for their defense. Old
Smoke reminded those assembled, "We have no interest to intermeddle
in the White people's disputes on either side."[55]

White Skin, likewise, denounced Butler and his motives. "We are
imposed upon, deceived, & bewitch'd by a trifling fellow," the sachem
insisted. He asked his brothers and sisters to shun Butler, whose "Heart
is deceitful." The Oneida leader predicted that "[w]e shall be ruin'd forever if we listen any longer to him." White Skin also urged the Six Nations to forbid their dependent tribes from attending Butler's councils
or listening to his words.[56]

Much to White Skin's delight, the council agreed to support the
Oneida position. The Iroquois leaders, in their public statement, reiterated their declaration that "they have no business to join either side in
the present war." They agreed to attend Schuyler's but not Butler's
council that summer. The sachems also issued an alert for both sides:
"We will not suffer either the *English* or the *Americans* to march an
army through our country." Should they do so, "they must abide by the
consequences."[57]

Schuyler's council got off to a troublesome start. The Iroquois arrived at
German Flatts in dribs and drabs, and as the days rolled by, the commissioners had to feed those present, despite very limited resources. To
compound the problem, some drunken Mohawks fired on and sank a
flat-bottomed boat, a bateau loaded with flour for the assemblage. Ultimately, nearly two thousand Iroquois men, women, and children would
attend. Everyone—Indians and soldiers alike—had to accept reduced
rations.[58]

By early August 1776, as the last Iroquois reached German Flatts,
word about the collapse of the rebel campaign in Canada had spread
throughout Iroquoia. This news certainly did not strengthen Schuyler's
position, an indication of which occurred just prior to the formal opening ceremony. Some sachems proposed that everyone present participate in a condolence ceremony for a fellow sachem who had died in
the fighting against the rebels in Canada. An ireful Schuyler rejected

this request, and the sachems dropped the matter; however, none of these events boded well for patriot plans to encourage neutrality or, as many now wanted, to get the Iroquois to favor the rebellion actively.[59]

Substantive meetings began with a statement regarding why the colonists had recently decided to establish the "Independent States of America." Schuyler then offered a litany of violations to the agreements made at the Albany council the previous summer. Various Iroquois had fought and killed rebel soldiers, confronted and threatened them and their emissaries, shot and sunk a supply craft, and aided Sir John Johnson in his efforts to arm and train Tory elements for war. In the end, various nations, including the Mohawks, admitted to misdeeds by some of their brothers. The Oneidas, led by the sachem Jimmy Tayaheure and chief warrior Good Peter, reiterated their declaration of neutrality, and their fellow Iroquois did so as well, pledging to "restrain our warriors."[60]

The problem lay with the amount of freedom accorded tribal members, especially young warriors anxious for combat. Sachems could agree to neutrality, but warriors did not feel bound by that commitment. Good Peter insisted on speaking, and he offered a plan intended to accommodate differences. He explained that the Oneida chief warriors had counseled their younger men to avoid entering the conflict. "If any of our young warriors should, contrary to the advice we have given them, interfere in your quarrel and fall," he promised, "it will not disturb our minds; neither will we regard it, nor will it break the friendship that now subsists between us." Since "[y]oung warriors know the danger of going to war," Good Peter elaborated, death in combat is "what they have to expect, and what often happens." Because such troublemakers "are sensible to our agreements with you, and the friendship that subsists between us," tribal members should dismiss such warriors as "instigated by the devil." As such, their deaths should not result in traditional condolence ceremonies and retribution—a viable way to deal with wayward warriors and to preserve neutrality. Except for the Tuscaroras, none of the other nations endorsed Good Peter's proposal.[61]

Before officials extinguished the council fire in mid-August 1776, Adam Wavonwanoren of Oquaga raised the old issue of land violations. The colonists were continually transgressing the boundaries established by the 1768 Treaty of Fort Stanwix, and he demanded redress. The commissioners guaranteed that the Continental Congress would "put a stop to these wicked practices" and punish all violators.[62]

Rebel officials then distributed the customary gifts, approximately two thousand British pounds worth of goods plus cash, and the attendees scattered to their homes. Although General Schuyler failed to make headway on the subject of Iroquois involvement on the rebels' side, he did obtain admissions of wrongdoing and a promise to admonish warriors to remain at peace. From the Oneida standpoint, the council had preserved the policy of neutrality, so critical to the Iroquois nation's welfare, if only for the moment. But that sentiment faded quickly.[63]

Within a few weeks, many of these same Indians, especially from the more westerly nations—Senecas, Cayugas, and Onondagas—gathered at Niagara to hear John Butler's enticing words. Joining them were members of some western and northern tribes, with a smattering of representatives from the Mohawks and Tuscaroras. Only a handful of Oneidas attended, led by a pro-British chief named Shagoghnatskecham.[64]

Butler continued to ply his persuasive logic, employing skillfully blended arguments about tradition, loyalty, and self-interest. The great military success of the king's forces in Canada, combined with the defeat suffered by Washington's army in the vicinity of New York City during late August, seemed to justify Butler's earlier assertions that additional imperial troops would turn the tide. With the St. Lawrence River open to commercial traffic once more and goods flowing steadily into Niagara, the British could offer a better selection at cheaper prices and more worthwhile gifts than could the resource-starved rebels.

Despite Whig promises to address territorial concerns, most Iroquois believed that colonist transgressions would increase. Violations of Oquaga lands remained unresolved, and rebel settlers were pouring into the Susquehanna Basin and tossing up small forts, menacing the Cayugas, Onondagas, and Senecas from the south. Regardless of what Congress did, the ever-encroaching settlement line strengthened the case for backing the British.[65]

Throughout the revolutionary crisis, Butler and other Crown officials kept raising the land-encroachment issue while blaming the rebels for virtually every act of territorial aggression. Patriots, loyalists, and disinterested folks alike had found ways to gain or steal tribal lands, yet the rebels, according to British leaders, were the ubiquitous culprits. During the Seven Years' War, French leaders had used this same exaggerated reasoning against the British and had induced some Indian nations to fight for France while discouraging others, even longstanding friends of the British, from choosing sides. The French ploy had not escaped the attention of Sir William Johnson, and Butler and the surviving members of the Johnson family had learned from the deceased master how to blame their adversary for all instances of grabbing Indian lands.[66]

This time, too, Butler reaped the benefits of a committed core of western and northern Indians, whose members cast their lot with the British. Traditionally, these natives had subordinated themselves to the New York Iroquois; this time, as the Six Nations struggled to hold on to a common course, their western and northern "children" acted on their own. With such substantial support from the north and west, the pressure proved irresistible for many Iroquois. Casting aside their pledges to the rebels of the previous month, many Senecas, Cayugas, and Onondagas proclaimed their allegiance to the British.[67]

By the early autumn of 1776, the Oneida struggle to maintain Iroquois neutrality had suffered a staggering blow. Many warriors from four of the original Five Nations now vowed fealty to the Crown, along with a smattering of defiant Oneidas and Tuscaroras. Caught between pro-rebel and pro-British forces, the Oneidas lacked the power to play one side off the other, as the Iroquois had done for so many decades with the British and French. They could continue to work for neutrality, or they could succumb to the pressures around them and choose a side, either way pitting themselves against a muscular foe right at their doorstep. Even as the prospect for continued neutrality dwindled with each passing day, the Oneidas clung to that option as the best means of staving off disaster. How much longer they could hold out now depended as much on the will of their fellow Iroquois as on their own desire for a peaceful existence amid all the feuding combatants.

6

TIGHTENING BONDS
WITH THE REBELS

General Philip Schuyler was born in November 1733 into one of the most prominent Dutch lineages in provincial New York. His pedigree, education, professional accomplishments, and marriage into the Rensselaer family all made him a preeminent member of the colonial elite. As befitted his high station, he assumed many leadership roles in promoting the welfare of the colony, and he expected lesser persons to defer to his judgment.[1]

When the war broke out, Schuyler took on two daunting assignments. Not only did he agree to command the Northern Department of the Continental Army, but he also became the acknowledged lead commissioner to the Six Nations. As he was beset by health problems that limited his capacity to provide battlefield leadership, some critics intimated that he leaned toward Toryism. In reality, Schuyler was a thoroughly committed patriot who served the cause well, despite various attempts to blame him for military setbacks in the northern theater.[2]

Schuyler often bristled over slights from fellow citizens, and he also complained about what he viewed as rude remarks and insensitive conduct by various Indians. Proud as the Six Nations were of their heritage and independence, the Iroquois frequently refused to accord Schuyler the degree of deference he thought was appropriate. Seeming disrespect from "savages" could elicit caustic commentary from him. "I do solemnly declare that I would rather be the proprietor of a potato Garden & literally live by the sweat of my Brow," grumbled the patrician general, "than be an Indian Commissioner at a Time when you cannot prudently resent an Insult given by these haughty princes of the Wilderness." Discreet in public for the good of the rebel cause, in private Schuyler described Indians as "a Compound of all the Vices without a Single Virtue."[3]

These harsh judgments were representative of the attitudes of most European American patriots living in central New York. From their perspective, Indians impeded expansion into fertile territory, a forested wilderness out of which thousands of Europeans could carve splendid farms. The shame, they thought, was to leave so much valuable acreage in the control of scattered tribes of Indians.[4]

Few colonists were comfortable in the presence of Native Americans. Most believed that the less they saw or dealt with Indians, the better off and safer they were. Still, to maintain decent relations with the Iroquois and other Indians, they had to follow Schuyler's example and control their personal prejudices and display outwardly tolerant behavior toward the native populace.

Back in mid-May 1776, before Colonel Elias Dayton's Continentals left Albany to enter Iroquoia, both officers and soldiers had received specific warnings about their treatment of the resident Indians. "Your men are frequently to be Cautioned against offering any Insult or abuse to the Indians," General John Sullivan directed, "as one act of Rudeness in a Soldier might Involve America in a Dangerous war with a Savage Enemy." By late June, as patriot troops prepared to occupy Fort Stanwix, these instructions would become very important.[5]

Fort Stanwix, or Fort Schuyler, as the Continentals rechristened this edifice in honor of Philip Schuyler, had fallen into disrepair in recent years. As with most military posts, its value lay in its location. The earth-and-timber bastion dominated the Oneida Carrying Place, the portage that interrupted the only viable direct water route from the Hudson River to Lake Ontario. From Stanwix, the hike was relatively short to the village of Oriska and about seventeen miles to Kanonwalohale. Thus, the reoccupation of the fort placed rebel soldiers very near the heart of Oneida territory.

Both soldiers and Indians harbored suspicions of one another. Dayton's troops were from New Jersey, and few of them had experienced any contact with Native Americans. The Oneidas, by comparison, had befriended many colonists over the years, but Dayton's men were armed soldiers who had no ties to the area. Still, both sides reached the conclusion that their continued survival depended on mutual respect and cooperation. Rebel troops with Dayton would soon come to view the Oneidas and Tuscaroras as "the best friends we have among the Indian nations."[6]

Disrespect quickly evaporated after Good Peter and the Oquagas arrived at German Flatts for Schuyler's council in mid-July 1776. On the first day, these Indians industriously threw up housing to shelter their families. The next day, at a social gathering, Good Peter and seven others in his party impressed the patriot officers with their politeness. Within forty-eight hours, the natives' actions had begun to shatter the colonial stereotypes of the lazy, unkempt, boorish, and brutal savage.[7]

A week later, White Skin, fresh from the emergency council at Onondaga to deal with warrior violations of neutrality, visited Schuyler and his senior officers. The Oneida sachem brought along Grasshopper. Grasshopper was Odatshehdeh, the first sachem of the nation. He also served as the premier spokesperson, an elected duty accorded to an individual of proven leadership and unbounded wisdom. In time, Grasshopper became one of the most influential Oneida friends of the patriot cause.[8]

Among the Oneidas, no one impressed Continental officers and soldiers more than Skenandoah. Although into his eighth decade of life, he still possessed extraordinary physical skills. The Continentals respected his military reputation and admired his vigor in scouting for enemy raiders. The chief's powerful attachment to the rebel cause, and to reformed Christianity, earned him, as with Good Peter, widespread praise among patriots.

One officer, Captain Joseph Bloomfield of the Third New Jersey Regiment, formed a friendship with the esteemed chiefs. On a trip to Kanonwalohale, he visited Grasshopper and Skenandoah. That evening, Bloomfield lodged at Skenandoah's residence — "a good house built in the Dutch fashion." Bloomfield judged his hosts "very good Company." When Skenandoah attended the council several weeks later, Bloomfield spoke with him frequently. One evening, these two friends dined together, and the Oneida chief presented Bloomfield with a red sash of beads "as a Testimony of his regard" for the captain. Two months later, after completing a scouting mission Skenandoah and some Oneidas paid Bloomfield a visit at Fort Schuyler. Along with Samuel Kirkland, they chatted the evening away together. As they conversed, Skenandoah gave Bloomfield "his present true Name which He would ever after call me by." The chief asked Kirkland to write out the word — "Aoghwaenjondawetha & is thus pronounced, Aw-vogh wun joon daw wat haw" — so that Bloomfield would not forget it.[9]

As other Indians trickled into German Flatts, the large numbers and distinctions among Iroquois nations opened entirely new vistas for observant soldiers. The troops enjoyed attending various Indian functions, including dances in which the rhythmic beat and intricate steps of the participants amazed persons accustomed to more staid European movements. Lacrosse games drew substantial crowds and some hefty wagering, as did other exhibitions of athletic prowess, such as foot races.[10]

On the Sabbath, officers and men flocked to the Oneida divine service, expecting to witness some quaint rituals. Instead, the beauty and solemnity of the occasion humbled them. Kirkland, who directed the religious celebration, alternated between the Oneida and English languages. The Indian congregation opened by singing a hymn, "at which they excel any white people I ever heard for melodiousness of music," one officer attested. Kirkland then prayed in both languages and preached in Oneida. Once he had completed his sermon, "[a]n Indian, who is a headman amongst them [probably Good Peter], got up and spoke for some time." The service concluded with a prayer and more singing.[11]

Captain Bloomfield, who was in attendance, wrote that the "devout Behavior of those poor Savages" served to rouse "the steady attention & admiration of all present, & was an Example to the whites & at the same time a Reproof to the Christians, who . . . frequently behave with the greatest Rudeness during Divine service." He then remarked, "Though I did not understand a word that was said, Yet I never paid greater attention or was more improved in attending divine Worship." Nor could he and others help contrasting this service at the Oneida camp with a scene a short distance away, where some Senecas, Onondagas, and Cayugas were singing, drumming, and carousing around "in the most Profane Manner." They were "abusing" God's day, concluded an officer, who viewed the Oneidas as more purposeful and cultured because of their Christian faith.[12]

Exposure to select Oneida practices piqued the rebels' curiosity. At Oriska, some soldiers examined the rough huts and two "Dutch houses" that composed the village. A few officers explored Kanonwalohale, at the center of which they found "a Miserable old long Hutt" that functioned as the council room. Residences varied in size from "huts" to European-style houses. Furnishings, they noted, were sparse. Aside from pots and jugs, dwellings contained beds consisting of two or three sheepskins and a fireplace in the center. Outside the village lay fields in cultivation and a "Very large cleared Field in which all their Horses & Cattle graise promiscusly." Dogs, chickens, and hogs also ambled about freely, both in and out of homes.[13]

Almost no aspect of the Indians' lives escaped scrutiny. When Continental soldiers observed scalps hanging in homes, they gained insight into the central role of warfare in Iroquois society. These trophies testified to combat prowess, as did the way warriors stepped forward during dances to recount their martial feats for those present.[14]

Captain Bloomfield also described physical differences between Indians and European Americans. The Iroquois, he stated, had reddish brown skin, darkened by the use of bear fat and paint. None had facial hair; they removed it with a wire device. Their natural hair was long and black, although many eliminated that as well. The Iroquois were taller and better proportioned than Europeans, with the Senecas the tallest among them. "Their bodies are strong," he judged, "but of such a species of Vigour, as is rather adapted to endure much hardship, than to continue long at any servile works." Their "strength [is] of a beast of prey, rather than a beast of burden," an image Bloomfield used to compare the Iroquois hunter with the colonial farmer. From infancy they ingrained toughness in themselves with the intent to "form their Bodies & Minds to endure the affliction of the greatest evils."[15]

Extensive interaction between the Oneidas and the Continentals helped engender mutual understanding. At the same time, the restoration and reoccupation of old Fort Stanwix caused inadvertent problems for the Oneidas: the refurbished bastion represented a symbol of patriot power in the region, and the fort seemed to tie the Oneidas closely to the patriot cause. Even though the edifice rested on land the Oneidas no longer owned, rebel enemies assumed that General Schuyler would not have reactivated the post without Oneida consent. The fort thus focused British attention more closely on that sector, in the midst of Oneida lands, and came to serve as a giant bull's-eye for British forces and their loyalist and native allies.

On the whole, though, the Oneidas viewed the fort's revival positively. Although still favoring neutrality, they had also concluded that staying out of the conflict was not possible unless all the Six Nations adhered to that course. Any attempt in the region by either British forces or American rebels to strike the other would almost certainly provoke forays into Oneida territory anyway, and the troops stationed at Fort Schuyler could help ward off any attacks aimed at the Oneidas.[16]

John Butler was among those who viewed Fort Schuyler as an alluring target, but he lacked the capacity to mount a major military operation during the summer and fall of 1776. What the British could do was continue their policy of scouting the countryside for intelligence. They drew upon the skills of the Mississauga Indians, who resided near present-day Toronto and had good relations with the Six Nations. In conversations with other natives, parties of Mississaugas would gather information on the deployment of rebel forces. Occasionally, when circumstances were favorable, the Mississaugas would employ traditional Indian-style warfare by striking isolated companies of soldiers before disappearing into the woods.[17]

Since these Indian scouts usually targeted the area around Fort Schuyler, they had to travel into Oneida territory. In response, the Oneidas adopted a more aggressive scouting program of their own.

Sometimes working in concert with rebel troops, small bands of Oneidas fanned out northward, occasionally spying on the British trading post of Oswego itself, at the southern edge of Lake Ontario. Because of their skills as hunters and trackers, the Oneidas frequently conducted reconnaissance missions in dangerous regions, usually undetected. Among their most active scouts were the aged Skenandoah and the blacksmith Thomas Spencer.[18]

With hostile bands moving surreptitiously across the landscape, white settlers, Indians, and soldiers alike felt heightened stress. Mere suspicion of nearby enemy activity stirred up the most horrid images of human butchery, in turn producing pangs of terror.

Oneida leaders realized that their close cooperation with rebel forces was undercutting their preferred course of neutrality. Even though security depended on advance warning, combined scouting operations were having the effect of moving the nation precariously close to active participation in the war. As a result, in September 1776, a group of forty sachems, chiefs, and warriors led by White Skin approached Colonel Dayton and told him that while they wanted to maintain a rapid communication system with the rebels, they felt they had to scout alone.[19]

Although the Oneidas tried to avoid provocative acts, events and the conduct of individual warriors kept them tied to the conflict. When some Tories fleeing to Canada stumbled into Kanonwalohale, the Oneidas detained and then turned them over to Whig officials. As Oneida reconnoitering activities continued, their parties sometimes exchanged gunfire with hostile Indians, and they regularly swapped information with the rebels. Although not at war, the Oneidas were effectively acting as more than disinterested neutrals.[20]

The Oneidas' traditional allies, the Iroquois Confederacy and subordinate peoples, expressed little tolerance toward any Indians who maintained cordial relations with the rebels. In a circular letter prepared at the end of John Butler's council in September 1776, pro-British natives called on all Indian nations to join forces against the American revolutionaries. For those Indians who ignored or rejected this demand, they warned, "we shall Imagine that our Road of peace is Entirely stopped and it will oblige us to act accordingly." In October, the Oneidas received this letter along with a pointed threat. Should they refuse to join their pro-British brethren, they "should be attacked," and ultimately "not a child's life would be then spared."[21]

A few weeks later, a small Indian party headed by a Mohawk warrior hoped to strike a blow for the British cause, while also offering a huge insult to the Oneidas, by kidnapping both Samuel Kirkland and Thomas Spencer. En route to Oneida country, the raiders bragged about their proposed scheme. An Onondaga chief overheard the plan and sent word to Kanonwalohale. Immediately, two Oneida sachems and three warriors raced westward to confront the Mohawk and "forbid his coming into *Oneida* or any of his party."[22]

The heightened state of alert in the Oneida Nation and the attention lavished on scouting parties generated ample activity and recognition for the warrior class. Even with occasional skirmishes with the Mississaugas, none had yet lost their lives, so the matrons had no cause to demand retributive strikes to bring closure to the mourning process. So long as the Oneidas did not lose control of circumstances by letting their limited involvement turn into full entanglement, neutrality, their leaders believed, remained the wisest course for them—and for the rest of the Six Nations.

In late October 1776, fresh rumors about a large-scale attack by British and Indians, instigated by John Butler, panicked local whites. Fearing the worst, the Tryon County militia threatened to lay down their arms unless General Schuyler assigned Continental troops to help them meet the supposed assault. To learn the truth about the offensive and Butler's intentions, the sachem and counselor Grasshopper volunteered to undertake an intelligence mission. He possessed the perfect cover. Since he was the leading member of the Oneida Nation, no one would challenge his right to visit Niagara and confer with his Iroquois brethren.[23]

Early in November, Grasshopper began his journey into the heart of Seneca territory. He traveled no farther than Cayuga. There, the sachem received the news he and Schuyler sought. The western warriors had returned home on Butler's recommendation to hunt all winter. They had no plans, Grasshopper stated, to "proceed to *Albany* the ensuing winter, the season being too far advanced." In addition, he reported that the Senecas "have all agreed to side with the King"; on the other hand, sources told him that most Cayugas and Onondagas still "are friendly to the *Americans*, and regard the treaty at *Albany* and *German-Flatts*" as inviolate.[24]

Grasshopper's observations offered little solace for those still hopeful of neutrality by all the Six Nations. In words that prompted an initial sigh of relief, but that on deeper reflection hung like a pall over the heads of Oneidas and rebels alike, the nation's counselor predicted, " 'Tis my opinion that you will have no trouble from the enemy this way till next spring."[25]

Because of efforts such as those of Grasshopper, the Oneidas were gaining a special standing with Schuyler. As freezing weather descended on central New York, the general worried about how his Indian comrades would cope with the elements. Unsettled conditions and the heightened state of alert had adversely affected the hunting season, so much so that the Oneidas had little to offer at the trading table. Even those hunters fortunate enough to have a few furs could procure little in exchange, since the rebellion had disrupted trading networks with Britain, which not only reduced supplies on store shelves but also resulted in skyrocketing prices. Schuyler hoped to alleviate the Oneidas' suffering. "They are such good Friends," he explained to the Continental Congress, "that I wish to have it in my power to give them some cloathing."[26]

Taking steps to address the problem, Schuyler established a trading post at Fort Schuyler, which eased the burden somewhat. Officers and soldiers, too, dabbled in trade, exchanging blankets and other goods for furs. Unfortunately, Schuyler's appeals to Congress, local merchants, and nearby states for woolen goods produced few items. To Congress he issued a blunt warning: "Unless Clothing & Covering can be found soon the Indian interest *will* be lost."[27]

Schuyler appreciated that without clothing to offer Indians as gifts or in trade, the patriots were in danger of pushing many members of the Iroquois Confederacy toward the British. "To transact Business with Indians," he grumbled to Congress, "with Empty hands greatly Increases the Difficulty" of maintaining neutrality let alone securing allies for the rebel cause.[28]

Signs of native frustration with the American patriots appeared when Schuyler attempted to use Washington's turnabout victories at Trenton and Princeton to press once more for the confederacy's favor or neutrality. Along with a keg of rum for each nation to toast their friendship, he prepared an exuberant address detailing the patriots' twin triumphs and their effect on the war. Schuyler also tried to gain favor with the Iroquois by suggesting that the French might go to war against England, an obvious boost for the revolutionary cause. "Altho' we do not want Men from the French King," the general postured, "yet if he makes war with England, the English war ships will not be able to prevent our Merchantmen from bringing us Blankets and other woolen Goods, which are scarce." Stating that the rebels would abide by their agreements with the Iroquois, he called on Oneida couriers to memorize the message and distribute it, with a keg, to each of the nations.[29]

The Oneidas rejoiced at Washington's success. In celebration, they fired a cannon three times: one salvo for Congress, a second for "your Chief Warrior" Washington, and a third for Schuyler. The other nations cheered the gift of rum, but the contents of Schuyler's message inspired considerably less enthusiasm. News of Washington's victories had little impact. Schuyler hoped that word of possible warfare between France and Great Britain might exploit old friendships, especially among the Senecas, who had maintained the closest relationship with the French in Canada. That, too, failed to impress the Iroquois.[30]

During the winter months, the British cause seemed to gain momentum at the expense of the neutralists. In January 1777, a horrible tragedy afflicted the central Onondaga castle. An undetermined malady, probably smallpox, struck down ninety villagers, including three of the principal sachems. Not only did some of their peace advocates succumb to the illness, but the passing of so many Onondagas required extensive condolence activity. In many instances, only combat could bring closure to the mourning process. The British proposal to join a spring campaign against the rebels could provide that opportunity.

In circulating word of their calamity, the Onondagas announced that the "Grand Council Fire at Onondauguas was extinguished."

While it burned, the council fire symbolized that the Six Nations were of one mind; when the fire no longer blazed, it indicated that each of the Six Nations could freely decide its own course.[31]

After reporting this news to Kirkland and Colonel Samuel Elmore, the new commander at Fort Schuyler, the Oneidas indicated privately to the missionary their own concerns. They suspected that "dissolving their *Body-politic*, or extinguishing the Council Fire at Onondaga is only a pretext by which they will repair to Niagara & then renew their ancient Covinant with the British King," Kirkland relayed to Schuyler.

To repair some of the damage, Kirkland encouraged the Northern Department commander to conduct a condolence ceremony to replace, at least symbolically, the deceased Onondaga sachems. Even though Iroquois tradition demanded that the opposite moiety perform requickening rites, Sir William Johnson had adopted this practice of officiating as well. By stepping into Johnson's role, Schuyler would signify his authority and remind the Six Nations that Albany remained the seat of power among them. "Either of your Oneida friends," Kirkland advised, "the Grasshopper or White Skin will model the Speech agreeable to Indian Traditions." Whether Schuyler conducted such a ceremony remains unclear. If he did, this action may have helped deter the Onondagas from aligning completely with the British.[32]

Also tilting the Iroquois toward the British was Joseph Brant, who had resumed his efforts to build support for the Crown among the Six Nations. After a harrowing return from England, he fought gallantly in the Battle of Long Island during late August 1776. Three months later he and the Mohawk Valley loyalist Captain Gilbert Tice disguised themselves and journeyed overland through rebel lines to Oquaga, where the residents greeted them warmly.[33]

Besides their split over religious doctrine, the Oquagas were dealing with other vexing problems. They felt the wartime pinch in trade goods, with gunpowder and ammunition now at a premium. In June 1776, five Iroquois held in high esteem by the rebels—the Oneidas' Good Peter, Adam Wavonwanoren, Beech Tree, and Hendrick, and the Tuscarora Seth—explained that gunpowder, musket balls, and flints were in short supply. They urged patriot officials to get them some soon, "for if we do not find these, we shall not have any skins to buy goods with in the fall." Seven weeks later, New York's Provincial Congress allocated two hundred pounds of gunpowder and a sufficient supply of shot and flints to meet their immediate needs. The Congress did so despite objections that the Indians would use the ammunition to butcher white settlers.[34]

The Oquagas also faced difficulties with encroaching European American settlers. Local militiamen, fearful of surprise raids, had adopted a policy of shooting at Indians they spotted in the woods who carried weapons, wore head feathers, and painted their faces. For many generations, Iroquois adorned with paint and feathers had hunted in the region, and they were loath to abandon the tradition. In a letter of complaint, the Indians spoke of their exhausted patience. Having tried to convince the colonists of their peaceful intentions, "[w]e know no reason why we should stay from our hunting or leave off painting according to our custom."[35]

Land encroachments, always a sore subject for the Oquaga residents, had heated up again, fostering deep suspicion among the Indians. Neither New York, Pennsylvania, nor the Continental Congress had addressed the problem of squatters on Indian lands. Even in territory to the south and west over which Oneidas did not lay claim, the rebels had built forts that seemed to threaten Oquaga.[36]

By these types of actions, the revolutionaries facilitated Brant's mission by alienating local Indians. At Oquaga, Brant already had extensive connections, through his wife and children, his Oneida father-in-law, Old Isaac, and his many relatives and friends. He soon forged a power base there by building on the substantial Mohawk population, the large number of Anglicans, and other disaffected elements in the community.

Brant was maneuvering to get these Indians to join British forces for the 1777 campaign effort. As the story filtered back to the Oneidas at Kanonwalohale, he told the Oquagas that the king both valued and hoped to strengthen the Covenant Chain with the Iroquois. As such, divisions among the Six Nations upset the Great English Father, and George III considered the behavior of the Oneidas and their Tuscarora

friends particularly reprehensible. Endeavoring to embarrass the Oneidas and Tuscaroras living at Oquaga into renouncing their neutralist
stand, Brant chided them for tromping on the Covenant Chain. "The
King was very sorry to hear that two nations of the Confederacy had for-
saken him and joined with those in rebellion and deserved to die,"
Brant avowed. "The conduct of these two were too notorious & could
not be denied."[37]

Brant's stirring stories of combat at such places as Long Island tanta-
lized warriors with the prospect of hostile action, once the weather
warmed. By the time Brant was ready to travel to Fort Niagara, he
had convinced large numbers of Oquagas to align with the British
cause.

For the final leg of his journey, Brant took along Tice, Old Isaac,
and a substantial party of Oquagas who hoped to conduct business with
British traders at the fort. On their way, they visited several Delaware
and Seneca villages, proselytizing with the same gospel for the king's
cause. Just before the new year, Brant and his group trudged through
the gates of Fort Niagara. The Mohawk leader had taken thirteen
months, seven thousand miles, and two battles to complete the circuit.[38]

Tall, handsome Brant received a cool reception at Niagara. When
he presented his oral instructions from British commander in chief
William Howe and Superintendent Guy Johnson about rallying the Six
Nations, John Butler viewed him as an interloper trying to muscle in on
his authority. After all, Butler had been working for months to cultivate
native support. He seemed vexed that Brant, an Indian no less, might in
some way supersede him.[39]

Offended by Butler's brusque manner and feeling unwelcome,
Brant prepared a belt in accordance with Guy Johnson's instructions
for deposit at Onondaga, to solemnize the messages of General Howe
and the superintendent. He then undertook a journey with the intent of
traveling the length of Iroquoia to generate participation in the upcoming campaign.[40]

At a predominantly Tuscarora town near the Oneida-Onondaga border, Brant requested that some Oneidas, especially his kin Skenandoah,
head warrior William Kayendalongwea, Good Peter, and Good Peter's

brother Thomas, meet with him there. He hoped to convince them of the rightness of the British cause. None of the four consented to meet or discuss the subject with Brant. Other Oneidas viewed the request as insulting. Should Brant want to speak with them, they asserted, he could come to Kanonwalohale. Evidently, Brant feared for his safety there, but the Oneidas dismissed this concern as ludicrous. As with all guests in their village, the nation would protect him.[41]

Ultimately, some Oneidas did travel to the Tuscarora castle to meet with the Mohawk chief warrior. Brant explained "how unjust the greater part of people in England considered the Rebels cause and that they could not expect Success." In response, the Oneidas reminded him of their neutrality, insisting "they were Friends to both King & Americans." With neither side conceding anything, the meeting ended with an exchange of harsh words.[42]

Near the time that Brant approached the Oneidas, an Onondaga chief arrived at Kanonwalohale, bearing a message from John Butler. The British agent had decided to invite some sachems and chief warriors to a council at Niagara, scheduled to commence during the second week of February. Butler asked to have Jimmy Tayaheure, Niklasko (Nicholasera), and young Kanaghwaes attend, and he requested that they bring as many warriors as were willing to come.[43]

When Kirkland reported news of the Onondaga emissary, he described Jimmy, Niklasko, and Kanaghwaes as "the only three Tory Chiefs the Oneidas have & their Influence is not very great." By labeling them loyalists, Kirkland simplified a convoluted situation. Unlike the chief warrior Old Isaac, who never wavered in his support of the British position, each of these leaders had originally advocated noninvolvement. In June 1775, twelve of the nation's leaders had affixed their signatures to the Oneida declaration of peace and neutrality to the governors of New England. Among the signatories were Jimmy and Niklasko.[44]

These three leaders came from two different communities and had experienced varying levels of contact with Kirkland and the American rebels. Jimmy, a sachem and prominent Oneida leader before the war,

resided at Kanonwalohale. In early 1775 he had defended the missionary's conduct against Guy Johnson's accusations and had been the first
Oneida to sign a letter justifying Kirkland's behavior. By contrast, the
youthful Kanaghwaes had taken the place and name of a sachem who
had leveled the charges of misconduct against Kirkland. Like this predecessor, Kanaghwaes likely grew up in Old Oneida. First introduced to
rebel leaders by Jimmy at the May 1776 council in Albany, young
Kanaghwaes then traveled to Philadelphia, where he met with Washington and the Continental Congress. Niklasko also came from Old
Oneida, where he was a longtime associate of the previous Kanaghwaes. Of the three, he seemed the most disposed to support the Tories,
although he kept hesitating to commit himself.[45]

Among those Oneidas who ultimately supported the British, most
would abandon neutrality with reluctance. They now saw the Iroquois
tide shifting in favor of the Crown, and they could not break with their
brethren in the Six Nations. As Oneida adherence to neutrality slowly
collapsed, Old Oneida residents were most likely to favor the British.
By contrast, an overwhelming number of inhabitants at Kanonwalohale
and Oriska ultimately aligned themselves with the rebels. Oquaga remained split, but a great many of the Oneidas there followed Good Peter's course and aided the revolutionaries rather than stand alongside
Old Isaac and Joseph Brant.[46]

By 1777 the highly politicized atmosphere caused by the American
rebellion had penetrated into every aspect of life in the Oneida Nation.
Everyone had to consider what was the best course for himself and for
the Oneida people. No Oneida was more influential than Grasshopper,
a powerful friend of the rebellion, who not only was Odatshehdeh, the
first sachem in the nation, but also served as the head counselor for all
Oneidas. Other recent selections for sachemships, too, reflected a widespread consensus about favoring the patriots, should neutrality fail.
Thomas Sinavis, a fervent supporter of the rebels and a member of the
Bear Clan, had recently been confirmed as a sachem. Even young
Kanaghwaes, despite his ultimate decision to side with the Crown, exhibited open-mindedness toward the American patriots. The Oneidas
expected their leaders to reflect the nation's will. Their collective reasoning finally determined that with the breakdown of neutrality, align-

ing with the American rebels represented the safest and most sensible course for the People of the Standing Stone.[47]

The Oneidas revered their elders, especially the matrons, senior sachems, and chief warriors. Years of experience had trained these leaders to serve responsibly as the nation's sages. Younger Oneidas, including warriors, had learned as they grew to adulthood not to disregard their elders' opinions. Even though young Oneida warriors had the right to act on their own feelings, following the pathway of their elders' wisdom caused the bulk of them to link arms with the rebels.[48]

In the early months of 1777, the Oneidas learned that a Mohawk and two Seneca spies had entered Fort Schuyler. Their intent was to assess the garrison's size and strength, an indication of a major British-Indian assault, most likely through the Oneida homeland. Less than two weeks later, the Oneidas found out that Brant had communicated with the Mohawks in their Upper and Lower Castles with the intent of freeing them from the rebels' clutches. "I intend to go with the Indians to deliver my brothers the Mohawks, who I imagine are prisoners," he wrote to his sister Molly. According to Oneida sources, she replied that he must delay any such action because the Mohawks could not escape from Canajoharie and Tiononderoga until springtime. Pulling the strands together, the Oneidas concluded that Brant hoped to extract the Mohawks and then lead a major force against Fort Schuyler.[49]

These conclusions were not that far-fetched. The British were in the process of planning a major offensive in northern New York for that spring and summer. The strategic objective was to gain control of the Hudson River waterway, thereby severing New England, the hotbed of revolution, from the rest of the rebellious states. British naval forces could then blockade New England's ports, cutting off supplies. Any rebel troops in New England would wither away or surrender to superior British strength, and the general populace would likely give up in the wake of desperate shortages of food and related necessities.[50]

The dandyish British officer-politician "Gentleman" John Burgoyne had returned to England from Canada during the winter of 1776–1777 to convince the ministry to pursue this plan—with him, of course, at the head of British forces. His concept was hardly novel. For more than a century, French, Indian, and British war parties had employed the Richelieu River–Lake Champlain water route to travel from Canada to upper New York and the Hudson River.[51]

At the end of February 1777, ever-ambitious Burgoyne submitted his "Thoughts" on the campaign. He proposed an army of approximately twelve thousand soldiers and Canadian militiamen and one thousand Indians. The troops would move across Lake Champlain in available watercraft and capture Fort Ticonderoga. Then they would proceed to Albany, ultimately joining with Howe's command somewhere along the Hudson River. As a diversionary force to help divide rebel resisters, Colonel Barry St. Leger, in company with Sir John Johnson, would lead a smaller number of king's regulars, loyalist partisans, and Indians, most likely from the Six Nations, from Fort Oswego to besiege Fort Schuyler, and after subduing that post, through the Mohawk Valley to link up with Burgoyne in the area of Albany.[52]

British Secretary for American Affairs George Germain and King George endorsed Burgoyne's plans, but with fewer troops. Conflicting strategies and the lag in communications to and from America resulted in some important changes. General Howe called for a vigorous offensive against Philadelphia. In the process, he hoped to speed the revolt to an end by destroying Washington's army. The disadvantage was that Howe would be moving thousands of regulars away from Burgoyne and not leaving enough troops in New York City to aid the invading force from Canada, should it run into trouble. Seeking to quash the rebellion before the French formally entered the struggle, Germain concurred with Howe's scheme.[53]

The Oneidas, meanwhile, stepped up their scouting and exchanged information with rebel leaders as the threat of invasion from Canada became more of a likelihood. Grasshopper alerted the patriots to the spies who had examined Fort Schuyler, and "a particular [Oneida] friend" of Schuyler's passed on word about the messages between the Brant siblings. Oneida scouts also picked up bits and pieces regarding Burgoyne's preparations. Like most intelligence, the details in themselves did not explain the larger plan but were tantalizing enough to encourage the Oneidas to keep piecing together the jigsaw puzzle.[54]

Seeking to protect themselves from all sides, the Oneidas did more than just collect intelligence. They also sought accurate information regarding the rebels and their reputed military strength. Brant and his followers had repeatedly argued that the revolution could not possibly succeed, that once the king introduced sufficient troops in America, resistance to imperial authority would crumble. The Oneidas wanted to check on patriot forces for themselves and then present their findings to their fellow Iroquois.

In January 1777 some Oneida chiefs and warriors proposed a trip through New England and into northern New Jersey, where Washington's army lay encamped. They also hoped to find proof to rumors that the French were covertly assisting the rebellion with money, supplies, and a few volunteers. For public consumption, an Oneida spokesperson explained that they had sent Chief Warrior Skenandoah to view patriot soldiers a little over a year before, "but upon his Return they tho't his report was more than *one pair of eyes* could see." Skenandoah had witnessed much; others wanted confirmation.[55]

With Washington's and Schuyler's blessing, Kirkland headed a small delegation that included the Oneida head warrior William Kayendalongwea, Beech Tree, and Hendrick. Traveling mostly by sleigh, the party arrived in Boston on February 17. Schuyler had written in advance to Major General Artemas Ward, urging him to "impress upon them with Ideas of Friendship" and grant them "some genteel present." Ward accommodated the Oneidas and even sent them aboard a patriot warship, where the captain ordered cannon shots fired to honor Congress, Washington, and the Six Nations.[56]

In Providence, Rhode Island, their next important stop, the Oneidas boarded another vessel and observed some shelling of British positions. While in Providence, chief warrior William Kayendalongwea addressed the General Assembly, with Kirkland acting as the translator. Nearly sixty years old, William purportedly had engaged in combat some fifty times, which gave him considerable credibility with his audience.[57]

William explained how the rebels' enemies had taken great pains to arouse the Six Nations against the patriots. Local Tories had claimed that the patriots suffered from a shortage of serviceable cannons and defective gunpowder that "would not carry the Ball beyond the End of the Gun." They also said the Revolution was "in a most forlorn & dispairing State." By visiting various sites, the Oneidas could see that these reports were false. Their hope was to "Put an End to the Life of Lies" and to present accurate information to the rest of the Six Nations. In gratitude, the legislature authorized money for expenses and awarded William an elegantly decorated musket.[58]

From Rhode Island, the Oneidas and Kirkland traveled westward to Lebanon, Connecticut, for a meeting with Governor Jonathan Trumbull. From there, they continued their journey to Peekskill, New York, where the group crossed the Hudson River and continued southward into New Jersey. By March 22, they had reached the Continental Army's headquarters, in Morristown.[59]

Well aware of the importance of maintaining Iroquois friendship, the commander in chief personally hosted the Oneidas. "I shewed them every civility in my power and every thing that I thought material to excite in them an Idea of our strength and independence," Washington informed Congress. He also advised his visitors that "France was assisting us & about to join in the War," news that "highly pleased" the Oneidas.[60]

Traveling next to Kingston, where the New York Provincial Congress was meeting, William and Kirkland stayed there for a few days while the rest of the group, including Beech Tree and Hendrick, pressed on to Oneida to communicate what they had seen. William took the opportunity to address the Congress. "The King of Great Britain has spread lies through the Six Nations," he elaborated. "Your people, or the superintendent at Albany, have not told us one lie." William promised that he and the other Oneida visitors would apprise their Iroquois brothers and sisters of their findings, but he admitted to deep divisions among the Six Nations. "We Indians are more jealous of each other than you white men," he confessed. In an oblique way, William was letting the Congress know that the report would have much greater influence with the Oneidas than with the other nations.[61]

While the Oneida emissaries conducted their investigation of rebel military strength, Schuyler convinced other Oneidas to keep gathering intelligence in Canada. Before the group left, James Dean equipped them with snowshoes and provisions; Schuyler gave them nearly twenty questions for which he sought answers, ranging from the disposition of Crown and Indian forces to the prospect of a sizable British force invading through the Mohawk Valley.[62]

With Thomas Sinavis in the lead, the Oneida spies trudged through snow and stinging cold northward along Lake Champlain into Quebec Province. Crown officials, who kept "a very watchful Eye" on Indian movements, learned of their presence and closely monitored their activity during their visit with the Kahnawakes. To speak privately with their Kahnawake brethren, Sinavis actually had to slip through windows in the dead of night to avoid British surveillance. Others in the village were "so much overawed by the King's Troops" that some of Sinavis's best friends acted as if they did not know him.[63]

Before the party returned home, they received a message from Governor Guy Carleton for distribution to the Oneida Nation. The document read like a final warning. The king "understood that their Nation, alone, espoused the cause of those Traitors." They served as "mouths for those Rebels," Carleton charged, since "the Language they utter is the Language of Rebellion." By the laws of nations, Oneida behavior represented a capital offense. "To take up arms against their King," declared Carleton, "is death." Aiding and assisting the American traitors in any way was punishable by execution. Thus far, the king had "spared the shedding of their blood" so he could "restore them to a proper sense of duty and obedience." However, "[i]f their blood should be spilt in large quantities," he warned, "they will bear witness to one another, that it was because they could not be reduced by gentler methods to a due sense of their duty." The only way to avoid such a catastrophe, Carleton stated, was to stop circulating patriot "lies" and to permit British and Indian forces to pass through their homeland so that they could wipe out rebel resistance in their region.[64]

In the minds of British officials and their native allies, all who were not with them were now against them. The People of the Standing Stone, therefore, were in the rebel camp. The only way to avoid destruction was to stand aside when Crown and Indian forces arrived in their territory, at which point they would be expected to join British arms against the revolutionaries.

When Sinavis and his band returned to Fort Schuyler in late May, they brought much valuable intelligence. The British invasion was just a few weeks away, they reported, confirming many rumors to that effect. Even more pressing for the Oneida Nation, Carleton's threatening message helped transform continued thoughts of neutrality into a delusion. Potent forces—political, geographic, economic, religious, and cultural—would not leave the Oneidas and their homeland alone. For the nation and for individuals, they had to choose one side or the other.

In mid-March 1777, to help forewarn both the Oneidas and the Fort Schuyler garrison of the ever more likely attack, White Skin suggested that a few Oneida warriors maintain a regular watch along the St. Lawrence River between Lake Ontario and Montreal, in Quebec Province. Everyone agreed that such reconnoitering of likely British movements made good sense.[65]

Other Oneidas, meanwhile, journeyed to Niagara to treat with John Butler. He had postponed the council, originally planned for mid-February, because of supply shortages. Throughout this April gathering, Butler worked both public and private agendas. According to the Oneidas, he talked "to them nothing but peace" and advised them not to meddle in the war. Behind their backs, however, and apparently undetected by the Oneidas, he spoke with selected Iroquois regarding the coming offensive, dangling before them patriot scalps and the prospect of liberating their Mohawk brothers and sisters from rebel oppression. Until the British were ready to move, they had to keep everything a secret. Then, to all in attendance, Butler announced plans for "another meeting before long which is to be held at Oswego." He did not hint that his intention at the next council was to deluge the natives with presents and induce them to take part in the invasion, with glory and plunder as their trophies.[66]

Although Butler managed to keep the Oneidas in the dark, other sources provided enough information to tip them off to British plans. The Oneida representatives passed the critical news along to rebel leaders, as they had always intended. "The Indians in Canada who are now out upon their hunt there are all directed to return by the first of may," they apprised James Dean, "when it is reported among them that the King's Troops are to attack Ticonderoga and Fort Schuyler, from there they are to march to Albany there to be joined by General Howe, who at the same time is to march up from New York."[67]

During May 1777, some three hundred representatives from the Six Nations, disproportionately Oneidas, traveled to Albany to report on the Niagara council. In their meetings with the Indian commissioners and Major General Horatio Gates, temporarily in command of the Northern Department while Schuyler was attending the Continental Congress, Iroquois spokespersons addressed Butler's public and confidential statements. The commissioners ridiculed such apparent duplicity, hoping to discredit Butler with the Iroquois. They should never trust him, since "[h]e publickly advises you to peace," they stated, "but privately asks you to join the Kings Army From Oswego to Fort Schuyler."[68]

Gates, who as a British officer had been posted for a time at Fort Herkimer during the Seven Years' War, knew some of the chiefs and warriors dating back two decades. In his speech, he reminded them of his extensive military experience and asked them not to let "any Evil Spirits . . . lead You into War" on the British side, which would "End in your misery." Gates then predicted a great patriot triumph. To reinforce his words, he closed the council with a military exercise that included the firing of twenty cannon salvos from a sloop of war stationed on the Hudson River.[69]

While Butler lined up Indian allies for the summer campaign, Joseph Brant returned to Oquaga irritated about Butler's callous treatment and concerned about the safety of his fellow Mohawks. Since his last visit, bad feelings toward the rebels had become even more pronounced. Brant easily organized some one hundred Mohawks and even a few Tuscaroras and Oneidas into a fighting force. Together, they watched as he hoisted the Union Jack over Oquaga, signaling Tory control of that community. As summertime approached, Brant kept adding numbers of loyalists and Indians to his force.[70]

Although appalled by news of Brant's takeover at Oquaga, the Oneidas pleaded with General Schuyler not to allow rebel troops to "commit any Hostilities" there "as they are trying to compose matters." Spilling Iroquois blood would only generate further support for Brant and produce retaliatory strikes. They also sent a party to Oquaga to urge their fellow Oneidas to eschew Brant; and Thomas Spencer, with four other Oneidas and a Mohawk acting as his guards, traveled throughout Iroquoia to spread word that Schuyler wanted to hold a council in Albany during mid-July. Events, however, had moved beyond the talking stage, and that conference never took place.[71]

In June, the sachem Thomas Sinavis, acting on a request from Schuyler, agreed to lead yet another reconnaissance party into Canada. He was the logical choice, since he knew the region and its native inhabitants well. Further, he was "a well affected friend of our cause," as a member of the Tryon County Committee of Safety stated, and, therefore, regarded as completely trustworthy.[72]

Sinavis set out on June 18 with four other Oneidas. Should they uncover vital information, one or more of these warriors could report back to Schuyler while the others continued the mission. At the village of Saint Regis, near Kahnawake, friends of Sinavis welcomed him but also warned that Tory leaders Sir John Johnson and Daniel Claus were there visiting them. From a hidden position on the second floor of the council house, Sinavis heard Claus encouraging those present to join him in the campaign that Colonel Barry St. Leger was about to lead against Fort Schuyler. Claus declared that the fort would fall easily, without casualties. Likewise, he pointed out that many Indians had agreed to fight with Burgoyne's army, and he asserted that Fort Ticonderoga would surrender with virtually no losses.[73]

With much intelligence in hand, the five Oneidas returned home, reaching Kanonwalohale near mid-July. By that time, St. Leger, Sir John, and Claus were moving toward Fort Oswego, where Joseph Brant and his followers would rendezvous with them. Once fully assembled, St. Leger's force would consist of about 750 King's regulars, Hessians, and loyalists (Sir John's Royal Greens) and somewhere between eight hundred and a thousand Indians.

In reporting back to the Tryon Committee, Sinavis said he expected Butler to join St. Leger's force after offering willing listeners among the Iroquois the hatchet to strike at the patriots. Unless the rebels acted in a "spirited" fashion and "encourage[d] one another to march on in assistance of Fort Schuyler . . . before it is too late," all could be lost. Should the Mohawk Valley's rebel colonists not "come soon without delay to assist this place," Sinavis warned, the Oneidas could not "stay longer on your side." Rather than see their homeland desecrated by St. Leger's invading force, they would either "be obliged to join [the British], or fly from the castles, as we cannot hinder them alone." Either alternative would be disastrous for both the Oneidas and the settlers, who could expect to be destroyed by the advancing enemy force. The only sensible course, the sachem concluded, was mutual assistance. "We are heartily willing to help you," Sinavis stated in suggesting united opposition, "if you will do some efforts, too."[74]

The prospect of a military disaster in New York, for the Oneida and patriot cause alike, was real and very much justified Thomas Sinavis's fears. By mid-July, Burgoyne's main force of eight thousand British and Hessian soldiers and Indian allies had moved southward across Lake Champlain and easily taken Fort Ticonderoga from outnumbered rebel resisters. Burgoyne was now positioning his force for its final push to Albany. St. Leger's diversionary column, still gaining strength at Oswego, would include many Iroquois warriors, a reflection of Joseph Brant's actions and John Butler's ceaseless efforts to entice the Six Nations into the war on Britain's side. By early July, the Oneidas were hearing that neutralists among the Senecas had lost much favor. Proof ultimately came in regarding that nation's lack of interest in accepting Schuyler's invitation to attend a council in Albany.[75]

In mid-July at Irondequoit, on the southern bank of Lake Ontario about halfway between Niagara and Oswego, Butler met with the Senecas and revealed his trump card. With a flair for the dramatic, he produced the belt that symbolized the ancient covenant between the Six Nations and the king, and reminded the Senecas of land en-croachments and the rebels' inability to sustain meaningful trade. Meanwhile, he plied them with alcohol and lavished them with pres-ents and trade goods. The attack on Fort Schuyler would be easy, he told them, and would produce much plunder for all. Seneca warriors would be able to display their worth in battle, and combat would en-able them to bring closure to the grieving process for Senecas already lost during the war. After much debate, the Senecas elected to seize the war hatchet.[76]

Later that month, near Fort Oswego, Butler convinced additional warriors from the Six Nations to join St. Leger's expedition. This time Butler spoke from a position of strength, since the Senecas had already committed to the campaign. In the debates, the Oneidas reminded their fellow Iroquois of their common pledge of neutrality and urged everyone present to cling to that policy. Their words had little effect. Butler rallied many of those present to the British banner, including most Cayugas, half the Onondagas, some Tuscaroras, and even a few Oneidas led by Rail Carrier (Kahkodinoiya).[77]

Schuyler's hopes for a mid-July council in Albany thus had crum-pled under the weight of events. The patriot general was staring into the ugly countenance of a two-front invasion from Canada. As for the Oneidas, their worst nightmare was also coming true. They had a siz-able enemy force gathering at their doorstep, with Iroquois brethren prominent among the invaders. Fatefully for all the Six Nations, even a semblance of neutrality was no longer an option as they now faced the reality of combat among themselves.[78]

7

DEFENDING THE
ONEIDA HOMELAND

Chief Warrior Han Yerry had long since chosen the side he would favor should his fellow Oneidas enter the war. After the skirmishes at Lexington and Concord, he raised a band of Oneidas who were "friendly to the Americans in their struggle for liberty." Initially, their purpose was to scout and defend the homeland. With St. Leger's expeditionary force making its way along the water route from Fort Oswego in late July 1777, now literally trespassing on Oneida territory, Han Yerry and his followers felt the time was at hand to embrace the fight.[1]

Born about 1724, somewhere in the Mohawk Valley, Han Yerry was likely the product of a mixed relationship, with a Mohawk mother and a father of German descent. He thought of himself as an Oneida, and the People of the Standing Stone concurred, as he later emerged as a chief warrior of the Wolf Clan. The Oneidas referred to him as Han Yerry Tewahangarahken, or "He Who Takes Up the Snow Shoe." Many others, especially local whites, called him Han Yerry Doxtader, a reflection of his supposed German heritage.[2]

Sometime in the 1750s, Han Yerry married an extraordinary woman named Tyonajanegen, or "Two Kettles Together." The couple settled at Oriska, counting themselves among those who had founded that castle. Over the years, they had three sons and a daughter. Two Kettles Together and their elder sons, Jacob and Cornelius, by the mid-1770s in their mid- to late teens, also favored the rebel cause.[3]

Few surpassed Han Yerry in reputation among the Oneidas. In

young adulthood, he exhibited exceptional courage and coolness in combat. As the years passed, he lost some of his physical vigor but not his mental and emotional edge. In his fifties during the Revolution, he was remembered by one observer decades later as an "ordinary sized" fellow and "quite a gentleman in his demeanor." An Oneida friend, Hendrick Smith, honored him when he said, "Hon Yerry was too old for the Service, yet used to go fearlessly into the fights."[4]

At Oriska, Han Yerry and his family prospered on an expansive farm, catering to travelers and people at nearby Fort Stanwix. By 1777 he and his family lived in a substantial frame house, had a barn, and owned fifteen horses, a half dozen cattle, sixty hogs, two sheep, six turkeys, and a hundred chickens. The family grew a variety of crops and owned an assortment of farm implements, including a wagon and a sleigh for winter travel. Two Kettles Together cooked meals in brass and copper kettles and served guests on pewter plates. Han Yerry had become one of the wealthiest of all Oneidas.[5]

Although he had flourished economically under British rule, Han Yerry disliked the Crown. Like other Oriska residents, he resented Sir William Johnson and his government for their actions in negotiating the Treaty of Fort Stanwix during 1768. The superintendent had wanted an eastern section of Oneida territory, including lands that encompassed Fort Stanwix and Oriska, to be available for Crown development and future settlement. At first, the Oneidas refused to cede this section, but Sir William coerced them into acquiescence. The people of Oriska were furious that they now owed their continued presence there to the goodwill of the British government. Alienated from the Johnsons, Han Yerry and other Oriska inhabitants gravitated toward the rebellious Whigs. By 1777 the Oneidas at Oriska, including the emissary Henry Cornelius, Han Yerry's brother Han Yost Thahoswagwat ("His Lip Followed Him"), Hendrick Smith, and Blatcop Tonyentagoyon (also called Platcoff, Henry Trathoop, and "Old Legs"), all prepared themselves to fight alongside Han Yerry against St. Leger's force.[6]

In planning to resist the British-Indian invasion, Han Yerry and his associates would need to cooperate with a new Continental regiment and commander at Fort Schuyler. Back in April 1777, as the terms of service for Samuel Elmore and his New Jerseyites expired, General Schuyler assigned the Third New York Regiment, under Colonel Peter Gansevoort, to replace them.[7]

Gansevoort, a local product from nearby Albany, was born in 1749 into a prominent Dutch lineage. He boasted not just a brother in New York's Provincial Congress but also an uncle, Volkert P. Douw, who was vice president of that congress and one of the Indian commissioners working in conjunction with Schuyler in the Northern Department.[8]

When the rebellion erupted in 1775, twenty-six-year-old Gansevoort opted for military service. Serving as a major during the rebel invasion of Canada, he gained the rank of lieutenant colonel in 1776 and assumed command of Fort George. Gansevoort earned a reputation as a sensible officer with an unflappable temperament, and he knew how to instill confidence in his troops. These qualities caused Schuyler to assign him to the Fort Schuyler command.[9]

Among Gansevoort's key responsibilities was maintaining solid relations with the Oneidas. His predecessor, Colonel Elmore, counseled him to "be Friendly to the Indians as it is of Consequence, and helpful to the cause." Schuyler seconded Elmore's advice, instructing his subordinate to "keep up a friendly intercourse with the Indians."[10]

Gansevoort continued the policy of issuing rations to Indians who visited or who undertook work for the government. He authorized scouting missions and paid Oneidas promptly for their services, sometimes out of his own pocket. His attentiveness preserved the healthy exchanges his predecessors had initiated.[11]

Like other European Americans, however, he bore the customary markings of prejudice against Native Americans. His deep-seated mistrust of all Indians convinced him to act cautiously. He fed the Oneidas, offered them supplies when necessary, and treated them with appropriate outward respect, but he maintained his distance with regard to personal friendship. He did not want to be deceived into missing possible signs of treachery.[12]

Gansevoort also focused his energies on the continuing process of rebuilding Fort Schuyler, especially with the threat of an invading force looming in the background. He and his troops labored diligently to restore the bastion by replacing rotting timbers, and they rebuilt or added several buildings with freshly cut logs. Outside the fort, they needed all new pickets—obstructions composed of rows of logs laid vertically and buried partially in the ground to secure them. The soldiers filled in eroded areas and sodded the slopes to help protect the structure from enemy cannon fire. Work details began improving the road to Fort Dayton at German Flatts, some thirty miles away to the southeast, to facilitate the arrival of reinforcements; others chopped down trees along Wood Creek to hinder water passage from Oswego.[13]

Britain's Indian allies offered Gansevoort's troops little rest. Using the wilderness to conceal themselves, small parties of Mississaugas and Iroquois maneuvered around Oneida scouts and attacked soldiers and civilians who foolishly wandered away from the fort. On June 25 a captain and a corporal slipped out after breakfast without permission to go hunting. At about 10:00 a.m., two Indians surprised them, killing and scalping the corporal and shooting the officer in the back and tomahawking him before taking his scalp. Only by feigning death did the captain survive.[14]

This incident placed the Oneidas in an awkward position. Gansevoort and his Continentals were upset, and the Oneidas felt the need to deflect any culpability from the Six Nations. The problem was that even if their brethren in the confederacy had not committed the act, Mississauga Indians could not have undertaken such a raid without the former's tacit approval or open encouragement.

A day or two later, some sachems and warriors from Kanonwalohale and Oriska visited Gansevoort to condole the garrison for its loss. They hoped to defuse bad feelings by claiming to speak for the Six Nations and expressing their sorrow and innocence. Blame, they insisted, should rest exclusively on the shoulders of such Tory-backing Indians as the Mississaugas. Had Generals Schuyler and Gates not urged them "not to take part in the war," the Oneida leaders claimed that Han Yerry and other scouts would have pursued the murderers immediately. Nonetheless, the Oneidas promised to send runners to each of the Six Nations, informing them of the incident and seeking their help in locating the culprits.[15]

Gansevoort remained unconvinced. While he expressed appreciation for the Oneidas' sympathy and efforts to identify the killers, his distrust of Indians dissuaded him from automatically accepting any claims of innocence. "I hope the mischief has been done," the colonel stated, "not by any of our good friends of the Oneida nation, but by the Tories, who are enemies to you as well as to us, and who are ready to murder yourselves, your wives, and children, if you will not be as wicked as themselves." As for other confederacy Iroquois, they would have to prove their own innocence. "When your chiefs convince me that Indians of the Six Nations have had no hand in this wicked thing, and shall use means to find out the murderers and bring them to justice," he declared, "you may be assured that we will strengthen the chain of friendship, and embrace you as our good brothers."[16]

Less than a week later, Gansevoort received confirmation of his misgivings. Barry St. Leger, carrying the temporary rank of brigadier general, and Daniel Claus, who had received orders to take charge of Indian allies under St. Leger's command, sought to obtain detailed intelligence about Fort Schuyler's condition and troop strength. They sent out forty Iroquois warriors led by Mohawk John Oteronyente. Weaving through the Oneida scouting screen undetected, the party pounced on a rebel work crew—sixteen privates and an ensign—cutting sod about three-quarters of a mile from the fort. When shots rang out, Gansevoort ordered out two rescue parties, but they arrived too late. Half a dozen men lay butchered, and another five, including the ensign, had fallen prisoner. These captives, after some torture, provided the information St. Leger and Claus wanted.[17]

The soldiers did not fault the Oneidas for letting the war party sneak past them, but this raid sent shock waves through Tryon County and beyond. Coming in the wake of the seizure of Fort Ticonderoga by Burgoyne's southward-advancing army, the attack helped instill an entirely new level of fear throughout the region. Refugees from the hinterland, seeking safety, abandoned their homes and crowded into safer places such as Albany, where all was confusion. Local committees of safety bombarded state and Continental officials with demands to send reinforcements and return militia units to their own communities. The British troops scared them; Tory elements panicked them; Indians horrified them.[18]

New York's patriot leaders winced at the level of local hysteria. "I am exceedingly chagrined at the pusillanimous spirit which prevails in the county of Tryon," Schuyler commented. The New York Council of Safety announced that no major troop reinforcements were available. Locals would have to stand up for themselves. "Let not a timidity unworthy of the cause . . . and unbecoming the character of freemen, deprive you of" your own defense, the revolutionary government chided.[19]

When Schuyler ordered Nicholas Herkimer to dispatch two hundred militiamen to Fort Schuyler, the local Committee of Safety stopped the movement. Herkimer protested and eventually carried the argument, but the committee's interference revealed the doubts Mohawk Valley settlers had about being able to protect themselves and their families. Their overriding fear was that "if they would gather themselves together to appear" for militia duty, as Herkimer explained, "their poor Wives and Children would be left helpless and fall a prey to the merciless Savages."[20]

Fear added fuel to their deeply ingrained anti-native prejudices, causing local colonists to blur the boundaries separating Indians sympathetic to the rebellion from those supporting the Crown. They wondered just how trustworthy, reliable, and dependable the Oneidas would prove to be when confronted by their Iroquois brethren in St. Leger's force. Most settlers suspected that the Oneidas, rather than fighting against other Iroquois, would join in attacking the white inhabitants of Tryon County. These doubters were anything but ready to depend upon ostensibly friendly natives for succor of any kind.

Among those who doubted Oneida constancy was Gansevoort's fiancée, Catherine Van Schaick. Gripped by the same prejudices against Indians that afflicted most whites, she perceived all natives as dishonorable and eager to erupt in flashes of brutality. Catherine admitted to a "Faint Heart" with St. Leger's column approaching Fort Schuyler. "I hope you [will] not put much trust on Our Indians they are a Sett of people not to be trusted on," she warned. "All my fear is that you will be blocked up in the Fort and will be forced to Surender for the want of provision and left to the Mercy of those brutes." At that point, she could only imagine her beloved Gansevoort being slaughtered and scalped by bloodthirsty natives.[21]

On July 27 another gruesome attack took place outside the fort. Three young girls wandered about a half mile away to pick raspberries. Four Indians surprised them. Once again, shots rang out, alerting the troops to danger. A rescue party rushed out to find two girls tomahawked and scalped. One was dead; the other, her breathing labored, expired within a half hour. The third girl suffered two musket wounds in her shoulder, neither of them fatal. "It is equally the same to them if they can get a scalp," vented an enraged Continental, "whether it is from a soldier or an innocent *babe.*" The next day, Gansevoort transported all the garrison's mothers and their children along with the scalped officer and the wounded girl to a more secure location near German Flatts. Before the month ended, he also gained more reinforcements, giving him a total of about 750 defenders, and he prepared to receive seven bateaux loaded with ammunition and provisions coming up the river from Schenectady.[22]

As Fort Schuyler braced for the attack, the Oneidas caucused at Kanonwalohale, seeking to chart a unified course. None of the options was appealing. At this juncture, the prospect of swaying a majority of the Six Nations back toward nonalignment was nil. If the Oneidas remained neutral, they would have to endure the humiliation of an invasion of their homeland—a prospect that mortified the warriors. By doing so they would tacitly be admitting a lack of courage with regard to defending the sanctity of borders that their ancestors had established, which generations of forebears had protected, and where Oneida spirits now resided. Equally undesirable, by granting St. Leger the right of passage, they would alienate the rebels and place the People of the Standing Stone in jeopardy from retaliatory strikes.

Another alternative called for them to resist St. Leger's force, even to the point of combat, a position Han Yerry and others advocated. This prospect reflected the will of most Oneidas, who leaned toward the rebel cause anyway. Further, they would be actively shaping their own destiny, rather than sitting by passively while others molded their future for them. If they challenged the British onslaught, however, the Oneidas would be forever abandoning their neutral course while placing themselves at odds with many of their confederacy brethren and converting their homeland into a battleground.

By July 29 the Oneidas had formulated their strategy. They would send a delegation to meet with fellow Iroquois now attached to St. Leger's army. They realized how slight their prospects were of reawakening their brethren to the sagacious course of confederacy neutrality. "When we come there and declare we are for peace," the Oneida chiefs predicted, "we expect to be used with indifference, and sent away." Still, they felt compelled to explore that option. If others in the Six Nations rejected their proposal, at least the Oneida people would know they had made a final effort to ensure peace, which would help unify them behind the option of armed defense. As expected, when their sachems presented their arguments at Three Rivers, near Oswego, their Iroquois brethren curtly dismissed them.[23]

Meanwhile, the Oneidas strengthened their ties with the rebels. Their nation's leaders asked Thomas Spencer to draft a letter for Gansevoort. Without formally declaring their support, they offered the colonel information that only a close ally would provide. They stated that St. Leger's force would likely reach Fort Schuyler within four days, and they encouraged Gansevoort not to be intimidated by the firepower of the British Army. They then exhorted the officers "to exert themselves" and "be couragious" in defending "the Fort." Schuyler, they suggested, should send out a relief force, and they encouraged the Tryon County Committee of Safety to "[l]et the Militia rise up and come to Fort Schuyler to morrow." The chiefs also warned that reinforcements should "take Care of their March as there is a Party of Indians to stop the Road below the Fort about 80 or 100" of them. In closing, the Oneidas included "a belt of eight rows to confirm the truth of what we say."[24]

Without stating what was obvious, the Oneida Nation had altered its policy. No longer would neutrality encumber the warriors. Under the duress of an invasion, individual Oneidas could now freely choose their own course of action, which meant they could fight alongside the rebels with their leadership's blessing. Immediately, a number of warriors volunteered to join the patriots, ready and willing to serve as spies, messengers, and scouts. Soon they would find themselves heavily involved in resisting St. Leger's army as that force began to besiege Fort Schuyler.[25]

On August 2 the lead elements of the British Army under Joseph Brant and Lieutenant Henry Bird approached the fort. The Oneidas had dispersed themselves throughout the nearby woods as pickets and spies, and a seventeen-year-old named Paul Powless (Tegahsweangalolis, "The Sawmill"), a member of the Bear Clan who resided at Kanonwalohale and known for his great foot speed, made first contact with the British. Powless and several of Brant's party spotted each other a few miles from the post. Before the young warrior could flee, Brant himself hailed Powless and called for a meeting. A bit cocky, yet sensibly distrustful, Powless engaged in a conversation with Brant. Still, he never let the Mohawk come close to him, and he kept his musket cocked and his finger on the trigger at all times.[26]

Brant tried to tempt Powless with rewards for shifting sides and helping to win the Oneidas over to the British. Powless demurred. "He and his Oneida brothers had joined their fortunes with those of the Americans," he proclaimed, "& should share with them whatever good or evil might come." As he had often done, Brant described the enormous power of the king, and he predicted the destruction of the Oneida Nation if its people persisted in their course. Powless replied that "[h]e & the Oneidas would persevere, if need be, 'til all were annihilated." With neither Brant nor Powless budging, the two soon parted company.[27]

Powless made a hasty retreat toward the fort, with Brant and his associates in hot pursuit. Using his great speed, Powless alerted the Oneida pickets of the enemy's presence just before the British and their Indian allies started firing at them. The Oneidas took up the fight. Heavily outnumbered, they escaped by maneuvering around the fort and gaining safety in the edifice from the opposite side.[28]

About the time that Powless was conversing with Brant, some bateaux loaded with supplies reached the Upper Landing on the Mohawk River. About one hundred reinforcements who were guarding the boats and another hundred troops from the fort began unloading the goods and hauling them inside the bastion. As they lugged the last of

the food and ammunition toward the main gate, the soldiers heard musket fire in the distance—the shots aimed at Powless and his fellow
Oneidas. Just as they completed the task, Brant's warriors struck the
bateaux men who dawdled at the landing. These civilians suffered two
wounded, one killed, and their leader captured. As for the 750 rebels
inside the fort, they now had up to six weeks of provisions to sustain
them during any attempted British siege.[29]

Brant and Bird spread their small numbers of troops around the bastion to challenge the defenders until St. Leger came up with the main
force. They had hoped to surprise the garrison, and if that failed, to
control the landing site on the Mohawk River and sever ties with the
colonial communities to the east. Now, given their small numbers, they
could not prevent Oneida messengers from passing through their lines.
Two Kettles Together slipped out of the fort and maneuvered her way
through the woods to Oriska. A fine horsewoman, she obtained a
mount there and rode to Fort Dayton and beyond, notifying everyone
along the way that the enemy was at hand. Under cover of darkness,
Powless also got past the assailants. Like Two Kettles Together, he secured a horse and galloped all the way to Schenectady to warn patriot
officials and seek help.[30]

Over the next two days, St. Leger came forward with the main body
of his command, estimated from 1,300 to about 1,700. This total included about two hundred British regulars, Sir John Johnson's loyalist
Royal Greens, a company of Tory rangers, a German light infantry unit,
a handful of Canadians, and approximately eight hundred Indians,
mostly from the Six Nations. Among them were two hundred Senecas
with John Butler. Because of the obstructions deposited in Wood Creek
by Gansevoort's axemen, St. Leger's artillery and supplies would be delayed, as his column labored feverishly to clear the waterway and restore a pathway to the fort. It took several more days before the
guns—two six-pounders, two three-pounders, and four 4.4-inch "Coe-
horn" mortars—reached the fort, and they lacked the firepower to dis-
lodge the rebel defenders.[31]

Brant's advance party had assumed positions amid clumps of bushes
and behind logs, stumps, and trees, and began sniping at the garrison.
The arrival of the main British and Tory units made it possible to fill in
the gaps and open the siege. Seeking a speedy capitulation, St. Leger

sent Captain Gilbert Tice into the fort under a flag of truce. Armed solely with a vainglorious pronouncement that St. Leger had plagiarized from Burgoyne, Tice urged Gansevoort to surrender to overwhelming force, or St. Leger would execute "the vengeance of the state against wilful outcasts." The offer, so noted a rebel officer, was "rejected with disdain."[32]

Gansevoort had reason to dismiss the proposal peremptorily. Besides 750 troops, he had the added benefit of numerous Oneida supporters. Some of them remained in the fort, ready to fight, deliver messages, or spy on the enemy. Outside the gates, other Oneidas kept careful watch and harassed St. Leger's force whenever opportunities presented themselves. Gansevoort had ample quantities of musket cartridges. His only shortage was cannon balls, which he decided to ration at nine per day. Also, the fort itself offered a huge advantage. In its refurbished condition, it provided excellent protection against enemy fire, and St. Leger's cannons lacked the punch to breach its walls.[33]

Despite his superior numbers, St. Leger thus had many challenges. Unfortunately for the British cause, a catastrophic blunder he had committed even before the campaign began was now haunting him. After interrogating the prisoners that John Oteronyente's reconnaissance party had captured a month before, St. Leger knew the strength of Fort Schuyler's defenses. He also realized that the artillery he planned to take on the campaign was insufficient to force a capitulation. A prudent decision would have been to wait for more muscular ordnance. Convinced of the inherent inferiority of rebel leaders and troops and the widely acknowledged colonial fears of potential Indian savagery, St. Leger counted on superior numbers and a surprise appearance to compensate for his lack of firepower. Once deployed at the fort, his only real option, besides using bluster, was a drawn-out operation. He would lay siege to the bastion and keep moving his force in closer, probing for exploitable weaknesses and squeezing the garrison until its worn-out defenders could endure no more.[34]

Even before the British-Indian force reached Fort Schuyler, Nicholas Herkimer was back in German Flatts organizing assistance for Gansevoort. On July 17 he published a proclamation, alerting the people of

Tryon County about a likely attack while exhorting them to respond "for the just defense of their country." All men in good health between sixteen and sixty should gather their weapons and accoutrements and be prepared to "march to oppose the enemy with vigor, as true patriots." On July 30, when Herkimer received a copy of Spencer's message from the Oneida chiefs that the British were four days away, he immediately called out the militia for service, to rendezvous at Fort Dayton.[35]

The citizens who comprised Herkimer's command were mostly farmers, with a handful of skilled and unskilled workers thrown into the mix. Although nearly all of them worked manually, and may have been in good health for everyday physical labor, they lacked the necessary conditioning for soldiering. Rarely did citizens walk ten to fifteen miles a day, carrying twenty-five pounds of equipment. Just to reach Fort Dayton, a large number of them had to travel substantial distances. By the time Herkimer's "army" gathered and marched for Fort Schuyler, many of these citizen soldiers were already fatigued.[36]

At Fort Dayton, some eight hundred arms-bearing militiamen assembled. They began their journey on August 4, along a trail through flat terrain on the northern bank of the Mohawk River. The next day, they pressed on and crossed the Mohawk River at a ford near Old Fort Schuyler (modern-day Utica). The column then continued on a winding, northwesterly course and finally bivouacked on the evening of August 5 with the head of the command near Oriska. By this point, the pace and hilly terrain were taking their toll. Summer heat, high humidity, and long distances hauling heavy loads caused some citizen soldiers to fall out of the march. A handful may have caught up that night, but most were probably too incapacitated to regain contact with the main column.[37]

Even as stragglers fell out, Herkimer picked up some fresh fighters along the way. Joining him near Oriska were a number of Oneidas, estimated at between sixty and one hundred persons, and at least one Kahnawake, Louis Atayataronghta. Included among the Oneida participants were Chief Warrior Han Yerry, his wife, Two Kettles Together, sachem Henry Cornelius, Han Yost Thahoswagwat, Hendrick Smith, Blatcop Tonyentagoyon, and Thomas and Edward Spencer.[38]

That night, Herkimer called on three trusted men—Adam Hellmer,

John Demuth, and John Adam Kember—to carry a message to Fort Schuyler. The general wanted Gansevoort to know that his column was nearing the fort. To prevent the British and Indians from ganging up on his force, Herkimer requested that the colonel fire a cannon salvo to signal that he had received the letter and then send out a party of raiders to distract and confuse the enemy.

Unfortunately, once they reached the fort, the three couriers did not know how to sidestep the attackers and gain access to the works. Not until mid- to late morning of the next day did they get inside the walls and hand Gansevoort the message, much later than Herkimer had anticipated.[39]

The final leg of the journey, the pathway from the Oriska area to Fort Schuyler, snaked its way through thick forests. The primitive road coursed up and down hills and through occasional gullies that glaciers and spring streams had gouged out over thousands of years. Maples, oaks, birches, beeches, hemlocks, and pines lined the route. With the trees in full foliage, Herkimer's column had limited visibility from the roadway into the timber, and the dense net of branches blocked out the sunlight. The contrast between the more sunlit path and darker woods gave a decided advantage to anyone looking out from the timber toward the road.[40]

Just why Herkimer neglected to have Oneida scouts, who were much more familiar with the terrain, fan out well ahead and beyond the flanks of his troops on the morning of August 6, 1777, will forever remain a mystery. Deep down, the fear of Indian treachery may have deterred the militia commander and his officers from placing Oneida skirmishers on their front and flanks. Although they heard stories about Oneida loyalty, they were not willing to risk their lives by assigning these Indians responsibility for the column's security. The Oneidas, after all, could be leading them into a trap, especially if blood ties to fellow Iroquois proved more powerful than friendship with the rebels.

Herkimer himself was also serving under a cloud of suspicion. Some of his relatives had sided with the British, and his own brother, Joost Herkimer, was then under arms with St. Leger. As such, unwarranted hesitation or signs of too much caution on his part might cause his subordinates to question his loyalty.[41]

As for the militiamen, they had come out in impressive numbers to arrest Sir John Johnson in 1775, but, since then, their enthusiasm and aggressiveness had waned dramatically. Charges of faintheartedness in serving the cause of liberty cut deeply at them, even threatening their sense of masculinity. True men, their critics said, would never endure a loss of liberty, which was tantamount to slavery. True men would fight courageously to defend their hearths, their homes, their families, and their freedoms. These slurs wounded stalwarts and grumblers alike, challenging them to prove that they genuinely merited that liberty.

Intent on demonstrating anew their resolve, Herkimer's officers and men applied tremendous pressure on him to move forward aggressively. When he insisted on waiting until they had heard the cannon salvos from the fort, his officers demanded that they press on anyway; and when he still hesitated, they accused him of Tory leanings and cowardice. Under a barrage of insults and insubordinate remarks, Herkimer finally yielded. "March on!" he announced, to the cheers of his troops.[42]

Topography and time, too, played key roles in Herkimer's decision not to send out scouts. The scouts' hiking off the main roadway in cut-up terrain, skirting huge tree trunks, stumbling over protruding roots, climbing over fallen timbers, and circumventing underbrush could needlessly delay the entire command. The slower Herkimer's column advanced, the greater the likelihood St. Leger could mass superior troop strength and firepower against the militia column.[43]

Focusing on speed rather than caution, the column lurched forward to assist Gansevoort and his troops. Although the old roadway between Forts Dayton and Schuyler had its twists and turns, soldiers had labored hard to improve the route before the campaign began. They had cleared fallen limbs and logs and used branches and other materials as corduroy to firm up mud patches and fill in small craters. With only a few miles left to reach Fort Schuyler, the improved trail seemed like the most expeditious route to traverse that morning.

———————

Warm, humid air and overcast, threatening skies, indications of stormy weather in the making, greeted the rebel militia early on the fateful morning of August 6. As they began their advance, Herkimer, on horseback, positioned himself near the head of his command. His forward guards were likely the half-Oneida brothers Thomas and Edward Spencer, but after the insinuations of cowardice by his troops, he was not far behind them. The column soon began to stretch out, with the rear companies dragging far behind. Undisciplined militiamen failed to maintain tight formations, and everyone behind proceeded as fast as the slowest soldiers ahead of them. "Carelessness," as Daniel Claus later reported, perhaps best described Herkimer's approach.[44]

About six miles from the fort, the road angled slightly to the northeast as it cut across a ravine. The terrain sloped downward from Herkimer's left to his right, broadening into flatland that extended toward the Mohawk River. The highest elevation was to the rebel left, about forty feet above the trail and obscured by tall trees. The road dipped down steep banks into the ravine, bending first toward that high ground and then curving away from that height as travelers moved up the opposite side. Coursing through the lowest part of the ravine was a stream, with marshy land cushioning both sides. A corduroy bridge, composed of logs and just wide enough to accommodate wagons, enabled people to cross over the water and muck.[45]

At about 10:00 a.m., the lead elements of Herkimer's force plunged into the crevasse, strode across the log bridge, and started scaling the opposite incline. Breathing heavily, they did not dawdle. Moments later, just behind the head of the column, an eruption of musketry fire shattered the calm. Herkimer had stumbled into a classic ambush.[46]

The previous afternoon, Joseph Brant had received news from his sister Molly that Herkimer would be within ten or twelve miles of the fort that night with about eight hundred rebel militia. He recommended a surprise attack, and St. Leger concurred. Early the next morning, after much wrangling, Brant convinced the Senecas to participate, and they joined Sir John Johnson and a company of light infantry, which had moved out toward the ambush site the previous evening. All told, the

Crown marshaled about five hundred men, four-fifths of them Indians, to attack Herkimer's force. Not all the Indians had muskets; some carried only tomahawks and spears. Although Johnson was technically in command, the Iroquois designed and executed ambushes better than anyone, and Sir John wisely yielded battlefield leadership to the Seneca chief warriors Cornplanter and Old Smoke.[47]

The Seneca chiefs chose the ground at the ravine for their trap. They placed their force in a U-shaped formation that straddled the morass, with the curving road between the U's posts. The base, or the bottom of the U, lay beyond the ravine's western bank. To guarantee control of the best terrain feature—the high ground that would be on the rebels' left as they marched along the road—the Senecas extended their upper prong from the western ridge to that high point. Because the stream and quagmire were nearly impenetrable and would prove a poor escape route, the lower prong required fewer warriors. Still, these experts placed enough fighters there to effect a devastating crossfire.[48]

The object was to let the rebel militia march between the two prongs toward the base. Once the rear of Herkimer's column passed the tips of the U's prongs, every person along the Senecas' line would fire a volley and then assault the unsuspecting militiamen. Indians on the eastern edges would work their way around and close off the open end, encircling Herkimer and his command. In an effort to avoid premature detection and to prevent pro-British Indians from firing into one another, the attackers hid behind trees and undergrowth about forty yards or so from the road, with a clear line of sight.

The first blast caught Herkimer's militiamen and the Oneidas completely unaware. Then came the chilling shriek from Iroquois warriors, as some attackers continued to rain musket balls down on the citizen soldiers while others closed on their prey with tomahawks and spears. Rebel survivors, stunned by the initial barrage, staggered off the road and crawled for cover. Others bolted for the rear, only to find the trail obstructed by their own wagons. Bunched together in a logjam, these militiamen made ready targets for Indian marksmen until they mustered enough good sense to seek shelter in the trees. Left behind in both instances were their wounded comrades, who lay completely exposed, along with dozens of dead citizen soldiers.[49]

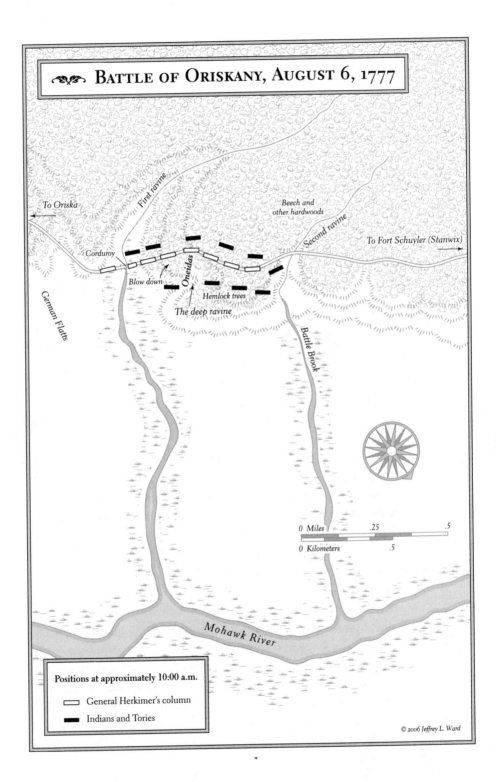

BATTLE OF ORISKANY, AUGUST 6, 1777

To Oriska

First ravine

Beech and
other hardwoods

Second ravine

To Fort Schuyler (Stanwix)

Corduroy

Blow down

Oneidas

Hemlock trees

The deep ravine

German Flats

Battle Brook

0 Miles · .25 · .5

0 Kilometers · .5

Mohawk River

Positions at approximately 10:00 a.m.

☐ General Herkimer's column

■ Indians and Tories

© 2006 Jeffrey L. Ward

When Herkimer heard the thunder of musketry to his rear, he swung his large white horse around and reentered the ravine. A splendid target, the general did not last long. A musket ball shattered his leg about six inches below his knee. The same ball killed his beautiful mount. Rebel fighters carried Herkimer up onto the western ridge and leaned him against a beech tree, with two Oneidas standing guard over him. From that spot, he calmly puffed on his pipe and tried to direct the fighting, but limited visibility and utter mayhem on the battlefield restricted his influence.[50]

Gruesome fates awaited the Spencer brothers as well. At the head of the column, they too returned toward the sounds of gunfire. How they went down, and whether it was the same musket volley that felled Herkimer, no one knows. A week earlier, the blacksmith Thomas had expressed his hope that "all Friends to Liberty and that loves their Families will not be backward but exert themselves as one Resolute Blow would secure the Friendship of the Six Nations and almost free this Part of the Country from the Excursions of the Enemy." Edward and Thomas Spencer—half Oneida, half European American—had lived and gained respect in both worlds. They died fighting for both peoples that day.[51]

Those in the rear of Herkimer's column resisted briefly but then fled in panic. Apparently, the pro-British Iroquois warriors had opened fire too soon, before the back portion of the rebel force had entered the snare. Some Iroquois broke away from the main element in pursuit, cutting down and scalping those they caught. With the loss of Herkimer's back units and so many early casualties, the general's numbers may well have declined by more than 50 or 60 percent just thirty minutes into the battle.[52]

The pro-British Iroquois, stripped to breechcloths and their skin covered in war paint, descended on the citizen soldiers, taking them on hand to hand while hoping to retrieve some scalps and firearms from the dead and wounded. Experienced warriors, they waited until a militiaman had discharged his musket and then they attacked. During the twenty to thirty seconds needed to reload, the rebel was virtually defenseless. He could swing his musket like a club or employ his fists. In either case, the advantage lay with the Indian warrior wielding a tomahawk or spear.[53]

The Oneida Blatcop Tonyentagoyon rushed into the melee, armed only with his tomahawk. Regarded as "a very able warrior," he enhanced his fighting reputation that day. A man of ordinary height but "heavy, vigourous" in his frame, Blatcop took three passes through the chaos, "Knocking right & left" as he went. At one point, he tomahawked a pro-British Indian, breaking his own arm in the struggle. An Oneida friend had to come up and help him "dispatch" the wounded native.[54]

Louis Atayaaronghta, the Kahnawake warrior who spoke Oneida, English, and French fluently, fought valiantly from a longer range than Blatcop. He observed an enemy shooting down rebels with consummate skill. "Every time he rises up," Louis complained to a nearby militiaman, "he kills one of our men." Thoroughly frustrated, he vowed, "Either he or I must die." As the warrior lifted up to fire yet another round, Louis discharged his own weapon, and the Indian crumpled over the limb of a tree. Louis gave out a whoop, raced forward, scalped the victim, then announced, "That fellow will do no more harm."[55]

About three hours into the struggle the skies opened up on the combatants, and passing thundershowers provided timely relief for the weary, causing an hour-long lull in the fighting. Visibility declined, and heavy rains moistened gunpowder, especially in flashpans, making muskets nearly impossible to fire. The break greatly aided the rebels, who caught their breath while regrouping and pairing up so they could more effectively ward off Iroquois tomahawk attacks. Herkimer was also able to organize the survivors into defensive circles for better protection.[56]

Amid the noise of battle and stormy weather, Han Yerry represented the ideal of calmness. Mounted on horseback, a sword dangling from his waist to indicate his leadership as a chief warrior, he had his wife, Two Kettles Together, on one side and his son Cornelius Doxtader on the other. All three fired at the enemy, Han Yerry and Cornelius employing muskets and Two Kettles Together using two pistols. When a musket ball struck Han Yerry in the wrist, Two Kettles Together took over the duty of loading for him while the chief continued to shoot. Before the battle ended, he also fought the enemy with his tomahawk and sword, swinging both with his uninjured arm. Han Yerry killed as many as nine enemy fighters with his musket that day. His son Cornelius, who brought down two more, gained his first combat laurels.[57]

When the rains subsided, the fighting began again and soon reached its earlier ferocity. Almost as quickly, the rage of battle began to fizzle out. Neither side could sustain the same level of intensity after the bloodstained morning engagement, and the heavy casualties on both sides were taking a psychological toll.

Just as exhaustion was setting in, a detachment of Tory fighters reached the field. With fresh troops, Sir John and others decided to attempt one final drive. By reversing their jackets, they hoped to confuse the rebels just enough to catch them in another surprise attack. The ruse failed. The citizen soldiers recognized the challenge from their former neighbors, and once again they clashed with musket butts and knives.

By this time, the pro-British Indians, sensing that they could inflict little additional damage without serious losses themselves, decided to pull back. They may also have detected some commotion to their rear near the fort, which caused them to break off to investigate. Cries of "O:nenh," the departure signal, circulated around the battlefield. As they retreated, so too did their British allies. The bloodstained Battle of Oriskany ended almost as suddenly as it had begun.[58]

Herkimer's citizen soldiers had held the battlefield, but they had no victory. Seven decades later, the horror of that clash continued to linger in the mind of the Seneca warrior Blacksnake. Never before (or since) had he seen so many dead bodies in one place. "I thought at the time the Blood Shed a Stream running Down on the Descending ground," the aged Blacksnake recounted. At least two hundred rebel partisans lay dead, with scores more wounded or captured. Most of those taken prisoner, according to John Butler, faced summary execution and scalping from Indians enraged by their own losses. About 150 militiamen walked off the field at the end of the day, and they carried about 50 wounded friends and neighbors with them. Since few British and loyalist soldiers fought, their casualties probably amounted to about twenty-five or thirty. As many as three dozen Senecas perished in the fight, including six chiefs. When these warriors returned home, recalled the white Seneca Mary Jemison, "our town exhibited a scene of real sorrow and distress." The Senecas engaged in "mourning" that was almost "excessive," which they "expressed by the most doleful yells, shrieks, and howlings, and by inimitable gesticulations." Perhaps an equal number of fellow Iroquois never returned home. Although these numbers pale by comparison with the dead militiamen, they were devastating losses for so small a population group to endure.[59]

After fighting all day, Two Kettles Together still possessed enough energy to jump on a horse and ride full tilt to notify local Indians and rebels of the battle's outcome. Patriot survivors hauled at least some of their wounded and dying to Oriska for the night. Herkimer, his leg shattered, refused to leave the field until the fight had ended. That evening and into the next day, soldiers carted him homeward. Ten days after the battle, a surgeon unsuccessfully attempted to amputate the militia general's shattered leg. Herkimer bled to death, a Bible clutched in his hands and his family gathered around him.[60]

Because most historians over the next century either ignored or did not know about Oneida participation in the battle, there were no tabulations of Oneida losses. The Spencer brothers gave their lives; Han Yerry was shot in the wrist; and Blatcop suffered a broken arm in the fight. Doubtless other Oneidas incurred wounds as well, and perhaps some even died at Oriskany. Posterity will never know.

8

ALLIED WITH THE REBELS

Back at Fort Schuyler, a little after dawn on August 6, the patriot defenders observed a large body of Indians shifting around toward the landings to the southeast. Once Adam Hellmer and General Herkimer's other messengers got into the bastion that morning, Peter Gansevoort began to piece everything together. With Herkimer's relief column camped eight miles away the previous night, the pro-British Indians had left their camps to launch an attack. Gansevoort decided to send out a force under his second in command, Lieutenant Colonel Marinus Willett, to link up with the citizen soldiers in accordance with Herkimer's instructions. Also, as the general had requested, Gansevoort ordered the firing of a signal—three cannon shots. By that time, however, the din of battle drowned out the salvos.[1]

An articulate and charismatic officer, Willett, a native of Long Island, had just celebrated his thirty-seventh birthday. As a young man, he had gained military experience in the Seven Years' War and had participated in the rebel campaign to take Canada in 1775. Now, with 250 New York and Massachusetts troops and a three-pounder cannon, he formed ranks inside the fort to deliver a diversionary blow. Just as his column planned to march, however, the thunderstorms struck. After stewing for an hour waiting for the rain to let up, Willett's force moved out toward the southeast, surprising and dispersing the token resisters in Sir John Johnson's camp near the Mohawk River. Willett and his soldiers plundered the camp, destroying anything of value they could not carry back to the fort.

Interrogating some captives, Willett learned that Herkimer and his troops had earlier suffered a devastating ambush. Although he could do little to help them, he realized that his sortie had caught the British and their Indian allies off guard. Should he push his troops out farther, they might be able to inflict serious damage on St. Leger's army by destroying critical supplies. Willett elected to proceed.

Gathering up plundered goods, the column pressed on to scatter some pro-British Indians from their campsites. As they rummaged through the native possessions, they found the scalps of the two girls from the fort who had been attacked while out picking raspberries. Rage bubbled up, but through sheer force of will, Willett kept his troops under control. Again they took whatever of value they could find and moved on to the next Indian encampment.[2]

Having wreaked much havoc while also seizing St. Leger's revealing correspondence, Willett's troops finally decided to return to the fort. En route, they spotted some British combatants trying to set a trap. With the fire from Willett's cannon and some well-directed rounds from Gansevoort's post artillery, they squelched the ambush. Moments later, they passed through the fort's gates loaded with British and Indian property and four prisoners. Their haul included "upwards of fifty brass kettles, and more than 100 blankets, (two articles which were much needed,) with a quantity of muskets, tomahawks, spears, ammunition, clothing, deerskins, a variety of Indian affairs, and five colours." Willett's column, moreover, did not suffer a single casualty.[3]

When the pro-British Indians who had fought at Oriskany returned to their camps and discovered their possessions stolen, they were furious. The British had convinced them to join the campaign by insisting that Fort Schuyler would capitulate easily, with ample bounty for all. Instead, they had taken heavy casualties in the battle, and the rebels had plundered their property. The pain of loved ones lost and the humiliation of having their camps ransacked slowly festered with the Indians, in time fomenting much dissension between them and their British allies.

Inside Fort Schuyler, many Oneidas accepted refuge alongside the garrison force, even as St. Leger's troops kept trying to effect a capitulation. No one knows how many Oneidas sought sanctuary there or helped defend the fort. Among those who volunteered their services were Cornelius (Clanis Kahiktoton), Anthony (Shonoghleoh), and Big Bear (Aughneonh). Also taking shelter in the bastion during the siege was Hanyost T,hanaghghanegeaghu, one of the Oneidas' best warriors.[4]

St. Leger tried various means to convince the garrison to surrender. Two citizen soldiers captured at Oriskany, Colonel Peter Bellinger and Major John Frey, signed a letter describing severe losses at the battle and encouraging Gansevoort to capitulate or face extermination. The rebel colonel dismissed the document as a likely forgery or a statement written under extreme duress.[5]

On August 8, John Butler entered the post under a flag of truce to offer Gansevoort an opportunity to give up. The Indians, Butler explained, were wrathful over their losses. Not only did they want to exterminate the fort's defenders, but they also were demanding revenge by launching a raid on German Flatts with the intent of plundering and killing everyone they encountered along the way. St. Leger had held a council and convinced them not to undertake such extreme action until he had given the garrison a final chance to surrender. After pretending to mull over the proposal for a day, Gansevoort first insisted that the surrender terms be put in writing. Then he rejected them. "It is my determined resolution with the Forces under my Command," he declared, "to defend this Fort & Garrison to the last extremity."[6]

British musket and cannon fire kept the rebel troops and Oneidas inside the fort close to the bombproofs. Indian and British marksmen directed sniper fire at everyone who exposed themselves, and artillery rounds inflicted both physical and psychological damage. Although St. Leger lacked the artillery strength to blast a pathway into the fort, twice he ordered all-night shellings, hoping to wear down the defenders with sleeplessness and anxiety. During daytime, the booms of cannon reports and the crackle of musketry offered the defenders steady reminders of their besieged circumstances.[7]

Even as St. Leger's campaign settled into a traditional siege, the Oneidas inside and outside the bastion worked in concert with the rebels. Clanis Kahiktoton performed "extraordinary service" by shuttling messages between the fort and German Flatts. Oneida scouts continued to harass British soldiers and their Indian allies. Others carried intelligence to key patriot military leaders and civilians. Two Oneidas and seven Kahnawakes provided estimates about British forces under St. Leger and General John Burgoyne, and they lobbied General Schuyler in Albany to send out troops to raise the siege. Various Oneidas also urged the people of Tryon County to keep resisting the Crown's forces, despite the slaughter at Oriskany. "They furnish us with several useful pieces of intelligence," a local official said of the Oneidas, "and beg us to stand with firmness."[8]

Schuyler, too, as head of the Northern Department, bore responsibility to help repel St. Leger's command. With the reluctant consent of his ranking officers, he ordered a brigade of nine hundred Continentals from his army, then dueling with the major British force under Burgoyne, to go west and relieve Gansevoort. Dividing his force in the presence of the enemy was a bold decision, but Schuyler felt he had no choice. If the fort surrendered, patriot settlers throughout the Mohawk Valley, and possibly even people in Albany, would be exposed to British-Indian raids. Further, the revolutionaries would be reckoning with an enemy in their front as well as their flank and rear.[9]

To Schuyler's delight, his most talented subordinate, Major General Benedict Arnold, volunteered to lead the relief campaign. Since Schuyler could spare only nine hundred Continentals, Arnold would have to depend on other sources to supplement his troop strength. He called out militiamen along the route and absorbed the small garrison force at Fort Dayton. Neither provided an appreciable increase in his manpower base.

Schuyler advised Arnold to encourage the Oneidas to join the relief expedition. He hoped the Battle of Oriskany had wiped away all thoughts of neutrality, especially after the loss of such Oneida warriors as the Spencer brothers and the invasion of the Oneida homeland. "The Oneidas have friendly sentiments towards us, and must be cherished," Schuyler counseled Arnold. "They may perhaps be induced to take an active part in our favour." He gave Arnold one thousand dollars in specie to "conciliate" and recruit the Oneidas and a belt to deliver to them, asking for a council at Albany in mid-September. There, the commanding general hoped to convince two hundred to three hundred Oneidas to join the rebel army.[10]

Advancing as rapidly as the muddy roads would permit, Arnold found a band of Oneidas waiting for him at German Flatts, armed with fresh intelligence. One warrior had just come from the British camp outside Fort Schuyler. He estimated St. Leger's force at about 1,700 fighters—1,000 Indians and 700 whites. Marinus Willett, who had slipped out of Fort Schuyler to seek assistance, confirmed these figures.[11]

Even though the rebels were considerably outnumbered, Arnold met with his officers and urged immediate action. With the slaughter at Oriskany fresh in their minds, the officers demurred, preferring to hold their position at Fort Dayton and seek reinforcements. Arnold was in a frustrating position. He knew that Fort Schuyler needed relief, yet his officers would not support bold action. Nor could he rely on additional support from his direct superior. Congress had voted to replace Schuyler with Horatio Gates as the Northern Department commander. Arnold suspected that the less-than-dynamic Gates would not have divided the northern force in the first place, so he was unlikely to endorse the diversion of yet more troops from Burgoyne's front.[12]

Just when the situation looked bleakest, Arnold stumbled onto a solution. John Butler's aggressive son Walter had undertaken a risky mission to encourage support for St. Leger. He carried a proclamation from Sir John Johnson, Daniel Claus, and his father to the people of Tryon County, demanding that they press the Fort Schuyler garrison to surrender. If they did not, the Indians would wreak vengeance on all patriot settlers—men, women, and children—in the region. Instead, local rebels seized Walter Butler and those persons with him, and Arnold ordered them tried as spies. A court-martial convicted Butler and his cohorts and sentenced them to death.[13]

Among those found guilty was a local man named Hon Yost Schuyler. A distant relative of Philip Schuyler, Hon Yost had a reputation for addled thinking. Some considered him witless if not insane. His mother and brother approached Arnold, seeking clemency. After some resistance, Arnold agreed to talk to Hon Yost, who actually exhibited unusual clarity of thought. In return for his freedom, Hon Yost offered to foment unrest among the Indians with St. Leger by claiming that a massive rebel army was approaching rapidly from the east. As further corroboration, two Oneidas volunteered to rush into the camp from different directions and circulate the same tale. Lacking other options, Arnold agreed to the plan.[14]

On August 22, Hon Yost and the two Oneidas played their parts to perfection. The Tory fell in with an Indian scouting party and warned of Arnold's impending arrival. Before long he found himself before St. Leger, to whom he spoke dramatically of his arrest, conviction, and alleged narrow escape. Because he was known as a dedicated loyalist, his saga seemed convincing. When the two Oneidas confirmed the story of a vast rebel army charging toward Fort Schuyler, Indian support quickly crumbled.[15]

The Iroquois and other natives were fully disillusioned with the campaign and St. Leger's leadership. Instead of a speedy, bloodless adventure with much booty for the trade-starved Indians, they had suffered heavy casualties and lost many of their possessions. Accustomed as the Iroquois were to swift, punishing strikes, the glacial pace of the siege had worn down their patience. Word of an enormous rebel army closing in on them drained their remaining resolve.[16]

St. Leger quickly called a council, hoping to use the influence of Sir John, Daniel Claus, and John Butler to keep the Indians at their assigned posts. While the four Britons debated, some two hundred natives decamped. Not long thereafter, St. Leger later reported, his Indian leaders "insisted that I should retreat or they would be obliged to abandon me." During the next few hours, discipline gave way to panic, and the campaign collapsed.[17]

Late that day, several British deserters approached the fort, seeking asylum and notifying Gansevoort that St. Leger had evacuated. Wary of a trap, the colonel sent out a party of sixty soldiers, who reported back that the enemy camp was empty. Later that evening, Han Yost entered Fort Schuyler and told the commander of Arnold's approach.

Gansevoort, who by then had expunged any doubts he harbored about the Oneidas, dashed off a note to Arnold and entrusted its delivery to two Oneidas, Anthony and Big Bear. Although the British army had departed, bands of pro-British Indians were still roaming through the woods, so the mission required continued vigilance. The two Onei-

das traveled south, passing below their own village of Oriska "to escape
the scouts & reconnoitering parties of the enemy." They kept slipping
south and east, and then swung northward to meet the rebel army,
which was finally moving forward. According to Anthony and Big Bear,
they "very narrowly escaped being taken" just before making contact
with Arnold's column, still twenty miles from Fort Schuyler.[18]

The next day, Arnold ordered a forced march to reach the fort. By
then, Gansevoort had sent out squads to capture enemy stragglers and
gather abandoned equipment. Some prisoners indicated that disgruntled Indians had begun to attack their British comrades during the retreat. Once at Fort Schuyler, Arnold dispatched a party of Oneidas to
track St. Leger's force, and he sent out an expedition of five hundred
troops to pursue the enemy as far as Oneida Lake. Heavy rains forced
them back, but St. Leger's minions were already long gone.[19]

By the end of St. Leger's campaign, the Oneidas had gained praisewor-
thy reputations among the rebels. Besides Han Yerry, Two Kettles Together, their two sons, and Blatcop Tonyentagoyon, patriot leaders later
acknowledged the contributions of Clanis Kahiktoton, Anthony, Big
Bear, and Hanyost T,hanaghghanegeaghu. "The Oneidas and Tuscaroras have been exceedingly friendly to us in the present dispute," Arnold
wrote to Gates. By comparison, he declared, "the other tribes of the Six
Nations are villains and I hope will be treated as such."[20]

Their fellow Iroquois, too, took notice of Oneida activities during
the campaign. Before they evacuated northward, as payback for the
Oneidas' assistance to the rebels, an Iroquois war party attacked Oriska.
With no men present to defend the castle, women, children, and the
elderly fled to the woods. According to Claus, the pro-British Indians
"burnt their houses, destroyed their fields, crops, &c killed and carried
away their Cattle." They confiscated Blatcop's horses and assorted
livestock belonging to Big Bear. Raiders set Henry Cornelius's small
hewed-log home ablaze. Also destroyed was the frame home and accumulated goods and memories belonging to Han Yerry and Two Kettles
Together. Oriska existed no more.[21]

As the Oneidas sifted through ashes and charred remains looking for personal valuables that might have survived, they grew increasingly angry. Not only had they endured an invasion and lost the lives of some of their kin, but now this act of sheer vindictiveness had converted dozens of them into homeless and propertyless refugees. At the same time, over at German Flatts and other Mohawk Valley settlements, hundreds of white families began picking up the pieces of their shattered lives. They laid to rest their dead husbands, fathers, brothers, and sons, and wept at their graves. Both groups vowed revenge.

To exact retribution, they needed to look no farther than the Mohawk settlements. Molly Brant, Sir William Johnson's former wife-mistress, had converted Canajoharie into a kind of Tory base in the heart of rebeldom. Molly had fed critical intelligence to the British, including word of Herkimer's approach. Moreover, after Sir John Johnson's flight to Canada, she functioned as a key figure in encouraging loyalty to the Crown. Once St. Leger retreated, Molly surmised that she could not remain safely at Canajoharie. She packed a few items and took flight for Onondaga.[22]

By this time, nearly all residents had moved from the Upper Mohawk Castle, and holdouts did not tarry long. Most relocated to Oquaga or Niagara even before some wrathful rebels and Oneidas swarmed into Canajoharie in search of plunder. Led by Peter Dygert, chairman of the Tryon County Committee of Safety, patriot advocates absconded with livestock and appropriated crops, and removed other valuables, even from those who had not vacated their homes. Dygert encouraged Han Yerry and other Oneidas to retrieve their losses in double at the expense of pro-British Mohawks. For each cow lost, the Oneidas should take two, and so on for horses, hogs, and sheep.[23]

Han Yerry concentrated on the property Molly left behind. "Amongst a number of things he has taken from Molly Johnson," commented a local inhabitant, "is a purse of gold, all Sir William's papers, nay, even his will, and not a jot will he return, till ample satisfaction is made him for the loss of his house, barn, grain, horses, cows, &c. which the enemy took and destroyed at Oriskie." Han Yerry and his family even took up temporary residence in Molly's home.[24]

Not long after Molly abandoned Canajoharie, her brother Joseph returned to the Lower Mohawk Castle, Fort Hunter, to escort those

Mohawks to safety in Canada. Brant hurriedly shepherded one hundred of them northward, leaving behind Little Abraham and a few others who refused to break with neutrality and abandon their homes. For their stance, they became the butt of barbs and venom from fellow Mohawks. Within days of Brant's departure, local white settlers decided to "liberate" the unguarded and unused property, just as they had done at the Upper Mohawk Castle. Painting their faces black, they converged on the community at night and pilfered the vacated domiciles before escaping unrecognized.[25]

In the midst of these retributive acts, some three hundred Iroquois men, women, and children prepared for the lengthy trek to Albany for Schuyler's mid-September council. No meeting of reconciliation with the Six Nations, the council would be attended largely by Oneidas, with some Tuscaroras, a handful of Mohawks, and an Onondaga sachem. The men brought their weapons with them, a good sign for the hosts. Several even confessed a desire to visit the rebel army resisting John Burgoyne's force north of Albany.[26]

Within official patriot circles, Schuyler had intimated the possibility of getting several hundred Oneida warriors under rebel arms. Then, on September 14, Gates sent a message to Schuyler specifically asking for native recruits. "At this Time Some Faithful Indians would be of Infinite Service to this Army, to Assist Colonel [Daniel] Morgans Corps as Spies & Guides," Gates indicated. "I wish they could be immediately provisioned & sent . . . to my Camp." After speaking with those Indians coming in for the council, Schuyler was not sure he could obtain many recruits, since the Oneidas in particular expected "Fort Schuyler will soon be again attacked." Still, he promised to "strive to procure some of them to join you, but cannot advise you to depend upon them for *guides*, as they are unacquainted with the part of the country you are in."[27]

When the council officially opened, Schuyler offered the customary welcome. In response, the Oneidas symbolically took the Six Nations' axe "out of the heads" of the rebels and proclaimed "it should be stuck in no more." As the day proceeded, Schuyler sounded out some of the

This undated lithograph, entitled *General Lafayette's Visit (Erie Canal)*, captures the excitement that the marquis generated everywhere he traveled during his yearlong tour of the United States in 1824 and 1825. (© Museum of the City of New York, Print Archive)

The Indian agent Henry R. Schoolcraft (1793–1864) first viewed the Oneida Standing Stone in 1845, then located at the top of Primes Hill several miles south of Oneida Lake. This drawing first appeared in Schoolcraft's *History, Conditions, and Prospects of the Indian Tribes of the United States, Parts 1–6* (1851–1857). The stone represents the nation's strength, durability, and adaptability through the ages and today may be found next to the Oneida Nation's council house in Oneida, New York.

Seneca artist Ernest Smith (1907–1975) depicts the Six Nations' Creation Narrative in his painting *Sky Woman*. Having become pregnant through magical means, Sky Woman falls toward Earth after her jealous husband pushes her from their village in Sky World. She falls onto the back of Turtle, who saves her from death. (From the Collection of the Rochester Museum & Science Center, Rochester, NY)

Warrior chief Good Peter Agwelentongwas (ca.1717–1793), as drawn by John Trumbull in Philadelphia during 1792. He was an early Oneida convert to Christianity, worked on behalf of the rebels during the Revolutionary War, and until his death devoted himself to saving what he could of the Oneida homeland. (Yale University Art Gallery, Trumbull Collection)

Augustus Rockwell's painting *Reverent Samuel Kirkland,* ca. 1873. As a New Light missionary, Samuel Kirkland (1741–1808) brought reformed Christianity to the Oneidas in the 1760s, and as a patriot, he encouraged the Oneidas to align with the rebels. (Hamilton College Collection. Commissioned by the Reverend Amos Delos Gridley)

Sir William Johnson (1715–1774), as depicted by John Wallaston, ca. 1750–1752. A native of Ireland, Johnson migrated to New York colony, where he acquired vast property holdings and developed close ties with the Six Nations. As England's Superintendent of Indian Affairs for the Northern Department, he worked to keep the Iroquois loyal to British interests. (Albany Institute of History & Art, Gift of Laura Munsell Tremaine in memory of her father, Joel Munsell)

Johnson Hall, the baronial frontier home of Sir William Johnson, still stands in modern-day Johnstown, New York. It served as a location for Indian councils with the Mohawks, Oneidas, and other peoples of the Six Nations. This rendering, by Edward Lamson Henry (1841–1919), is entitled *Johnson Hall (Sir William Johnson Presenting Medals to the Indian Chiefs of the Six Nations at Johnstown, New York, 1772)*. (Albany Institute of History & Art Purchase)

Wealthy Albany, New York, resident Philip Schuyler (1733–1804) served as a major general in the Continental Army and also as an Indian agent from the Continental Congress to the Six Nations. (Library of Congress)

A Mohawk warrior who had grown up under the tutelage of Sir William Johnson, Joseph Brant (1742?–1807), also known as Thayendanegea, was a loyalist and deadly foe of patriot interests. Brant sat for this painting by the renowned artist Gilbert Stuart in 1786. (Fenimore Art Museum, Cooperstown, NY)

As the Revolutionary War unfolded, George Washington (1732–1799) developed warm relations with the Oneidas; and as the nation's first president, he signed federal legislation designed to protect all Indian peoples from having their ancient tribal lands taken from them by manipulative speculators and state agents. (Independence National Historical Park)

The French aristocrat Marie Joseph Paul Yves Roch Gilbert du Motier, the Marquis de Lafayette (1757–1834), sailed for America in 1777 and soon received a major general's commission in the Continental Army. Oneida warriors served under him at the Battle of Barren Hill, a source of their lifelong friendship. (Independence National Historical Park)

John Sullivan (1740–1795), Continental Army major general from New Hampshire, failed to convince the Oneidas to join an expedition in 1779 that had as its primary target pro-British members of the Six Nations. Most Oneida warriors wanted to avoid combat with their Iroquois brethren. (Independence National Historical Park)

While serving as governor of Quebec Province, Sir Guy Carleton (1724–1808) encouraged Indian nations in Canada and New York to align with the British. In early 1777 he proclaimed the Oneidas to be traitors, deserving extinction because of their close ties with the American rebels. (Library and Archives Canada, C-002833)

When Sir Frederick Haldimand (1718–1791) became governor of Quebec Province in 1778, he actively encouraged violence against frontier settlements in New York and Pennsylvania and advised the Oneidas to forsake their rebel allies or face destruction. (Library and Archives Canada, C-003221)

Jean-Baptiste-Antoine de Verger (1762–1851), a French soldier who sailed to America in 1780 to serve the rebel cause, drew sketches of several Oneidas, Tuscaroras, and Kahnawakes, including these two showing the Indians in light summer dress, slightly painted and with weapons in hand. (Courtesy of Anne S. K. Brown Military Collection, Brown University Library)

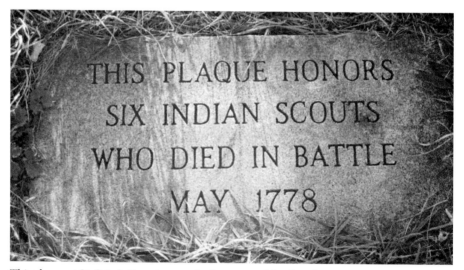

This plaque at St. Peter's Cemetery marks the graves of the Oneida warriors who were killed at the Battle of Barren Hill, Pennsylvania, on May 20, 1778. Even though the plaque does not specifically mention the Oneidas, it represents the only commemoration by European Americans of Oneida military service in the Revolution. (Photograph by Sarah A. Jones)

attendees on the prospect of their entering the war. When he received a favorable response, he prepared a belt and a speech under Gates's name.[28]

At the war feast the next day, alcohol flowed freely as Schuyler delivered "Gates's address" to cement the arrangements. Speaking as one warrior to others, Gates maintained that the patriots had always wanted neutrality, while the selfish king had prodded them to fight. The Six Nations had now done so and lost some of their most esteemed chiefs and fighters. "To avenge yourselves of those People who have deceived You, & to turn that Vengeance upon Their heads which they so well deserve, I now put into your hands this Axe," Gates challenged them. "Show yourselves therefore Men and use it with all your strength against your enemies and ours." "Our Cause is the same," Schuyler elaborated for Gates, "and We have nothing to hope for but Tyranny & oppression should we be defeated." Visibly moved by these words, the Oneidas and Tuscaroras seized the belt that symbolized the axe and sang their war song; the Onondaga sachem refused, despite Oneida entreaties that he do so. In time, they deposited this war belt at Onondaga, in accordance with confederacy practices.[29]

In private, the Oneidas and Tuscaroras explained part of their motivation to the Onondaga chief. They had not given up on securing peace among their Six Nations brethren but had accepted the ceremonial axe to use against the Crown's soldiers. Rebel authorities, they pointed out, were holding captive a Mohawk, Onondaga, and Seneca from Walter Butler's party. What the Oneidas intended to do was to capture some British soldiers, whom they would then exchange for their incarcerated Iroquois brothers. This action, they hoped, would prove their desire "to continue in peace with all the Indians" and ensure goodwill among all Iroquois. A campaign against the Crown, moreover, would enable the Oneidas to condole those grieving families who had lost loved ones during St. Leger's campaign.[30]

On the night of September 19, as Schuyler and others dined with several chiefs, news reached Albany about a major battle at Freeman's Farm (the first Saratoga battle), in which Burgoyne failed to pry open the route to Albany. Exploiting the moment, the commissioners encouraged the Indians to set out immediately for Gates's army on Bemis

Heights, located some thirty miles north of Albany. They concurred. By traveling all night, 112 Indians, mostly Oneidas, reached Gates's head-quarters the next morning. That evening, another 40 strode into the camp, bringing the total to about 150 warriors ready to fight against Burgoyne's army.[31]

The Oneidas and their comrades' arrival at that time was fortuitous. Most of the natives traveling south with Burgoyne's army had grown tired of the campaign and recently returned to Canada. Food supplies were running low, but lacking sufficient Indian scouts ("his eyes"), Burgoyne found that his foraging parties were having ever-increasing diffi-culty slipping out of camp and safely returning with provender.[32]

Day after day, the Oneidas and other Indians clipped the British wings as Burgoyne's force reached out for foodstuffs and useful intelli-gence from its defensive position at Freeman's Farm. Simply put, the pro-rebel Indians controlled the region outside British lines. Alone or in small groups, the king's troops fell victim to swift, powerful strikes from the Oneidas and their allies. On their first full day on duty, for in-stance, the Oneidas grabbed two Tory soldiers. The next day, they cap-tured a pair of British regulars and took the scalp of a third one.[33]

The act of scalping raised a serious issue between the two allies. For some time, the American rebels had complained about British toler-ance—and payments—for scalping. The Six Nations, however, consid-ered the practice standard in warfare, with the scalp representing the conquest of an enemy's spirit. When the Oneidas first took a scalp at Saratoga, a commissioner in Albany wrote Gates, advising him to deal with the matter delicately. The commissioner hoped Gates could reach a solution that "will not deprive them of trophies of war like achieve-ments." Gates formulated a sensible policy. He offered a cash bounty for each prisoner of war—but no money for scalps.[34]

Unlike their Iroquois brethren at Oriskany, the Oneidas at Saratoga did not go about executing their prisoners. Their objective was to cap-ture enough British troops to exchange for members of the Six Nations recently taken by the rebels. Also, to help obtain possible intelligence, the Oneidas would frighten their prisoners, playing on British stereotypes of savagery to instill utter horror but leaving them relatively un-harmed physically. The day after the Oneidas arrived, Arnold let them have one of the Tories they had captured. The Indians buried him up to his neck and held a powwow around him. Then "they had him up and Laid him a side of a great fire & turn'd his head & feet a while to the fire, hooting & hollowing round him." They later handcuffed him and sent him to jail in Albany. The next day, they painted the faces of two British regulars to resemble their own warriors and brought them into camp. Another time, the Indians marched three prisoners into camp with ropes around their necks. In each instance, the captives doubtless recalled whatever useful information they had about possible actions by Burgoyne's army.[35]

Earlier in the campaign, the rebels lived in fear of brutal sorties by Burgoyne's Indian allies. "The Damn'd Copper heads are trouble-some," growled a Continental surgeon, "not a day but a scalp or two taken near our very encampment." With so many of the Canadian Indi-ans withdrawing and the arrival of the Oneidas and Tuscaroras, intimi-dating acts of harassment now became an important patriot weapon. War parties struck hard and sometimes deep, instilling panic among British and Hessian regulars. On September 24 pro-rebel Indians pene-trated Burgoyne's rear lines and snagged eight loyalist soldiers. The next day, they mounted a raid in concert with rebel troops, killing or wound-ing eight and seizing one prisoner. The day after that, morning and af-ternoon sorties resulted in their largest haul: sixteen prisoners and two more scalps.[36]

Like ghosts, the Oneidas and Tuscaroras popped up from nowhere, attacked furiously, and vanished with their prisoners. They "Brought in more or Less Prisoners Every Day," commented patriot officer Henry Dearborn. Friends of the rebel cause touted their achievements, de-lighted that they finally had the capacity to deliver strong doses of terror to Burgoyne's army. The efficient aggressiveness of the Oneida and Tuscarora warriors impressed even the most experienced Continental soldiers.[37]

Then, just as suddenly, many of the Oneidas and Tuscaroras an-nounced that they were leaving. During the previous two weeks, their concern over another invading strike into their own territory had not diminished. More than one hundred miles away from their villages, they worried about how to protect their families should British and Indian forces appear again. Part of the hunting season, too, had passed, and the prospects of stalking fattened bear and deer, which had gorged on bountiful autumn forage, proved very tempting. If the warriors did not hunt these animals soon, their larders would be barren over the winter. Equally important, they felt that they had accomplished a key mission. They had accumulated plenty of prisoners for the exchange.[38]

The Oneidas and Tuscaroras asked Gates to turn over ten prisoners to them so that they could obtain the release of the Iroquois captives. Although Gates wanted the Oneidas to remain with the northern army, he yielded and granted their request. He also provided them with provisions and some ammunition for their journey home. During the annual hunt, the general realized, the Oneidas could continue to perform vital service for the rebel cause. Scouring the woods in search of game, they could likewise function as scouts for Fort Schuyler and German Flatts.[39]

The pro-rebel Indians marched the frightened British captives down to Albany, where the prisoner exchange took place. The Oneidas remained optimistic that getting the three Iroquois warriors released would open the pathway to fixing their deeply strained relations with the other confederacy nations.[40]

Although the bulk of the Oneidas and Tuscaroras headed home, a few stayed with Gates's army to help finish off the enemy. They worked with the Stockbridge Indians and continued to scout, raid, and seize prisoners, and occasionally take scalps. "They [were] Brave men," stated a rebel participant, "and fought Like Bull dogs till Burgoine Serrendert."[41]

As the defeat of Burgoyne's army became all but certain after the second great battle at Freeman's Farm on October 7, 1777, Gates paid homage to the Oneidas and their allies for their assistance. To Congress, the general declared, "[t]he Six Nations having taken up the Hatchet in our favour has been of great Service & I hope the Enemy will not be able to retreat from them." Gates's adversary, Burgoyne, indirectly praised the Oneidas and Tuscaroras when he confessed that rebel forces had launched "concerted attacks on our advanced picquets" and "no foraging party could be made without great detachments to cover it." The British general concluded that after the September 19 engagement, his opponent's plan was "to harass the army by constant alarms, and their superiority of numbers enabled them to attempt it without fatigue to themselves." Trying to retreat northward, his command finally gave up under unending annoyance and sniping fire. On October 17, Burgoyne formally surrendered his entire force.[42]

Saratoga was arguably the most consequential triumph for the revolutionaries in their pursuit of independence. The victory convinced French leaders to recognize American independence and to engage openly in war against their ancient British enemy. Heretofore, the French had offered covert aid to the rebels, but now they would add critical muscle to the patriot cause by committing their own land and naval forces to the contest, making the British task of quashing the rebellion that much more difficult. Further, during the autumn of 1777, Washington's Continentals fared poorly in challenging British forces around the rebel capital of Philadelphia, which the British captured in late September. Saratoga thus offered much cause for hope at a low point in the rebel war effort.

A portion of the credit for the defeat of Burgoyne's army belonged to the Oneidas. During their service at Saratoga, they and other pro-rebel natives killed about a half dozen British troops and captured between thirty and forty more. They suffered one wounded warrior. Among those who distinguished themselves were Han Yerry and Two Kettles Together. Despite his wound at Oriskany, Han Yerry served as a head warrior throughout the campaign. Two Kettles Together assisted him and shuttled messages for the rebels. To reward her services, Gates directed Gansevoort to "deliver to her Three Gallons of Rum, for a Winter's supply for her Family." He also encouraged the Fort Schuyler commander to issue "a small supply of the Provisions now on Hand to such of the faithful Indians as may be in Want."[43]

Of all the Oneidas, no one performed more valuable service for the Northern Department army than the warrior Peter Bread (Kaunaudauloonh). A resident of Kanonwalohale, Bread exhibited an extraordinary ability to infiltrate enemy positions and spring ambushes on unsuspecting troops. Because of his outstanding contributions in leading parties of Oneidas on raids and seizing prisoners, George Washington would personally decorate him with "a handsome belt."[44]

The Oneidas reveled in the Saratoga triumph. Through cooperation, sacrifice, and courage, they helped to stave off the enemy and, ultimately, to secure two exceptional victories at Fort Schuyler and Saratoga. The sachems White Skin and Grasshopper pronounced, "It is great news!" Trying to protect their homeland even though losing a village in the process, they had helped defeat powerful enemy forces. "This is the fortune of war," the sachems commented, and concluded, "Those who are too proud, are sometimes humbled—It has proven true in this instance—and it is perfectly right."[45]

The warrior class likewise delighted in the victory. Commenting for all, Good Peter and Hendrick declared to General Gates, "We rejoice greatly in your success—It revives our minds."[46]

Samuel Kirkland, meanwhile, asked head warrior William Kayendalongwea to travel to Onondaga with a belt to announce Burgoyne's surrender. Joseph Brant happened to be there, lobbying to bring those who would listen into the war on the British side. According to one sachem, the Onondagas "spared no pains in advising & reproving him & dissuading him but all in vain," since Brant persisted in his "obstinacy." When William appeared, proclaiming the news about Saratoga, Brant quickly departed. Acting pleased with William's report, the Onondaga sachems directed six runners to spread the tidings of the rebel triumph throughout Iroquoia.[47]

In an official comment, the Onondagas applauded the victory. The British, "once very strong in that quarter, are now subdued—this is a matter of great rejoicing," Onondaga sachems and warriors stated. Like the Oneida sachems, they had detected a cockiness about Burgoyne and St. Leger that boded poorly for their success. The British officers had boasted " '[t]hat they would trample all down before them, and at the first sight of them the fort would vanish.' " With their crushing defeats, "now the proud are brought low!" Such humiliation was "right," stated the Onondagas, before disingenuously wishing the American rebels "a continuation of success."[48]

Even if the victories at Fort Schuyler and Saratoga earned some momentary goodwill among the Onondagas, the Senecas and Cayugas were still reeling from their losses. After attending Schuyler's gathering in mid-September, a leading Onondaga sachem rekindled the council fire in hopes of reviving the neutralist stand of the Six Nations. "I sent a second and a third message to the Senekas & Cayugas to repair to it," he explained, "[b]ut my words had no effect." He waited three weeks, then gave up and extinguished the flames. Their battlefield losses with St. Leger had triggered the condolence cycle, which encouraged acts of retribution and further military action. "The Senekas appear very obstinate," the Onondaga sachem advised the patriot Indian commissioners before reporting that "they have sent the war hatchet both to the southward & westward to collect the foreign Indians for bad designs by next spring."[49]

In early December 1777, representatives of the Six Nations gathered again at Niagara for a council with John Butler to rebuild relations and replace the goods lost by the warriors around Fort Schuyler. Besides the usual assortment of Mohawks, Senecas, and Cayugas, "all the Onondaga and Tuscarora chiefs with the greatest part of their young men attended." Only two Oneidas made the journey to the British post.[50]

Butler began with a solemn condolence ceremony for those warriors lost at Oriskany and Fort Schuyler. He presented scalps and belts as mourning gifts and urged the Indians to name those "you think will act with the same spirit as those whose places they are now to fill." Gazing about the crowd, Butler wondered why Oneidas and Tuscaroras, who had taken the hatchet from Schuyler, were in attendance. This gathering was only for friends of the Crown, he pronounced, and only those persons could expect to receive the king's gifts.[51]

An Onondaga sachem, the same who had congratulated the rebels so warmly, exhibited the belt Schuyler had offered that symbolized the war axe. The Onondagas, he explained, had refused to take up the hatchet. As for the Oneidas and Tuscaroras, they had seized the belt to attack and capture British troops to be exchanged for their fellow Iroquois. The Onondagas had stored the belt until the Oneidas obtained the warriors' freedom; then, the Onondagas rolled it up. Most of all, this sachem wanted to assure everyone present that the Onondagas had no ties with the American patriots and thus were fully deserving of gifts. So he now repudiated the Oneidas. "We promise in this meeting never to go again to the Councils of the Oneidas or of the Rebels, and in token of our sincerity We now deliver to You the Axe given to us by them."[52]

At a session with only the chief warriors present, a Tuscarora spoke along similar lines. "We now take the Axe out of your heads & assure you & our brothers here now assembled, that we will stick it into the heads of the Rebels," he proclaimed, "when you and the rest of the Chiefs shall think proper." The Tuscarora chiefs then relinquished their belt from the rebels and picked up the one Butler offered.[53]

By the end of the council, Butler could crow to Governor Carleton, "I can truly inform you that the whole of the Six Nations except the Oneidas are determined to act heartily and with vigor this winter." The other Six Nations had repudiated the Oneidas, whose attempt at reconciliation through the liberation the three Iroquois warriors had completely failed.[54]

During the long, cold winter, the Oneidas wrestled with the physical and emotional hardships of the war and the widening fissure between them and the rest of the Six Nations. They understood that any isolated declaration of neutrality would now be worthless and would only expose them to the humiliation of possible invasions from both sides. With so many alienated Iroquois brethren, they gravitated toward the only people who would embrace them—the American rebels.

The Oneidas who had called Oriska their home endured a difficult winter season. "About fifty in number, including women and children, had all their Habitations stock and provisions destroyed by the Enemy because they had joined General Herkimer," Schuyler explained to the Continental Congress. Few of them sought shelter at other villages; they preferred to remain near their old homes and the fort. When the homeless requested basic subsistence from Schuyler, the Indian commissioners could hardly refuse. They called upon Gansevoort to supply the Indians' needs until Congress formulated a plan to care for them. The colonel, now an active friend of the Oneidas, provided what he could.[55]

Except for Oriska's destruction, the Oneidas had emerged from the 1777 campaign relatively unscathed. Neither Kanonwalohale nor Old Oneida had suffered any damage. Because women tended the crops and livestock, the involvement of males in military activities had caused minimal disruption to agriculture. Warriors had lost out on part of the fall hunt and missed much of the salmon catch, which had reduced winter food supplies and the number of pelts for trade. Otherwise, the Oneidas were in good physical shape.

Oquaga had also survived the campaign but was no longer an attractive place for its Oneida residents. Over the past two years, they had grown tired of opposing Anglicanism, Toryism, and the predominant influence of Joseph Brant's Mohawks and other cohorts. Migration to Kanonwalohale, where they felt welcome, became their preferred course of action. Then, in August 1777, even the missionary Aaron Crosby, the remaining bulwark of grace-oriented Presbyterian faith and Whig feelings in Oquaga, gave up and vacated that community.[56]

As everyone knew, Oquaga had become a staging area for the launching of British-Indian raids, with Mohawks and growing numbers of Tuscaroras and Delawares banding together under Joseph Brant. When the Oquaga elders, including Old Isaac, who maintained his loyalty to the Crown, asked for neutral standing from New York late in the summer of 1777, the Council of Safety called this proposal "an insult" and "inconsistent with the honour and interest of the State to consider them in a state of neutrality, while their warriors are engaged against us." The Oquagas, as such, did not receive any guarantee of peace, so long as Brant's warriors were in the field.[57]

For the vast bulk of the Oneidas who were now aligned with the rebel cause, especially those at Kanonwalohale, they, too, had lost any assurance of peace. In assuming the perils of combat, Oneida warriors were also exposing their communities to retaliatory actions, as had hap-

pened at Oriska. Every time the warriors embarked on a hunt, scout, or
more formal expedition, they left their loved ones vulnerable to attack.
To keep contributing in the field, they needed reassurance that their
friends and families would somehow be secure.

In mid-September at Schuyler's Albany council, the Oneidas
broached the notion of constructing defensive works in their castles.
Having witnessed the capacity of Fort Schuyler to resist a powerful enemy force, they proposed that "some fortifications may be made for the
security of such villiages [*sic*] as have or may send out their warriors."
The commissioners considered the request reasonable, since "[s]uch
means of defense have been made for them in like cases in times past
and as they will be exposed without them." By late January 1778, the
Oneidas had also suggested that the rebels build and occupy a major
fort at Kanonwalohale.[58]

The exposed location of Kanonwalohale placed those Oneidas in a
particularly vulnerable situation, since most of Iroquoia viewed that
community as a hotbed of rebel sentiment. Should the Senecas, Cayugas, and Mohawks assemble their full strength and launch a strike
against that village, the Oneidas probably could not repulse them. Nor
could the limited number of Continentals at Fort Schuyler, located
some seventeen miles away, provide much assistance in an unanticipated strike. The Oneidas thus could suffer devastating losses, as an entire community might well perish in vengeance for the nation's
attachment to the patriot cause.[59]

Both the Continental Congress and New York officials, in gratitude
for the Oneidas' contributions to the Fort Schuyler and Saratoga campaigns, had pledged friendship and assistance to the nation. Because
they were "our trusty friends," broadcast Congress in early December,
"we shall protect you; and shall at all times consider your welfare as our
own." Furthermore, early in September, the New York Council of
Safety resolved as follows: "That the Oneida nation are the allies of this
State, and that we shall consider any attack upon them as an attack
upon our own people."[60]

Certainly the rebels and their governmental bodies recognized the
great benefit of having the Oneidas as friends and allies. Since before
the Seven Years' War, the People of the Standing Stone had acted as a

shield for German Flatts and other European American settlements. Their warriors detected enemy advances and alerted settlers in time to adopt countermeasures. With the Oneidas now engaged in the war on the rebels' side, locals had another layer of defense and an early-warning system, since invaders had to pass through Oneida territory first.

In time, rebel leaders concluded that the only way to halt British-Indian raids was to launch massive preemptive strikes. Government officials contemplated major campaigns against such enemy strongholds as Niagara, unless the Six Nations stopped actively supporting the British. At the moment, however, these were paper threats. The patriots had yet to designate a single soldier or stow away a solitary morsel of food for such operations.[61]

Even as rebel leaders reviewed the Oneida request for a fort at Kanonwalohale, General Schuyler and the other Indian commissioners decided to give the Iroquois a final opportunity to recant their support of the Crown. Schuyler prepared a belt and a speech calling for a new council and passed them to James Dean for circulation to each of the Six Nations. The Oneidas warned the rebel interpreter that he should not travel deep into Iroquoia, as he might be killed. They and the Tuscaroras agreed to serve as messengers.

The response was frigid. The Onondagas "took little notice of the message and the Quiyugas [Cayugas] none at all," reported the Oneida couriers. Seneca leaders stated that "they had not forgot the Blow the Bostonians gave them last Summer but still felt its Smart." They promised to solicit the opinion of fellow Senecas at Genesee, one of their principal villages, before formally responding, but the Oneida courier seemed sure that they would not participate. He intimated that the Cayugas and most of the Onondagas would follow the Senecas' lead.[62]

In mid-March 1778, some 732 members of the Six Nations attended the council sessions at Johnstown. The Oneidas came in significant numbers, as did the Tuscaroras. Approximately one hundred Onondagas along with a handful of Mohawks and Cayugas made the journey. Even though the Senecas and most Mohawks and Cayugas stayed away,

Schuyler knew that information regarding what transpired there would reach them. He offered to make copies of the commissioners' speeches and provide supplies for anyone traveling to Niagara.[63]

Joining the commissioners in attendance was a twenty-year-old French gentleman and aristocrat, the Marquis de Lafayette. Having volunteered for Continental service in the summer of 1777, he had served with George Washington in New Jersey and Pennsylvania, received a battlefield wound at Brandywine, and spent the first part of the winter of 1777–1778 at Valley Forge. Lafayette then came north to Albany with the assignment of assembling a force to invade Canada in another attempt to bring Quebec Province into the rebellion. The invasion plan quickly collapsed for lack of resources, including troops. Now Schuyler and the other commissioners hoped that Lafayette's rank as a Continental major general and especially his French nationality—an identity that once held favor with numerous Indians, including the Senecas—might help diminish the intensity of anti-rebel ire felt by so many Iroquois.[64]

From the very outset, the commissioners directed most of their words to pro-British Iroquois, very few of whom were in attendance. According to one observer, the opening address conveyed "a Tone becoming the Dignity of Congress and the Spirit and Power of the United States," reflecting newfound confidence after the great Saratoga accomplishment. The rebel delegates even employed threats "as the only means left short of actual chastisement to induce them to observe a strict neutrality." Despite the bloodshed they had caused, Schuyler later explained, the Six Nations who were supporting the Crown could atone for their actions. They had to bury the war axe and return to a peaceful posture, or the rebels would target them for destruction in future operations.[65]

This kind of scolding tone vanished when the commissioners mentioned the Oneidas and Tuscaroras. They referred to these nations as "excepted and distinguished," extolling their "Courage & Fidelity" and applauding them for their "Integrity and Firmness." They assured them of "our Friendship and Protection," and at various times during the council they actively solicited the Oneidas' thoughts and opinions.[66]

A day after the commissioners delivered their opening speech, an

Onondaga sachem named Tuhuasquachta agreed to take the belt and message to the other Iroquois for their consideration. He blamed the abandonment of neutrality on overeager, especially younger warriors. Recalling the once-prevalent Iroquois reliance on rank and age grades, he lamented, "Times are altered with us Indians. Formerly the Warriors were governed by the wisdom of their uncles the Sachems but now they take their own way & dispose of themselves without consulting their uncles the Sachems—while we wish for peace and they are for war." Tuhuasquachta admitted that "the answer is attended with many Difficulties for even my Nation are divided in Sentiment as well as white people."[67]

In private meetings, the Oneidas warned the commissioners to be wary of the Onondagas and their contrite pledges of neutrality. The Oneidas now viewed most Onondagas as "Enemies," and they "affirmed that there was not the least doubt but that they, the Senecas, & Cayugoes, would renew their Hostilities early in the Spring." John Butler, they predicted, would probably occupy Oswego again, and the rebels should prepare themselves for ongoing hostile strikes.[68]

As the council proceeded, the Oneidas and Tuscaroras asked the commissioners to reopen trade at Fort Schuyler. The British were taking full advantage of the rebels' incapacity to offer basic wares for exchange. The commissioners agreed and reported to Congress that trade goods were essential to improving relations with disaffected Iroquois. As for the Oneidas, they also disliked being overly dependent on patriot gifts of blankets, clothing, gunpowder, and ammunition. Keeping their economic autonomy would help them avoid becoming a client state to their rebel allies. From the commissioners' point of view, as they wrote to Congress, making merchandise available would reduce expenses for presents and also undercut British commentary that the rebellious colonists could never supply Indian needs.[69]

On the second day of the council, Grasshopper assumed center stage. The previous year he had led a delegation of Senecas to Washington's army, but his hopes of brokering a peace among all the Six Nations had failed. Now Odatshehdeh spoke only for the Oneidas and Tuscaroras and addressed the council "with a Spirit and Dignity which would not have disgraced a Roman Senator," according to a rebel onlooker. He regretted that the other Iroquois had fallen under Butler's spell and feared they were sowing the seeds of their own destruction. He declared the resolve of the Oneidas and Tuscaroras to hold fast to the Covenant Chain with the rebellious Americans and "with them to be buried in the same Grave; or to enjoy the *Fruites* of Victory and Peace." To secure this partnership, he asked the patriots to build a fort in Oneida country and provide a small garrison force as well. When the commissioners concurred, Grasshopper pledged Oneida friendship and cooperation with the rebels against common enemies.[70]

Although Grasshopper's oration focused on the strengthening of ties, he also chided the warrior class for its precipitous behavior. Like the Onondaga sachem, he lamented how warriors during wartime disregarded the advice of their elders, especially the sachems. Both he and his friend White Skin recognized their almost inevitable loss of standing during times of war, a vestige of the perennial power struggle between traditional leadership and the warrior class.[71]

Even though Grasshopper agreed with the Oneida warriors' aligning themselves with the rebels, he believed that in their fury for combat, they had cast aside the need for rational judgment, including prospects for neutrality. "Formerly, the Sachems were instantly obeyed by the Warriors," Odatshehdeh pointed out to the assemblage, "but now the latter have thrown off all Regard to their council." By doing so, the warriors had lost access to the collective wisdom that the sachems had attained through decades of experience.[72]

Before the entire gathering at Johnstown—sachems, chiefs, warriors, matrons, women, children, and patriot attendees—Grasshopper warned that the impetuousness of the warriors would come to haunt native peoples in important ways. As a pragmatic leader, he understood why the Oneidas had entered the conflict, and he felt that their decision to ally themselves with the rebels was the most sensible course. Yet, more generally, eager Iroquois warriors, forsaking neutrality, had boxed the Six Nations into a set of horrible options—war, destruction, and divisiveness or virtual enslavement. They had placed themselves above the well-being of their people, had dissolved unity among the Iroquois, and had caused brothers to kill one another. Peace and neutrality, Grasshopper declared, would have much better served the long-term interests of the Six Nations.[73]

In concluding, Grasshopper warned the younger men about their destructive example for future generations, who would be more likely to commit the same errors. "Brother Warriors reflect for a moment that at a future Day your Locks will be silvered by age and then . . . will you deplore the neglect which your Elders now experience from you," stated Odatshehdeh. "The Rising generation will imitate your Example and you will then be incapable of enforcing your advice by the measures you now pursue."[74]

Odatshehdeh's words were full of meaning, but they had little immediate impact or influence. War had overtaken the People of the Standing Stone, and the warrior class was in the ascendancy.

9

ASSISTING CONTINENTAL FORCES
AT VALLEY FORGE

Once again, the Oneida sachem Thomas Sinavis volunteered to serve, this time with rebel forces at Valley Forge. Earlier in the conflict, he had traveled to Canada for the revolutionaries, once in 1776, seeking to preserve peace, and twice in 1777, to gather intelligence about pending British invasion plans. After Barry St. Leger's retreat, when General Schuyler asked for warriors to aid the northern patriot army then resisting John Burgoyne's minions at Saratoga, Sinavis proposed that the rebels become directly involved in defending Oneida communities by constructing forts. Then warriors could turn out in large numbers with less worry about the security of their families and fight against the British without having to keep casting anxious glances toward their own home front.[1]

Now, in the spring of 1778, Commander in Chief George Washington asked to have Oneida and Tuscarora warriors join his army at Valley Forge, near Philadelphia. The plan to employ Indians in the main Continental Army germinated from an idea Washington expressed to a congressional committee then at Valley Forge—the Committee at Camp—in late January 1778. British detachments were willfully roaming the countryside around Philadelphia, confiscating supplies, seizing stragglers, acquiring intelligence, and harassing civilians. The rebels needed to counteract these raids. Certainly native warriors had repeatedly proved themselves as exceptional scouts and superb small-unit fighters. Besides helping to thwart enemy raiders, "would it not be well," Washington asked, "to employ two or three hundred indians against General Howe's army [in] the ensuing campaign?" "Such a body," he elaborated, "joined by some of our woodsmen would probably strike no small terror into the British and foreign troops, particularly the new comers." If the Indians served in the field a long way from home, too far for them to wander in and out of the army, Washington felt sure they would prove to be a valuable and cost-effective asset.[2]

The Committee at Camp had several reservations. Aside from language differences that would require translators, the members worried that distinct cultural practices, such as scalping, might cause friction and even some erosion of support for the patriot cause. They also expressed concern that pro-rebel Indian warriors roaming through the countryside would discourage enemy desertions.[3]

On the other hand, the committee agreed that if Washington could employ some four hundred Indians in conjunction with light infantry units, the Continentals could better control the hinterland around Philadelphia. As scouts and raiders, the Indians could check enemy foragers, depriving Howe's army of needed supplies. With their capacity to strike quickly, they could snatch prisoners who could then provide information about enemy plans. From select vantage points, they could also monitor any British movements, and their presence as advance pickets might discourage attempted desertions from the Continental Army.

Indian warriors could also have a terrifying psychological impact on enemy soldiers. "There is great Reason to believe the Novelty of their Appearance in the Field, the Circumstances of Horror & Affright which attend their Attack, will have a great effect Upon the Minds of Men wholly unacquainted with such an Enemy," concluded the committee. "When we consider upon what trivial Circumstances the Fate of Battles often turns," then anything that can "discompose & terrify" enemy troops would serve rebel military operations well. For all those reasons, they recommended this experiment in Indian usage. Two weeks later, Congress approved the proposal.[4]

The Committee at Camp viewed the Oneidas as trustworthy warriors for the rebel cause, but patriot leaders realized that the proximate threat of British and Indian forces to exposed Oneida villages would

limit the prospect for service so far away. The committee knew the
Oneidas were "threatned [sic] by surrounding Tribes" and speculated
that ultimately, "unless we can protect them, they must however reluctantly take up the Hatchet against us or be intirely cut off." If a fort
could not be built and garrisoned at Kanonwalohale, one solution was
to relocate the Oneidas to safer territory closer to Albany. With their
families secure, the warriors might then be able to join the main Continental force in considerable numbers.[5]

In mid-March 1778, with congressional approval secured, Washington asked Schuyler and the other Northern Department Indian
commissioners to recruit approximately two hundred warriors. "The
Oneidas have manifested the strongest Attachment to us throughout
this Dispute," Washington stated, "and I therefore suppose, if any can
be procured, they will be most numerous." He suggested that Samuel
Kirkland accompany the Indians to Valley Forge, and that they should
arrive by mid-May in preparation for the new campaign season.[6]

Even before Washington's letter reached Albany, the Marquis de Lafayette learned about the commander's thinking. On his own initiative
during the mid-March council at Johnstown, he raised the possibility of
having some Oneidas join him in Pennsylvania. A handful of warriors
agreed.[7]

In contrast to Lafayette, the more staid Schuyler, who had actual responsibility for recruiting the Indians, offered a pessimistic analysis.
The war had placed the Oneidas in a complicated predicament. They
and the Tuscaroras had publicly proclaimed their bond to the revolutionaries. At the same time, Schuyler explained to Washington, their request for assistance to build a fort at Kanonwalohale "strongly indicates
the Hostile Intentions of the others and leaves me but little Room to
hope that we shall be able to prevail on them to join you." Even such
committed revolutionaries as Thomas Sinavis needed to know that his
fellow Oneidas would be secure at home in his absence.[8]

As both Schuyler and Lafayette comprehended, the Oneida petition
for a fort and troops reflected fears that angry Iroquois brethren, especially the Senecas, Cayugas, and Mohawks, might strike at Kanonwalo-

hale anytime they chose. The Oneidas had witnessed the value of strong fortifications the previous August at Fort Schuyler, and they had endured the destruction of the lightly defended and unfortified Oriska castle. The need for a defensive structure seemed obvious.[9]

The request for rebel military assistance raised important social, cultural, and diplomatic issues. For a proud and independent people to ask for this kind of assistance was an admission that the Oneidas were becoming dependent on Continental resources for their safety. Implicitly, warriors were conceding an inability to protect their own people against an attack by their Iroquois brothers. The Oneidas had come to the aid of the revolutionary cause in the previous campaign season. Reciprocity, they believed, demanded that the American rebels return the favor.[10]

The call for support also indicated that the Oneidas had accurately gauged the strengths and weaknesses of their own fighting skills in relation to those of the rebels. The Indians excelled as scouts and in furtive raids, but they lacked the disciplined patience for such sedentary duty as garrisoning forts, which Continental troops had the training to perform. This was not an embarrassing confession—the Oneida leadership was merely acknowledging the limitations of its own warriors and objectively assessing patriot capabilities.

At the same time, the presence of European Americans in the midst of their principal village was an uncomfortable prospect. Back in the 1750s, the Oneidas had accepted the construction of Fort Stanwix in their territory, but those circumstances were different. Few Oneidas lived that near to the Carrying Place between the Mohawk River and Wood Creek. This time, however, rebel troops would occupy a post in the midst of the Oneidas' major castle. Once the rebels were present, the People of the Standing Stone would likely lose some of their valued independence and control.[11]

A fort and rebel troops would also paint a bull's-eye on the heart of the Oneida homeland. Yet the Oneidas had long since surmised that Kanonwalohale had become a target for the enemy, that it was simply a matter of time before the Crown attacked the castle. At least, then, the fort and troops would offer some semblance of protection, especially if the warriors were off fighting in other locales.

For all the possible trouble that might ensue, the Oneidas concluded that having a fort with rebel defenders at Kanonwalohale represented the best of various undesirable alternatives for their nation's protection. Basic security needs overrode all other considerations.

Lafayette understood the Oneida dilemma, and he developed a genuine interest in providing for their defense. He was not yet in the Mohawk Valley when the Indians first introduced the idea of constructing a fort and obtaining some Continentals for garrison duty, but he heard Grasshopper restate the appeal at Johnstown. "Every body wants forts," the young general observed, but for him the request "of the Onoyedos seems [to] Me the most important."[12]

A few days after the end of the Johnstown council, Lafayette initiated steps to build a small citadel at Kanonwalohale while also recruiting the warriors whom Washington sought. To fulfill these twin missions, he called on three of his countrymen, Lieutenant Colonel Jean Baptiste Gouvion, Captain Louis Celeron, and A. Louis de Tousard. Each was a trained engineer who had served in the French Army. With them they carried belts that conveyed Washington's greetings and some gold coins as recruiting inducements. Always enthusiastic, Lafayette vowed to Washington to "bring down to your excellency some scalping gentlemen for dressing the fine hair of the *Howe*."[13]

Lafayette's plan was to have Gouvion design and supervise the construction of the fort. The Oneidas had already cut down the timber for the project. Lieutenant Colonel Marinus Willett, then acting commander at Fort Schuyler, would furnish the tools, and Lafayette solicited some Tryon County militiamen to provide additional labor. Tousard, meanwhile, was to oversee the enlistment and movement of the Oneida warriors to Valley Forge and to aid Gouvion in any way while he was still at the village. Celeron would shuttle messages between Kanonwalohale and Fort Schuyler.[14]

Despite Lafayette's optimism, fulfilling a request for two hundred warriors was far more complex than obtaining commitments from a few volunteers. When Schuyler received Washington's directive on Indian recruitment, he sent a speech for Willett to share with the Oneidas.

The lieutenant colonel traveled to Kanonwalohale and presented the potentially controversial message.[15]

As Willett expected, the magnitude of Washington's request—two hundred warriors—jolted the Oneidas. At the time, few of the Oneida leaders were around, and the remaining sachems, chiefs, and matrons asked Willett to be patient. Many of the men had gone off for the spring hunt, they explained, and the prospect of two hundred Oneidas serving in Pennsylvania with the enemy so close by demanded very deliberate consideration.[16]

The People of the Standing Stone welcomed the French officers into their village with very polite hospitality. Throughout their month-long stay in April 1778, the Oneidas treated their French guests like brothers, including them in council meetings and providing for their wants. "We are at present in plenty of Corn, which we receive from the Ingians them selves, who made a prohibition to receive any money for it," Tousard wrote to Willett, "and every day they Carry Corn much more than we want for fitting our horses."[17]

The arrival of the engineers indicated that after all their lobbying, the Oneidas would finally secure the defenses they so badly wanted. Assuming the rebels would now see to the fort's construction, the Oneidas in turn promised to send a respectable number of warriors to Pennsylvania. Everyone seemed satisfied with this mutually beneficial arrangement.[18]

Once launched, however, the building project quickly stalled. Gouvion did his job. He designed the miniature bastion and staked the ground. Almost nothing else happened. No rebels appeared to perform the labor, and no one offered explanations as to why. Barely a month after Lafayette had heard Grasshopper's request, he received orders to return to Valley Forge and could no longer monitor the fort's progress. Military officers at Fort Schuyler were ready to lend tools but felt they could not spare soldiers. Because of transfers and attrition, the number of troops on hand was "not half sufficient to man the internal works" of Fort Schuyler, so wrote Colonel Gansevoort. The Tryon County militia commander likewise grumbled about a lack of troops. Recent Indian raids along the Pennsylvania and Virginia frontier and anticipated strikes in the Mohawk Valley had so badly frightened locals that militia

officers refused to send their troops too far from their home communities. In addition, most of the militiamen were farmers, and the planting
season was at hand. Military service and numerous casualties from the
previous year had badly disrupted harvesting activities and produced
food shortages. Leaders pointed out that another lean agricultural season could cause starvation among families and animals in the region.[19]

At the moment, then, few white settlers were available to engage in
militia service. If the rebels could not come up with persons to help
construct the fort, there was likewise little hope of assembling a detachment of Continentals to occupy that edifice, especially with Fort
Schuyler short on troops. The Oneida fort thus stood dangling in
limbo.[20]

Back in March, during the Johnstown council, the Indian commissioners had delivered a stern warning to all pro-British Iroquois Indians in
New York. If they wanted to avoid becoming targets of major rebel offensives, they had to stop participating in the Crown's military operations and, at a minimum, return to the course of neutrality. The
commissioners asked the Indians to hold a grand council meeting at
Onondaga so that all Iroquois leaders would consider and, hopefully,
agree to this proposition. Schuyler and the other commissioners were
"inclined to believe that the Indians will commence Hostilities," but
they felt they should make one more attempt to restore peace before
the hand of unremitting warfare swung with devastating force at the
pro-British Iroquois.[21]

The Oneidas, like the patriot commissioners, did not expect the ultimatum to have much effect. They were aware that most Mohawks
were bitter enemies of the rebellion, and that nearly all of them had
abandoned their homeland for sanctuary among the British. Still seeking revenge for their losses during St. Leger's campaign, the Senecas
had refused an invitation to attend the most recent council fire. The
Cayugas had expressed virulent opposition to the rebels and their
Oneida brethren for supporting the revolutionary cause. Only a change
of allegiance by the Senecas could possibly redirect their thinking. The
Onondagas had become very divided but with a sizable number still

clinging to neutrality. Publicly, the Tuscaroras were following the Oneida lead, yet some of their warriors had joined forces with the Crown. In short, the Oneidas were sure that words alone would not persuade the other confederacy nations or their warriors to return to the pathway of neutrality.[22]

In mid-April 1778, the Indian commissioners met in Albany with James Duane, a member of Congress, to assess the situation. They would inform Washington that because of troop shortages, "the protection requested . . . by the Oneidas and Tuscaroras from the united States has not been granted them," even though both nations "seem to be fully persuaded that they themselves will be attacked." The commissioners promised to do what they could to recruit some warriors for Continental duty, but they also observed that "it is not reasonable to suppose that they will march to the Southward and leave their Families defenceless."[23]

The commissioners were right. With no positive news from Onondaga and with Gouvion stifled in Kanonwalohale, the outlook was bleak for Tousard and his recruiting mission. What the commissioners misread, however, were Oneida values and the depth of their commitment to the rebel cause. The request to serve with Washington's army struck a cultural chord in the Oneida Nation, specifically in the form of obligation in discordant conflict with opportunity. All warriors felt the duty to protect their loved ones, but the prospect of Continental service was very tempting. The chance to travel to Pennsylvania, see the main Continental Army, and serve at the specific request of Washington, the "Great Chief Warrior," aroused their sense of adventure. Warriors could demonstrate their martial prowess before thousands of witnesses, enhancing the reputation of individuals and the entire nation among friends and enemies alike. Deep down, too, the Oneidas realized that the concept of reciprocity demanded that they assist their revolutionary friends and allies. Washington had said he needed their assistance. Somehow, the Oneidas concluded, they had to accommodate the commanding general while also shielding their families from their enemies.[24]

After days of conversation and debate, the Oneidas sent a delegation to meet with Marinus Willett at Fort Schuyler and respond to the patriot request for warriors. As a principal sachem, White Skin offered the customary greetings. Deacon Thomas, Kirkland's assistant, then acted as primary spokesperson. He apologized for Grasshopper's absence, pointing out that Odatshehdeh was ill and could not travel. Evidently, Deacon Thomas noted, some confusion had developed regarding what the Oneidas had stated to Lafayette at Johnstown. He hoped to clarify matters. The Oneidas had agreed to send some warriors to Washington's army, but "we do not remmember [sic] that we Promised that so large a number should go with the Mar.s [Marquis]." Two hundred warriors were far beyond their means to furnish. "We are but a small People, and we think that matter was not rightly understood."[25]

In addition, the present and near future appeared very uncertain for the Oneidas, representing another reason they were hesitant to promise so many warriors. "We don't know what will happen," Deacon Thomas observed, "but we are determined to Lay our bones in the American cause." Their immediate problem was that their settlements were "in the front of those who hate us and a number of news carriers say there are many troops in Canada." Still, the Oneidas wanted to assist the rebel cause, thereby remaining "true to . . . the Americans."[26]

In response, Willett asked "if they would assist us after there [sic] Fort was built." The Oneidas replied, "Yes." To his superiors, the acting post commander predicted, "I think some of them will follow the Mar Defayette Immediately." Congressional delegate James Duane was not quite so sanguine. "If they see a prospect of Tranquility on their own Borders," he surmised, "some of them will turn out & Join our Arms with alacrity, otherwise it is hardly to be expected."[27]

To everyone's surprise, the prospect of tranquility suddenly seemed possible. The Oneidas received a message from the head Onondaga sachem, Tehosgweatha, indicating that the Senecas and Cayugas might very well attend a grand council. Oneida leaders deemed this prospect so important that they immediately dispatched two of their own, William Kayendalongwea and Skenandoah, to Fort Schuyler to share the news. When the two Oneida chiefs arrived on April 22, they extended some wampum strings and summarized the message from the

Onondaga sachem. "The Council fire at Onondaga has been for a long time kindled up & repeated messages sent to the Senekas," they reported. "There now appears some probability of their attending."[28]

The Oneidas interpreted this surprising development with cautious optimism. Getting the Senecas to attend a grand council meant hope for renewed Iroquois consensus, nothing more. "What their sentiment will be, remains yet very uncertain," William and Skenandoah indicated. "However, some late accts. [accounts] afford a gleam of hope, they may be friendly." The two chief warriors then urged Willett and others to be patient and adopt a wait-and-see attitude.[29]

The following day, a large number of Oneidas and a few Tuscaroras appeared at Fort Schuyler. Rebel officials at the Johnstown council had lacked sufficient goods to offer presents. Once they obtained these wares, they asked their native allies to come and retrieve them.[30]

In addition, the Oneidas traveled to Fort Schuyler for a second reason, to bid farewell to their warriors who had volunteered to fight with Washington's army. That morning, Marinus Willett was hoping to send off twenty Indians to Valley Forge. Caught up in the enthusiasm of the moment and what appeared to be positive news about the Senecas, forty-seven Indians, almost all of them Oneidas, agreed to follow the Frenchman Tousard to Pennsylvania. Among them was their captain, Han Yerry, the reliable Thomas Sinavis, Han Yerry's brother Han Yost Thahoswagwat, the English-speaking Jacob Reed, Henry Cornelius, Blatcop Tonyentagoyon, Kirkland's assistant Deacon Thomas, Skenandoah's son Daniel (Teouneslees), and, according to Oneida lore, an Oneida woman named Polly Cooper.[31]

The Oneida leaders carried a message apologizing to Washington and Lafayette for not contributing more warriors. "Should matters take a favourable turn in a Convention of the six nations now setting at Onondaga," their message relayed, "His Excellency may expect a Considerable number of their best warriors to repair to his Camp."[32]

Grasshopper, still quite weak from illness but determined to carry out his responsibilities, stepped before the gathering and performed the time-honored ritual of addressing the warriors. He reminded those departing, especially the younger men, that they had a long march ahead and would be exposed to sundry hardships and temptations. The eyes of the rebel Americans and the French would be scrutinizing their conduct. "Keep in mind that warriors sustain an important character," he counseled them. "They can do much good or Commit Great Enormities." Warriors were also to eliminate "such evils as threaten the peace of the Country. . . . Here they may display the hero, but private revenge is to be Carefully avoid'd." Any act of "abuse or plunder" against innocent and helpless persons was "beneath the Character of a Warrior."

He reminded them that Oneidas would be fighting in the "Grand army of America" under the watchful eye of General Washington. Their behavior would reflect on the entire Oneida Nation. "Any misconduct in you, if only a little, will be of Extensive Influence," Grasshopper cautioned, "The reproach not Easily Whiped [wiped] away." The warriors had to function in perfect harmony as a team. "Don't let every one think himself a head warrior or that he may use all those freedoms which are Indulged at home," he warned. Younger warriors were to obey the instructions of their leaders.

Grasshopper also implored them to avoid alcohol. No doubt, they would gain access to hard liquor during their journey, but they had to resist "the Common beguiler of Indians," he intoned. Drinking would only lead to personal embarrassment and possible disaster for all of them. Good order and sobriety, on the other hand, were ideals to which they should aspire. Everyone expected them to "play the man"—to exhibit courage in the face of danger, and compassion and charity toward those in need. "Your deportment in this Case," he concluded, "will resound through the american army, be noticed by General Washington the Chief warrior and finally reach the ears of our father the french King—and we Sachems shall then rejoice to hear from you."[33]

The warriors responded by thanking Grasshopper, acknowledging the wise council of their sachems, and promising to act with one mind. Before embarking on their southward journey, they offered their own council to the sachems. They exhorted the hereditary leaders to "maintain one Uniform line of Conduct in their deliberations, pursue them with resolution and not restrain the warriors." This was wartime, and the chief warriors had to decide how best to defend the Oneida homeland. They expected the sachems to adhere to these judgments.[34]

The next morning, April 25, the party began the lengthy land journey of more than 250 miles to Valley Forge. They took very few horses with them and, according to Oneida tradition, they also brought along some quantity of corn. The Oneidas had enjoyed an abundant corn crop the previous year, and they knew about the food shortages facing Washington's army. The lone woman on the expedition, Polly Cooper, joined to show Continental soldiers how to prepare the hulled corn soup that served as a mainstay of the Iroquois diet.[35]

For weapons, the forty-seven warriors carried firearms, tomahawks, knives, and bows and arrows, a lesson from last year's campaigning. For long-range skirmishes and open-field combat, they preferred muskets. Those Oneidas who had fought at Oriskany had observed the disadvantage of slow-loading muskets when ambushes evolved into lengthy engagements. Skilled use of the bow, an art all Oneida boys mastered, delivered a firing rate with arrows that no one could match with muskets and easily surpassed the effectiveness of hatchets. Since Washington hoped to employ the warriors in small-unit raids and ambushes, they felt that they could better attack and defend themselves with traditional weapons. Bows and arrows were hidden killers. They made virtually no noise and did not emit a large cloud of smoke that exposed the location of the shooters.[36]

En route to Valley Forge, Tousard and the Oneidas strove to "Keep the Whole party sober" so that none would be accused of "abusing the people in the Country." They succeeded. No civilians complained of mistreatment or plundering, although a few warriors ignored Grasshopper's warning and drifted behind the column, perhaps hoping to obtain alcohol. Overall, though, Tousard insisted "the totality behaved well enough" along the trail leading them to southeastern Pennsylvania.[37]

About a day's journey from Valley Forge, the party settled into a small Pennsylvania farming community for the night. With nearly fifty fully armed Indians in their midst, the local European American settlers were apprehensive. Tousard advised the residents that under no circumstances were they to give the Oneidas any alcohol, "which was easy to obey," commented one man, "for it is very scarce and expensive."

Before sunset, the Oneidas took to the woods to hunt game, mainly squirrels and birds, for their evening meal. "These they cooked over a fire in the evening and devoured without any European ceremony," a witness recorded. In search of fresh milk, one Oneida visited a home. The woman who answered the door stunned the warrior by speaking some Iroquois phrases to him. She had spent her childhood days in central New York and knew a modest amount of Mohawk, which is very similar to the Oneida language. The two of them exchanged some pleasantries, and she served the warrior a helping of bread and milk. The grateful Oneida thanked her in song before politely exiting.

That night, local whites slept fitfully. "We feared that the Indians would give us a restless night but, God be thanked, it was altogether quiet," a German clergyman sighed with relief. The next morning, the Oneidas bid the local settlers farewell and completed their journey to the American cantonment.[38]

Since late December 1777, Washington's army had resided in winter quarters at Valley Forge, about twenty miles northwest of Philadelphia. Back in September, the potent British force of Sir William Howe had compelled the rebels to abandon their capital city of Philadelphia. Congress escaped, and Washington eventually settled the main Continental Army into Valley Forge. With fresh water, plenty of timber, and easily defensible hilly terrain, the site represented a strong location from which to monitor British movements.

On May 15, 1778, the Oneidas passed through the army's pickets. As they approached the massive encampment, the sight of thousands of troops impressed the warriors, if they did not look too closely at the soldiers' tattered appearance. They also observed wooden shanties speckled throughout a sea of mud. Everywhere their eyes gazed, tree stumps reminded them that this was once an elegant land. "A Noxious Stench" from five months of poor sanitation reduced the glamour of the occasion. Every evening, according to one officer, horrid vapors rose and spread through the cantonment, and only "the Sunshine of the day" dispersed them.[39]

Ill-clad soldiers, when not drilling, milled about everywhere, now rejuvenated by warmer temperatures and more abundant rations after a demanding winter that had featured a breakdown of the army's supply system. These troops had seen Indians before; a few Stockbridge Indians were serving with them at the time. Still, the Oneidas, from the famous Iroquois Confederacy, drew much attention, and the soldiers seemed to appreciate their arrival. "A few days ago, 40 Indians, of the Oneida nation, arrived at our Camp," commented one Continental. "They are to join Col. Morgan's corps, and to scout near the lines; to check the unlawful commerce, too much carried on at present, between the country and the city." The Oneida presence, this soldier also stated with pleasure, had an additional benefit: "This will make the tories fear for their scalps."[40]

Soon the Oneidas began poking about the camp, inspecting everything and visiting with officers and soldiers. Washington had no objection to their curiosity, so long as they did not lay their hands on alcohol. The day after the Oneidas arrived, army headquarters issued a directive that "[n]o sutler or soldier are to give or sell any rum or Liquors to the Indians on any pretence whatever." Three weeks later, the commanding general again reminded everyone about the policy, but no violations appeared to have occurred. Whether voluntarily or as a result of their lacking access, the Oneidas stayed away from alcohol—and trouble.[41]

Both Washington and the Congressional Committee at Camp had anticipated some Oneida customs and were careful not to offend anyone. Each warrior wanted to meet the "Great Chief Warrior" Washington, and he treated them with kindly respect. Their first full day in camp, the commander hosted the Oneida leader Han Yerry at supper. For the others, Washington extended every reasonable courtesy, and his openness bolstered the Indians' admiration for him.[42]

The commanding general was busy planning for the upcoming campaign season, but he drew on his well-tried sense of patience to avoid any awkward situations. Accustomed as Oneida chief warriors were to participating in council gatherings, one tried to sit in on a planning session. Washington calmly thanked him, escorted him to the door, then continued the meeting. On another occasion at a headquarters supper, an Oneida invited himself to join Washington's gathering.

He entered the room, circled the table to examine the feast, and grabbed a slice of meat. When others offered to remove the warrior, Washington demurred. He was not going to anger his Oneida allies over so trivial a matter as a piece of beef.[43]

While the Oneida warriors familiarized themselves with Washington and his army, Polly Cooper went to work preparing hulled corn soup for the hungry soldiers. Although the Oneidas lacked the corn and transportation capacity to feed the entire army in Pennsylvania, any little bit helped in a time of need. The small amount of corn they brought from New York was a magnanimous gesture from one friend and ally to another. Polly shelled the ears, ground the kernels into meal, boiled the corn soup, and mixed these items with available fruits and nuts, all with the intent of showing the soldiers how to improve the nutritional quality and taste of their sparse diets.[44]

As with the Oneida warriors, Polly Cooper would accept no payment for her services. Word of her generous deeds so impressed Washington and his staff that according to oral tradition, the commanding general's wife, Martha, gave Polly a shawl, a gift that the Oneida people still cherish.[45]

Washington had not intended to bring Oneidas into the army only to have them lie around camp. After a few days' rest, he directed them to participate in a reconnaissance-in-force mission under the command of Lafayette. Intelligence reports were indicating that the British had plans to evacuate Philadelphia, and Washington wanted an advance force to observe any movements, cover his army at Valley Forge, and harass enemy foraging parties in their attempts to gather food and intelligence. The commander enjoined Lafayette, who had pressed for this active command assignment, to be alert to possible surprise attacks. "A stationary post," the former counseled, "is unadvisable, as it gives the enemy an opportunity of knowing your situation and concerting successfully against you."[46]

Along with the Oneidas, Washington committed 2,200 soldiers, including Enoch Poor's New Hampshire Brigade, Captain Allen McLane's Independent Partisan Corps of 150 troops, 600 militia, and

5 artillery pieces. Some ten Frenchmen volunteered to join Tousard and the Oneidas. Lafayette, in turn, attached the Oneida-French contingent to McLane's Partisans.

Late on May 18, Lafayette marched his detachment eastward from Valley Forge, wading the Schuylkill River at Swede's Ford. The column advanced along Ridge Road into a hamlet called Barren Hill, approximately halfway between Philadelphia and Valley Forge and within two miles of British outposts. Here, at Barren Hill near midday on May 19, Lafayette called a halt.

From a tactical standpoint, Lafayette selected well when he occupied Barren Hill. Overlooking the Schuylkill River, the tiny village lay at the junction of three land routes coming in from the south and east. The road from Whitemarsh entered from the east. Just southeast of Barren Hill, the thoroughfare running up from Germantown first crossed the Whitemarsh Road and then formed a bypass, skirting to the north and west around Barren Hill. The Ridge Road, the direct avenue from Philadelphia, ran roughly parallel along the course of the Schuylkill River. This pathway entered Barren Hill from the south and bisected the community. Just north of town, the Ridge Road intersected the Germantown Road before extending on in a northwesterly direction to Swede's Ford. From its crossing with the Ridge Road, the Germantown Road angled to the west to the Schuylkill River and Matson's Ford, about two miles north of Barren Hill. For Lafayette, even though he would maintain stationary headquarters, vigilant scouting, spying, and harassing parties could easily carry out assigned missions from Barren Hill without risking a major enemy attack.[47]

Many of the Continentals now experienced their first extended contact with the Oneidas. Connecticut enlistee Joseph Plumb Martin described them as "stout-looking fellows and remarkably neat for that race of mortals," although he could not resist tossing in the caveat, "but they were Indians." Before occupying scouting positions, the Oneidas entertained some troops with feats of marksmanship with the bow and arrow. At an old and abandoned stone church, the Oneidas struck suggested targets inside and outside the structure. When one of the soldiers asked an Oneida to fire into a black mass dangling from a corner of the roof, the warrior agreed. The arrow hit the target, stirring up a hoard of bats.

"The house was immediately alive with them, and it was likewise instantly full of Indians and soldiers," noted Martin. "The poor bats fared hard; it was sport for all hands," he recorded. "They killed I know not how many, but there was a great slaughter among them."[48]

Lafayette, meanwhile, posted his detachment throughout the community. On the high ground just west of the Ridge Road, he located his main body of troops. In advance of that line, he placed his field pieces, so that their fire could rake the Ridge Road, the most obvious route for any concentrated enemy advance. The Schuylkill River and the steep incline up the hill protected his force's right flank. Lafayette positioned the Pennsylvania militia to his left. He ordered them to report possible enemy movements along the Whitemarsh and Germantown Roads and block any thrust toward Swede's Ford. Since the primary threat would likely come from Philadelphia, Lafayette directed McLane's corps and the Oneidas to scout southward along the Ridge Road. For added precaution, he familiarized himself with the nearby thoroughfares and his potential escape hatch, Matson's Ford.[49]

As May 20 dawned, Lafayette could feel trouble in the air. First, McLane brought in two prisoners who claimed that a major attack was about to begin. Not long afterward, the marquis received an account of red-coated cavalrymen riding along the Whitemarsh Road. The general discounted this report, since some of the mounted Pennsylvania militiamen assigned to guard that route wore red jackets, and no exchange of gunfire had occurred. Still, Washington had told his youthful subordinate to act with prudence, so Lafayette sent out his scouts. Suddenly, the scouts returned frantic with news that the British were advancing in large numbers toward the American left flank. Lafayette had no clue how the enemy troops had gotten there or what had happened to the Pennsylvania militia.[50]

Local spies had informed British officers in Philadelphia about Lafayette's expedition. Generals Howe and Sir Henry Clinton, who was about to replace Howe at the head of His Majesty's forces in North America, sensed a splendid opportunity to ensnare a sizable portion of the rebel army in one bold stroke. The two generals ordered three columns to descend on Lafayette's force at Barren Hill. The largest contingent would approach from Whitemarsh and then swing around

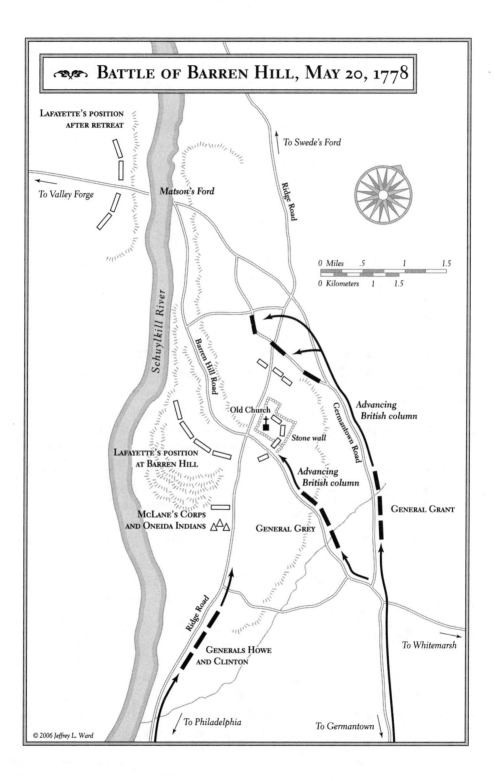

BATTLE OF BARREN HILL, MAY 20, 1778

LAFAYETTE'S POSITION
AFTER RETREAT

To Swede's Ford

To Valley Forge

Matson's Ford

Ridge Road

Schuylkill River

0 Miles   .5   1   1.5
0 Kilometers   1   1.5

Barren Hill Road

Old Church

Germantown Road

Advancing
British column

Stone wall

LAFAYETTE'S POSITION
AT BARREN HILL

Advancing
British column

GENERAL GRANT

McLANE'S CORPS
AND ONEIDA INDIANS

GENERAL GREY

Ridge Road

To Whitemarsh

GENERALS HOWE
AND CLINTON

To Philadelphia

To Germantown

© 2006 Jeffrey L. Ward

the bypass to block the Ridge Road on the north side of town. They were to repel any attempted rebel retreat to Swede's Ford and eventually seize Matson's Ford, cutting off Lafayette's escape routes. A second detachment, consisting of infantry and a small number of mounted dragoons, was to press in from the Germantown Road and threaten Lafayette's left flank. These were the soldiers the patriot scouts first detected. As for the third column, Howe and Clinton decided to accompany this element, which approached from Philadelphia along the Ridge Road. The combined British troop strength totaled more than eight thousand—four times Lafayette's numbers.[51]

The three columns synchronized their movements well. When Lafayette at last observed the middle British prong bearing down on his main line, the largest enemy detachment had already gained access to the bypass road undetected and was sliding around the rebel rear. Because of the disappearance or flight of the Pennsylvania militia, by the time Lafayette fully comprehended the magnitude of his force's predicament, the British lead elements had also gained control of the road to Swede's Ford.[52]

At this critical juncture, the marquis reacted effectively. To meet the British force advancing on his left flank, he shifted some troops from his main line over to the area around the old church and cemetery, where they occupied a good position behind a stone wall. He also sent parties into the woods north of town, there to act as decoys against the enemy column encircling him. If the British believed these bands were part of a larger attacking force, they might halt the march and prepare for battle. That distraction and delay could provide just enough time to plan and execute an evacuation.[53]

Salvation lay in Lafayette's exploration of the local roads and Matson's Ford. With British troops commanding the line of retreat via Swede's Ford to Valley Forge, the remaining pathway of escape was to cross over Matson's Ford. A road led from Barren Hill down a steep slope to the Schuylkill River and Matson's Ford. Although the forward British elements were just as close to that crossing as Lafayette's troops, they were not aware of this potential getaway route. When the British paused in reaction to what seemed like a significant rebel movement to the north, the Continentals gained the necessary time to reach Matson's Ford first and wade across the Schuylkill before the king's troops could cut them off.[54]

Lafayette withdrew his soldiers from the main position first, then those to the north and at the cemetery. He conducted the difficult movement skillfully, pulling troops out from their battle lines while preserving reasonably good order. As they plunged into the swift river, all were "in a Fluster." The water was waist deep, and the soldiers had to hold hands to keep the current from dragging them downstream. At any moment, they expected the British to open with heavy fire while they were still vulnerable to slaughter. Stumbling out of the Schuykill's waters, they formed into a defensive position on higher ground and held themselves ready for an attack that never came.[55]

In comparison with their compatriots, the Oneidas did not fare quite so well. That morning, they and part of McLane's corps were scouting two miles south along the Ridge Road, with the Oneidas well in advance. About the time that Lafayette realized his army's state of jeopardy, the column under the command of Howe and Clinton approached, with some cavalry in the vanguard. The sounds of the hooves of a couple of hundred horses provided ample notice for the Oneidas. The warriors prepared to spring an ambush, concealing themselves among the trees lining both sides of the road. As the British riders approached, out of the woods came a flurry of gunfire and arrows, followed by ferocious shouts from the warriors.[56]

Fifty years after the battle, Lafayette wrote in his memoirs: "The war cries on one side and the appearance of the cavalry on the other surprised the two parties so much that they fled with equal speed." Not a witness to the scene, Lafayette assumed that the Oneida warriors had not heard the enemy's approach. In reality, the Indians' unexpected barrage had staggered the horsemen. They stumbled backward, but then, fortified by the approach of the main column, they regrouped and surged forward once again.[57]

During the hiatus, the Oneidas quickly gathered up the cloaks and other equipment that the British had abandoned and fell back toward the main rebel force in traditional Iroquois fashion, darting from tree to tree for concealment while fighting when necessary. With no support, and against cavalry reinforced by two thousand foot soldiers, the retreat lapsed into a running fight toward Matson's Ford for the nearly fifty Indians and a handful of Frenchmen.[58]

Tousard, who thrust himself into the struggle alongside his Oneidas, praised the warriors' combat prowess. To the president of Congress, he boasted, "I have had the occasion to acquaint the british light horses with the hollow [holler] of the Indians, and their hability [ability] in firing." He attributed his own survival to two Oneidas and two Frenchmen who refused to leave his side after his horse threw him: while Tousard lay stunned and defenseless, his defenders shot and killed two attacking British cavalrymen. Although he could not offer an accurate account of how many casualties his men inflicted, Tousard stated that those with him "fired pretty smart though running away, and I have seen myself five or six killed." The Oneidas were among the last of Lafayette's troops to cross the treacherous Schuylkill.[59]

With the Continental force now posted on high ground across the river, the British commanders knew they had squandered a superb opportunity to devastate an overextended rebel force. After an all-night march designed to surprise Lafayette's detachment, they could not expect combat miracles from their exhausted troops. In addition, an assault across the river would have resulted in considerable casualties. Suspicions that Washington was nearby with the rest of the Continental Army, ready to spring his own trap on them, further discouraged additional action. Howe and Clinton broke off the effort, and the weary British Army marched back to Philadelphia. Soon thereafter, Lafayette reoccupied Barren Hill, mainly to make a statement, and then he returned his troops to Valley Forge.[60]

Because of their timely escape, patriot casualties were slight. Washington placed rebels killed, wounded, and captured at nine. He did not indicate if that number included any Oneidas. Lafayette told his wife that his detachment had suffered six or seven casualties, as compared with twenty-five to thirty for the British. According to British sources, two Oneidas fell into their hands. A Hessian officer mistakenly referred to these captives as Stockbridge Indians and described them as "hand-some and well-built people, who had a rather deep yellow skin." One of the Oneida prisoners was Jacob Skayowi:yo:h (Beautiful Sky), whom the British marched to Philadelphia stripped of his weapons and every-thing else except his breechcloth.[61]

Although no official reported the number of Oneidas killed in the fight, some years afterward Pennsylvanians placed a plaque at St. Peter's Church Cemetery in Barren Hill that memorialized the SIX INDIAN SCOUTS WHO DIED IN BATTLE MAY 1778. According to the church's official history, at least four of them had been buried there, their graves marked by ordinary headstones, all in a straight line. Among those Oneidas who gave their lives for the cause of liberty that day was the devoted rebel friend, the sachem Thomas Sinavis.[62]

Barren Hill turned out to be the only engagement in which the Oneidas fought as part of Washington's command. Even before they had arrived at Valley Forge, the commander had decided not to stretch out their service, at least for the present time. He had received a report from the northern Indian commissioners that reviewed the challenges facing the Oneidas: continued threats from the Crown and other Indi-ans, including their brother Iroquois, a shortage of Continental troops to assist them, and no fort for their immediate defense.[63]

That Oneida warriors, despite these circumstances, had left their homeland to serve in the Continental Army surely impressed Washing-ton. "The Oneidas and Tuscaroras have a particular claim to attention and kindness, for their perseverance and fidelity," he wrote to Schuyler. Still, for them to serve so far away from home was unwise, especially when trouble lurked in their own neighborhood. The commander asked Schuyler to stop any additional Indians who might be planning to join their warrior brothers at Valley Forge, and he would send back those with him very soon.[64]

"When my application was made for a body of Indians to join this army," Washington went on to explain, "our prospects were very differ-ent from what they are now." Since then, the patriot cause had become the beneficiary of a formal alliance with France, and Washington cor-rectly predicted that this invaluable pact would change the entire na-ture of the conflict. Until British leaders decided how to cope with direct French intervention, they would likely keep their forces on the defensive, he stated. As such, Washington thought "[t]here will be very little of that kind of service in which the Indians are capable of being useful." "To bring them such a distance, while there is likely to be scarcely any employment suited to their active and desultory genius," he concluded, "could answer no valuable purpose; but would be productive of needless expence, and might perhaps have a tendency to put them out of humour" with regard to their affirmative feelings about the rebel cause.[65]

Washington worried about the Oneidas' reaction when they learned that he no longer needed them. He urged Schuyler to cast the news in very positive terms. The latter should emphasize the treaty with France, Washington advised, and explain to the Oneidas that the patriots wished them to concentrate on protecting their homeland while also preparing for any possible future combat in conjunction with patriot forces.[66]

The Oneidas at Valley Forge agreed that they should return home. During the month that followed Barren Hill, the Continental Army remained dormant, awaiting British movements. The warriors disliked such inactivity. The structure, regimen, and pace of the European's brand of military life exasperated them, and the novelty of serving in the army had worn off. If Washington was not able to employ them, they could better assist their own nation. As reports of bloody actions near their homeland filtered down to them, concern for family and friends weighed more and more heavily on their minds as well.[67]

In mid-June, thirty-four of the original forty-seven Indians began the long trek home under Ensign Jacob I. Klock. Within a month or so, those who remained elected to return to central New York as well. They left behind a very favorable impression in the mind of Washington and his army, two prisoners of war, and the bodies of their fallen brothers, Thomas Sinavis among them.[68]

10

THE ENEMY OF OLD FRIENDS

Word spread like wildfire through Kanonwalohale—the warriors were returning from Pennsylvania. Mixed waves of excitement and trepidation swept over the residents. Young and old hastened to the outskirts of the castle to greet their loved ones. Among them was the Bear Clan matron Wale, sister of Thomas Sinavis. She and everyone else wanted to hear about what the warriors had experienced with the Continental Army. Their collective fear was that some of their kin had died along the way, either during their journeys south and back north, in the rebel camp at Valley Forge, or in combat. The news for Wale could not have been worse.

Since mid-June, the warriors had traveled the long route back home. Their return trip took close to three weeks, since they first stopped in Albany to share information with the Indian commissioners. On July 1, 1778, twenty-one warriors with Deacon Thomas strode into town; six days later, Han Yerry's party of twelve arrived. Both groups met with Philip Schuyler and Volkert P. Douw. The two Indian commissioners listened to their reports and messages, fed them well, and sent them on their way home.[1]

As accounts of the expedition and resulting casualties spread among the Oneidas, wails of mourning quickly drowned out the shouts and chatter of joy. The time would come to speak of martial achievements and to exhibit the trophy leggings the warriors had made from British blankets and cloaks, but this moment belonged to the family and friends who had lost loved ones. Grief-stricken people like Wale poured out their emotions regarding fallen relatives buried so far away, with only their names and spirits left to remember.[2]

The loss of Thomas Sinavis generated a particularly powerful outpouring of sympathy. Despite his youth and brief tenure as a sachem, Sinavis had demonstrated unusual leadership ability. In some ways, his selection as a hereditary titleholder represented an accommodating gesture toward pro-rebel warriors, an attempt to renew the bonds of respect between the traditional leaders and the hunters and fighters.[3]

Sinavis's death also represented a tragic loss for the rebels. An ironclad supporter of the revolutionary movement, he had fought in two military campaigns over a nine-month period, unusual for a sachem. He had also provided astute advice to the Indian commissioners, besides carrying out missions to Canada. Louis Atayataronghta, the Kahnawake warrior, could take over negotiations for the rebels with his own people and possibly other Canadian tribes. An outstanding warrior, he could also aid the cause in various military functions. Sinavis, however, possessed two distinct advantages over Louis: he was an Oneida, and he held the title of sachem. Together, these factors provided him with a higher level of credibility when he addressed the Kahnawakes, speaking as a hereditary leader and a diplomat from the most powerful Indian ally of the American rebels.[4]

Because of Sinavis's status, his family received the comfort of an elaborate condolence ceremony. Tradition called for the senior moiety to oversee the event and requicken a replacement during the upcoming autumn or winter seasons. Most likely, some Onondaga hereditary leaders joined Mohawk sachem Little Abraham in conducting the ritual. The Indian commissioners, who appreciated the importance of paying proper respect to kin, also attempted to ease the pain for Sinavis's family. Commissioner Douw issued three pounds to James Dean for the purchase and distribution of gifts to the grieving family. More symbolic than valuable, the presents represented concern and sympathy for those in deep grief.[5]

Unfortunately, in distributing the condolence items, no one gave a present to Sinavis's sister Wale. All she wanted was some small gift from the rebel government as acknowledgment of her brother's contributions and his ultimate sacrifice for the patriot cause. When she received nothing, she spoke with Schuyler, who pledged to correct this oversight. This pledge soon proved a forgotten promise, and Wale had to wait several years before anyone fulfilled her modest request.[6]

Even as the Oneidas mourned, the returning warriors offered stirring accounts of the territory they had seen, the people they had met, and the battle they had fought. In turn, those who stayed at home described events of the past two months that boded poorly for the welfare of the Oneidas. The warriors had left for Pennsylvania amid glimmers of hope that a grand council at Onondaga might actually restore harmony among the Six Nations. Nothing except deception had emerged from that gathering.

Initially, a report from Onondaga indicated that the Senecas and Cayugas might attend the council fire. Over the next few weeks, the Cayugas informed the Oneidas of their willingness to participate, even suggesting they had the consent of John Butler. Soon the Oneidas learned that this news was not only misleading but intentionally deceptive. Knowing how much the Oneidas desired a return to a unified confederacy, the Cayugas used the story as a distraction while some of their warriors slipped southward for raids into Pennsylvania and Virginia.[7]

Despite warnings from Skenandoah and other leaders about the intentions of the Cayugas and Senecas, the Oneidas had fallen for the ruse. Living in daily fear of vengeful attacks from the British and from their own Iroquois brethren, they had allowed wishful thinking to undergird their hopes for peace. Early reports about the rebel alliance with France further convinced them that their fellow Iroquois would realize that returning to the course of neutrality would be best for the Six Nations. Schuyler and others encouraged this thinking. Suffering from their own paroxysm of optimism, rebel leaders wanted to believe that all the Iroquois would accept the decreased likelihood of British success with France formally entering the fray. The pro-British Iroquois warriors, wrote Schuyler, might even begin bearing arms alongside the revolutionaries to atone "for past Offences."[8]

By mid-May, the bubble had burst. The Oneidas received word that the pro-British Senecas and Cayugas would not attend the proposed council, and news of a patriot alliance with France had little impact. Equally distressing was information that the Cayugas, the Oneidas' brothers in the junior moiety, had purposely misled them. "The Oneidas now find they have been very much imposed upon by their Brothers the Cayugas," who had fabricated a "great part of that speech sent to you with four strings of Wampum," Kirkland wrote to Schuyler. Those Cayugas who had not used the possible gathering to camouflage their raid were meeting with John Butler to plan upcoming martial campaigns.[9]

Not to break off communications completely, the Oneidas listened when a small delegation of neutralist Senecas approached them for assistance. Their leader, a chief warrior named Great Tree, asked them to broker a prisoner exchange for a prominent Seneca chief named Atskearax, who had been wounded and captured by the rebels during a raid into Virginia. Great Tree felt that if his party could help effect the release of Atskearax, they would gain heightened credibility among the Senecas in pushing for neutrality. The journey required to broker the prisoner exchange would allow the Oneidas to retrieve the handful of warriors who had stayed behind with the Continental Army.[10]

With Schuyler's blessing, two Oneidas and ten Tuscaroras, Onondagas, and Senecas set out for Washington's force. On June 21 they located the commander in chief in New Jersey. The Continentals were on the march in pursuit of the British, who had recently evacuated Philadelphia and were making their way back to their main base of operations in New York City. Great Tree explained his purpose, seeking the indulgence of one chief warrior for another. Washington knew nothing about Atskearax's whereabouts. He recommended that the Indians travel on to Philadelphia. Perhaps patriot officials there might have information. As for the Oneida warriors who had remained with his army, they had gone on to Philadelphia with Tousard, he told the Indians. The Oneidas would find them there.[11]

During this meeting, Washington gestured toward his army and leveled a threat. The Senecas had committed hostilities at Oriskany and elsewhere, the commander stated. "If they did not immediately cease them," he warned, he "would turn our whole force against them and the other Indian Nations, who have taken a like bloody part against us and cut them to pieces."[12]

In Philadelphia, the two Oneida emissaries rendezvoused with their warriors and advised them to return home. Three had already left, and those who had remained behind agreed to do so shortly. Before the delegation departed, rebel officials showered the Oneidas and Tuscaroras with gifts while offering nothing to the Seneca and Onondaga representatives.[13]

The journey generated few positive results. The Senecas eventually learned that Atskearax had died. Any favorable impressions the visit to Washington's army generated also soon evaporated. Great Tree returned to his homeland, vowing to expand his neutralist party. By autumn, however, he took up the war axe when some Pennsylvania rebels appeared ready to invade the Seneca homeland from the south.[14]

Even while the Oneidas were at Valley Forge, Joseph Brant struck the opening blow in what became a full campaign season of ruthlessly bloody warfare along the New York and Pennsylvania frontier. In May, Oneida scouts detected the initial Indian-Tory movements and warned rebel officials about an impending raid in the German Flatts region. The alert came too late.[15]

From their operations base at Oquaga, Brant and his followers, about three hundred in number, struck the German Flatts–Schoharie settlements, spreading devastation and terror in their wake. Brant lured a small Continental detachment into an ambush and crushed it at Cobleskill, west of Schoharie. After torching nearby homes and barns and confiscating livestock, the Indian-Tory force pushed westward, killing and scalping two riders near Cherry Valley. Loaded down with plunder, Brant's force returned to Oquaga before continuing with more bloody forays. Over the next few weeks, Indians and loyalists raided along the Mohawk Valley and even near Fort Schuyler. Brant had effectively put the whole region on edge, with everyone nervously wondering where his path of destruction would next lead to more mayhem and death.[16]

At the end of June 1778, a larger force of nearly six hundred

Senecas, Cayugas, and loyalists under the command of John Butler and the Seneca chief warrior Old Smoke thrust to the south and west into Pennsylvania. For a decade before the war, many persons, mostly migrating from Connecticut, had settled along the Susquehanna River in the Wyoming Valley. Under wartime fears, these European Americans had built fortifications for community defense. The Iroquois viewed these settlers as potential threats to their welfare. The water route from the Wyoming Valley could provide an invader with a direct avenue into the "underbelly" of Cayuga and Seneca territory. Earlier in 1778, after some discussion, these Iroquois deemed the Wyoming Valley settlements such a danger that they determined to eliminate the threat.[17]

Once in the valley, the Indian-Tory force wreaked massive destruction. Through sheer intimidation, Butler coerced two forts to surrender. Then he induced the rebels in a third fort to come out and challenge his force on ground of his own choosing. These defenders stumbled into a death trap—as many as 376 of them lost their lives, and the pro-British Indians returned home with 227 scalps. Virtually all other patriot resisters and civilians fled the valley. After seizing what they could of value, including livestock, the Indians and Butler's Rangers torched all nearby buildings and trampled maturing crops. The Wyoming Valley settlements lay in total waste.[18]

The People of the Standing Stone interpreted this new season of frontier warfare as a serious threat to their own safety. In late May 1778 an enemy party fired on two young Oneida warriors not far from Kanonwalohale. Darkness enabled both men to slip away and return to the village unhurt. Still, James Dean reported to Schuyler that this incident caused "great apprehensions of danger" among the Oneidas. With the failed effort to hold a grand council and an end to prospects for renewed Iroquois neutrality, Dean reported to New York governor George Clinton that "[t]he Oneidas expect nothing but a vigorous war will be commenced between the United States and the Six nations."[19]

The Oneidas continued to view themselves as likely targets for pro-British Tory and Indian attacks, so they again addressed their concerns about defending their people. In early May, the Continental Congress had voted to offer them assistance in their defense, but nothing had happened. In mid-June, frustrated Oneida leaders called on patriot New York officials to "think of some means for their safety." They proposed either temporarily moving the nation's populace eastward into the Mohawk Valley or positioning rebel troops in advance of Kanonwalohale. Both ideas generated little enthusiasm among patriot leaders.[20]

At the same time, the Oneidas offered to scout in the Schoharie and German Flatts regions and provide warnings to European American settlers in the event of further Indian-British raids. Four Oneida and Tuscarora chiefs advised Schuyler that since "all Hopes of bringing the Cayugas and Senecas to peaceable Sentiment are lost they are now ready to join our [rebel] Arms & assist us in punishing them." Wanting to avoid direct martial confrontations with their Iroquois brethren, how- ever, the pro-rebel Indians said they would conduct offensive opera- tions only against British and loyalist strongholds. Through such targeted military action, they hoped to avoid offering pro-British Iro- quois any reason to assault Oneida communities.[21]

Once they had decided to become more active in support of the rebels, the Oneidas did not appreciate a challenge to their loyalty ema- nating from Fort Schuyler. In early September 1778, after a party of en- emy Indians killed and scalped a soldier not far from the gate, some soldiers in the garrison charged the Oneidas with complicity. The accu- sation stung so much that a party of sachems and warriors met with the acting post commander, Major Robert Cochran. They explained that they "were Sorry any Suspecions [sic] should be entertained that they had the least knowledge of any thing being Intended against any body here."[22]

Voicing their irritation, the Oneidas pointed out that previous com- manders had treated them respectfully, but "we are sorry you Neglect us now." "When your affairs were in a worse Situation you courted us and our Interest," stated the sachems and chief warriors. "But now you are prosperous you Don't know us." Nevertheless, the Oneidas had made an agreement with Schuyler and the commissioners to "be friendly and not Strike the ax at each other," and they promised to con- tinue to abide by that arrangement.[23]

Cochran reassured them of rebel friendship and urged them to dismiss the words of ill-informed soldiers. All societies have some "[b]ad people," he stated, and the Oneidas should give no weight to their opinions. The Indian leaders replied they would henceforth only listen to the fort's commander, not his troops, and then they drank toasts to mutual friendship. Still, that Continental soldiers would blatantly question their commitment was very irksome, especially in the wake of their battlefield contributions and losses at Oriskany and Barren Hill.[24]

For weeks the Oneidas had wanted to launch an attack to help bring closure to the condolence process for persons who, like the Bear Clan matron Wale, had lost relatives at Barren Hill. The warriors kept turning their eyes southward to identify a place where a strike would also aid the rebellion. About twenty miles northeast of Oquaga, on the Susquehanna River, was the heavily loyalist stronghold of Unadilla. Inhabitants there often joined forces with Joseph Brant in his various assaults on rebel settlements. The town represented both an advance base of operations for Brant and an apparent safe haven for disaffected loyalists. For some time, as the Oneidas were well aware, patriot leaders had expressed a desire to see Unadilla demolished.[25]

In mid-September 1778, Brant set out from Oquaga with a force of more than four hundred Indians and Tories, destined for an attack on German Flatts. Along the way, his force stumbled across five Oneida scouts in the woods and took them prisoner. Brant's Indians refused to bring the Oneidas on the expedition, so they left several guards behind to keep their captives from warning the local populace of their approach.[26]

Not long afterward, Brant's contingent skirmished with some rebel scouts. They killed several of them and dispersed the others, but one eluded the attackers and warned the settlers around Fort Dayton, on the northern bank of the Mohawk River. Word spread rapidly, so that when Brant's command struck early the next morning, nearly everyone had found refuge in Fort Dayton or Fort Herkimer, on the river's south side. With soldiers and civilians holed up inside the forts, Brant's followers had their way with the settlements. They torched sixty-three homes, fifty-seven barns, and four mills, and ran off over seven hundred horses, cattle, and sheep.[27]

While Brant and his raiders carried out their destructive operations at German Flatts, the Oneida prisoners slipped from their captors' grasp and reported all they knew back at Kanonwalohale. Since Brant had left no significant rearguard to protect the British strongholds, the Oneida chief warriors saw an opportunity to deliver a heavy blow for the rebel cause. Now was the perfect time to target Unadilla.[28]

A few days later, a fast-moving Oneida and Tuscarora war party raided a portion of Unadilla and the area just to the northeast called the Butternuts. Lightly defended, these places represented easy pickings. The warriors burned some homes and barns, gathered and led off live-stock, seized ten prisoners, and freed a prominent local rebel, William Dygert, whom Brant had captured nine weeks earlier.[29]

Although the Unadilla operation was limited in scope and scale, the Oneida and Tuscarora warriors inflicted substantial damage before withdrawing. Still, they made no effort to torch both areas in their entirety, and they showed compassion. "Our Warriors were Particular that no hurt should be Done to Women & Children," an Oneida leader explained. "We Left four old men Behind who were no more able to go to War."[30]

The war party took the prisoners back to Kanonwalohale to let the community determine their fate. Ultimately, the warriors turned over eight prisoners to Major Cochran at Fort Schuyler. While meeting with Cochran, the Oneidas again referred to doubts about their commitment to the rebels. "We hope," their spokesperson emphasized, "you are now Convinced of our Friendship towards you & your Great Cause." As for the other captives, they gave one to some Kahnawakes then visiting from Canada. The last captive, William Lull, experienced a different lot. Grasshopper took a liking to the young man and brought him into his household, adopting Lull as his own son.[31]

Certainly Washington held no doubts about the Oneidas. "I am very glad to hear of the blow struck by the Oneida Indians upon the rear of Brant's Party," the commanding general expressed to Major General John Stark, Lafayette's successor as commander of the Northern Department. Finally, someone on the frontier had attacked the always menacing Tory bases.[32]

Two weeks later, in early October 1778, a rebel force set out to complete the task of eliminating Brant's strongholds. With 266 officers and men, Lieutenant Colonel William Butler of the Fourth Pennsylvania Regiment attacked Oquaga under cover of darkness. With riflemen on the flanks and infantrymen with bayonets fixed in the center, Butler's troops waded through the brisk, chest-deep Susquehanna River and stormed the village. No one was there; all the residents had fled.[33]

At daylight, Butler and his troops gained a full view of the size and construction of Oquaga. "It was the finest Indian town I ever saw; on both sides the River," he jotted down in his journal. "There was about forty good houses, Square logs, Shingles & stone Chimneys, good floors, glass windows, &c." His soldiers gathered up livestock and started torching the buildings. Before nightfall, Butler's command vacated the town, sparing only a single home—owned by an Oneida— probably Good Peter's old place. Although no longer an Oneida stronghold, Oquaga joined Oriska as yet another Revolutionary War casualty.[34]

For local rebels, the success of the Oneida-Tuscarora foray against Unadilla blended together with William Butler's expedition against Oquaga three weeks later. The patriots rightly viewed both communities as bases for the launching of Indian-Tory attacks. Their destruction, rebel leaders had concluded, would help improve security for the region's European American residents.[35]

For the Oneidas, however, the leveling of Oquaga occasioned a new set of physical and emotional challenges. Their kin had lost their homes, blankets, clothing, household goods, farm animals and implements, and the entire harvest from 1778. No one knows how many Oquaga Oneidas migrated to Kanonwalohale and Old Oneida as refugees, but go there they did.[36]

They did not arrive at a prosperous time. Food production had fallen off as the year progressed, mostly because threats of attack had kept warriors nearby rather than ranging to the best locations for game and pelts. The fall salmon harvest had yielded smaller-than-usual quantities, also a reflection of a heightened sense of alert and additional scouting. Fortunately, crop yields were fairly abundant. Some of the problem lay in the Oneidas' traditional practice of raising just enough corn, beans, and squash to satisfy basic needs. They invariably assumed that ample quantities of meat and fish would be available, but when that amount fell below expectations, everyone had to make due with less. The unanticipated population influx from Oquaga worsened the shortage.[37]

Clothing shortages had also reached a near-crisis point. The British had obstructed much of the importation of garments and blankets. Runaway inflation and restricted supplies drove the price of cloth goods to exorbitant levels, beyond the means of most Oneidas. In mid-April 1778, the Indian commissioners advised Congress that the Oneidas and Tuscaroras "are now naked and destitute and it cannot be expected that they will long persevere in their Attachment without some Assistance." Ten days later, the Indians received a limited issue of clothing items at Fort Schuyler. Still, during the spring and summer months, many Oneidas dressed in tatters, and sometimes with almost no covering whatsoever. As autumn descended on them and inevitable frigid winter temperatures eventually froze the landscape, the Oneidas struggled to keep themselves and their refugee kin from Oquaga minimally outfitted and warm.[38]

Hoping to reduce governmental expenses and provide for immediate Oneida needs, Schuyler again called for a trading post operation at Fort Schuyler. Indian friends could swap furs for garments and blankets at "reasonable" prices. The skins would help defray the cost of operating the exchange and would allow the government to purchase additional necessities, while also reducing the expense of a costly handout program.[39]

After securing congressional approval and start-up funds, rebel officials stocked the shelves and began operations in mid-October 1778. The prices, even at cost, shocked the Oneidas. Not many had secured pelts, and those who did could not see trading them for so little. Some Oneidas had earned small amounts of money from the commissioners for various services performed on behalf of the rebels, but these sums were insufficient to purchase enough blankets and shirts to satisfy family and community needs. In the end, only a few used money or furs to obtain goods. The trading post failed to ease Oneida shortages.[40]

In late October, Good Peter led a delegation of three Oneidas, two Kahnawakes, and a Tuscarora to Albany for a meeting with the Indian commissioners. Atop their list was the treatment of Oneidas who had lost homes and property at Oquaga. "Many of the Indians who lived at *Ochquaga* are as true Friends to the thirteen united States as any of us," declared Good Peter. The chief warrior compared these Oquagas to patriot supporters who could not remove themselves from their communities when Tories seized control. He also sought to protect them from rebel harassment, requesting papers that would identify each friendly Oquaga as "under the protection of the united States and that they are not to be molested."[41]

Next came clothing shortages. Although the pro-British Iroquois regularly received garments and blankets, Good Peter stated, "we are obliged to use Grass for Garters & that we shall soon be destitute of Stockings." The Oneidas needed to have a secure clothing supply, not just for the upcoming winter but also for months and perhaps years to come. "We imagine that if the War continues it will be extremely difficult for us to procure clothing," the chief predicted. The Oneida expectation was that the rebels, as their allies, would work to find the means to remedy this pressing deficiency.[42]

Speaking for the Oneidas at Kanonwalohale, Good Peter complained about Samuel Kirkland's prolonged absences. The war had transformed the clergyman's role from ministering to the Oneidas to caring for the spiritual needs of Continental troops. Although Kirkland had devoted time to his Oneida flock during the previous winter, other demands kept him away from Kanonwalohale during most of the summer and autumn of 1778. Further, with the constant threat of Iroquois attacks, Kirkland had to be careful about his travels. After all, his capture would have represented an invaluable prize in pro-British Iroquois circles.[43]

Meanwhile, the Oneidas seemed to be languishing in their Christian faith. To fulfill military and diplomatic duties, warriors and sachems were often absent from home, ranging from a day or two to weeks at a time. With the men around less, church attendance dropped off, particularly among the warriors' mothers, wives, and sisters, even on those days when Kirkland was present. The Oneidas, male and female alike, needed the missionary's abiding presence to sustain their faith.[44]

For Good Peter, a practitioner of new-birth Presbyterianism for twenty-five years, his convictions were unshakable. By comparison, many Oneida converts had accepted Christian beliefs only more recently. Without frequent nurturing, their faith lacked deep roots, and the pressures of the rebellion and war only further diverted them from continuing their religious development. Good Peter, for one, viewed the Oneidas as slipping into a kind of religious vacuum, caught between Christian teachings and traditional beliefs. He beseeched the commissioners to encourage Kirkland to "[c]ome up to us at Oneida only for two or three Sundays." For the latter's safety, Good Peter said that Oneida warriors would travel to Fort Schuyler and escort the minister to Kanonwalohale and back. "You may assure him that he need not be afraid," the Christian chief pledged. "We shall take Care of him and die to protect him."[45]

Commissioner Douw responded the next day. He apologized for the damage to the property of friendly Indians during the Oquaga raid. Douw handed Good Peter multiple copies of a document and authorized the Oneida chief to distribute them to all Oquaga residents who "have evinced a constant Attachment to the Cause of the Liberties of this Country." The paper stated that Good Peter, "one of the Oneida Chief Warriors," and "a steady and sincere Friend to the thirteen united States of America," had represented the holder as a devoted supporter of the rebellion. "By the Fate of War their Houses and possessions have lately been destroyed and that they will be obliged to seek for protection amongst their Neighbours and Friends, particularly among the Oneidas." Douw requested that all civil and military officials and "every Well-Wisher to his Country" offer protection to these displaced Oquagas.[46]

The commissioner indicated that clothing shortages would persist, at least in the short run. Although prices at Fort Schuyler were high, so

were payments offered the Indians for their beaver pelts. At least the
Oneidas could buy clothing, he consoled. "Our poor cannot either purchase or procure it." Nonetheless, Douw promised to look into lower-
ing prices. Six weeks later, Congress authorized the commissioners to
distribute free all clothing on hand to Indians who "have been faithful
and steady in their attachment to these states." Congress also wanted
the Oneidas to know that the rebel government had ordered from
France "a large assortment of Indian goods, suitable for, and adequate
to the supply of their wants."[47]

Concerning Kirkland, Douw promised to relay the message and
urge the minister to visit Kanonwalohale regularly. Unfortunately, Kirkland could spare few days because of numerous other assignments. As a
consequence, Christian religious fervor at Kanonwalohale continued to
decline, even with the influx of devoted Christian followers from
Oquaga.[48]

During this Albany gathering, the watchword was *harmony*, with an
emphasis on helping the Oneidas reconcile themselves to the destruction of Oquaga. What Good Peter, Volkert P. Douw, and others did not
yet know was how extensive and gruesome the repercussions would be
for the burning and sacking of Oquaga and Unadilla.

In early November 1778, an Oneida warrior named Nicholas Sharp,
also called Saucy Nick and Loghtaudye (He Continues Speaking), conveyed important intelligence to Peter Gansevoort, commanding at Fort
Schuyler. An Onondaga Indian had just returned from the Susquehanna Valley and described a "great Meeting" in which Indians and
Tory rangers decided to attack Cherry Valley. Gansevoort rushed the information to the rebel commander at Cherry Valley, Colonel Ichabod
Alden. With gross incompetence, Alden refused to shelter local settlers
in the fort recently built there, and he and other officers kept their bil-
lets in a private residence some distance away.[49]

The British had assembled more than five hundred Indians, Tories,
and regular soldiers for the attack. Captain Walter Butler, who had escaped from the patriots back in April, assumed command of the expedition, more in name than anything else. Haughty and arbitrary, he was

in charge only because his father, John, was suffering from a severe bout of rheumatism. Young Butler quickly alienated the Indians and many of the loyalists. Ninety of Brant's Tory followers refused to fight under Butler and went home, despite the latter's threats to treat them like traitors to the king. Friends implored Brant to remain. He did so grudgingly.[50]

Shortly after dawn on November 11, the British force swooped down on the settlers of Cherry Valley. Those in the fort were able to repel the assault. Outside the fort, the affair turned ugly. Indians and Tories began slaughtering men, women, and children. From house to house they tomahawked, scalped, plundered, and spread flames. Whether intending to or not, they had converted Cherry Valley into the devil's dominion. Efforts by Butler and Brant failed to restrain the attackers. When the smoke cleared, the Crown raiders had butchered thirty-one residents and grabbed seventy-one prisoners, thirty-eight of whom they later released. In addition, twenty-six rebel officers and soldiers, including Alden, lost their lives, and fourteen more became prisoners. The Indians and Tories stripped the area of livestock and left almost no structures standing.[51]

When Butler evacuated the charred remains of Cherry Valley, he left behind a letter for Schuyler, attempting to rationalize what had happened. He absolved himself of culpability and shifted the onus onto the rebels. His Indians and Tory rangers had committed their butchery because "[t]hey were so much incensed by the Destruction of their Village of Auquaga by your People." Evidently recognizing the shallowness of his defense, Butler later asserted that rebel forces had torched such communities as Oquaga with malicious impunity, as if such premeditated property destruction justified the unbridled human carnage that had occurred under his command at Cherry Valley.[52]

Within a few weeks after Cherry Valley, pro-British Iroquois decided to use the massacre there as a threat to prevent rebel forces from attacking other Indian villages. Speaking for the Mohawks and Senecas, four chiefs warned revolutionary officials not to disturb some Indians living along the Delaware River, or "you be worst delt with, then your Nighbours the Charyvalle People was." Nor would winter conditions deter them from retaliating, since they had "Big Shouse [shoes] and can come in a few day to your place," they reminded their patriot enemies.[53]

As the devastation intensified, the other Six Nations became increasingly angry with the Oneidas. They could not understand why the People of the Standing Stone would break with three hundred years of tradition and side with the European American settlers; and they were suspicious that the Oneidas had joined in the destruction of Oquaga, or as rebel allies they had somehow helped plan its wreckage.

In mid-December 1778, a pro-British Oneida named William Johnson visited Kanonwalohale, bringing with him a belt and a message from the Cayugas. Through Johnson, the Cayugas reminded their junior moiety brothers that they had long-standing, intimate ties.

Not mentioning the Iroquois invasion of the Oneida homeland, the Cayugas grumbled about the Oneidas providing the revolutionaries with regular intelligence and warnings of Indian attacks that were "hurtful to us." They even accused the Oneidas of having persuaded Nicholas Herkimer and his Mohawk Valley militiamen to relieve the Fort Schuyler garrison and of having alerted the rebel settlers of German Flatts and those of Cherry Valley of impending attacks. For that reason, "we must think that you only are to be blamed for the Death of all the Warriors we lost in our Engagement with him [Herkimer]."[54]

Through such treacherous acts, the Oneidas "had Exposed themselves to the severe Resentment of the other tribes." So far, the Cayugas claimed, they had shielded the Oneidas from reprisals, but "the Conduct of the Oneidas in Carrying Information to the Americans" and other forms of assistance to the rebels "had proved them to be so Notoriously Disaffected to the Confederacy that it was neither their interest nor Indeed in their Power to protect them any Longer." The Cayugas urged the Oneidas to reconsider their behavior and "Reunite with their antient friends & allies in a vigorous opposition against the Common Enemy of the Confederacy." If they would not pick up the hatchet against the rebels, then they should at least abide by the solemn promises of neutrality that they had made to the Six Nations. Should the Oneidas choose neutrality, the Cayugas advised, they should "move down to the Susquehanna [River], that you may not be trodden under Foot by the Kings People who intend to pass by you in the Spring."[55]

The Cayugas had given the Oneidas abhorrent alternatives: either fight your patriot friends or abandon your homeland. The consequences of not pursuing one of these courses would be severe. "They should not see another spring in peace," threatened the Cayugas, "but that this winter should Determine their fate."[56]

The Oneidas recognized the hypocrisy of these threats. Their Iroquois brethren had not lived up to their promises either, to make war against whichever side sent troops through any portion of Iroquoia. However, the Oneidas also realized that this was no time for reason, logic, or argument. They were not going to convince their brothers and sisters in the Six Nations to appreciate their point of view. The Oneidas had received an ultimatum, and they would have to make a critical decision.[57]

After much caucusing among themselves, the Oneidas held a formal two-day council in mid-January 1779. Each person had the opportunity to express his or her viewpoint. They agreed that anyone who wished to join the pro-British Iroquois could freely withdraw from the community, as a few dozen had done earlier in the conflict. Meanwhile, the Oneidas agreed upon "a unanimous Resolution to stand by each other in Defense of their Lives and Liberty against any Enemy that might be disposed to attack them."[58]

With Oneidas who lived at Kanonwalohale and Old Oneida in unified agreement, they then crafted a response to the Cayuga message. Since the People of the Standing Stone had conducted themselves in such a peaceable manner toward their fellow Iroquois, they expressed dismay that their brothers and sisters found their behavior reprehensible. They had worked strenuously to preserve neutrality and had exerted themselves to gain freedom for Iroquois warriors captured by the rebels. After several years of war, the Oneidas saw virtually no prospect for the confederacy to reconcile with the American revolutionaries. Their best hope was that some of their Iroquois brethren might abandon the Crown. Then the Oneidas made their position perfectly clear. "They would never violate their Alliance with the American States," they vowed, "and that tho' they would not be the Agressors or wantonly provoke any Tribe to War, yet they should henceforth be on their guard against any Enemy whatever."[59]

Knowing full well their words would reach British officials, their statement was both powerful and courageous. Of all the Iroquois, the Oneidas were the only nation solidly in the rebel camp, and they would remain so, even in times of desperate need. After the destruction of Oquaga, nearly three hundred former residents, mostly Mohawks and Tuscaroras, had migrated to Niagara and drew supplies from the Crown that winter. Another 142 Tuscaroras from villages near Kanonwalohale had abandoned their homes for British protection. By comparison, only fifty Oneidas had accepted clothing, weapons, or ammunition at Niagara, and just ten of these were men. Some of the Oneida women likely had husbands from other Iroquois nations.[60]

In mid-February 1779, John Butler boasted to General Frederick Haldimand, who had became the governor of Quebec Province, that most of the Iroquois had promised to persevere and "never come to terms with the Rebels." However, "[t]he greatest part of the Oneydas," he continued, "seem resolved to adhere to the Enemy." To the Crown, the Oneidas remained a festering sore. As long as they supported the rebels, their example kept alive the possibility that numbers of their Iroquois brethren might again embrace neutrality or even switch sides.[61]

The People of the Standing Stone thus played the dual role of protector and proselytizer. They encouraged other Indians to become neutral or to support the rebel cause, and they offered friendship to those who did. Both sides knew that the Tuscaroras who aided the patriots could not sustain their position without Oneida backing, and the Oneidas had absorbed all the Oquaga refugees who had declined Crown protection at Niagara.[62]

As the principal pro-rebel link to other Iroquois peoples, the Oneidas also rendered a vital service by maintaining an open communication channel. They encouraged and helped bolster a substantial neutralist faction among the Onondagas. During the Oneida debates over the Cayuga ultimatum, seven principal Onondaga chiefs stopped at Kanonwalohale while en route to Albany. After listening to the Oneidas explain their thinking, these Onondagas proclaimed a shift in their own policy. Speaking only for themselves, not the whole nation, the visiting chiefs, according to James Dean, "let go their Hold of peace." Now they "were determined to join their Children the Oneidas and Tuscaroras to oppose any Invader." In response, the Oneidas invited these chiefs and any other Onondagas to come live at Kanonwalohale. Some twenty or so accepted the offer.[63]

By taking in their kin from Oquaga and these Onondagas, the Oneidas were reinforcing their own modest numbers. They also retained strong ties with their old allies the Kahnawakes. This relationship gave them indirect influence with the other Indians of the Seven Nations of Canada. Before his death, Thomas Sinavis had worked diligently to preserve that friendship. Then the Kahnawake Louis Atayataronghta had stepped forward to keep open communication lines among his own people and the Oneidas, the rebels, and, circuitously, the other Seven Nations.[64]

Despite pressure from the Senecas, the Kahnawakes held firm to their commitment of mutual defense with the Oneidas. A small number of Kahnawake and St. Regis Indians even took up residence among the Oneidas and scouted and campaigned with them. Most, however, tried to maintain a low profile and avoid the wrath of the pro-British Six Nations while also assisting the Oneidas and rebels in subtle ways.[65]

Both the Oneida and Kahnawake nations repeatedly worked together to strengthen each other. When Continental soldiers seized a Kahnawake warrior allegedly spying for the British near Fort Schuyler, the Oneidas intervened. Good Peter traveled to Albany and met with Volkert Douw, reminding the commissioner of the service the Kahnawakes had performed and how important were strong relations with them. As a "compliment to our Oneida Friends," Douw secured the warrior's release. A few months later, the Kahnawakes repaid the favor by sending a message to the Cayugas, attempting to convince them to renounce the British and join the Oneidas and the rebel cause. The Cayugas ignored this request.[66]

Trying to reward longtime service and strengthen the Indian-rebel alliance, Philip Schuyler explained to Congress in March 1778 that "[s]ome of the chief warriors of the six nations held Captains commissions under the former government." The Indian commissioners thought "it would be advisable . . . to give a few to some of the Chiefs whose Fidelity may be depended on." The delegates took thirteen months to respond, but in April 1779 they finally sent Schuyler a dozen blank commissions.[67]

Responsibility for making nominations fell to James Dean, who wisely asked the chief warriors in the Oneida and Tuscarora nations for recommendations. Dean forwarded their list in early June, and Congress promptly ratified the choices. Han Yerry, who had distinguished himself at Oriskany and Saratoga and led the Indian column to Valley Forge, along with John Onondiyo (Silversmith), known as a savvy leader, James Wakarontharan (One Tree Lodging Against Another), and Tewagtahkotte (The Standing Bridge) accepted commissions as captains for the Oneidas. Both Clanis Kakektaton (Cornelius) and Han Yost Thahoswagwat had distinguished themselves in resisting St. Leger's force around Fort Schuyler. They, along with other active warriors Christian Thonigwenghsoharie (Kristianko, or Washer Away of Blood), Totyaneahani, Joseph Banghsatirhon, John Sagoharasie, and Cornelius Okonyota, gained the rank of lieutenant. Just Nicholas Cusick of the Tuscaroras received a lieutenant's commission, reflecting both the subordinate position of his people and their smaller contributions in combat.[68]

The Oneidas and Tuscaroras only considered their own warriors. No one remembered the Kahnawake Louis Atayataronghta, who had fought, scouted, and negotiated so ably. Since everyone called him Colonel Louis, and in appreciation of his excellent service and multilingual talents, Schuyler secured him a lieutenant colonelcy a month later.[69]

Understandably, the appointments pleased those who received them, while those who lost out felt slighted. Among the Oneidas, Jacob Reed had the most reasons to complain. Because he could read and write in English, he had acted as an interpreter and had also served at Saratoga and Valley Forge. On other occasions he had led scouts and accompanied diplomatic envoys. No doubt, with his skills, Reed had been one of the most active and enterprising pro-rebel Oneidas. Furthermore, he insisted that Lafayette had earlier issued him a warrant and promised him a captaincy. The omission so deeply disappointed him that several years later he filed a petition with Congress asking for a captain's commission. The delegates never acted on this request.[70]

In addition to commissions, rebel officials showed renewed concern about protection for the Oneidas. When the Cayugas delivered their ultimatum, the Oneidas approached Schuyler once more about defensive assistance, effectively reviving the moribund plan to construct a fort at Kanonwalohale. This time, the rebels followed through. Schuyler wrote both George Washington and John Jay, his old friend and the new president of Congress, about their needs. A committee contacted Washington, and together they authorized building a "picket Fort" at Kanonwalohale "should they find the other Nations inclinable to put their threats in execution." However, no Continentals were to be made available for post duty there. The Oneidas would have to defend themselves, but at least they would have somewhere to shelter their people in the event of an attack.[71]

In late January 1779, Brigadier General James Clinton ordered construction to commence. A detail of fifty troops, headed by Captain John Copp from Fort Schuyler, joined the Oneidas to perform the labor. Over the course of a few weeks, soldiers and Indians toiled side by side, chopping down trees, skinning bark, slicing planks, and securing posts and walls in the ground. Sometimes the work so consumed their energies that all hunting ceased, and they had to haul food from Fort Schuyler to feed everyone.[72]

Copp located the fort a short distance from the houses and huts of Kanonwalohale. Inside the walls in two places, work parties built swivels—platforms for small, maneuverable cannons. (The Continentals never provided the ordnance pieces.) They also implanted outside pickets, or sharpened logs, to obstruct concentrated enemy assaults. When they had finished, the crews had fashioned a substantial wooden fortress, large enough to contain the villagers. In mid-February, after some Oneida scouts reported an enemy party of Indians and Tories nearby, the soldiers spent the night inside the structure. Copp reported that "our Quarters are not very agreeable but we are nevertheless contented." Even though the finished "bastion" hardly compared with Fort Schuyler, the Oneidas gratefully viewed the fort as an affirmation of patriot concern about their welfare.[73]

Copp and his Continentals remained at Kanonwalohale for nearly two months. They observed the marvels of Oneida scouting and the threatened state under which these Indians lived. The captain and his soldiers gained feelings of respect for the Oneidas' commitment to the cause and for their martial talents. In time, Copp felt confident serving alongside them. When intelligence in February 1779 indicated the approach of a hostile force, he expressed little trepidation. "If the same fidelity continues in these people as I have now the satisfaction to observe," stated the captain, "I doubt not if we should be attacked but we shall be able to give a good account of the Enemy if not too strong."[74]

Eventually, Copp received orders to return to Fort Schuyler, leaving the Oneidas to defend themselves, if need be, from inside the newly constructed fort. Rebel officials did not worry about the structure's elemental size or absence of artillery. The post represented a hastily assembled defensive work meant to help toughen the Oneidas' resolve and provide them with a greater sense of security until the patriots implemented a much bolder war plan designed to break the will of the pro-British Iroquois. What the revolutionary leaders did not anticipate was how their upcoming offensive operations into Iroquoia would place the Oneidas at even greater risk of retaliation from their British-Indian enemies.

11

WARFARE BY DEVASTATION

Gosen Van Schaick, better known as Goose to his friends, was a fervent patriot. From one of Albany's elite Dutch families, Van Schaick was the son of a mayor of that community. Born in 1736, Goose took an active part in the Seven Years' War, eventually rising to the rank of lieutenant colonel in the First New York Regiment. He sustained a nasty combat wound to his left cheek that forever marred his appearance. In July 1775, he accepted a commission as colonel of the Second New York Regiment. A burly person with command presence, he led his Continentals into Canada in support of the rebel invasion of Quebec Province, and he later sustained a wound in the fighting at Saratoga in 1777. Van Schaick was still in active command when the Cherry Valley massacre occurred in November 1778.

Van Schaick and other rebel leaders felt profoundly frustrated by their inability to check British-Indian-loyalist raiding forays. Congressional delegate and Indian commissioner James Duane complained that the troops on garrison duty at Fort Schuyler "might as well be in the moon." Enemy forces, whether large or small, simply skirted the bastion and struck where they pleased. Nor did seeking out and attacking such parties in the dense forests offer much prospect for success. "We may as well hunt the Eagles of the air as Indians in the woods," Duane sighed three months later. The Indians, he elaborated, possessed two superior attributes in war, their skill in staging ambushes and "the nimbleness of their Heels."[1]

After the Cherry Valley disaster, Duane, Van Schaick, and others had to accept the obvious shortcomings of maintaining so porous a defensive posture. Crown forces had too many viable invasion routes, and the rebels could not muster enough Continentals and militiamen to check these penetrations. If the rebels were going to protect their settlements, they would need to adopt a new operational approach. "I am perfectly convinced," Washington stated in the wake of Cherry Valley, "that the only way of preventing Indian ravages is to carry the war vigorously into their own country."[2]

The commander in chief had already begun to accumulate information from Philip Schuyler and others about invading the Iroquois country. Early in 1779 he issued orders to stockpile necessary supplies and transportation, and by May he had mapped out the course of invasion. Because the British had begun to shift the primary focus of their campaign efforts to the southern states, Washington could release some of his own troops for the operation.[3]

"The object of the expedition," the commanding general explained, "was to give peace and security to our frontiers by expelling the Indians and destroying their principal point of support." The primary thrust would focus on Cayuga and Seneca territory, with troops invading from north-central Pennsylvania, through the Susquehanna River Basin. The commander, Major General John Sullivan, would gather troops and supplies in the Wyoming Valley and move northward to Tioga, where his command would join a column under Brigadier General James Clinton, coming down from the Mohawk Valley. All told, Sullivan and Clinton had about 4,500 effectives, so they were to concentrate on wreaking havoc in the Iroquois homeland, not on taking out Fort Niagara. To help disperse any attempted concentration of British-Indian pressure on Sullivan's force, a supporting column under Colonel Daniel Brodhead would proceed north from Pittsburgh up the Allegheny River.[4]

As a separate but related part of the campaign, at Schuyler's insistence, Washington decided to order a surprise hammer blow against the Onondagas. Unlike the Cayugas, Senecas, and nearly all the Mohawks, the Onondagas were split in their loyalties. Just a few months earlier, a small number had joined the Oneidas and pledged support to the rebellion. Still, Schuyler believed that chastising the Onondaga Nation would cause pro-British Iroquois to seek neutrality and peace with the patriots. He could not have been more wrong.[5]

The rebel leadership knew the Oneidas would look askance at any of these plans. Any thought of a massive, destructive invasion of Iroquois territory, with the prospect of a calamitous loss of life, would anger and pain the People of the Standing Stone. Success for the rebels, therefore, depended on concealing their plans. Goose Van Schaick, whom Schuyler and General Clinton selected to direct the campaign against the Onondagas, certainly understood. Yet maintaining secrecy would only camouflage invasion preparations to a limited extent. Many Oneidas visited Fort Schuyler regularly, and their warriors continually scoured the woods for raiders and game. The intricate network of scouts, spies, and kinship ties ensured rapid communication, especially between the Oneidas and their Onondaga neighbors.[6]

If the rebels hoped to surprise the Onondagas, they had to distract their Oneida allies. Circumstances seemed to work in Van Schaick's favor. In March 1779 a rebel detachment that included fifteen Oneidas left Fort Schuyler to strike at British soldiers garrisoned along the St. Lawrence River at the Indian village of Oswegatchie. Two days out, five more Oneidas caught up with the band. They had evidence that pro-British Indians and Tories were gathering in Seneca country to attack Kanonwalohale and the Mohawk Valley. The sachems wanted them to come home. After some debate, the warriors agreed to obey their hereditary leaders, which upset Lieutenant Thomas McClellan, the commander of the attack force. He urged them to continue, then "Begd for one of them to go as A Guide, but they Sed they must and woulde Return." The mission collapsed, leaving McClellan cursing the fifteen Oneidas as "Infernil Villins."[7]

A month later, after the reports proved false, sixty-three Oneida men and women decided to visit Fort Schuyler. They apologized for not following through on the Oswegatchie raid. Spotting obvious signs of an impending campaign, they asked Van Schaick if they could participate. The colonel insisted that he "was not going on any Expedition," a claim that "almost satisfied them," recorded a lieutenant.[8]

Over the next few days, the Oneidas continued to mill about the fort. During that time, twenty more Oneida and Tuscarora warriors appeared, also eager for service. Finally, the Oneida chiefs suggested an operation of their own against the British at Oswegatchie. Van Schaick blessed the undertaking as an ideal diversion. He issued food and ammunition and assigned two officers, McClellan and Lieutenant Thomas Hardeman, and thirty-two enlisted men to join the sortie.[9]

Amid mid-April snow flurries, the column of some one hundred Oneidas, Tuscaroras, and Continentals angled northward. A week of rapid travel through the forest brought the detachment close to Oswegatchie. On April 25, the party snatched a canoe out of the St. Lawrence that contained two Onondagas. Under questioning, the pro-British Indians divulged that the garrison force at Oswegatchie consisted of about forty soldiers with four cannons under the command of Captain James Davis.[10]

Suspecting that the British were aware of their presence, McClellan and his Oneida and Tuscarora allies decided they would try to lure the king's soldiers away from the post and into an ambush. Before they could act, however, a squad under Davis stumbled onto some Oneidas and Tuscaroras about four hundred yards from the fort. During the ensuing firefight, the Indians killed two British soldiers. Davis and the others scampered back to the bastion, protected by the garrison's cannon and musket fire.

All told, the rebel-Indian raiders inflicted eight casualties on the British, six of them taken prisoner, and suffered no losses. At the insistence of the Oneidas and Tuscaroras, McClellan released the two Onondagas. The Oneidas had trophies enough: the British captives. The lieutenant granted them permission to show off these prizes at Kanonwalohale, before turning them over a few days later. More important to the Continental officers, the venture against Oswegatchie had diverted the Oneidas and helped preserve the secrecy of Van Schaick's punitive expedition.[11]

When the Oneida-Tuscarora warriors returned home, they caught the first whiff of the assault on the Onondagas. On April 19, the day after they had left for Oswegatchie, Van Schaick and his command of

558 soldiers moved out from Fort Schuyler toward the Onondaga homeland. Two days later, the advance company approached a sizable Onondaga castle. Within moments, the alarm sounded. Blasts of gunshot reverberated throughout the community. Some Onondagas dropped to the ground, dead or wounded, and others fell into rebel hands, prisoners of war. Most residents took flight into the surrounding woods.

In pursuit of his prey, Van Schaick unleashed pincer columns with instructions to capture or kill as many Indians as they could and to destroy homes and confiscate usable property. Combing a large area, the rebels plundered and torched two villages and numerous isolated houses. They incinerated the large longhouse that housed the council fire symbolic of a united league of Six Nations. All told, the rebel force killed a dozen Indians and captured one white man and thirty-three Indians—two sachems, six warriors, twelve women, and thirteen children. The soldiers slaughtered livestock and scorched large quantities of corn and beans. Van Schaick and his troops crowed over their seizure of ammunition and guns, as if these weapons were proof of Onondaga complicity with the Crown. Had they searched the same residences during peacetime, they probably would have uncovered a comparable haul. Three days after their attack, they returned triumphantly to Fort Schuyler, prisoners and plunder in hand, and without a single casualty.[12]

Just two and a half months earlier, rebel leaders had expressed hope that the shift of some Onondagas to the side of the Oneidas would initiate the return of many more Iroquois to the course of neutrality or even to supporting the rebel cause. Just three weeks before Van Schaick's attack, James Dean advised Schuyler that "the Onondagas seem determined to make peace with the United States." Patriot opinion hardened noticeably, however, when pro-British Onondagas participated in small-scale raids. So determined were Schuyler and others to avoid a repetition of more devastating incursions, such as the bloody massacre at Cherry Valley, that they ignored Dean and refused to delay the raid. Brutal punishment, they concluded, was about all that unfriendly Iroquois would understand.[13]

When Washington learned about the results of Van Schaick's expedition, he declared, "[t]his tribe has been very hostile and has met with the chastisment [*sic*] they deserve." Such evident satisfaction, however, belied the true character of the raid's consequences. Since the outbreak of the rebellion, the Onondagas had aided the patriots through their Oneida nephews and nieces. As keepers of the council fire, the Onondagas kept acting as peace brokers and conduits between the Oneidas and Tuscaroras on one side and the pro-British Iroquois on the other. Since most Oneidas were no longer welcome in Cayuga or Seneca territory, the Onondagas served as an information source regarding news from Niagara and the sentiments of pro-British Indians. Now that vital channel, from which the rebels likewise had benefited, was gone.[14]

As for Crown officials, they took perverse pleasure in Van Schaick's raid, since its wanton destructiveness actually strengthened their ties with the Indians. By obliterating the neutral fence that so many Onondagas had straddled, the attack choked off any possibility of drawing the Onondagas toward the rebel cause. They now overwhelmingly identified with the Crown. As for other pro-British Iroquois, they considered the assault an unjustified act of needless brutality, which only hardened their resolve to serve the king's side.

Perhaps worst of all, in the rebels' haste to lash out at all Onondagas for the behavior of some, they had attacked the wrong people. Most of those who suffered in the strike were neutrals or friendly toward the patriots. "It is probable that the Affair of Onondago will serve further to confirm the Indians in their Attachment to Government," loyalist John Butler explained to General Frederick Haldimand, "as the People Killed & taken at that place were chiefly in the Rebel Interest."[15]

The destruction compelled the Onondagas to flee their ancient tribal lands. One hundred and twenty-six, including thirty-four warriors, arrived on the Oneida doorstep, where the People of the Standing Stone welcomed them. Back in early April, to counteract the momentum the rebels seemed to have in luring Onondaga warriors to Oneida territory, John Butler had invited the Onondagas to move to Seneca and Cayuga lands and bring the Six Nations' belts—their archives— with them. Before the Onondagas had made up their minds, Van Schaick's force struck, which settled the issue. Most displaced Onondagas migrated to Fort Niagara, seeking British aid and protection, while feeling nothing but anger and wanting revenge against the European Americans who had plundered and murdered their kindred.[16]

Other Iroquois, too, reacted bitterly. Multiple sources reassured Daniel Claus that "the Rebels have incensed the five Nations and their Allies to Desperation by that Blow at Onondaga, and carry off twenty odd old Women & Children which latter exasperates them most." One British officer declared that the assault had stripped the Indians of their complacency. Now when they campaigned, the Onondaga disaster would keep reminding them of the consequences of defeat.[17]

After the bloody raids of the previous year, Mohawk Valley patriots had let their wrath blot out attempted diplomatic overtures in favor of military operations. A few weeks before Van Schaick's raid, the Cayugas had sent vague peace feelers to the Oneidas and Onondagas, suggesting that the two nations help initiate discussions with rebel leaders. Even as Schuyler was meeting in Albany with Oneida, Tuscarora, and Onondaga sachems, talking over how to bring the Cayugas to a negotiating council, Van Schaick's column strode triumphantly into Fort Schuyler. This offensive vanquished any possibility of successful deliberations with the Cayugas.[18]

The assault on the Onondagas upset, even angered the Oneidas. As soon as the news reached Kanonwalohale, they sent Good Peter, Skenandoah, and James Dean to Fort Schuyler to meet with Van Schaick. Good Peter asked whether the Continental column had made some horrible mistake in executing this destructive mission. Van Schaick replied that the Onondagas had broken their promise to preserve neutrality, that they "have been great murderers." He justified this charge by claiming that "we have found the scalps of our brothers at their Castle," a point he failed to mention in his various reports and letters on the campaign. The assault, he declared, was "not by mistake, but by design—I was ordered to do it—and it is done."[19]

The Oneidas felt that the rebels had exploited the Oneidas' desire to contribute to the war effort by sending them off on a risky mission as a way to distract them. The attack had destroyed the Oneidas' efforts to strengthen patriot rapport with the Onondagas and slaughtered and injured people who were mostly innocent of crimes against the revolutionaries. Two of Joseph Brant's friends, an Oneida and a Cayuga, passed through Kanonwalohale several weeks after the raid. They claimed that some Oneidas were now threatening "to act with the rest of their [Iroquois] Brethren" against the rebels, "if they do not release those they have taken Prisoners."[20]

Local patriot leaders failed to appreciate the complexity of internal divisions within the various nations of the Iroquois Confederacy. Although the Oneidas and others repeatedly advised them that sentiments varied widely, just as they did among the whites, patriots too quickly branded entire nations as friends or foes. This stereotyping benefited the Tuscaroras, whose service the rebels viewed as friendly, even though close to a majority were assisting the Crown by 1779. By comparison, rigid branding worked against the Onondagas, even though numbers of them favored neutrality. Except for those Onondagas who demonstrated good faith through actual deeds, that nation remained an enemy.[21]

For the Oneidas, British soldiers and their Tory accomplices were the true adversaries, not their Iroquois brethen. Unlike European American rebels, the Oneidas could view the other Six Nations in all their complexity and diversity. Each nation had its share of persons who did not despise the rebels and their cause. With proper cultivation, the Oneidas believed they could coax these and other Iroquois brethren to see the advantages of neutrality, if not pro-rebel activity. After the assault on the Onondagas, they knew their chances of getting other Iroquois peoples to listen to them were remote at best.

The Oneidas realized they could not undo the damage done. They did, however, try to ease the pain among the displaced Onondagas. Grasshopper convinced Van Schaick to permit Onondaga prisoners to stay at Kanonwalohale a few days, to help comfort them about their plight and console them for their losses. The Oneidas immediately began to negotiate with the Indian commissioners for the release of these Onondagas into their custody. Slow to respond, patriot leaders finally agreed in mid-August to turn over those Onondagas whose families resided with the Oneidas, as long as they pledged never to support the enemy. The commissioners would continue to hold the other Ononda-gas for prisoner exchanges with the Crown.[22]

Despite Van Schaick's punishing assault on their fellow Iroquois, most Oneidas remained aligned with the rebels. They understood that any hope of all the Six Nations returning to a neutral posture was gone, particularly after the internecine spilling of Iroquois blood at Oriskany. The Oneidas could guess as well that strongly pro-British Iroquois were already accusing them of having secretly conspired with rebel leaders to plan the deadly attack on the Onondagas. Resentment and bitterness, perhaps even acts of revenge, would greet them if they now submitted to the will of the other Six Nations. Further, the Oneidas saw no advantage in becoming Crown allies, since the British had failed for four years to break the rebel will of resistance. If anything, the most reasonable option was to maintain their current alignment with the expectation that, in the long run, the American patriots would prevail, thereby earning for the Oneida people all sorts of benefits for having stood with the revolutionaries as invaluable allies.

In May 1779, in continuing to work with the rebels, five Oneidas scouted Buck Island, located among the Thousand Islands close to where the St. Lawrence River connects with Lake Ontario. They seized three British soldiers and procured intelligence about enemy strength at the island and possible war plans for that summer.[23]

Several weeks later, the Oneidas sent Deacon Thomas and another Oneida to Kahnawake, to exchange information. Soon after their arrival, British colonel John Campbell learned about the Oneidas' presence. Assuming they were spying, he invited them to a meeting. When the Oneidas declined, Campbell sent a detachment of twenty-one soldiers to seize them. The troops entered the village at night and surrounded the council lodge. At sunrise, they ordered the two Oneidas to surrender. Both refused. A firefight erupted, and during the exchange Deacon Thomas suffered a fatal wound. The troops also shot the other Oneida, but he apparently survived.

Campbell reported the incident to Governor Haldimand, noting that "[t]he Indian who is killed I am informed was the right hand of

Parson Kirkland." Haldimand sharply rebuked Campbell for sending armed troops after the Oneidas, an act that would alienate their hosts, the Kahnawakes, and infuriate the Oneidas. Such stern words brought little consolation. A prominent Oneida had fallen, and the deed had happened at Kahnawake, where all tribal emissaries assumed they would be safe.[24]

Haldimand's reaction did not mean that he now viewed the Oneidas in a more favorable light. Earlier in the year, he had prepared an ultimatum, giving them one final opportunity to align themselves with the Crown. Faulting them for failing to adhere to their pledge of neutrality, the governor demanded an immediate response "whether you mean to persist in this your daring and insulting course," or whether "you will accept this my last Offer of reuniting and reconciling yourselves with your own Tribes the five Nations." If the Oneidas failed to break their rebel ties, "I shall soon convince you that I have such a Number of Indian Allies to let loose upon you, as will instantly convince you of your Folly when too late, as I have hardly been able to restrain them from falling upon you for some time past."[25]

Haldimand called on a party of Canadian Indians to carry his decree to central New York, but not to Kanonwalohale. The governor sent word to have the Oneidas meet with his native representatives in Cayuga territory, where these Indians were to convey the governor's seriousness. Oneida leaders, however, fearing the British had some sort of trick in mind, declined to send out a delegation. Instead, they dispatched two messengers but no sachems to receive the printed message. The People of the Standing Stone would neither accept the belts nor treat with these Canadian Indians, whom they viewed as British pawns and unrepresentative of Canada's Seven Nations.[26]

Although in public the Oneidas handled the delicate matter with aplomb, in private Haldimand's threat shook them. The governor of Quebec Province, an experienced military leader, had vowed to unleash Iroquois and Canadian warriors against them. Since St. Leger's campaign, the Oneidas had lived in daily fear of an assault on their homeland. They recognized that they had many British, Tory, and native enemies who might tap into the severity of Haldimand's threat as an excuse to crush them.[27]

In the wake of these events, a small but steady number of reports started dribbling into Niagara from the Oneidas and Tuscaroras, each voicing doubts about the patriot cause. The Oneidas talked more to visiting Indians regarding what they had learned about rebel plans that summer. When a Mohawk chief passed through an Oneida village, people "were very friendly to him, said they did not mean to quarrel with the Indians, & that it was merely for their own safety that they acted in favor of the Rebels." After Haldimand's threats, some Oneidas notified the Senecas that "they would come away with their Families and live among them, and act in conjunction with them for the future." John Butler doubted the seriousness of these persons and assumed they were simply buying time so they could better protect themselves. Then, two weeks later, forty Tuscarora warriors plus their families secretly expressed a desire to join the Senecas. They planned a fake fishing trip to the head of Oneida Lake "to disguise their real design from the Rebels," which was to migrate to the Seneca homeland.[28]

More and more, concern about a retaliatory strike gnawed at the People of the Standing Stone. To prevent what seemed like the inevitable, several Oneida and Tuscarora chiefs visited Colonel Van Schaick at Fort Schuyler. Because of their attachment to the American Whigs, their nations had become "an Object of resentment" to other Iroquois people, and they were sure, especially in the wake of Haldimand's pronouncement, that the Senecas would attempt to destroy their villages. Events had convinced these chiefs that only force of arms would settle the dispute, and they promised to join the rumored campaign against their western brethren.[29]

Yet when Clinton's Brigade launched its journey in mid-June 1779 to link up with Sullivan's force at Tioga, the Oneidas hesitated. At Lake Otsego, where Clinton and his troops remained for more than a month, James Dean arrived with thirty-five warriors headed by "the famous *Honyary*." The Oneidas apologized for not having more warriors with them. A rumored assault from Canada compelled their leaders to hold back the bulk of their fighters. As usual, the Oneidas were also reluctant to participate in a campaign to destroy fellow Iroquois. They shared a heritage, a culture, and a confederacy with the Senecas. Over the centuries, they had built powerful bonds, and the Oneidas simply could not bring themselves to strike first.[30]

In mid-July, a large force of Canadian Indians did assault Fort Schuyler, seizing twenty-one prisoners and taking several scalps. After the fray, some Oneidas came out of the fort under a flag of truce and parlayed with their native foes. They learned that Crown officials had placed enormous pressure on these Indians to attack the Oneidas, but they had resisted this demand.[31]

The news had a chilling effect on the Oneida Nation. By the time Clinton moved out for Tioga, only two Oneidas remained, "& these are of the lower class," complained the general. The rest returned to Kanonwalohale, to defend the castle and determine how "to revenge the death of a chief who was lately massacred by the British," specifically Deacon Thomas.[32]

On August 25, three more Oneida warriors joined Sullivan and Clinton at Tioga. One officer described them as "men of integrity and sobriety." Two of them were Lieutenant Han Yost Thahoswagwat and an active young warrior named Bluebeck.[33]

The day after the Oneidas arrived, Sullivan and his 4,500 effectives began their advance into Iroquoia. On August 29, the Continental command ran into organized opposition. About 500 Indians under Joseph Brant's command, along with a handful of British regulars and about 180 Tory rangers led by John Butler, had fortified a position at the native village of Newtown (modern-day Elmira, New York). With vastly superior numbers, Sullivan's force drove them back by an attack in front and on the flank. The British-Indian combatants, shaken by the rebels' strength, kept their distance from Sullivan's column for the rest of the campaign, focusing instead on evacuating inhabitants while harassing their adversary around the edges. They could do little else in the wake of the rebel juggernaut, which torched villages and homes and destroyed fields, orchards, and food stockpiles everywhere the troops went.[34]

Even with the easy triumph at Newtown, Sullivan knew that he needed knowledgeable guides as his force moved deeper into western Iroquoia. He sent Bluebeck back to the Oneidas with a scolding

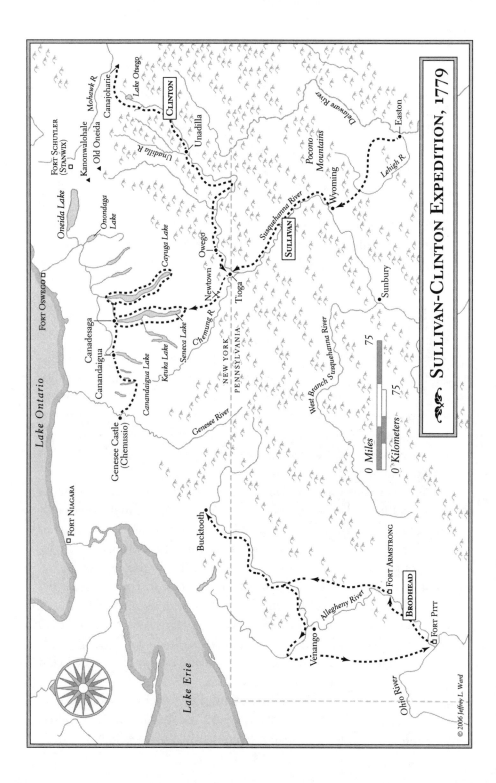

SULLIVAN-CLINTON EXPEDITION, 1779

Lake Ontario

Lake Erie

Fort Niagara

Fort Oswego

Oneida Lake

Fort Schuyler (Stanwix)

Kanonwalohale
Old Oneida

Onondaga Lake

Mohawk R.

Canajoharie

CLINTON

Lake Otsego

Unadilla R.

Unadilla

Delaware River

Easton

Pocono Mountains

Lehigh R.

Wyoming

SULLIVAN

Susquehanna River

Cayuga Lake

Seneca Lake

Owego

Newtown

Chemung R.

Tioga

Sunbury

NEW YORK

PENNSYLVANIA

Canadesaga

Canandaigua

Canandaigua Lake

Keuka Lake

Genesee Castle (Chenussio)

Genesee River

West Branch Susquehanna River

75

75

0 Miles

0 Kilometers

Bucktooth

Fort Armstrong

BRODHEAD

Allegheny River

Venango

Fort Pitt

Ohio River

© 2006 Jeffrey L. Ward

message. The general reminded them of their vow to assist the expedition: "It is with no small degree of surprise that I find, though I have far advanced into the enemy's country, that only four of your warriors have joined me, and they totally unacquainted with every part of the country through which I have yet passed," Sullivan wrote. He implored the Oneidas to send forward warriors with knowledge of the region. Little interested in their worries about defending their own homeland, Sullivan used harsh words: "Unless this is complied with I shall be compelled to think that the chiefs of your warriors, if not really unfriendly to us, are very inattentive to their own interest and safety, as well as indifferent with respect to the interest of the United States."[35]

While Bluebeck made his way across the wilderness toward Kanonwalohale, the other four Oneidas continued with the rebel force as guides, scouts, messengers, and translators during prisoner interrogations. On September 12, Sullivan ordered Lieutenant Thomas Boyd to lead a small scouting party toward the town of Chenussio, the principal Seneca castle and capital located on the Genesee River. Sullivan assumed Boyd would take along two or three soldiers, a guide, and Han Yost Thahoswagwat.[36]

An experienced warrior, Han Yost was not that familiar with the region but thoroughly understood Indian practices and methods of warfare. Since the early days of the rebellion, he had scouted in his brother Han Yerry's "company." After distinguishing himself in the fighting around Fort Schuyler in 1777, he most likely participated in the Saratoga campaign and traveled with his brother to Pennsylvania. Because of his war record, the Oneida chief warriors nominated him for a lieutenancy. In 1779, Han Yost moved out from under his brother's shadow, electing to join Sullivan's campaign. Colonel Philip Van Cortlandt, a regimental commander on the expedition, fondly recalled Han Yost as "my favorite Indian."[37]

Confused about Sullivan's intentions and insecure about entering the woods with such a small detachment, Boyd took twenty-five soldiers with him, including two Indians, a number that seemed to trap him in a manpower no-man's-land: too large to perform the kind of concealed scouting Sullivan sought and not large enough to protect itself against nearby Indians and Tories. The party slithered its way to the castle, now located in a different place from where the rebels anticipated. Evidence of a hasty removal indicated that the inhabitants had recently abandoned Chenussio. Boyd sent back four soldiers to notify Sullivan, while he and the rest of his company hid near the village. Not long afterward, four Indians rode by them. Unwisely, Boyd's party fired on them, killing one and wounding another. By discharging their weapons and permitting three mounted Iroquois to escape, they exposed their presence and position.[38]

At this critical juncture, Boyd disregarded the advice of his more experienced fighter, Han Yost. The Oneida urged him to retreat rapidly to the main body, but Boyd adopted a leisurely pace. Han Yost found fresh footprints, indicating the presence of a large war party nearby; Boyd dismissed this evidence as proof of a retreating enemy. After a few more miles, Boyd halted and sent ahead a couple of messengers to alert Sullivan of his location. The pair soon encountered a few Indians and reported back to Boyd. Han Yost warned him about a trap, but Boyd refused to listen and ordered an attack. Moments later, he realized that Han Yost was right. They had stumbled into an ambush from which they could not extricate themselves.[39]

John Butler had conceived and executed a classic snare, and Boyd had jumped at the bait. Only a handful of the rebel scouting party escaped. Fourteen fell on the spot, most of them shot from close range and then scalped. Among those killed at the ambush site was Lieutenant Han Yost Thahoswagwat. In vengeance over his participation in the expedition against the Six Nations, the Indians removed his scalp and dismembered his body. Boyd and a sergeant were taken alive. Hauled back to Chenussio, both suffered horrible torture before being dispatched. His body completely mutilated, Boyd also had his head decapitated and skinned, and his eyes bored out.[40]

After discovering the corpses and solemnly burying the remains, Sullivan's troops scoured the local area, gathered all the foodstuffs they needed and burned the remaining crops, using them as fuel to torch every structure in Chenussio. They had achieved their deepest penetration into Iroquois country. On September 15, Sullivan ordered his army to pivot and commence the return march home.[41]

Three days later, Bluebeck appeared with an Oneida chief, Teheaniyoghtiwat, and two other warriors. He had traveled all the way to Kanonwalohale, the weary Oneida reported, and delivered Sullivan's message. "The warriors expressed great joy, both on account of your success and the opportunity now given them to testify their friendship to the American cause," he told Sullivan. Seventy Oneidas had set out with him to reach the rebel force, with thirty more preparing to leave the next day. Along the way, they had met a pro-rebel Kahnawake who came from the army and informed them that Sullivan and Clinton no longer needed their services unless they could act as knowledgeable guides. Except for Bluebeck and his three companions, they all then returned to Kanonwalohale.[42]

In times past, Oneida warriors would have continued the journey. Their spirit of adventure and desire for opportunities to engage in combat would have spurred them forward. Their hearts, however, were not in the work of joining an expeditionary force charged with devastating other peoples of the Six Nations. Sullivan's words had shamed them into action; leaders felt pressured to let the warriors go, even if against their better judgment. As the warriors wound their way through forests and across rivers that generations of Iroquois had walked and ancestral spirits haunted, they lost their ardor. When the warriors met the Kahnawake that September day, they simply accepted his words, without questioning him or his information. He was offering them a way out of a delicate predicament, and they gladly abandoned the enterprise.

Teheaniyoghtiwat and two others continued on with Bluebeck to deliver a message from the Oneida chief warriors, based on what the Kahnawake had told them about Sullivan electing to show clemency toward the Cayugas. "We are glad you manifest such a disposition, and are willing to make peace with them," Teheaniyoghtiwat stated to the patriot general. The Oneidas knew that a portion of the Cayugas advocated neutrality, and they promised to round them up and escort them to their homeland. "We therefore request that you would not for the present destroy their cornfields," the chief urged, "as we cannot furnish them with provisions should we be able to find them and bring them to our town."[43]

After discussing this proposal with his senior officers, Sullivan responded by thanking the Oneidas for their loyalty to the rebellion, even though a "groundless report" had turned their warriors back. He also praised Bluebeck, "who bore my messages to the Oneidas, & who on several occasions has proved himself the faithful friend & brave warrior." Then he rejected the request that his troops preserve Cayuga villages and fields. His orders from Congress and Washington directed him "totally to extirpate all the unfriendly nations of the Indians, to subdue their Country, to destroy their Crops, and force them to seek habitations where they would be less troublesome to us & their allies." The Cayugas were well known as inveterate enemies. "But when they found that our army had proved victorious," he declared, and "that the enemy were flying like armed women before us, & that we were spreading desolation thro' their whole Country, then & not till then did those Cayugas begin to express their friendship for us and perhaps solicit the interest of the Oneidas to save their Country." He thus wondered "if their friendship was sincere, why did not they, like the Oneidas, declare it in season."[44]

Sullivan was sure the Oneidas felt obligated to help stave off disaster for their Cayuga brothers and sisters. Since he had upbraided the People of the Standing Stone in his previous message, this time he modified his tone and expressed only dismay that his Oneida allies were being "deceived" by professions of neutrality from the Cayugas. He promised, though, that those Cayugas who acted in a "friendly" manner would receive the protection of Congress.[45]

Sullivan broke off two sizable detachments to dole out punishment to the Cayugas. Colonel Henry Dearborn guided a force along the western bank of Cayuga Lake, and Lieutenant Colonel William Butler, who had directed the destruction of Oquaga the previous year, led a column along the eastern course. As instructed, they burned villages and homes, consumed or torched food in storage, trampled fields, and girdled the trunks of fruit trees. They met no resistance; all the Cayuga inhabitants had fled.[46]

First Dearborn and then Butler reunited with the main force; and two days later, on September 30, the combined column reached Tioga. Over the month-long campaign, Sullivan estimated that his command destroyed some forty-one villages, innumerable scattered dwellings, 160,000 bushels of corn, and vast quantities of vegetables and fruit trees. He boasted in his comments to Congress, "we have not left a single settlement or field of Corn in the Country of the Five Nations."[47]

On October 1, Sullivan spoke to those few Oneidas who were present with his force. Thanking them for their assistance, he encouraged them to welcome and aid those Cayugas who sought shelter with their Oneida brothers and sisters. Sullivan also justified his decision to devastate the Cayuga homeland. In longhouses, his soldiers had found fresh scalps, he claimed, seeming proof that these Indians were enemies of the rebellion and the Oneidas.[48]

Teheaniyoghtiwat replied by admitting that Sullivan's "suspicions" about the Cayugas were "not without foundation." The Oneida chief applauded the policy of letting Cayuga refugees relocate in Oneida territory. He was sure the Oneida people, although suffering many shortages, would find some way to provide for their junior moiety brothers. However, Teheaniyoghtiwat also believed that the destruction of Cayuga homes and fields would cause these Iroquois brethren to become even more dependent on the British, and stronger Crown allies.[49]

Teheaniyoghtiwat's observations were accurate. Certainly Sullivan's expeditionary force produced panic among the Senecas and Cayugas as well as among other Iroquois living among them, but the raids did not break their will. Even before the campaign ended, John Butler wrote to Haldimand: "Notwithstanding the losses the Indians have suffered by the destruction of their Corn and Villages I am happy to acquaint your Excellency that they seem still unshaken in their attachment to His Majesty's Cause." In time, as the initial shock wore off, morale improved as the British provided for the five thousand Iroquois refugees who flocked to Niagara with little more than the clothes they were wearing and a few of life's necessities. Just as Butler thought would happen, once the warriors were sure older persons, women, and children had their basic needs met, they would "take revenge of the Enemy."[50]

From their perspective, the enemy now clearly included the Oneidas. Lieutenant Colonel Mason Bolton, the British commander at Fort Niagara, posited to Haldimand that if Sir John Johnson led an attack on them, the Six Nations "would readily join him." A few days later, Haldimand wrote to Guy Johnson, who had recently returned to Niagara, that "a stroke against the Onidas [sic] should be undertaken this winter." Said the governor, "[t]he Mohawks, and many of the Senecas are well disposed to bring them to their Senses, and they have had long Experience that it cannot be accomplished by Persuasion."[51]

Although both Guy Johnson and his brother-in-law, Sir John, wanted to deliver a devastating blow, they agreed that most Iroquois warriors would not willingly attack their Oneida brethren. Guy Johnson informed Haldimand that many of the Six Nations, "even of those who Condemned the Oneidas," were unenthusiastic about wiping out Kanonwalohale, and the Canadian Indians felt similarly. On the other hand, he had "good hopes that large party's may be made during the Winter, composed solely of those who are determined Enemys to the Oneidas, by which business may be effected." Hoping to generate participation for an assault on Kanonwalohale, Haldimand directed his subordinates to blame the Oneidas for the killing of the Onondagas and the destruction of their settlements.[52]

In November 1779 a raiding party captured and brought back to Niagara three rebel Indians—two Oneidas and a Tuscarora. Haldimand ordered them "kept in secure confinement as Hostages for the Conduct of their Nation—and to answer with their Lives for any that may be taken of the Five Nations by their means." By such actions, Crown officials began to convince more and more Iroquois warriors that the Oneidas were much worse than errant kinfolk; rather, they were treacherous enemies.[53]

That fall and winter, the Oneidas could almost hear the animus building to a crescendo against them at Niagara. Even though they had mostly stayed away from Sullivan's campaign, in the eyes of other Iroquois the Oneidas had to assume some responsibility for the rebels' destructive campaign. After all, they reasoned, the Oneidas had not remained in political alignment with their Iroquois brothers and sisters and, as a result, had torn apart a confederacy that had held fast against external threats for hundreds of years.

Attuned to the sentiments of their fellow Iroquois, the Oneidas braced themselves for retaliation. They realized they could not fend off a large-scale strike. Certainly their little fort at Kanonwalohale could only offer them minimal protection. The Oneidas thus took a dramatic step in February 1780. They asked the rebel Indian commissioners to "lend us a piece of land for a year or two where we may plant & live till we can return in safety to our own Country." The decision to evacuate their homeland did not come easily because they did not want to abandon their ancestral spirits. However, having reckoned with the obliteration of Oriska and Oquaga, besides numerous other Iroquois settlements, they concluded that protection for the living superseded all other considerations. With no truce in sight, Grasshopper, as the nation's spokesperson, declared that the Oneidas "shall not dare," at least until peace returned, to continue "to plant in our own Country."[54]

The commissioners expressed concern but pointed out that "such alarms must be expected in time of war." They were positive that pro-British Iroquois and others the Oneidas "feared had smarted too much from the Blow our brave Army had just given them, to venture into the Country." Still, the commissioners promised that "whenever you find it necessary to remove nearer to us we shall provide you with Land to plant and live upon till you can return to your own Castle without Danger." The Oneidas welcomed this commitment from the rebel leaders.[55]

A couple of months earlier, two neutral Mohawk Indians, Little Abraham and Johannes Crine, living at the Lower Castle, had suggested to Philip Schuyler that they be permitted to journey to Fort Niagara to propose a truce. Schuyler doubted whether such an effort would have positive results, but after thinking over the matter, he saw no reason why these two trusted Mohawk leaders should not try.[56]

Independent of the Mohawk proposal, Schuyler had determined to send two Oneidas with a message to Niagara. He and Crown officials had recently communicated about exchanging prisoners. A timely letter from Guy Johnson offered the rebel general a chance to broaden the peace delegation by having two eminent Oneidas travel along with the Mohawks. The Oneidas would deliver the reply to Johnson regarding the exchange of captives.[57]

Schuyler communicated with the Oneidas about the purpose of the mission. In turn, they met in council and chose Grasshopper and Good Peter to make the lengthy winter trek to Seneca country. Grasshopper asked to have another go in his stead, stating that as the ranking sachem he must care for his people at home. He recommended Skenandoah as his replacement, and the elderly chief warrior assented.[58]

Good Peter acquiesced grudgingly. "He did not want to be required to go to his Enemies," he indicated. "It was a hard request," Good Peter stated, but he wanted to "do everything for the good of his Country & therefore he agreed to go & do his best." The septuagenarian Skenandoah had similar feelings, and he did not like the prospect of traveling such a long way at the height of winter, but he would not try to evade an assignment that might help save his people.

As the council continued, various Oneida constituencies offered advice to the messengers. Grasshopper, on behalf of the sachems, urged them to "remind the Onemy [Enemy] Indians how great they were while they held fast of the Covenant Chain that they coud then light their Council fire in any part of the Continent." Times had changed. "Now," he continued, "they had lost their Country by Joining the King and were suffering the greatest hardships." Grasshopper wanted the messengers to urge their fellow Iroquois to "act wisely," make peace, and then return to their homelands "for the sake of their wives & children" and for generations to come.

The warriors asked Good Peter and Skenandoah to direct their comments to the Iroquois fighters who had joined the enemy. They were particularly "distressed" that their fellow Six Nations brethren "would finally be destroyed." The British had misled them about the rebels. "The war had already lasted five years & they saw what the Americans were able to do." The conflict was really "the Kings fault." True, "the King was very Rich" and had lavished them with gifts to secure their services, but it was "high time" to disengage, not only "for the sake of their wives & children" but before they lost everything of value in their lives.

The matrons then presented advice regarding the critical matter of long-term Iroquois survival. "They the Women brought forth the Men," a clan matron stated. So much warfare had stripped the Iroquois of too many of their finest males. Only healthy, stable family lineages in peacetime would offer the Six Nations the circumstances they needed to recoup these tragic population losses. Warriors fighting in "the Interest of the Enemy" thus should declare their neutrality and reoccupy their territory so that "they woud be able to get more men."

The two Oneidas listened to all these comments and to summary thoughts from Grasshopper, who reiterated that their fellow Iroquois brethren should put down the war hatchet and return to their lands to end their own suffering. Further, if any Iroquois delegation wished to travel to Albany and negotiate a return to neutrality, he promised that the Oneidas would guarantee their safety.[59]

In company with Little Abraham and Johannes Crine, Good Peter and Skenandoah trudged through thick forests and across icy streams. Winter winds, reinforced by frozen moisture, howled at them while arctic-like temperatures chilled them to the marrow. After two weeks of agonizing travel, the four emissaries approached Fort Niagara. On February 12, 1780, just a few miles away, they bumped into Joseph Brant and a war party. Brant delayed them for a day until military escorts could accompany them to Niagara.

At the fort, the Oneidas and Mohawks spoke frankly about their intentions, even in the presence of Guy Johnson. They also delivered Schuyler's letter. Johnson, in response, belittled them about their pro-rebel conduct while contending that the Iroquois there had no interest in their words. He even claimed that the guard had escorted them "for Fear they should feel the Effects of that resentment which their Behavior must have excited in the Indians now at this place." Johnson consulted with Aaron Hill, a Mohawk chief, and they agreed to deny the emissaries free access to the other Indians, since their statements were likely to contain nothing of merit.[60]

The next day, Guy Johnson spoke with the Seneca Old Smoke, who said he would talk to the other chiefs and obtain their sentiments. Meanwhile, they interrogated the four Indians separately. Skenandoah endured the first grilling, with Old Smoke rebuking him for not obeying the will of the other Iroquois and failing to protect the eastern door. The others followed, with neither side offering to compromise its thinking.[61]

Another two days passed before Johnson allowed the four emissaries to speak before a dozen Crown and Indian leaders. After the usual formalities, Little Abraham told the gathering that the Iroquois had no business taking part in the white man's war. Had they behaved prudently and remained neutral, as the rebels had originally requested, they would still be occupying their homelands. He urged them to relinquish their weapons and proclaim their neutrality, at which point they could live in peace. In concluding, Little Abraham made an unfortunate misstatement when he said that the Oneidas and Lower Castle Mohawks had been consistently neutral.

Good Peter rose and applauded Little Abraham's words. "The Great Spirit," he suggested, "loves People who will attend to good Advice." The pro-British Iroquois had acted too much in the extreme and, as a result, had put their future at risk. To survive, let alone prosper again, they had to reclaim their status as peaceful neutrals. Handing over a belt to make a record of his oration, Good Peter then shared the concerns of the Oneida matrons, who "wanted them to comply with the offer now made them."

Little Abraham finished the presentation by indicating that they had received assurances of generous treatment from the Continental Congress and the Indian commissioners. Rebel officials were waiting for their visits to Albany so that peace terms could be framed, and they had promised not to detain or arrest any chiefs who participated in these negotiations.

Once the Mohawk sachem sat down, Guy Johnson became all bluster. He would never accept belts from "People of their Character" and threw the belts back at the four emissaries. In a more civilized manner, Old Smoke announced that the Oneida and Mohawk emissaries would have an answer once the pro-British Iroquois had considered the speeches. Revealing his own feelings, the Seneca chief called for alcohol and offered a toast to the good health of all those in attendance except the four diplomats.

The next day, having conferred among themselves and with Guy Johnson and John Butler, the pro-British Iroquois offered their first reply via Old Smoke. He spoke of the "Insolence in such an inconsiderable People as you are to tell us what we are to do." He dismissed their thoughts as a "great presumption in you to pretend to dictate to the Six Nations." Mohawk chief Aaron Hill then orated at length for the "Mohawks, Part of the Oneydas, the Onandagoes, Senecas, Cayougas, Tuskaroras, Nanticokes, Shawanese & Delawares." In accord with Old Smoke, he said that "we will take no Notice of your Message." Aaron insisted that the Oneidas were the real culprits in violating sacred obligations, since harmonious ties between all the Six Nations and the king extended back "for many Ages."

The two Oneidas and two Mohawks had visited Niagara, Aaron declared, only to spread falsehoods. "You say you come for the Sake of Peace & Quietness, and for the Good of the Six Nations but at the same Time bring a false Heart & a flattering Tongue to breed confusion amongst us." Referencing Little Abraham's speech, he accused the Oneidas of lying when they claimed to be neutral. "Have you not taken Prisoners and Scalps at Oswegatchie?" he asked sarcastically. "Did you not fight against us at Fort Stanwix? Did you not go out to War against the Kings People at Saratoga, the Highlands and other Places? And did not some of you even join the Rebels who invaded our Country and assist them to destroy us?" Aaron declared those whom the four emissaries represented to be a "Deceitful Set" whose real purpose was not to unite the Six Nations but to provoke more division.[62]

With Aaron's pronouncements, the Iroquois ended the meeting, but not before again tossing belts back at the Oneida and Mohawk emissaries. Then Aaron informed Good Peter, Skenandoah, Little Abraham, and Johannes Crine that they could not return home. How long they would have to remain at Niagara, the Mohawk chief would not say, should "we let you leave at all." Guards then hauled them away and cast them into the fort's dungeon. The four emissaries had failed to open a pathway toward peace and had become Crown hostages, portending much additional turmoil and bloodshed in the days ahead.[63]

12

VENGEANCE AND VICTORY

Little Abraham had a widespread reputation as a mesmerizing orator, but during the remaining winter months of 1780, the Indians in the vicinity of Fort Niagara would not let him speak. Along with Good Peter, Skenandoah, and Johannes Crine, he languished in a prison cell area commonly called "the black hole." Beneath the south redoubt in the cellar at Fort Niagara were four-foot-square compartments. With stone walls all around, all light disappeared when guards closed the ceiling doors. Lieutenant Colonel Mason Bolton, the commander at Fort Niagara, opposed flogging, instead using these black holes to punish unruly soldiers, confining them for days on end to break them.

British officials lowered the Oneida and Mohawk emissaries into the damp, cold darkness, and kept them there for about 150 days. The four elderly Iroquois suffered horribly. In later life, Good Peter rarely mentioned the experience, except to say that "[t]he Distresses of a Prison are great" and that "our Confinement was long and Rigorous." Skenandoah was in his mid-seventies, and the harsh elements wreaked havoc on his well-worn joints and bones. Crine, too, emerged with damaged health but survived the torture. As for Little Abraham—the Mohawk sachem who defied his kinspeople by holding fast to the prospect of peace—he never walked away. The black hole claimed his life.[1]

At Kanonwalohale, meanwhile, the residents waited eagerly for reports from the four delegates, even as weeks turned into months. By early April, they began to worry that the Crown was holding the emissaries against their will. Fearing the worst, the Oneida leaders could only conclude that a British-Indian force would soon attack Kanonwalohale. They started planning to remove their families to a more secure location.[2]

Earlier in the war, the prospect of temporarily leaving the Oneida homeland had been met with stiff opposition. By the spring of 1780, the war had become especially ugly. Both sides had burned villages, slaughtered civilians, and destroyed crops and farm animals. So much deliberate brutality compelled the Oneidas to reconsider moving to a less vulnerable locale. The Cayugas, Onondagas, and nearly all the Mohawks had done so. For pro-rebel Oneidas, relocation, at least temporarily, seemed like the most sensible action.

Pro-British Iroquois, although initially jolted by Sullivan's expedition, soon were preparing to resume their attacks along the frontier. Word filtered back to rebel leaders that the Indians at Niagara "boast of their intended revenge as soon as the Lakes and Rivers are clear of Ice." In late March 1780, Governor George Clinton told New York's delegates in Congress that Sullivan's campaign was already producing even more intense warfare, certainly not neutrality or peace. Crown officials, by comparison, rejoiced that not only were the renewed raids inflicting mayhem and death on the rebels but that pro-British Indian losses were inspiring an even more frenzied desire to seek revenge.[3]

Revenge was not the only motivation. In failing to resist Sullivan's expeditionary force, Iroquois warriors had suffered a devastating psychological blow. They felt as though they had failed in their primary function, to protect their homeland and their families and friends from dangerous enemies. The warriors had to reestablish their lost masculinity and rebuild their self-image as fearsome fighters. In 1780 they could demonstrate their martial prowess anew by demolishing additional European American settlements and maiming, torturing, and slaying the inhabitants. At the same time, the thought of wiping out Kanonwalohale and inflicting on the Oneidas the kind of pain and humiliation the Iroquois warriors had so recently endured would help ease their deeply wounded pride.

Oneida warriors, meanwhile, continued their scouting forays in service for the rebels. When Sir John Johnson launched a raid that spring, Oneida trackers quickly gained intelligence about his force's strength and also helped deprive him of valuable support. Johnson wanted to involve a large number of Mississaugas, but they so feared the speed and stealth of Oneida warriors that they traveled too lightly and sustained frostbite injuries, rendering them unfit to join Johnson's column.[4]

Since early in the war, the Oneidas had corralled small groups of loyalists and Continental Army deserters for the rebels. On May 22, 1780, thirty-one men stationed at Fort Schuyler fled the fort, complaining of harsh living conditions. Rather than order his own depleted garrison to retrieve them, Colonel Goose Van Schaick asked his Oneida allies to track them down. With a Continental lieutenant in command, forty Oneidas went after the runaways under orders to bring back as many of the deserters as possible and, if need be, to pursue them until they surrendered or died. A few days later, at the Grand River, the Oneidas caught up with the deserters. Half had slipped across the waterway on a raft while the remainder waited their turn. The lieutenant offered the latter group a chance to surrender, but they refused. When the Oneidas closed in to gain a better position on these sixteen men, one soldier fired at them. The Oneidas responded with their own barrage. Once the smoke cleared, thirteen soldiers lay dead, and three had fallen into Oneida hands. Those already across the river scattered and apparently got away.[5]

The vigilance of the Oneida warriors suggested unity of purpose but actually camouflaged a serious underlying problem—the bonds among them had started to unravel. So many brutal wartime incidents, such as the destruction of the Onondagas and Sullivan's expedition against the Cayugas and Senecas, had begun to divide the People of the Standing Stone. Then they had to face the prospect of retaliatory strikes from Crown and Tory forces and their own Iroquois brethren without any significant commitment of protection from the European American patriots.

Going back to the spring of 1779, Indians living on Oneida land, perceiving virtually no benefits from supporting the rebels, started whispering about switching over to Niagara. As pressure mounted that winter and spring, private conversations blossomed into action. In February 1780 a small group of Onondagas packed up and moved to the British fort. Then, in mid-June, the entire village of Kanaghsaraga, made up of Tuscaroras and Onondagas, sought shelter at Niagara, which in turn convinced any remaining Onondagas and even some Oneidas to migrate to the British stronghold. Except for a handful of Tuscaroras and about a half dozen Kahnawakes, the Oneidas found themselves completely isolated from their Iroquois brethren.[6]

According to British count, 262 Onondagas and Tuscaroras migrated to Niagara. Thirty-two Oneidas joined them. Led by the sachem White Skin, the Oneidas included the immediate kin of Good Peter and Skenandoah. These families went to Niagara to be near their loved ones. White Skin, once a close friend and highly visible rebel advocate, had changed his thinking. At the war's outset, he had acted as a key spokesperson for the Oneidas. With the elevation of Grasshopper as head counselor, White Skin shared the center stage. Throughout 1777 he and Grasshopper stood on the same platforms and spoke as one. Early in 1778, when patriot leaders sought warriors for Washington's army at Valley Forge and Grasshopper was ill and Good Peter was unavailable, White Skin and Deacon Thomas filled their shoes. Since then, White Skin had become less visible, most likely because he now questioned the wisdom of aligning against the Six Nations. His resettlement at Niagara was a clear expression of his doubts.[7]

On July 3, 1780, these former neutrals and rebel allies assembled at Niagara before Guy Johnson. White Skin performed the condolence ritual and asked Johnson to "pity, & exuse [sic] them for having been so ignorant and foolish as to be persuaded & misguided by a Contemptible People, who by their Artifice had induced them to swerve from their Engagements both to him and the King." Johnson replied by rebuking White Skin, once so good a friend of Sir William Johnson. The superintendent then faulted the rest of those present for their "weakness and folly." To regain the king's good graces, he would require much salutary conduct from them. "Words will do no longer," he concluded, " 'tis actions must prove your sincerity." In reply, White

Skin compared Johnson's words to "a Light that has suddenly broke out of the ground" and promised absolute loyalty from all of them.[8]

By fleeing to the British, White Skin and his companions had reunited themselves with their Iroquois brethren more generally. The Oneidas remaining at Kanonwalohale enjoyed no such comfort. The evacuation of the Tuscarora-Onondaga village and the departure of several important Oneida kin threw the castle into turmoil. Continued reports that Crown forces intended to subjugate all those who failed to seek refuge at Niagara further aggravated the pro-rebel Indians' demoralized feelings.[9]

Even with their fort, the Oneidas knew they could not defend Kanonwalohale against a large, vengeful military force. The works could offer only temporary protection, nothing more. With the castle stretching along the old trail from the Mohawk Valley to Onondaga, everything else—homes, huts, barns, the church, fields, and livestock—lay completely exposed.[10]

Desperate for assistance, Grasshopper and three others drafted a declaration for the new Fort Schuyler commander, Colonel Cornelius Van Dyck, describing what was taking place. "This strange & sudden movement has alarmed us very much," they stated. "We are in great Consternation," and "we scarcely know who to trust among us in this Critical situation." The women "are much terrified" and wanted to abandon the village with the children. Many warriors concurred, knowing "[w]e are not able to defend ourselves . . . against the force we are sure will come against us." Once the Oneidas had settled their families in a safer location, they would then return to Fort Schuyler and perform military service in exchange for Van Dyck's help.[11]

Before Van Dyck could act, however, the crisis reached a decisive point. A Crown raiding force appeared in the area, consisting of some 110 Senecas and Mohawks and 70 Tory rangers under Captain John McDonnell and the Mohawk chief David. When they learned that so many Onondagas and Tuscaroras were migrating westward to Niagara, Chief David wanted to attack and destroy Kanonwalohale and force its inhabitants to join the migration to Niagara or flee eastward and become rebel dependents. In either case, British raiders would not have to worry about Oneida scouts and would gain an unobstructed pathway for unleashing yet more bloody raids on European American settlers throughout the Mohawk Valley.[12]

On June 24, 1780, a Tory-Iroquois war party appeared at Old Oneida, demanding a council. Convoluted discussions ensued, during which the pro-British Iroquois reminded the Oneidas of the latter's vulnerable situation and urged them to go to Niagara and rejoin the rest of the Six Nations. In reply, the Oneidas demanded information about Good Peter and Skenandoah and insisted on their release.

The next day, the Seneca chief Spruce Carrier appeared with an additional seventy warriors. A forceful speaker, he accused the Oneidas of scouting too diligently in their own territory and reporting on passers-by to Continental officers at Fort Schuyler. He demanded an end to this practice. Replying with equal vehemence, the Oneida sachems blasted back that these woods belonged to them. They had every right to range in them as they thought fit. To survive, the People of the Standing Stone had to hunt and fish for subsistence. For anyone to conclude that all Oneida males who moved about in their own territory were actually tracking Crown soldiers and warriors was ridiculous.

McDonnell gained the impression that once the Crown returned Good Peter and Skenandoah to them, the Oneidas would march en masse to Niagara and apologize for their misconduct. The Oneidas denied this claim, saying they had not promised to give a firm answer until they had consulted with their two missing leaders. The Oneidas were stalling for time by making vague statements that caused McDonnell to misunderstand their words. The British officer suffered from "the Fever and Ague these Ten days past, to an immoderate degree," which also affected his recollections. Regardless, Spruce Carrier promised to return with Good Peter, Skenandoah, and a large combat force in three weeks.[13]

As these discussions took place, the Oneidas collected valuable information away from the council fire. One warrior boasted to Grasshopper that "the Oneidas should not taste of their Cornfields this year unless they complied with their proposals." Two other warriors indicated that the British would not release Good Peter and Skenandoah until the Oneida Nation abandoned the rebel cause. They also bragged that a portion of their force intended to besiege Fort Schuyler.[14]

The Tory-Iroquois war party did not leave for Niagara empty-handed. Eleven warriors, eight of them Oneidas, joined them. The sachems feared the raiding force might slip southeastward and strike at European American settlements. Wanting to avoid any suspicion of Oneida complicity, they sent along additional warriors to escort their visitors part of the way to Niagara.[15]

Whether they lied, as Governor Haldimand later claimed, remained noncommittal, or negotiated well, the Oneidas gained several weeks of breathing space for their people. They used this critical time to pursue one of two options: move closer to the rebels for better protection or migrate to Niagara. Their overwhelming sentiment lay with the rebels. Captain John Onondiyo went to alert Van Dyck that they were abandoning Kanonwalohale and Old Oneida. Everyone hastily collected basic items, herded together as many cattle as they could find, and walked somberly toward the fort. They occupied an "Indian field" not far from the post, where they had often camped during overnight visits.[16]

The evacuation of their castles forced the Oneidas to abandon close to 120 horses and dozens of sleighs, wagons, saddles, harnesses, and plows. They left behind much of their livestock and virtually all their poultry, plus crops and food stockpiles. Lost, too, were tools, pots, pans, cutlery, clothing, and other household items.[17]

Over the next few weeks, the Oneidas maintained themselves near the fort as best they could. The women and elderly attempted to make their temporary quarters livable, while their warriors assumed defensive duties. Fifty Oneida fighters accompanied a party of sixty Continentals on a march to Fort Herkimer to escort supply boats back up the Mohawk River to Fort Schuyler. Others scouted or guarded work details outside the fort, all nervously expecting enemy reprisals.[18]

Once back at Niagara, the Tory-Indian detachment reported on the council with the Oneidas. The prominent Seneca chiefs Old Smoke and Kayashuta had long since asked to have the incarcerated diplomats released. So had White Skin. Guy Johnson, however, refused these en-

treaties. Now he relented. Good Peter and Skenandoah, in return for
their personal freedom after five months of suffering in the dungeon,
said they would travel to Kanonwalohale and try to convince their
Oneida brethren to relocate to Niagara. Most of all, the two chief warriors feared that a Crown-sponsored military force would destroy the
homes and possessions of their people and perhaps even kill some of
them, should they not cooperate with Johnson.[19]

Joseph Brant led the party to Kanonwalohale, bringing more than
three hundred fighters besides the two Oneida chiefs. So many months
in the black hole had so debilitated Good Peter and Skenandoah that
both men had to ride horses. When they arrived at the Oneida castle, they found the community abandoned. Ignoring pleas from the
two chiefs, Brant ordered a torch put to everything, including the fort
and a nearby Tuscarora village. The flames consumed all the Oneida
homes—some seventy in number and more than twenty of them
framed—most personal effects, the meeting house, the church, even
the bell Sir William Johnson had donated and inscribed.[20]

Brant soon learned that the residents had fled to Fort Schuyler.
Leaving Kanonwalohale behind in a heap of glowing embers, the Mohawk chief and his raiders pressed on to the outskirts of the post. At the
Indian field, with unenthusiastic support from Skenandoah, Brant attempted to persuade the Oneidas to switch their allegiance. One hundred and thirty-two agreed to join the Crown; the others resisted. As
tension mounted and the Oneidas felt more threatened, some at the Indian field started taking flight for the fort. Brant and his party pursued.
Most of the Oneidas were able to get inside the gates, but two were not
so fortunate. They were shot down before they reached the fort.[21]

For the next day or so, Brant's followers fired sporadically inside the
post, and the garrison responded with musket shot and cannon blasts.
After wasting much ammunition, the raiders then gathered up the
Oneida cattle grazing outside Fort Schuyler and vanished. Skenandoah, Good Peter, and a few guides led those Oneidas who had agreed
to switch allegiance, and the animals, to Niagara, while Brant directed
his warriors eastward, toward rebel settlements.[22]

Despite their rage against the Oneidas and the destruction of
Kanonwalohale, the British and their Iroquois allies left Old Oneida

standing. Throughout the Revolutionary War, its residents maintained a reputation for neutrality. Most of the military-age men, eager to earn esteem in combat, had already linked in some way to one side or the other. Old Oneida became a kind of haven for older people, women, children, and those who wanted nothing whatsoever to do with the war.

Among those who migrated to Niagara, a disproportionate number were women, children, and the elderly, in some cases sent west for their safety. Under pressure from Guy Johnson to prove their loyalty and contribute to the British war effort, these 132 Oneidas produced only 20 warriors for military campaigning. General Schuyler noted the imbalance, commenting a few weeks later that some pro-rebel warriors intended to "go in quest" of their wives and children who were "carried off by the Enemy."[23]

In early September 1780, Guy Johnson announced to Governor Haldimand, "The Oneidas are now once more united with their Confederates." Only a "small number," he asserted, remained tied to the enemy. A few days later, he stated "that the Small remains of that people are in no Capacity or Situation to give much Obstruction to partys." Johnson went on to claim that the pro-British Iroquois would consider any remaining pro-rebel Oneidas as refractory enemies who deserved death, should they meet them in combat.[24]

Regarding British tabulations about those who turned away from the patriot cause that spring and summer, Guy Johnson offered a total of "above Five hundred Souls." In mid-September 1780 he provided a more specific tally: 424 Indians. The actual figure was nearer to 440. Of these persons, fewer than half were Oneidas. Despite Johnson's claims, no more than two hundred Oneidas joined the forty or fifty already residing in the Niagara area. Combined with the small number of Oneidas whom Crown officials may have listed as Oquagas, the total number was somewhere between 250 and 300.[25]

Records do not indicate just how many Oneida warriors ultimately fought for the British. Samuel Kirkland placed the number at around 120, although his estimate was likely too high. Certainly a population of 250 to 300 would have struggled to yield nearly half its number in adult males of fighting age, especially when primarily Oneida women, children, and older persons sought sanctuary at Niagara.[26]

At the same time, some of the Oneida warriors who changed sides were very effective fighters. Longtime rebel friend Jacob Reed took his wife, two children, two sisters, and his male cousin to Niagara. Three Oneida warriors who had received patriot officer's commissions— Christian Thonigwenghsoharie, Joseph Banghsatirhon, and Totyanea-hani—also "deserted" to the British. What specifically produced their shift is unclear. Some no doubt listened to their fellow Iroquois and decided that the king's side would better protect their tribal interests; and others may have shifted to protect their families. In Reed's case, he likely migrated to Niagara to safeguard his loved ones. During the next three months, however, his conscience kept bothering him. Finally, with kin in tow, he slipped away from Niagara and returned to Fort Schuyler, a rebel ally once more.[27]

For the six hundred or so Oneidas still committed to the rebellion, remaining at their exposed location near Fort Schuyler was not possible. Initially, Schuyler had considered the Upper or Lower Mohawk Castles as possible resettlement sites. After some debate, the Oneida refugees decided to move to Schenectady, which they deemed a safer location and which lay closer to Albany.[28]

Within days of their arrival, Schuyler and the other Indian commissioners came out to visit them. The rebel leaders expressed disappointment over the loss of so many brothers and sisters to the British and sorrow over the destruction of Kanonwalohale. This home, they explained, would be temporary, and while the Oneidas remained at Schenectady, the patriots would attempt to obtain supplies for them.[29]

Unfortunately, the patriot leaders did not deliver much in the way of shelter or basic goods. Schuyler authorized the use of an old barracks for their lodgings, and he had already tried to negotiate for food and clothing. A month later, he learned that some four hundred Indians, almost all of them Oneidas, were barely eking out an existence. They lived in pathetic lean-tos, and virtually all their clothing was in tatters. Severe financial constraints had prevented the patriot government from paying the contractors for these items, so the latter refused to provide the goods.[30]

Many Oneida men and quite a few women were not present at Schenectady. Assuming that the rebels would care for their loved ones, warriors continued to scout and assist the Continental detachment at Fort Schuyler. Other adult males, along with a number of women, went off to hunt for desperately needed food. A few able-bodied males remained at the Schenectady campsite to help protect the people there and to assist them in adjusting to—and surviving under—their new living conditions.

Housing accommodations did not work out as Schuyler intended. White refugees had already laid claim to the barracks, so the Indians tossed up shanties on some hills in the southeast part of the town. In early November, the general reported that "the huts occupied by the Indians are so exceedingly bad that it will not be possible for them to pass the winter in them." He ordered the removal of those persons in the barracks and their placement in private homes, if necessary. "*They must comply*," commanded Schuyler, "for It is of vast Consequence to this State In particular and to all the states in General that these faithful Indians should be as well provided as the distressed circumstances we are in will permit." The barracks, however, offered only minimal relief. Although providing cover from rain and snow, there were no forests nearby. As autumn winds kicked up, warning of the approach of biting cold and winter storms, the Oneidas wondered how they would survive without firewood, especially in their ragged clothing.[31]

Underfed, exposed to the elements, and densely concentrated in ramshackle housing, the Oneidas found themselves mired in an ideal breeding ground for killer diseases, including smallpox. Roaring fevers, massive vomiting, and dehydration wreaked havoc among them. Many fought off the spiking temperatures only to fall victim to pneumonia or other respiratory ailments. Among those who perished that winter from an apparent case of smallpox was Lieutenant John Sagoharasie, one of the Oneidas earlier awarded an officer's commission.[32]

The horrible reality of rampant illness, food shortages, insufficient clothing, and inadequate housing served to magnify the psychological burden that already weighed heavily on the Oneidas after losing their largest castle. Kanonwalohale had blossomed into a prosperous settlement, earning the admiration of Indian visitors and European Ameri-

cans alike. Its sudden destruction induced wrenching sensations of violation and humiliation. Oneida warriors experienced deep anguish over
having abandoned their homes and personal property without a fight.
No longer in a place of security, hospitality, and nurturing, they addi-
tionally had to endure the painful images of fellow Iroquois warriors,
now their avowed enemies, vengefully torching their beloved community. They felt shame in having failed to protect their homeland. As the
warriors regarded how much their people were suffering, their emotional turmoil rose to the point of nearly immobilizing distress, and
they had no effective means to reduce their mortification.

Amid such mental agony, some Oneidas turned to alcohol for comfort. When they moved to Schenectady, Schuyler had "Cautioned
them against taking too much strong Liquor." The Oneidas were to remove those "in Liquor" from the streets to avoid any ugly confrontations. Unfortunately, unscrupulous local traders preyed on the Oneidas
in their weakened physical and emotional state, plying them with alcohol and convinced them in their drunken stupor to trade away their
weapons and any clothing they might have for triflings or more liquor.
The problem became serious enough for Marinus Willett to file a complaint with Schuyler. He hoped the general could get the New York
legislature to outlaw this destructive trade, which not only devastated
the health of once-reliable warrior scouts but also stripped them of necessities that rebel sources could not easily replace.[33]

Wounded emotionally and burdened physically, the Oneida refugees at
Schenectady did their best to care for one another. The matrons and
sachems persevered in their leadership roles and kept up morale as best
they could. Since the rebels could not provide for their basic needs,
many of the Oneidas took leave of Schenectady and moved northeast to
the Saratoga region for the winter. There, plentiful supplies of timber
provided them with building materials for huts and unlimited quantities
of firewood. The extensive wilderness offered more game than the over-
used woods near Schenectady. Even if this new location left them more
exposed to enemy attacks, the Oneidas accepted that risk as the price for
obtaining food, shelter, and warmth for their people.[34]

Unfortunately, the winter of 1780–1781 was particularly harsh. The severe weather destroyed some of the game, besides causing many animals to migrate southward. To procure necessary supplies of meat, warriors had to hunt for longer periods of time, which forced them to keep exposing themselves to brutal conditions with few garments to protect them from the frigid air and biting blasts of wind and snow.[35]

Even as the Oneidas attempted to provide for themselves, Schuyler kept trying to help. The Oneidas were the only Indians on whom the general felt he could rely, and he knew how much they had risked, how much they had lost, and how much they had contributed to the rebel war effort. "I feel myself deeply interested to relieve [their] distresses," he explained, "which I have been instrumental in drawing on them."[36]

Schuyler's inability to obtain supplies reflected the financial straits of the Continental Congress and so much destructive raiding in and around the Mohawk Valley. Before the war, New York's frontier region produced huge quantities of wheat, corn, livestock, fruits, and vegetables. After 1775, repeated attacks by Indians, loyalists, and British troops destroyed homes and barns and ruined fields. War parties either killed or confiscated domestic animals. On one expedition alone, in the fall of 1779, Sir John Johnson's command destroyed 150,000 bushels of wheat, plus other grains and forage, and 200 dwellings. As the number of acres under cultivation plummeted, local farmers strained just to feed their own families, let alone the growing number of displaced European American settlers.[37]

Dependent on Continental dollars that grew more worthless with each passing day, Congress struggled to procure something akin to minimal food and clothing for its own soldiers. Rebel leaders in the Mohawk Valley talked seriously about abandoning Fort Schuyler, since they could barely meet minimal supply needs for the garrison force stationed there. As such, they did not see how they could siphon off even a small portion of their own deficient allotments to assist the Oneidas.[38]

Schuyler, however, refused to give up. Back in October 1780 he had reminded Congress of the many contributions of the Oneidas and then urged that body "to attend to their situation and afford them some relief." With "few having clothing to render them comfortable at this season" and with their "poverty" making them a "spectacle of distress," he warned Congress that "their suffering will be great as the Cold weather advances."[39]

In early December, Schuyler advised Congressional leaders that "their case is at present much more critical." With the local cupboard all but bare, the situation was truly grim. "Their affection for us," he cautioned, "hath hitherto induced them to turn a deaf ear, to the repeated offers of the Enemy, and enabled them to support the misfortunes they experienced, with fortitude, and temper." If the rebels failed to find provisions, Schuyler feared that the Oneidas' "virtue will at last yield to a continuation of distress, which no human beings can endure, and that they will renounce an Alliance which has exposed them to such variety of Calamity, to form one" with the British, "who can amply supply every of their wants." All true patriots "are bound, by every principle of honor, as well as by considerations of Interest, to give them relief," concluded Schuyler, not only because the Oneidas had "made the Capital sacrifice of Abandoning their Country to follow our fortunes," but also because of the "reiterated promises on our part to afford them ample protection and support."[40]

Concern for the Oneidas reached down into the Schuyler household. Measuring up to his own words, the general dipped into his private larder, until he had doled out much of his personal stock of food. In mid-January 1781, he informed Congress that he would tap his own credit to purchase food and clothing, and he also drafted a personal note for a thousand dollars to acquire 200 blankets for his Oneida allies.[41]

As a veteran quartermaster, Schuyler knew how to scrounge from old supply depots and plead for handouts. By late January, he had procured shirts, breeches, coats, vests, shoes, and linen overalls. Some of this merchandise was shoddy but was better than nothing. Eventually, Congress approved Schuyler's actions, and the New York delegates promised that when some clothing arrived, "our Oneida friends will have a share." At that moment, however, when "it is impossible to Cover our own army," the Oneidas could not "expect to be provided for as their sufferings & their merits require."[42]

Despite their difficult circumstances, Oneida warriors did not shy away from military-related commitments. In October 1780, Sir John Johnson, Old Smoke, and Joseph Brant led a large body of regulars, Tory rangers, and Iroquois fighters on a raid of Schoharie. After massive devastation, the Crown force crossed the Mohawk River and crushed a patriot detachment at Stone Arabia. Rebel militiamen and sixty Oneidas under Brigadier General Robert Van Rensselaer pursued them across the river. On October 19, with the Oneidas in the lead, one scout detected the enemy force not far ahead. Just before sunset, the Oneidas opened the attack. The initial bursts of musket fire drew a "warm" response, recalled Van Rensselaer, but the Oneidas and their rebel allies pressed forward and started to overwhelm Sir John's left. Just as darkness squeezed out the last hint of sunlight, the Crown force fell back, leaving behind forty prisoners and substantial quantities of plunder. Van Rensselaer called off the pursuit until morning. For the next two days, the Oneida warriors tracked the enemy raiders, with additional troops behind them, until the rebel force ran out of rations.[43]

In the Battle of Klock's Field, also known as Fox's Mills, the Oneidas fought tirelessly. Several weeks later, Schuyler reported to Congress: "In the late Incursions of the Enemy they Joined our troops with alacrity, and behaved with a spirit, which drew the admiration of the officers under whose command they fought and bled." Governor George Clinton, who arrived just after the battle and joined in the pursuit, informed Congress that Sir John's force "would have completed the entire Destruction of Tryon County had not the Militia and Oneida Indians overtaken and obliged them to retire with precipitation."[44]

At the end of September 1780, before the Battle of Klock's Field, Guy Johnson had crowed to Governor Haldimand about the extraordinary turnaround of British fortunes. A year before, he remarked, the Iroquois were "uneasy and unsettled in their minds" after the destruction visited on them by Sullivan's expeditionary force. "The Oneidas &c.," he went on, "were in peaceable possession of their Fort and Town, which checked many, as the Majority certainly did not wish to fight them however they might condemn their measures." Retaliatory raids in 1780, he claimed, had put the pro-British Iroquois back in the ascendancy. From Sir John's perspective, the future seemed particularly bright.[45]

Haldimand disagreed. Much to his amazement, the wreckage of Kanonwalohale had failed to break the will of most Oneidas. Their "Treacherous Conduct," he complained to Lieutenant Colonel Mason Bolton, commanding at Niagara, "and the impossibility of effecting any thing against the Enemy in the Quarter they Inhabit, while they Remain in the Rebel Interest, has brought me to a Resolution to force them to obedience, or to Cut them off." The action at Klock's Field reinforced Haldimand's belief that the pro-rebel Oneidas had to be neutralized or destroyed.[46]

By comparison, the Oneidas who had fled to Niagara, according to Haldimand, were not very useful. Only a few warriors were among them, and British officials could not be sure of their loyalty and trustworthiness. Haldimand demanded proof through vigorous martial action, which never materialized. By October 1780 he suspected that the Oneidas had moved families to Niagara to feed them or burden the Crown by consuming resources. If the Oneida warriors did not fight out front in raids, Haldimand vowed, he would drive their families away from Niagara.[47]

That autumn, a few Oneida warriors joined Sir John Johnson's campaign against Schoharie. During the fighting, two of them were killed, prompting Guy Johnson to notify Lord George Germain, "[t]he Oneidas have behaved well Since they returned to our interest."[48]

The reality, however, was that only a small number of Oneida warriors engaged themselves vigorously on behalf of the Crown. Eight days after Johnson's observation, Haldimand charged a group of them with traitorous behavior. "Some Oneida Indians who have expressed great Concern for their bad conduct hitherto," he complained to Germain, "were with many others Received into favor at Niagara, from whence they deserted to the Rebels and alarmed the Country before Sir John Could arrive in it."[49]

Outraged by this alleged willful deception, Joseph Brant decided to "take Revenge on the rebel Oneidas for sundry Insults he as well as his Sister rece d [received] from them," Daniel Claus explained. To facilitate his objective, Brant "had determined to pick a trusty party of Mo-

hawks & other Indns. & go in search of their casle [sic] in the spring."
Although he learned that a great many Oneidas were waiting out the
winter season in the remote Saratoga region, he was not able to launch
his strike. Other demands temporarily pulled Brant away from his plan,
and a large number of Iroquois and Canadian Indians said that they
were reluctant to join any such assault. Then, as the weather started to
warm, many Oneidas drifted back to the more populous Schenectady
area, where they would be less exposed to surprise attacks.[50]

That spring and summer, the Crown did not press their offensives as
they had the previous year. Old Smoke and Joseph Brant led expeditions out west, and most of the raids in New York involved small parties
with limited objectives. In a strange way, the British had fallen victim to
their own success. Their retaliatory achievements of 1780 left far fewer
exposed targets in 1781.[51]

The calm offered various Oneida leaders the opportunity to visit
with patriot leaders in other locales. The year before, a delegation of
fourteen Oneidas and Tuscaroras and five Kahnawakes had traveled
eastward to view the French Army and Navy at Newport, Rhode
Island. Conversing with French lieutenant general Jean-Baptiste
Donatien de Vimeur, Comte de Rochambeau, and inspecting the
troops and warships, these Indians could now thwart British misinfor-
mation denying that the French were formally allied with the American rebels.[52]

During the summer of 1781, forty-four Oneidas, Tuscaroras, and
Kahnawakes journeyed to Philadelphia. General Schuyler encouraged
them to do so, hoping that a personal appeal might persuade Congress
to make greater efforts to supply their needs for the upcoming winter.
Led by Grasshopper and Lieutenant Colonel Louis Atayataronghta,
they declared their official intention "to manifest our friendship to
America & its Cause, and wait any orders Congress shall think proper
to give." Congressional leaders housed them in barracks and introduced them to various leaders. Among these was the French ambas-
sador, Anne-César, Chevalier de La Luzerne, who bestowed on
Grasshopper an elegantly embroidered uniform. On all important oc-

casions afterward, Grasshopper donned this apparel as a symbol of the Oneidas' friendship with France.[53]

The visitors soon had a meeting with members of the Congressional Board of War at the Pennsylvania Statehouse (Independence Hall). The patriot leaders lamented the loss of Kanonwalohale. "We hope the time is not distant when we shall amply avenge your injuries," besides seeing the Oneidas "restored to the peaceable enjoyments of your land." The board members apologized for wartime shortages but encouraged their guests to keep fighting "manfully" when they returned home. Once the rebels were triumphant, "[t]he faithfull Oneidas, Tuscaroras, and Cachnawagas [sic] will then experience the good consequences of their Attachment to us and yourselves and your Children, when they share in the blessings of our prosperity."[54]

Some among the Indian delegation announced they wanted to keep proceeding south to Virginia. While traveling to Philadelphia, they had learned that Washington's army had feigned an attack against the British in New York City before slipping southward. With Rochambeau's troops, they intended to entrap the army of Charles, Lord Cornwallis, some eight thousand strong, in the vicinity of Yorktown. The Indian leaders wanted to visit Washington and Lafayette, among others, and observe the martial action.[55]

How many Indians actually made the trek to Yorktown is unclear, but at least three, Grasshopper likely among them, remained for the duration of the campaign. Along with Washington, the Oneidas would have an opportunity to reunite with their French brother Lafayette, who commanded a light division during the siege operations.[56]

Surrounding Yorktown, they found a massive Franco-American force of nearly eighteen thousand, supported by more than thirty French warships. The magnitude of the confrontation amazed the Indian observers, accustomed as they were to smaller-scale warfare, especially as heavy-siege artillery boomed away at the enemy. Ultimately, Cornwallis accepted reality and asked for terms of surrender, since his troops could neither escape nor be rescued. On October 19, 1781, on a beautiful autumn day in Virginia, Washington's Indian friends watched as the British army marched out from its Yorktown lines and stacked its arms in complete capitulation.[57]

As the Indian observers celebrated with patriot and French forces at Yorktown, warfare was flaring up again along the New York frontier. A large Crown war party of almost seven hundred regulars, Indians, and Tory rangers raided around Durlach and Cherry Valley, burning some fifty homes and barns, destroying fields full of hay and grain, and confiscating more than two hundred cattle. Colonel Marinus Willett rallied local rebels and gave chase. At Johnstown, the two sides fought inconclusively.

As Willett prepared his four hundred troops to continue the pursuit, some sixty Oneidas entered the camp. Just two weeks earlier, the sachems had declined Schuyler's request to have some warriors join an expedition. Too many were out scouting and hunting, except for twenty who had stayed behind to protect the women and children. Somehow in this crisis, the chiefs had cobbled together a substantial reinforcement for Willett's command.[58]

The British and their Indian allies retreated at near breakneck speed, yet they could not elude Willett's pursuing force, with the Oneidas leading the way. At West Canada Creek, the British finally offered resistance. By defending a fordable crossing, they tried to delay the rebel pursuers long enough to allow their main column to escape. A bloody firefight ensued. Captain Walter Butler, commanding the British rearguard, held this position as long as possible. After he ordered his detachment to pull out, he turned to taunt his patriot enemies. An Oneida warrior named Anthony raised his weapon and fired from great range. The ball crashed into Butler's head, knocking him to the ground. His comrades instantly dispersed, leaving their stunned captain semiconscious but mortally wounded. According to Willett, another Oneida warrior rushed forward and "finished his business for him and got a Considerable booty," including young Butler's scalp and everything he had in his pockets. The scourge of Cherry Valley and one of the most detested Tories of them all lay dead at the hands of two Oneida warriors.[59]

After the engagement at the ford, Willett halted the pursuit. The swift marches had fatigued his command badly, and his supplies were dwindling. The British later indicated that they had suffered thirteen killed, twelve wounded, and forty-nine missing during this campaign. As for Willett, he reported thirteen rebels killed, twenty-three wounded, and five missing. He did not mention any Oneida casualties.[60]

In his after-action report, Willett spoke highly of the Oneidas. "Our Indians were very useful, and behaved with their usual alertness," he stated to his ranking officer, Major General William Alexander. "Your Lordship knows they are the best cavalry for the service of the wilderness."[61]

The Oneidas kept contributing all season long, scouting actively to the north and east, mostly in the area around Saratoga. In mid-May 1781 an Oneida warrior was killed when his party collided with an enemy contingent along the north branch of the Hudson River. During the summer, the Oneidas set up a forty-person ambush team near Crown Point to gather intelligence and intercept hostile raiders moving south from Canada. By autumn, so many Oneida scouts were scouring the woods that one rebel officer feared his own troops might encounter them and be mistaken for the enemy.[62]

With the Oneida scouts primarily shielding the Saratoga region, the rebels lost a significant part of their capacity to detect British-Indian raiding forces coming from Niagara. When General Washington started drawing away Continental troops for use in the Yorktown campaign, local commanders had to rely more heavily on militiamen, who were hesitant to scout in hostile territory and insisted on returning home for the harvest. The absence of the Oneidas enabled the Crown to establish advanced raiding bases, sometimes even using the former site of Kanonwalohale as a springboard for operations into the Mohawk Valley.[63]

British officials, meanwhile, fumed about the effectiveness of the Oneidas in tracking and disrupting raiding ventures coming out of Canada. During the summer, they again tried but failed to convince various Indian groups in Canada to seize the hatchet against the Oneidas. The British then modified their objective in one operation, seeking not just to destroy rebel property but also to deliver a telling blow against the Oneidas. Before the raiders departed, Governor Haldimand ordered them "to extirpate the remaining unfriendly Oneidas, who much impede our Scouts and Recruiting Parties, and are in many Respects useful to the Rebels." Somehow, the Oneidas evaded this force and suffered no casualties.[64]

Once word of Lord Cornwallis's defeat filtered back to Canada, British officials reduced the size, pace, and scope of their operations. Part of the slowdown was normal for wintertime, but Haldimand and other Crown officials were not sure what the home government planned to do. The British had lost their second army, and opponents of the war in England, growing increasingly powerful, would likely have the political strength to force the government into peace negotiations.

Haldimand and his officers also worried about the impact of the dramatic Yorktown triumph on their Indian allies, especially those in Canada. Substantiating these fears, Schuyler tried to exploit this circumstance by sending to Canada the Kahnawakes who had been at Yorktown, escorted by a group of Oneidas. Bad weather quashed this plan, but the Seven Nations had already learned about Cornwallis's surrender. Even though they were divided in their loyalties, the news convinced them to pull back into a posture of neutrality.[65]

The Oneidas, meanwhile, got through the winter of 1781–1782 more easily than the year before. Milder weather, fewer worries about enemy raiders, and a better supply situation improved their living conditions. Schuyler continued to lobby for the Oneidas, explaining to Congress's new Superintendent of Finance Robert Morris that "they have so firmly adhered to our cause," despite devastating shortages. All of Schuyler's efforts were finally beginning to show results. Subordinates and friends kept the Oneidas in mind whenever extra goods became available. As much as anything, however, reverberations from the victory at Yorktown prompted British home government leaders to loosen up their resistance to the flow of trade goods into America. As more supplies entered ports, some eventually made their way into Oneida hands.[66]

Nestled into the Schenectady area, the Oneidas had frequent contact with local European American residents and soldiers. Almost invariably, clashes occurred. The previous winter, Schuyler reported that an Oneida was "barbarously murdered and others Assaulted and dangerously wounded." Then, in the spring of 1782, a few local residents were killed, and rumors swirled about Schenectady that an Oneida was the perpetrator. Schuyler immediately asked Henry Glen, an army quartermaster and a respected leader in the area, to investigate. Glen concluded that the Oneida whom locals suspected was not responsible for the murders.[67]

Determined to prevent senseless, race-based violence, Schuyler circulated a letter to the inhabitants of Tryon County. He reported Glen's findings and reminded everyone how valuable the Oneidas were to the Revolution. "There may be villains amongst them," the general stated, "as well as amongst white Inhabitants." Schuyler stressed how "extremely Imprudent and Unjust" retaliation would be if the evidence showed that the suspected person was innocent. He also promised to keep taking the "necessary steps to bring the delinquents to justice."[68]

Amid this local turmoil, word reached the eastern Mohawk Valley in June that George Washington, who was present with the Continental Army in the Hudson Highlands, about one hundred miles away, intended to visit the Albany region. For some time, the commanding general had talked about traveling to the area where so much fighting had taken place. The slowdown in military operations made such a journey possible.

Sailing up the Hudson River in the company of Governor George Clinton, Washington arrived in Albany on June 26. For two days the locals fêted him, offering grateful thanks for his achievements and fond wishes for his future success. Then Schuyler, Brigadier General Peter Gansevoort, and about forty troops escorted the commander in chief, New York's governor, and various other dignitaries to Saratoga. There they toured the battlefield where the critical triumph over General John Burgoyne's army had occurred.[69]

The next day, Washington traveled overland to visit Schenectady. About five miles out, sixty of the leading citizens greeted him. As the party approached the city boundary, some one hundred Oneida warriors, in paint and frayed battle regalia, assembled to welcome the

"Great Father." Very pleased to see his Oneida friends, Washington presented them with a belt and urged them to target Oswego and Oswegatchie in their raids and seize as many prisoners as they could. Recent small-scale enemy attacks on various frontier communities had surprised the commanding general, and he wanted to put a stop to them. Grateful for the friendship he had exhibited over the years, the Oneidas accepted his charge. That evening, the city hosted the commanding general at a celebratory dinner, and the next morning, Washington wished everyone well and said goodbye before traveling back to the army.[70]

By the late autumn of 1781, Quebec Province governor Haldimand could tell that his allies among the Six Nations no longer showed much desire for combat. Cornwallis's defeat had cast a gloom over the British officer corps, and the Iroquois warriors could sense the feelings of despair. Like their British counterparts, they suspected that an unfavorable conclusion to the conflict was almost at hand.[71]

They were all correct. In March 1782, Parliament defied King George and Chief Minister Lord Frederick North, who wanted to continue the war, and voted to seek a peace settlement. This action produced resignations from North and Lord George Germain, the cabinet officer charged with providing overall direction to the British war effort. Momentarily considering abdication, King George quickly regained his senses and assembled a new ministry that soon began negotiations in Paris with designated American peace commissioners. By November 1782 a preliminary settlement was almost complete that, among its various provisions, granted the American revolutionaries their independence.

Unlike other pro-British warriors who were now less willing to take major risks, Joseph Brant wanted to keep fighting, no matter what. He had to use all of his persuasive talents to assemble 460 Indians, among them 3 Oneida chiefs and 22 warriors, to join a company of soldiers at Oswego for yet another strike into the Mohawk River Valley. Hesitant to undertake any operation that might provoke significant rebel retaliation or upset negotiations to end the war, Haldimand in late May 1782 decided to recall this expedition. His message arrived too late; Brant had already left. Later, in what seemed like a strange comment but reflective of the new reality, the British governor stated how pleased he was that Brant's raiders had failed to inflict significant damage on the rebels.[72]

A few months later, in mid-September 1782, Schuyler learned from a trusted source in Canada that Haldimand had received orders from England to stop all "incursions into your country by indians and small parties." Attempting to save face with their Iroquois allies, local British commanders told them that "they must not go to war as the King had compassion on his American subjects they having expressed their sorrow for what they had done." A Seneca sachem dismissed this commentary as pure nonsense. He observed that "the Americans and French had beat the English[,] that the latter could no longer carry on the war, and that the Indians knew it well & must now be sacrificed or submit to the Americans." He thought "it was time to attend to their own concerns and listen no longer to . . . lies."[73]

Not everyone, however, was willing to put down their arms. Joseph Brant remained determined to teach the Oneidas a painful lesson for having supported the rebels. In November 1782, he proposed an attack on the Oneidas who resided at Canajoharie, his sister Molly's old town. He requested snowshoes and canoes for the strike. Appreciative of Brant's wartime efforts, Haldimand had no objections, so long as the operation did not touch any rebel settlers. Brant's problem was his fellow Iroquois. Few of them bore his intense anger toward the Oneidas. They viewed such an assault as a useless, spiteful act. The plan thus remained stillborn, because of a lack of enthusiasm on the part of virtually all pro-British Iroquois except Brant.[74]

As for the rebels, they believed they still had more to accomplish. The British occupation of the fort at Oswego on the southern shore of Lake Ontario remained a potentially serious threat to the frontier region of New York. "While the Enemy remain posted in Force at Oswego," James Duane related to Governor Clinton, "we have nothing to expect short of total Desolation of the scattered remains of that once flourishing district" of Tryon County.[75]

In early 1783, to eliminate that source of danger, Marinus Willett proposed a raid against Oswego. Washington endorsed the plan and helped with its implementation. Since a siege was not possible, the attack force had to be large enough to take the fort by storm but small enough to preserve the secrecy of its presence. "I wish to impress it upon you," Washington forewarned, "that if you do not succeed by surprise, the attempt will be unwarrantable." The commander also stressed that success depended on "having good guides to Oswego" and "upon persons that can carry you without hesitation and difficulty to the points of attack."[76]

On the night of February 9, 1783, Willett moved out from Fort Herkimer, taking with him a small body of troops and three Oneida scouts, led by Captain John Onondiyo. They crossed Oneida Lake, and by mid-afternoon on February 13 they were camped without fires near Oswego Falls, some seven miles from their objective. There they built scaling ladders to storm the works.

Early in the evening, they resumed their advance, moving along the ice on the river, which made for easier travel than trudging over deep snow in the woods. About four miles from Oswego, the ice became thin, and the column had to move into the forest. At that point, Captain John Onondiyo became the lead guide. Over hills and into morasses the column pressed. On they went, even as Captain John insisted not much farther. Hours passed. When quizzed again, the Oneida scout declared they were within two miles of the fort. After another hour, Willett called a halt while Captain John advanced alone. Soon, he returned with a report, just two more miles. This time Willett and a few others accompanied him. Once again, after a while, Willett asked how much farther. Onondiyo replied, "Two miles." As sunlight began to crowd out the darkness, Willett realized that they were lost, that the enemy would soon know of their presence since daylight would make it impossible to conceal his troops in the woods.

Willett decided to abandon the strike and return to Fort Herkimer. "Whether it was careless designe or Ignorance it will not alter the Case with me," he later wrote in blaming Captain John for getting his column lost. "I had as high an opinion of his knowledge as a guide as of his fidelity & integrity." He had counted on the Oneida officer based on the latter's excellent war record and because "except in his last fatal stroke of sabotage he appeared to perform very well."[77]

Willett's Oswego expedition was the last attempted campaign of the Revolutionary War along the New York frontier. Two soldiers died from exposure, and others suffered severe physical repercussions from the freezing elements. "My enemies may rejoice at this misfortune," Willett stated angrily. Washington, his idol, consoled him that he had done all he could. Willett should accept that "some of those unaccountable events which are not within the control of human means" were commonplace in military life, demanding the "calm reflection of the philosopher to bear." Washington thought that Willett had exhibited zeal, perseverance, and intelligence, all that the general could ever want from his subordinates. Captain John's blunder, moreover, had saved lives. Storming the fort would have resulted in multiple casualties, and the treaty ending the war awarded Oswego to the revolutionaries anyway.[78]

Back on November 30, 1782, patriot negotiators John Adams, Benjamin Franklin, and John Jay initialed preliminary peace accords with British representatives in Paris. Both governments still had to review and ratify the treaty, which in its provisions acknowledged American independence and established boundaries that placed the lands of the Six Nations within the borders of the new American republic, the United States. In the rush to protect their own immediate interests, the British did not demand any form of protection for their Iroquois allies. The treaty, finally ratified in Paris on September 3, 1783, left the bulk of the Six Nations vulnerable to the potential wrath and ever-expansive land-grabbing predilections of those former British colonists who had now become citizens of the United States. As yet undetermined, however, was the fate of those Native Americans, most prominent among them the Oneidas, who had served as committed allies of the victorious European American rebels.[79]

13

FORGOTTEN ALLIES

The summer of 1783 wore heavily on George Washington. He again needed to get away from headquarters, this time because of the "distressing tedium" of "waiting for the definitive Treaty" amid never-ending requests for services that he lacked the resources to fulfill. As before, he chose to visit portions of northern New York. The commander set out from Newburgh in mid-July and traveled up the Hudson River and beyond to Ticonderoga and Crown Point. After examining the fortifications and walking the terrain of these memorable war sites, he swung around and explored the Mohawk Valley. His travels even took him along Wood Creek and to Oneida Lake.

Marinus Willett met Washington at Fort Herkimer and escorted him to Fort Schuyler, both to show him that edifice and to describe in detail the siege of 1777. There, the commander's Oneida friends turned out once more to greet him. This time, in remembrance of their wartime services, the commanding general ordered Willett to distribute three pounds of gunpowder and one pound of lead to each warrior. The Oneidas greatly appreciated this recognition from the "Great Chief Warrior."[1]

In contrast with Washington's kindly consideration, the New York troops who occupied Fort Schuyler that autumn did not treat the Oneidas nearly so well. When a few Oneida women came to the post to sell boots, some soldiers "with a vilinous & base intent . . . ill treated & disturbed" them. Precisely what the troops did, Willett failed to mention, but he rebuked them "for an action not only Brutal & inhumane itself but highly prejudicial to that friendly Intercourse which we wish to cultivate." Hoping to "prevent insults & abuses of this or any other kind in future," he warned of courts martial and severe penalties.[2]

Isolated events in themselves, these incidents came to represent the kind of treatment the Oneidas experienced in the postwar years. For the most part, the Continental Congress expressed interest in the well-being of the Oneidas and attempted to treat its wartime allies with respect. By comparison, local citizens and their leaders in New York viewed the Oneidas mostly as an annoyance and an impediment. Once the war ended, they began devising ways to force the People of the Standing Stone from their traditional homeland.

As the Oneidas and the rest of the Six Nations would learn, the peace settlement between Great Britain and the United States contained no provision for the protection of Iroquois interests. Nor did the document conclude peace between the pro-British Six Nations and the American revolutionaries. That issue would have to be resolved at some point in the future.

Not until the autumn of 1784 would the Six Nations and the victorious revolutionaries sit down together and thrash out an agreement. Meanwhile, misleading rumors swirled on both sides. The British offered advice, sometimes unwittingly poisoning the atmosphere. Self-appointed rebel negotiators interfered, and a befuddled Congress, often not having a quorum of states present to conduct its proceedings, took an inordinately long time to form a peace commission to treat with the Six Nations. Philip Schuyler and the other northern Indian commissioners likewise received virtually no direction from Congress. At the same time, New York state officials stridently staked their claim to control all aspects of Iroquois affairs, since the vast domain of Iroquoia rested within the state's borders.

During the winter and spring of 1783, a report reached Niagara that the Crown had turned over the Iroquois homeland to the rebels. The Six Nations told their British allies that if this report were true, they would "look upon our conduct to them as treacherous and cruel."

After all, the Iroquois "were a free people, subject to no power upon earth."[3]

Misleading information from three Oneida couriers heightened the tension. In early May, they reached Niagara with a letter from George Washington to Brigadier General Allan Maclean, announcing an end to hostilities. These messengers had relatives at Niagara—one a mother, another a wife, and the third a sister. While conversing with their family members, the three Oneidas alleged that General Schuyler had publicly declared that the revolutionaries planned to destroy the Six Nations. Since they had come as official representatives of Washington, their fellow Iroquois assumed that their tale was credible. Only extensive denials by local British officials calmed down their Indian allies.[4]

Six weeks later, two young Oneida warriors who had sided with the British visited relatives and friends in the Mohawk Valley. They returned to Niagara with bizarre stories of forty American workmen who intended to build a house for Schuyler at Onondaga and an announcement by the general that all natives who had left their homes for Niagara had forfeited their lands. John Butler told the Six Nations he could not deny these tales. He recommended that several chiefs visit the Oneidas and obtain further information. Once Maclean learned of this response, he faulted Butler for stirring up needless rancor when the Tory leader knew "in his Conscience . . . Every word of it to be untrue."[5]

Clearly upset, the Iroquois decided to send their two prominent Oneida hostages, Skenandoah and Good Peter, to meet directly with Schuyler. Since the summer of 1780, when Crown officials released the pair from prison, they had been under a kind of loose house arrest. The two moved freely about Niagara, but they could not leave the area without permission. Skenandoah even participated in councils and assumed his place as a leading warrior. His presence and prominence may well have offered some protection for pro-rebel Oneidas. Few pro-British Iroquois would deign to insult Skenandoah by raising the prospect of attacking his beloved brothers and sisters. Even Joseph Brant's last war plans to destroy the Oneidas originated away from Niagara. As for Good Peter, he took no part in pro-British Iroquois decision making, a stance that reflected his abiding attachment to the rebel cause.[6]

Skenandoah and Good Peter arrived in the Schenectady area in mid-July 1783. No one recorded how the Oneidas received them. No doubt a few cast suspicious glances at them, refusing to trust their old chiefs, who said they had come to communicate with Schuyler about rebel policies and intentions regarding the future of the Six Nations. Good Peter and Skenandoah prepared a speech that Jacob Reed wrote out and translated into English. They asked Schuyler to "send some of their great men to have some conversation with them." The two also passed along a message from Joseph Brant, stating that he was now in favor of peace and would rejoin the triumphant Americans in friendship.[7]

In reply, Schuyler stated that he had stopped sending any messages to Fort Niagara since the chiefs' brutal incarceration. From that point on, he assumed that the pro-British members of the Six Nations had "determined never to bury the hatchet." The authority to negotiate peace terms, he also explained, rested with the Continental Congress. That body had not yet given him instructions. He suggested that the Iroquois select a deputation of sachems and warriors to consult with the Indian commissioners, armed only with a sincere interest in peace. He also advised them to bring along all the prisoners they held as firm evidence of their conciliatory intentions.[8]

While Good Peter and Skenandoah were back east, Sir John Johnson worked with the Six Nations to ease their distress. He explained that the treaty boundaries would place their homeland within the United States, "yet you are not to believe, or ever think that by the line which has been described it was meant to deprive you of an Extent of Country." Nor did he think the revolutionaries "will act so unjustly, or impolitically as to endeavor to deprive you of any part of your Country under the pretence of having conquered it."[9]

Sir John's carefully chosen words helped soothe anxious feelings. However, nervousness again set in when Good Peter and Skenandoah returned with word that Schuyler was still waiting to hear from Congress. Two representatives sent directly from that body had recently appeared at Niagara, claiming "full power to treat on that subject." Now the Iroquois could not be sure who was in charge or what rebel officials might demand.[10]

Likewise, news of persons coming directly from Congress to visit with the Six Nations jolted Schuyler. He wrote the delegates and voiced his dismay, wondering why they had seemingly slighted him along with their other Indian commissioners. After years of dedicated service, he thought he deserved better treatment. Schuyler promised to keep working with the Six Nations, but he wanted clarification regarding his possible role in any congressional-sponsored negotiations.[11]

That winter, a small Iroquois contingent from Niagara, guided by Good Peter and led by a Seneca chief named Little Beard, arrived at Schenectady. As Schuyler described their message, they said they had now "plucked the Hatchet out of our Heads" and were seeking a formal end to hostilities. In response, the general, besides praising the Oneidas and Tuscaroras, stated that Congress, now finally in touch with him, "has never done any thing more than signify the intention of peace."[12]

Schuyler also commented on a letter he had received from Joseph Brant back in November. Brant had insisted that the Six Nations were neither "drunk" nor deluded when they joined the British, and he demanded peace terms that would be "honorable for both parties." The general explained that he and the other commissioners lacked authority to determine the agenda, and he advised the delegation that "the conditions doubtless will be such as Congress have a right to insist upon."[13]

Schuyler then addressed a key semantical point. In their communications, the Iroquois at Niagara kept calling themselves the Six Nations. This designation implied that pro-rebel Oneidas were some rump faction rather than mainline representatives of their own nation. Schuyler pointed out that two of the Six Nations, the Oneidas and Tuscaroras, were not a part of these discussions, and, therefore, he was correct when he referred to the Niagara Iroquois as "those Indians of the Six Nations who sent a Belt & speech."[14]

During interludes between formal sessions, Good Peter met privately with Schuyler and Grasshopper. After much discussion, they agreed to have Grasshopper extend an invitation through Good Peter for all Oneidas, Oquagas, Tuscaroras, and Kanaghsaragas at Niagara to resettle in their former homes. Schuyler promised them protection. When word of this offer became public at Niagara, the news "kindled some Jealousy" and "a good deal of uneasiness" among the excluded Iroquois, who anxiously wondered whether they would ever be allowed to return to their own homelands.[15]

Personally, Schuyler did not favor any attempts to take territory from the Six Nations. In a detailed letter to Congress, he mapped out his rationale. If the Indians removed to Canada, the government would lose the capacity to influence their conduct and yield the fur trade to the British. The Indians could cross the border and harass settlers with impunity, retreating in times of crises to their Canadian sanctuaries. Their reoccupation of Iroquois territory, Schuyler surmised, would not deter westward expansion. As settlers crowded in on their borders, game would become increasingly scarce. The Iroquois would have to abandon their territory for fresh land elsewhere, or their numbers would dwindle to the point that the government could purchase thousands upon thousands of acres for virtually nothing. The general accurately predicted that either way, European American speculators and settlers would eventually obtain the land peaceably.[16]

George Washington concurred, declaring that his position on Indian policy "coincides precisely with those delivered by Genl. Schuyler." Should the government try to bar the Six Nations from their traditional territory, an Indian war could erupt. Washington proposed a less violent plan to let the westward-moving flow of land-hungry European Americans ease the Indians out of the region. "The gradual extension of our Settlements," commented Washington, "will as certainly cause the Savage as the Wolf to retire."[17]

Congress, meanwhile, ignored Schuyler and the other Northern Department Indian commissioners when naming a delegation to construct a peace treaty with the pro-British Iroquois—Oliver Wolcott of Connecticut, Richard Butler of Pennsylvania, and Arthur Lee of Virginia actually served. Amid criticism for excluding the most knowledgeable and experienced person available, the delegates belatedly extended

Schuyler an appointment. By then, the New York general, having had his fill of Congress, declined the post.[18]

Before the congressional negotiators could arrange their council, the State of New York pressed into action. Leaders there disagreed with Congress regarding which political entity possessed the right to control relations with the Six Nations. According to the Articles of Confederation, Congress had the power to make war and conclude peace, and these were treaty negotiations. The Yorkers asserted that since Six Nations territory rested within their state's borders, decisions about the Iroquois belonged to them. State sovereignty, after all, was supreme under the Articles. To prove the point, in April 1784, Governor George Clinton advised the Six Nations to meet with him and other New York officials at Fort Stanwix (called Fort Schuyler during the late war) to construct peace terms.[19]

The two parties finally gathered at the end of August, but the Oneidas and Tuscaroras were not present. The Mohawks, Onondagas, Cayugas, and Senecas immediately complained that the former's absence was "contrary to the antient & usual Custom" of the confederacy. They particularly wanted the Oneidas to attend, since they had a good rapport with the state and might help secure more favorable terms for the pro-British Iroquois. The state commissioners dispatched two of their party to invite the Oneidas to participate. Three days later, their representatives arrived, and the council proceeded in earnest.[20]

The Oneidas had not initially attended because they had not been at war with the American rebels or the State of New York. New York's commissioners, however, assumed they had stayed away because of concerns that the state had designs on their lands. To reassure them, Governor Clinton expressed "gratitude" that the Oneidas "have often in the Hour of danger given indubitable proofs of your inviolable attachment to us and of your determination of living and dying with us." He claimed that stories about state plans to take their lands were false. "You must not believe it," Clinton declared. "We have no claim on your Lands; its just extent will ever remain secured to you." The governor pointed out that the state's constitution forbade the Oneidas from disposing of any of their lands to individuals without the legislature's consent. What the commissioners wanted was for Oneida leaders to trace out the boundaries of their holdings. That way, if New York appropriated chunks of land from the other nations, they would know they were not infringing on the territory of their Oneida friends.[21]

Grasshopper rose and thanked Clinton. On behalf of the Oneidas, he offered condolences for all the state's losses during the war. He admitted that the Oneidas had heard the rumors about the state seeking their lands but assured Clinton that "[w]e have utterly rejected and disbelieved these Reports." He endorsed the idea that no individual could purchase lands from the Oneidas without the government's knowledge, and he reported Colonel John Harper of Unadilla as an offender.[22]

In tracing their boundaries, the Oneidas made no special request for Canajoharie, where the displaced Oriska inhabitants had taken up residence after the destruction of their village. When Clinton pointed this omission out to them, they politely demurred. That land belonged to the Mohawks, and that nation alone could dispose of it.[23]

Over the next five days, the state commissioners negotiated with the other four Iroquois nations. The Iroquois admitted their confusion over two governments trying to treat with them. Their leaders preferred to reach an accord with the thirteen United States first and then attend to any remaining difficulties with New York. Clinton told them that in light of their wartime losses and debts, a cession of land from them was a "reasonable" request. Included in that proposed gift was territory around Niagara and Oswego. Joseph Brant replied that they had come to make peace. They were "not authorized, to stipulate any particular cession of Lands." They would, however, recommend this cession, as they, too, deemed the governor's suggestion "reasonable."[24]

Three weeks later, in early October 1784, the Six Nations began their next round of negotiations at Fort Stanwix, this time with representatives from the Continental Congress. Besides Oliver Wolcott, Richard Butler, and Arthur Lee as the designated commissioners, other notables were present. Among them were James Madison and the Marquis de Lafayette with a party of Frenchmen who happened to be touring in the area and decided to attend as well.

During the three-week interlude, the Oneidas had sought to reconcile with their Seneca uncles. Neither group had spoken to the other during New York's peace conference. Then one day, Grasshopper donned the uniform his French friends had given him and walked over to the Seneca camp. Five prominent Oneidas accompanied him, all dressed in their best, although tattered, finery. They moved about the Seneca campsite until one of the most distinguished chiefs, either Old Smoke or Kayashuta, emerged from a lean-to. The two leaders greeted each other, sat on the ground, and smoked the peace pipe. The next day, as a courtesy, the Senecas reciprocated, visiting the Oneidas and smoking a peace pipe. Having exchanged "apologies," they had officially restored their relationship.[25]

Unlike their Iroquois kin, who approached these negotiations with trepidation, the Oneidas had no qualms about this gathering. Although Schuyler was not present, their old commander and friend Lafayette was on hand, and he could remind everyone what the Oneidas had endured and achieved during the war.

Because of Lafayette's stature, various individuals suggested that he address the gathering. Uncomfortable about intruding, the marquis consulted with James Madison, then offered to meet informally with the assemblage. The Indians, however, insisted that a person of his importance required a prominent forum. The congressional commissioners thus invited him to speak on the first day.[26]

Seated on the ground around a fire in the chilly October air, the Iroquois listened attentively as Lafayette reminded them that seven years earlier he had counseled them that "the cause of the Americans was a just one." Although he had encouraged neutrality, many had chosen to align with the British, the losing side. Wondering what lessons they may have learned by "meddling with the quarrels of whites," he hoped they were wiser and would keep the peace among themselves. Engage in trade with the Americans, he encouraged them, and when "selling your lands take care not to fool them away for brandy." Soon he would return to France, but he would follow their fortunes from the other side of the Atlantic. Then, until they could smoke the peace pipe once more, Lafayette wished them "health, fortunate huntings, peace and plenty, and the fulfilling of Such of your dreams as foretell good luck."[27]

Over the next two days, various Indian leaders responded to Lafayette's words. A Mohawk chief admitted that they had "listened to the
wicked and shut our ears against thy voice." The Mohawks, he continued, "quitted the good path," and ever since they had been "surrounded by a black cloud." Speaking along the same lines, the Seneca
chief Towanoganda went on to encourage the United States to exhibit
some compassion. "Every nation is liable to err, and we have committed a great many faults, at the instigation of Great-Britain," he averred.
"We have been overcome, but it becomes all wise nations to forgive,
and particularly the victorious one."[28]

Soon the serious negotiations began. The congressional commissioners showed little leniency. They claimed sovereignty over all lands
and denied the right of the Six Nations to speak for the western Indian
nations in the Ohio country. All prisoners, including Good Peter, Skenandoah, and Johannes Crine, were to be returned immediately. The
commissioners also demanded a boundary adjustment—a portion of
the Six Nations homeland. Day after day, the Iroquois tried to dissuade
them. Ultimately, however, the power rested with the United States,
and its commissioners were able to dictate the terms. The Iroquois
could do little except acquiesce.[29]

In the Treaty of Fort Stanwix, signed on October 22, 1784, the Six
Nations yielded their claims in Ohio and turned over territory around
Niagara and Oswego to the United States. The agreement also specified that until the Iroquois released all prisoners of war, six of their people would remain behind as hostages. The commissioners, to prove
their "humane and Liberal views," promised to distribute valuable trade
goods as presents after the signing.

With peace declared, the Onondagas, Cayugas, Senecas, and Tuscaroras could return safely to their homelands. The same option applied to
the Mohawks, but they declined to do so. Prewar treaties had reduced
their territory to small parcels, and colonial settlers had pressed up
against their borders. Among all the Iroquois peoples, they had the
strongest ties to the British, and the prospect of having former rebels
surrounding them proved uninviting. When Governor Haldimand of-

fered to secure land for them in Canada, nearly all the Mohawks, Joseph Brant prominent among them, chose to relocate.[30]

Because the Oneidas were rebel allies and friends, the negotiations did not deal directly with them. Nonetheless, they did use the forum to secure various promises from the commissioners. If the government could provide resources to support Samuel Kirkland and help reconstruct the church that their enemies had destroyed, they would be extremely grateful. Several Oneida leaders asked to have a reward for James Dean, who had faithfully acted as their interpreter and adviser throughout the war. Because they had no money, all that the Oneidas could give him was a sizable grant of land—two miles square. They wanted Congress to authorize some funds for Dean so that he could begin farming operations near them and continue providing his services. The commissioners submitted these requests to Congress, where they languished amid many piles of unfinished business.[31]

In the treaty itself, the commissioners and, ultimately, Congress expressed their gratitude to the Oneidas. For a long time, leaders in Congress had sought an opportunity to "reward their Fidelity and encourage their Zeal and Exertions against the common enemy." At the peace table, they fulfilled this pledge. Article 2 specified that "[t]he Oneida and Tuscarora Nations shall be secured in the possession of the Lands on which they are settled." The reason, the commissioners explained, was that the United States should not "forget those nations who preserved their faith to them, and adhered to their cause." These people, "therefore must be secured in the full and free enjoyment of those possessions."[32]

News about the final treaty terms, while pleasing to the Oneidas, caused an uproar among the Iroquois at Niagara. They were indignant with their delegates for giving up so much and gaining so little. Since the new American republic possessed the power, the negotiators pointed out that the Indians had to accept what were dictated terms. Without a patron such as Great Britain to support their side, further resistance would be futile.

As a result of the Treaty of Fort Stanwix, the status of the Iroquois Confederacy declined, especially with regard to the confederacy's influence over Indian peoples in the Ohio country. In contrast, the Oneidas emerged from the treaty council in a much stronger position with the four upper Iroquois nations. Since the Oneidas had positive relations with various revolutionary leaders, the other Iroquois started relying on them to represent their concerns in state and national dealings.[33]

For much of the eighteenth century, the Mohawks and Oneidas were the primary source of confederacy leadership. In an understated way, these two nations were the most important among equals, the head of each moiety. With the decline of the Mohawk nation and its removal to Canada, the burden fell almost exclusively on the Oneidas. They now controlled the eastern door, historically the passageway of greatest threat to the confederacy. They also maintained the highest credibility with the new powers, the United States and the State of New York. The Tuscaroras and Cayugas had already acknowledged the Oneidas as their leaders. In 1785, the Onondagas likewise designated the Oneidas as the heads of the Six Nations. Only the Senecas reserved judgment about the leadership capacities of the Oneidas.[34]

Their newfound status among the Six Nations, however, plummeted rapidly as the People of the Standing Stone confronted the realities of postwar life. The Revolution had come at a delicate moment, when the Oneidas were straddling two worlds. During wartime, those who joined the rebel cause set aside their differences to concentrate on the common foe. Peace removed the reason for unity of purpose. Old, unresolved issues—such as the struggle between sachems and warriors or Western versus traditional values and customs—resurfaced. In effect, the war had only suspended the internal battle.

The American Revolution had also fostered new problems. The war left the Oneida homeland in a shambles. Only one castle remained standing, and the process of reconstruction would represent a painstaking challenge. The loss of life among the Oneidas was devastating. At the time of Lexington and Concord, they had a population of approximately 1,200 men, women, and children. By 1783 their numbers barely represented a thousand souls. Some had succumbed to killer diseases, and as many as three dozen warriors perished in combat. The Oneidas mourned their losses and consoled the living, yet they could not easily replace the lost talents related to the war's toll, including the likes of Thomas Sinavis and Deacon Thomas.[35]

The separation into pro-rebel and pro-British factions produced damaging and, in a few instances, permanent splits among the Oneidas. For some among those who went over to the Crown, the war generated too much bitterness for them ever to return to their homeland. The British government compensated them with £520 for their property losses, and these Oneidas took up permanent residence in Canada.[36]

Those who migrated back received chilly receptions. Pro-rebel Oneidas believed that their brothers and sisters had abandoned them while they were struggling for their survival. Those who had served with the Crown felt that their Oneida brethren had rejected their long-standing confederacy ties in favor of new, self-interested rebel friends. As they looked upon one another, the wrenching emotions from all the hardships—the violence, destruction, and death—came to the surface. Icy stares, harsh words, and vengeful acts were commonplace. As Lafayette commented to Washington, "the Whigg and tory distinctions Are kept up Among those tribes to an Amasing degree of private Animosities."[37]

One young Oneida warrior lost his life because of suspicions that he was pro-British. According to his mother, someone accused him "falsely" of "having imbibed something of the tory spirit & to have been accessary someway or other to the burning of our church." Another youthful warrior walked alongside him, conveying "all the appearance of friendship," and pulled out a dagger and plunged it into the alleged Tory, killing him. In 1784, Lafayette and his party witnessed two brothers squabbling. One had fought as a rebel and the other for the Crown. Fueled by liquor, they began to bicker, when one of them delivered a massive blow with a club that felled the other. The father and some women moved quickly to break up the fight. Some time later, the father convinced the brothers to smoke the peace pipe, which restored calm. "These quarrels are all the more frequent as they stem from the war," commented an observer. In denigrating tones, the Oneidas called each other Whigs and Tories, which "serve[d] to perpetuate the division and the violence even after the war is over."[38]

For several years afterward, uncompromising Oneidas even shunned Skenandoah or treated him with hostility. "Some of the Oneidas bitterly reproached him," claimed one source, "& one even knocked him over the head, felling him with his tomahawk, & came near killing him." Although they sympathized with his plight in prison, they were slow to forgive him for his active role in high-level pro-British circles at Niagara.[39]

Good Peter, by comparison, was the rare person whom the pro-rebel Oneidas almost immediately embraced. He had supported the British cause only as much as was absolutely necessary to survive. Compelled to accompany Joseph Brant in the raid that destroyed Kanonwalohale, Good Peter restricted his activity with the British to serving as a spokesperson attempting to broker peace when the fighting had ended— certainly honorable duty. His gentle, positive manner also helped him regain old friendships.[40]

As peace returned, the centuries-old power struggle between the sachems and matrons and the chiefs and warriors revived. During the Revolutionary War, the war chiefs had dominated Oneida decision making. Sachems served more in an advisory capacity while also planning and executing diplomatic missions. All in all, the pro-rebel Oneida leaders demonstrated a surprising degree of cooperation and cohesion. Few warriors exhibited greater commitment to the rebellion than Grasshopper, Thomas Sinavis, or Henry Cornelius, who were all sachems. One of them even gave his life for the cause. For their part, the matrons sustained morale at home despite wrenching human losses and massive property destruction. Disputes between the hereditary and the chosen leaders thus were comparatively few, a key to pro-rebel Oneida unity of purpose.[41]

When the war ended, many war chiefs refused to relinquish their authority. According to one observer, they were "aspiring after a monopoly of power." Furthermore, they had a built-in constituency, the warrior class, which preferred to see its leaders carrying the greatest influence. None of this assertiveness pleased the matrons and sachems, which resulted in much postwar bickering and divisiveness among not only the nation's leaders but also ordinary Oneidas who chose to identify with a specific matron, sachem, or war chief.[42]

Even among the chiefs, a struggle ensued. As a result of their war-time service, many younger, talented warriors had risen in esteem. By contrast, some older, proven chiefs had moved past their prime in bat-tle. In part, the internal contest for power represented a generational phenomenon, with elders reluctantly passing the torch to more youth-ful males. However, within particular age groups as well, command rivalries developed among chief warriors, tugging the Oneida commu-nity in numerous directions at once.[43]

Nor had the Oneidas resolved the clash between traditional beliefs and values and Western influences. Before the war, both Christianity and the private ownership of property had taken firm hold among vari-ous Oneida constituencies. Fascinated by European trade goods and weaponry, many Oneidas saw in these commodities better tools to serve their needs. Many of these same persons, as well as some others, refo-cused their long-held religious beliefs and forsook their communal modes of living, finding in the Christian faith greater spiritual consola-tion and in the European style of living expanded material benefits. The booming Oneida castle of Kanonwalohale epitomized all these changes, just as Old Oneida, the only castle still standing at the end of the Revolutionary War, remained a traditionalist bastion.

The rebellion erupted in the midst of this dissonant clash between Western and traditional ways. By breaking from the Iroquois Confed-eracy and joining forces with the rebels, most Oneidas had resisted hundreds of years of tradition and obligation. At the same time, the movement toward Western practices sustained a setback when wartime responsibilities diverted Samuel Kirkland from addressing the Oneidas' spiritual concerns. Christianity waned among them, and the destruc-tion of their villages and property demolished the steps they had taken toward private ownership and personal accumulation.

The Oneidas emerged from the conflict as a people confused about and, in some cases, divorced from their cultural and political founda-tions. In this unsteady state, the wartime tragedies and massive destruc-tion fostered a kind of consuming depression in many of them. Parents, spouses, and siblings struggled to accept that they could never replace lost loved ones. Those who had latched onto the material world of the colonists witnessed firsthand its ephemeral nature, even as they consid-

ered how the flames of war had consumed years of hard work and accumulation.[44]

In victory, too many Oneidas felt disillusionment, not the euphoria
of great hope for the future. This troubled atmosphere produced hostility and frustration, and factions started to tear the nation asunder. The
pall that postwar poverty cast over the nation deepened the wounds and
intensified the conflict. The Oneidas started to lose all hope of forging a new consensus about their customs, beliefs, values, and ways of
living.[45]

In olden times, those Oneidas who could not accept consensus or who
refused to live up to their obligations would simply move somewhere
else. After the Revolutionary War, however, such persons stayed in their
homeland but divided themselves into five separate communities. In
the future, a majority, not universal agreement, would decide the outcome of village and national debates.

The Oneidas' first task was to salvage what they could and rebuild
their communities. In 1783, Grasshopper directed the efforts of forty
to fifty families in an attempt to reconstruct Kanonwalohale. Without
proper tools or food supplies, these Oneidas failed to tame the over-
grown fields. They tried again the next year, somewhat better prepared
but not nearly as well supplied as Philip Schuyler believed was necessary. This time, the small settlement survived. Within a year, the Oneidas constructed four more independent villages to accommodate the
major factions.

Conditions in these castles bordered on the deplorable. Once again,
lean-tos, not houses, sheltered the Oneidas. The fields looked improp-
erly tended. Residents had almost no domestic animals, including livestock or poultry. The supply of wild game had fallen off, as wartime
raiding parties had hunted excessively in Oneida territory. The People
of the Standing Stone, stated an observer, were "wretchedly poor."[46]

Under these depressed conditions, some again turned to consuming
mind-numbing levels of alcohol for relief. Before the war, Samuel Kirkland had worked with the leading residents of Kanonwalohale to ban
liquor from the community. Both Christian converts and traditionalists

recognized alcohol's destructive effects. The shift back to massive consumption began during the war, when rebel traders around Schenectady offered them so much liquor. With no promise for the present and little hope for the future, some Oneidas consoled themselves by resorting to heightened overindulgence. When Brant passed through Kanonwalohale in 1784, he commented that "they are continually Drunk with Stinking Rum."[47]

In the late summer of 1785, Kirkland visited Kanonwalohale. He was aghast at what he saw. "The most of my people," he wrote to his wife, "are degenerated as much as our paper currency depreciated in the time of war." They were living in squalor, with little concern for their appearance, health, or well-being. "They are in plain english — filthy, dirty, Nasty creatures a few families excepted." Over the next two decades, Kirkland regularly commented on the widespread intoxication, among both men and women, as various Oneidas drowned their frustration and hopelessness in liquor. He likewise noticed how the internal divisions, rivalries, alliances, and poverty had broken the Oneidas up into five separate villages, each with its own leadership. Animosities among the castles only deepened the chasms separating these once-united people.[48]

In the midst of low morale and rampant squabbles, Governor Clinton asked the Oneidas to meet with him in a council at Fort Herkimer in June 1785. They thought the purpose of the council was to block an unauthorized land sale and to check encroachments on the Oneida estate. Clinton had something different in mind. His goal was to extract a massive land purchase from them.

At the time, the State of New York had an unclear title to the Six Nations lands. Administratively, the British had considered Iroquoia a part of the colony of New York, but the provincial charter failed to confirm that point. To ensure that the state was able to fend off all challenges by other states, specifically those with western land claims such as Massachusetts, New York's political leaders wanted to acquire as much land from the Six Nations as possible and sell it off to settlers, thereby guaranteeing a firm claim to the region.[49]

In his opening address, Clinton stunned the Oneidas by informing them of his desire to purchase lands in the Susquehanna Basin. After the Treaty of Fort Stanwix in 1784, the Oneidas had met in council and decided "never to sell any more of our land." When they responded negatively, the governor kept pressing them. One night, he met with Good Peter and tried to lobby him. The Oneida chief warrior would not cooperate, explaining, "We cannot part with so much of our Hunting Lands, which are dear to Us; as from thence We derive the Rags which cover our Bodies." Young warriors also objected. The loss of such a valuable tract for hunting would deprive them of the opportunity to demonstrate their prowess to their people. After much badgering, the Oneidas offered a compromise. They offered to lease a tier of farmland along their border, to block attempts by others from encroaching on their homeland.[50]

Confronted by the prospect of failure, Clinton launched a vigorous, multipronged attack. In public, he professed his indignation. He claimed falsely that the Oneidas knew full well why the council had gathered, and he insisted that they were wasting his time. Privately, he launched a campaign to discredit Good Peter, expressing "Astonishment" that this pious, Christian Oneida "who had been with the Enemy should speak so often." Then he brought selected Oneidas into his quarters and offered these poverty-stricken leaders money—and no doubt ample amounts of alcohol—in exchange for their support.[51]

The governor and his minions knew exactly what they were doing. They realized that Good Peter opposed the land sale and that his voice carried great weight in Oneida councils. Clinton's accusation of pro-British leanings was deeply insulting to Good Peter, who announced, "I will for the future no more speak in transacting Business with the Commissioners." Beech Tree took over as primary spokesperson. After extensive lobbying by those Oneidas who had accepted Clinton's bribes, Beech Tree declared that the Oneidas had consented to the proposed land sale.[52]

And so the pattern went. Representatives from the State of New York and others employed all means honest and dishonest to gain more and more Oneida territory. State leaders exploited the Indians' poverty, internal divisions, power rivalries, and fondness for alcohol. Good Peter grasped the problem clearly when he said, "[w]e Indians are unwise and our want of wisdom is owing to our want of knowledge of the ways of white people. White people say to us—, 'This Measure will be for your good.' And we have always been accustomed to obey this voice, without inquiring into it; as we verily thought our white brothers meant good to us; and hence we have been deceived in respect to our lands."[53]

Samuel Kirkland continued observing the moral and physical degeneration of the Oneidas, but he could not find any means to help reverse the downward spiral. Eventually, he convinced himself that the only hope for the Oneidas was the breakup of their holdings into individual family farms, like those of their European American neighbors. Perhaps private ownership would help in promoting a rekindled sense of personal worth, which he struggled so mightily to encourage. Kirkland aided those who sought tracts, and he even accepted a piece of land for himself.[54]

Many reasons account for the Oneidas giving up title to millions of acres. Some agreed with Kirkland and concluded that their best hope lay in the establishment of small farms and the full adoption of European American ways. Others were susceptible to bribery, or they viewed intrigues with powerful local and state leaders as a means of enhancing their own strength within the community.

In addition, the Oneidas had begun to lose their sense of spiritual connectedness with the land. Traditionally, the Iroquois revered their territory. The Great Spirit had granted them millions of acres to hold in common and to sustain them physically, so long as they treated the abundant, spirit-filled flora and fauna all about them with respect. Likewise, tribal lands provided a home for ancestors. Over the hills, through the valleys, and across rivers, lakes, and streams, the spirits of past generations roamed. In European practice, by comparison, parcels of land served the individual, based on the concept of private ownership. Owners could use their property as they chose, with or without reference to the welfare of the greater community. In Christian doctrine, the only sacred acres were church lands and cemeteries, since spirits, human and otherwise, did not inhabit the landscape.

These Westernized views of land use were already well known to the Oneidas when they endured three terrible years of forced separation from their homeland during the Revolutionary War. In abandoning their territory, they felt the searing pain of forsaking the spirits of their ancestors and leaving their beloved homeland totally unprotected. When they returned, they were a divided, poverty-stricken people, in many cases fully uprooted from tribal values and working at cross purposes with one another. Many did not seem to care as they once had about preserving and defending their homeland, whether for their ancestors, for themselves, or for future generations. Widespread despondency made it easier to sell off huge parcels of once-sacred territory to speculators and land agents of various kinds.[55]

With the loss of so much acreage, traditional hunting became more problematic. A higher concentration of people struggled to sustain themselves on shrinking land resources and a decreasing wildlife population. This situation produced more than just food shortages; without pelts, the Oneidas had nothing to offer at the trading table.[56]

Conditions worsened, and the Oneidas became more dependent on compensation for land sales to provide for themselves. Good Peter understood the direction his nation was going. The once proud and independent People of the Standing Stone had begun to suffer the indignity of becoming partial wards of the new American nation. In the eyes of some Oneidas, this growing dependency smacked of chattel slavery. Without hunting grounds for themselves, their children, and their grandchildren, they felt more and more as if they were becoming desperate beings, too reliant on the ever-increasing numbers of European Americans all around them for basic necessities.[57]

Spiraling downward, many Oneidas looked backward to regain some control. A religious and cultural revival swept the landscape, winning back hundreds of them to traditional ways. Among the proponents was Good Peter's son. He and others resumed ancient ceremonies and customs, as they sought to bring stability and meaning to their lives. By turning the clock back to better, more prosperous, more harmonious times, many found inner peace and happiness. The revival of older ways, however, added to the formation of factions among the Oneidas, and in the early nineteenth century they officially divided their reserva-

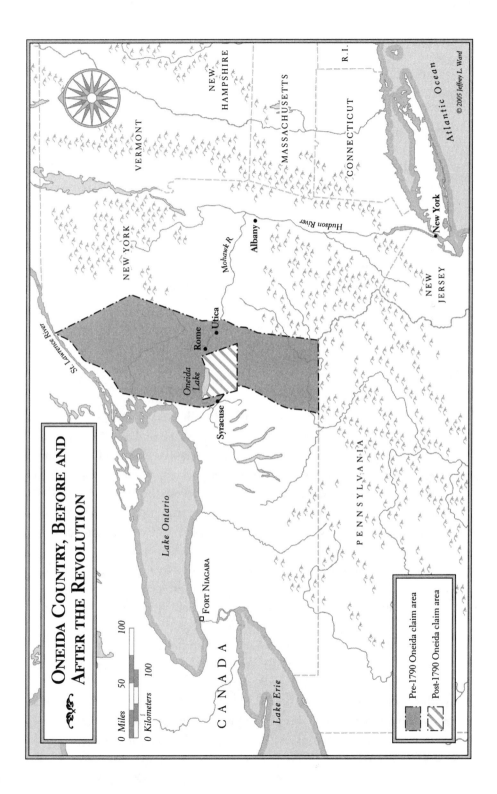

ONEIDA COUNTRY, BEFORE AND
AFTER THE REVOLUTION

© 2005 Jeffrey L. Ward

Pre-1790 Oneida claim area

Post-1790 Oneida claim area

tion, with one part called the "Pagan" and the other the "Christian" section.[58]

The United States government, meanwhile, continued to look favorably on its old allies. Upon George Washington's inauguration as the first president, the Oneidas sent him their congratulations. The press of business did not deter Washington from responding to his friends with a few pleasant words of his own. In 1790, Congress legislated and the president signed the Indian Nonintercourse Act, which gave the federal government exclusive rights to negotiate with the various Indian nations. Four years later, in the Treaty of Canandaigua, the federal government recognized the territorial claims of the Oneidas and the other Iroquois and guaranteed them the free use and enjoyment of their lands.[59]

That same year, Timothy Pickering, a special envoy to the Oneidas, negotiated a treaty to compensate the latter for their services and losses during the Revolution. They would finally receive reimbursement for the destruction of three castles and their property. The agreement authorized up to five thousand dollars to cover all individual compensation and one thousand to rebuild the church; and it also provided for the construction of a sawmill and a gristmill to replace those lost at Kanonwalohale. In systematic fashion, Pickering, Samuel Kirkland, and James Dean collected information on what each person had owned. Pickering then proportionally adjusted the figure to fit the five-thousand-dollar cap. Although the government's payout was not compensation in full, the Oneidas seemed satisfied with Pickering's figures.[60]

Among the funds was a small sum dedicated to a condolence gift for the Bear Clan matron Wale. Seventeen years after her brother Thomas Sinavis had died in combat, she finally received acknowledgment of her grief and appreciation for his service.[61]

Shortly after the war, the federal government had made sure that New York paid the Oneida officers their back salaries. They received the nonnative rate up through January 1, 1782. Why the government authorized payment only up to that date, when the officers actually served much longer, the secretary of war never specified.[62]

As New York did for all its Revolutionary War veterans, the state gov-

ernment awarded the Oneida officers land bounties. The tracts for the
Oneidas were nearly all swampland in Junius Township and are currently part of the Montezuma National Wildlife Refuge. Although
Philip Schuyler and others had sometimes paid Oneida warriors for
specific assignments during the war, those who had served as auxiliary
troops received no structured wages. Because they did not officially belong to organized military units or hold officer commissions, New York
declared them ineligible for postwar land bounties. The federal government rejected their requests for old-age pensions, claiming insufficient
proof of wartime service. Thus, Oneida warriors, some of whom had
fought more actively than those who gained land bounties or pensions,
received no veterans' compensation.[63]

Grasshopper, the sachem and head counselor, was the first to go. He
had used his status and persuasive skills to build and preserve a strong
coalition in favor of the rebellion, even after three of their four villages
were destroyed. Chiefs, matrons, and warriors alike admired and respected him, as did Schuyler. In 1786, Grosshopper visited the government for the last time, to renew the Oneidas' friendship with the
United States. That same trip, he petitioned Congress for personal financial assistance. During the war, he had lost everything, and he
asked for some reward for his services "to make his old age comfortable." Those twilight years did not last long. Grasshopper passed away
in 1788.[64]

Captain John Onondiyo's strong war record and leadership talents
enabled him to recoup his reputation after the Oswego scouting blunder. A devoted Presbyterian and an active chief warrior, he continued to
serve his people well during peacetime. When Kirkland decided to take
only one Oneida on a trip east in 1794, he chose Captain John as "a
young Chief of first abilities in the nation & a very influential character
and for an Indian, possesses an uncommon share of sensibility." With
Kirkland, Captain John visited Dartmouth College, where he elo-
quently addressed the president and the student body during commencement exercises. Then, at Harvard, he conversed impressively
with the school's president and other leaders. The following year, 1795,

he and other leading Oneidas traveled to Albany to conduct the nation's business. He and Skenandoah contracted an illness, probably smallpox. Skenandoah recovered; Captain John did not. He died on September 12, 1795, and was laid to rest in the Presbyterian Cemetery in Albany.[65]

As he had done before the war, Han Yerry assumed a leadership role in an Oneida village. In 1787 he journeyed to New York City to visit with Congress about a boundary dispute, and he lobbied for the appointment of a Superintendent of Indian Affairs. Three years later, Han Yerry and his community grew angry with some fellow Oneidas for selling land that his Wolf Clan had traditionally occupied. Eventually, Kirkland and Governor Clinton intervened to quell the dispute and restore the land to the Oneidas. Han Yerry, a great and seemingly ageless Oneida warrior, died around 1794. His extraordinary wife, Two Kettles Together, lost her eyesight in old age. She outlived her husband by nearly three decades.[66]

The postwar years proved unkind to Jacob Reed. For all his efforts, he failed to receive a commission as captain, although the Oneidas commonly referred to him by that rank. As a former scholar at Wheelock's school, Reed possessed valuable skills as an interpreter, but he could not resist "demon rum." Kirkland described him "as a person of good abilities & capable of rendering great service to this nation should he persevere in his resolution to lead a sober & virtuous life." Reed was on track to become one of the first councilors of the nation until the temptations of alcohol overwhelmed him. "His appetite for strong liquor returned & raged more violent than ever," Kirkland elaborated, so much so "that he has for some time given himself up to one continued scene of dissipation." A few years later, when discussing a shortage of Oneida translators, Good Peter mentioned Jacob Reed, "who can talk your language but we can never fix his attention" because of his alcohol addiction. Reed's wife, Hannah, endured much misery from her husband's constant drinking. "Except [for] a few intermissions," she stated tearfully, Jacob "was almost incessantly drinking for a number of years before his death" in the late 1790s.[67]

Good Peter never let all the pain and suffering of his fellow Oneidas destroy his optimism about life. As late as the 1860s and 1870s, many

Oneidas could still recall him from their childhood days, popping into homes, offering prayers and a kindly word, and then moving on to the next residence. His loving nature left a lasting impression. "By his excellent example," Skenandoah's granddaughter Christine recalled, "he did a great deal of good amongst his people." According to another Oneida, even dissipated persons respected Good Peter's presence. "He always had a few words of encouragement to offer," remembered Moses Schuyler, whose father was the celebrated warrior Blatcop Tonyentagoyon. In the evenings, villagers heard Good Peter singing hymns, and his Sunday sermons often surpassed Kirkland's in skillful delivery. He died in 1794, at Buffalo Creek, still working to improve the lot of his nation.[68]

The oldest of the group, Skenandoah, outlived them all. Until Good Peter's death, the two remained close friends. Others would criticize Skenandoah for having cooperated with the British, but Good Peter never did. Only he and Johannes Crine knew just how awful was the experience of spending five months in Fort Niagara's black holes. Skenandoah ignored those who treated him unkindly, but like Good Peter, he was outspoken about the damaging effects of so many land sales. "Our fires are put out, and our beds are removed from under us," he complained in council. "The graves of our fathers are destroyed, and the children are driven away."[69]

Skenandoah would survive for decades beyond his peers. Late in life, he described himself as "an aged hemlock. The winds of an hundred winters have whistled through my branches; I am dead at the top. The generation to which I belonged have run away and left me; why I live the great Good Spirit only knows." His sight abandoned him, and his body decayed, but he kept a crisp mind well beyond the century mark. On March 11, 1816, when he was about 110 years of age, the end came for Skenandoah. As he had requested, he would be buried alongside his other dear friend, Samuel Kirkland, who preceded him in death by eight years. James Dean, by then a county judge, acted as interpreter at the funeral.[70]

Although each one of these Oneidas witnessed the postwar distresses and crises that befell their people, none of them could have imagined how disastrous everything would become. Despite the federal treaties, the new Constitution of 1787, and federal legislation, the State of New York continued to press the Oneidas for land. In 1788, New York made false promises of protection and gained 5.5 million acres from them for $5,500 and a $600 annuity. This left the Oneidas with three hundred thousand acres, but over the years, those holdings dwindled to virtually nothing as well.[71]

In 1823, after negotiating the purchase of some land in Wisconsin, the first wave of Oneidas abandoned their homeland and headed westward. Within fifteen years, more than six hundred Oneidas had relocated south of Green Bay.[72]

Back in New York, conditions deteriorated so badly that another group of Oneidas purchased 5,200 acres of land south of the Thames River in the province of Ontario, Canada. In 1840 this fresh migration began, and in five years, four hundred more Oneidas had moved there.[73]

Fewer than two hundred Oneidas remained, and they were no match for the powerful State of New York or for land-hungry speculators and farmers. By the early twentieth century, the Oneida Nation in New York, which once called nearly six million acres its home, held only thirty-two acres of land.[74]

Deganawi:dah's sage words rang true. Unity would ensure a free, prosperous, and happy people. Divisions, both among the Iroquois Confederacy and within the Oneida Nation, would lead to their downfall. "The Great Spirit spoke to the whirlwind," the Oneida warrior Hanyost T,hanaghghanegeaghu had proclaimed, "and it was still." In time some would listen again, and those voices would be heard anew.[75]

EPILOGUE: FROM JUBILEE TO CENTENNIAL CELEBRATIONS AND BEYOND: TOWARD THE RESTORATION OF HISTORICAL MEMORY

... The Marquis de Lafayette's Utica hosts responded quickly to his request. Before long, on that beautiful June day in 1825, a handful of Oneidas came in from the countryside. Much to the amazement of the gathering, Lafayette, whom the Oneidas had named Kayewla, or Great Warrior, back in the days of the Revolution, recognized two of them, Blatcop Tonyentagoyon and Henry Cornelius. Both had fought at the Battle of Oriskany and later traveled to Valley Forge and served under the marquis's command at Barren Hill. Among the others was a son of the mighty warrior Han Yerry.[1]

Lafayette granted the Oneidas a private audience, a courtesy no other group received that day. They talked about their experiences during the rebellion as well as the plentiful times they had once known. The Oneidas mentioned how much territory they had lost, so much that they could no longer mount an effective hunt. Many, as a result, were moving west to Wisconsin territory. What Lafayette detected was a deep sadness, a longing for the old days before their world had begun to disintegrate in the midst of the American Revolution.[2]

At day's end, Lafayette and his party were on their way. After additional salutations and a blessing, the former major general boarded a craft bound for Schenectady, the next stop on his tour. As for the Oneidas, they took consolation that Kayewla had remembered their wartime services and met with them, even if their European American neighbors had no memory of their many contributions to the Revolution and the cause of liberty.

Wherever Lafayette went on his grand tour, his presence generated an emotional outpouring of gratitude, toward both him and the aging revolutionaries. The popular enthusiasm generated by the marquis, however, was modest when compared with the frenzied celebrations that denoted the centennial years of the American Revolution. Such was the case more than fifty years after the marquis's visit, at the site of the Battle of Oriskany on August 6, 1877, near where the Oneida village of Oriska had once stood. The current inhabitants had long since modified the Oneida word *Oriska* and named the battle and the sleepy little hamlet Oriskany.[3]

Few could have predicted the mammoth turnout. "There was no end to the stream of humanity," one eyewitness stated. Carriages and pedestrians clogged the roads for miles around; gridlock ruled the occasion. New York Central Railroad employees laid aside their labor disputes with Cornelius Vanderbilt to ensure that everyone who wanted to come by rail to Oriskany could do so. With the track barely three-quarters of a mile from the battlefield, one local wisecracked, "Herkimer displayed great good judgment in fighting his battle so near the line of the Central." Rail cars on all tracks were "packed to suffocation," and hundreds hitched rides on the roofs as the best available mode of transportation.[4]

Both the battle and its centennial commemoration took place on private property. At the time of the engagement, timber and undergrowth had filled the ravine and the high ground, making an ideal setting for a surprise attack. Much of the land was marshy, and a stream now called Battle Creek coursed through the main site along the lowest points of the gully. Over time, the owners denuded the area of nearly all its trees. Improved drainage had converted the swampy areas into firm earth. By 1877, the creek was flowing at about half its previous width.[5]

In the southwest part of the ravine, just north of the current road through the battlefield, locals constructed the western reviewing stand, where the most distinguished speakers would deliver their addresses.

Organizers set up a second platform, the eastern reviewing stand, in the ravine on the bank of Battle Creek a couple of hundred yards away. Less-noted orators and guests assembled there.

On Monday, August 6, the centennial anniversary day, the throngs of people, numbering as many as seventy-five thousand, came together for the great celebration. "It resembles Donnybrook Fair," a prominent citizen stated, "without the traditional shillelahs." The Rome, New York, *Sentinel* proclaimed the occasion "the largest gathering . . . ever held within the boundaries of the State."[6]

Local officials had carefully planned the program. Ex-governor Horatio Seymour headed the list of eminent speakers. At 10:30 a.m., cannons boomed, and a serpentine procession of uniformed militiamen from four counties weaved through the cheering masses. As they passed through the once-deadly ravine, the companies dipped their flags in commemoration of the heroes who had fallen there.

Thousands congregated by the western reviewing stand and hoped to bask in the public-spirited discourses from the distinguished speakers. After a local clergyman invoked God's blessings, orator upon orator delivered their addresses. Seymour spoke with the accepted patriotic tone, reminding all listeners what their revolutionary forebears had accomplished. Over the next few hours, others extolled the virtues of the citizen soldier as well as the liberties the United States of America had enshrined. They reminisced about General Nicholas Herkimer and his band of freedom-loving militia, and they recalled the deeds of Colonel Peter Gansevoort and Lieutenant Colonel Marinus Willett and their stalwart defense at nearby Fort Stanwix.

Over at the eastern stand, where the War of 1812 veterans sat, speakers of lesser renown, including historian Samuel Earl and Chancellor E. O. Haven of Syracuse University, expounded on similar themes. Both platforms concluded their festive speech making with dramatic poetry readings. By nightfall, the last stragglers among the celebrants had abandoned the field.

In reflection on the significance of the day's happenings, the *Utica Daily Observer* declared the commemoration a glorious success. "A few months ago," the editor noted, "the Battle of Oriskany was only a dim tradition to the three hundred thousand inhabitants of the Mohawk

Valley. Today it is a fixed historical fact." Those heroic pioneers who had fought one hundred years before had shown that "there are purposes worth living for,—and worth dying for,—which do not come within the scope of the practical world's view." Fortunately, too, the editor declared, the current generation had fulfilled its obligation to its ancestors and to its children's children "to revive the memories, to celebrate the work, of those who gave their lives to Liberty in the first great struggle against armed oppression."[7]

The seventy-five thousand participants had properly venerated the revolutionaries and "the story of their sufferings, their deeds of valor, their words of faith," the *Daily Observer* declared. Their collective memory, however, was highly selective. Noticeably absent from the day's activities was any tribute to the Oneida Indians. None of the speakers mentioned that one in every six to eight persons who fought with the rebels at Oriskany was an Oneida. Only the most casual reference by a single speaker acknowledged that Thomas Spencer, the Oneida blacksmith and respected translator, had lost his life there. The audience that day heard nothing about the exceptional service of Han Yerry, the heroism of his wife, Two Kettles Together, the raw courage of Blatcop Tonyentagoyon, or the valorous fighting of many other Oneidas.

The sole Oneida Indian to receive recognition that day was eighty-six-year-old Dr. Daniel Skenandoah. He sat at the eastern stand with fellow veterans of the War of 1812, and a local reporter incorrectly identified him as the son of a woman who had fought at Oriskany.[8]

The speakers and celebrants at the Oriskany centennial celebration recalled the American Revolution as a colonial uprising of transplanted Europeans against oppressive British policies, as a war among European Americans in which the liberty-loving colonists triumphed. For them, the Revolution represented a momentous victory for human freedom that paved the way for the establishment of the new American republic. Discarded along the way was any popular awareness, let alone remembrance, that the Oneidas had fought beside American rebels and helped them win their independence.

A century earlier, Philip Schuyler had told the Oneida Indians that "sooner should a fond mother forget her only Son than we shall forget you." Had the general still been alive at the time of the Oriskany centennial celebration, he would have seen for himself how unprophetic his words proved to be. The likes of Lafayette and a few others with more complete memories were long since dead and gone. Only a very few Oneidas now remained in the immediate region. Their forebears had become allies long since forgotten as European Americans rushed forward after the Revolution to obtain the bountiful territory of Iroquoia that had once contained the Oneida homeland.[9]

AFTERWORD: NEW BEGINNINGS AMID REVIVED MEMORIES

The descendants of the Revolutionary-era Oneidas held tightly to the dream of someday regaining possession of at least some portion of their homeland. At virtually every turn, however, federal and state sources kept impeding their attempted actions. Then, in 1970, the Oneidas filed a lawsuit in federal court against Madison and Oneida counties in New York. They alleged that a land sale of one hundred thousand acres to New York in 1795 was in violation of the Indian Nonintercourse Acts of 1790 and 1793, which Congress had passed and President George Washington had signed into law to protect Indian homelands from states and private citizens who preyed on unsuspecting and misinformed native peoples. In this test case, the Oneidas sought trespass damages for a two-year period, specifically 1968 and 1969, not only to gain compensation for their losses but also to establish the illegality of the 1795 transaction.[1]

The U.S. District Court dismissed the case, ruling that the trespass claim for damages was a state matter and did not belong in federal court. By a two-to-one majority, the U.S. Second Circuit Court of Appeals affirmed this ruling, but on review by the U.S. Supreme Court, the justices reversed the lower courts. In a unanimous decision rendered in 1974 and known as *Oneida I*, the Supreme Court ruled that the claim regarding trespass on the Oneidas' land rights was a federal matter. The justices ordered the case back to the U.S. District Court.[2]

In the ensuing trial, the Oneidas demonstrated that they had possessed these lands from aboriginal times and that New York had violated the Indian Nonintercourse Acts when the state obtained the one hundred thousand acres in question. In 1977, the U.S. District Court determined that the two counties had to pay the Oneidas a fair rental value for using these lands during the two-year period (1968 and 1969) covered in the suit. Four years later, the judge assessed $16,694 in damages plus interest and held the State of New York responsible for reimbursing Oneida and Madison counties.[3]

On appeal, the Second Circuit Court affirmed the district court's decision but returned the case to the lower court for a recalculation of the award. The Supreme Court took the case, and in 1985 the justices heard arguments in *Oneida II*. By a five-to-four vote, the court sustained the award of trespass damages against the counties. The justices also held that Madison and Oneida counties could not sue the State of New York for reimbursement. Their decision set the stage for continued Oneida legal actions seeking redress for allegedly unlawful land transactions by the State of New York as well as fair rental compensation covering some two centuries.[4]

Not wanting to oust the citizens of Madison and Oneida counties from lands they currently owned, the Oneidas sought to negotiate a settlement with the State of New York. In late 1998, the district court judge informed all parties that since talks had evidently failed to resolve the dispute, he would render a final verdict in the test case. Dissatisfied with the slow pace of the proceedings, the Oneidas continued to pursue various options, including additional litigation, to obtain an acceptable damages settlement in compensation for being deprived of their ancient tribal lands and current possessory rights.[5]

The Oneidas' legal activism upset local landowners in the two New York counties. Oneida leaders, including Nation Representative Ray Halbritter of the Wolf Clan, repeatedly stressed that the People of the Standing Stone had no desire to evict current residents from homes or lands. As standing proof of that key point, the nation had long since begun a vigorous land-purchasing program, reacquiring several thousand acres at fair market value that were once a part of the Oneida homeland.[6]

Regaining title through open-market transactions provoked additional controversy. The city of Sherrill, New York, located in Oneida County, sought to collect taxes on these properties. The Oneidas declined making such payments on the grounds that the parcels of land were part of their reservation holdings. Legal proceedings commenced, with Oneida leaders maintaining that these properties, lawfully in the nation's possession, subjected them to Oneida sovereignty, thereby precluding any requirement to pay taxes of any kind.

In the deliberations that followed, the U.S. District Court determined that the properties were not taxable, a ruling upheld by the Second Circuit Court of Appeals. The U.S. Supreme Court agreed to review this conclusion and announced its decision on March 29, 2005. In an eight-to-one vote, with the majority opinion written by Justice Ruth Bader Ginsburg, the court ruled against the Oneidas, declaring that the land purchases did not restore ancient sovereignty. Drawing upon an undefined principle said to be "evoked" by the doctrine of "laches," the justices held that the Oneidas had let their entitlement to sovereignty lapse by allowing nearly two centuries to pass before reasserting their claim. Accordingly, the justices concluded, the Oneidas had not acted in a timely fashion. Wrote Justice Ginsburg, the Oneidas' long period of inaction served to "preclude the Tribe from rekindling embers of sovereignty that long ago grew cold."[7]

The justices, on the other hand, were careful not to reverse their ruling in *Oneida II*, regarding the Oneida Nation's right to keep seeking damages in compensation for "the Tribe's ancient dispossession" from its homeland and for trespass on the Oneidas' continuing possessory rights. This litigation, carrying forward from the test case that resulted in the favorable rulings of *Oneida I* and *Oneida II*, is ongoing, focusing on the alleged unlawful conveyance of some 250,000 acres to the State of New York during the first half of the nineteenth century.[8]

During these various legal proceedings, the Oneida Indians reminded the courts that they had joined the rebel cause as allies during the Revolutionary War. This information did not escape judicial notice. In 1977 the district court judge recognized the Oneidas' "active participation in various battles in upstate New York" and stated that they "performed another valuable function for the Colonies—they prevented the Six Nations of Iroquois from taking a united stand as allies of the

British." A judge of the Second Circuit Court of Appeals echoed these words in 1983 when he wrote, "During the Revolutionary War, the Oneidas were active allies of the colonists," and "[t]heir support prevented the Iroquois from taking a unified stand against the colonists—an important achievement for the confederated states."[9]

In the 1985 majority decision of the U.S. Supreme Court (*Oneida II*), Justice Lewis Powell remarked that "the Oneidas . . . prevented the Iroquois from asserting a united effort against the colonists, and thus the Oneida support was of considerable aid." He pointed out that "[t]he United States recognized the importance of the Oneidas' role" through favorable treaty terms in 1784 that clearly confirmed them in their homeland. Once various Indian nations began losing large amounts of territory, Congress passed the Indian Nonintercourse Acts of 1790 and 1793, which established a "clear policy that no person or entity should purchase Indian land without the acquiescence of the Federal Government." Despite repeated "warnings," the State of New York had ignored these federal laws.[10]

Back in December 1777, the Continental Congress vowed to the Oneidas, "While the sun and moon continue to give light to the world, we shall love and respect you." For nearly two centuries after the War for American Independence, these forgotten allies endured dark days and darker nights while also being excluded from accounts of America's past. Through legal proceedings, even with setbacks, and the Oneidas' business initiatives in central New York and elsewhere, the darkness is finally giving way to new and brighter days. Likewise, with an end to historical amnesia, the rediscovery of lost memories, and the reconstruction of a historical record more inclusive of all Americans, the Oneida Indians have begun to reclaim their rightful identity as valued "allies in war" during the American Revolution while also receiving acknowledgment as worthy "partners in peace" with the modern United States.[11]

ABBREVIATIONS USED IN THE NOTES

NAMES

AL	Arthur Lee
AM	Allan Maclean
BA	Benedict Arnold
BSL	Barry St. Leger
CVD	Cornelius Van Dyck
DC	Daniel Claus
ED	Elias Dayton
EE	Ebenezer Elmer
EW	Eleazar Wheelock
FH	Frederick Haldimand
GCA	Guy Carleton
GCL	George Clinton
GG	Lord George Germain
GJ	Guy Johnson
GJB	"Gentleman" John Burgoyne
GM	George Morgan
GP	Good Peter
GR	Grasshopper
GVS	Gosen Van Schaick
GW	George Washington
HG	Horatio Gates
HL	Henry Laurens
JBL	Joseph Bloomfield
JBR	Joseph Brant
JBU	John Butler
JC	James Clinton
JDE	James Dean
JDU	James Duane
JJ	Sir John Johnson

JK	Jacob Klock
JST	John Stark
JSU	John Sullivan
MB	Mason Bolton
MDL	Marquis de Lafayette
MW	Marinus Willett
NH	Nicholas Herkimer
PG	Peter Gansevoort
PS	Philip Schuyler
RB	Richard Butler
RC	Robert Cochran
RS	Richard Smith
SE	Samuel Elmore
SH	Samuel Huntington
SKE	Skenandoah
SKI	Samuel Kirkland
TP	Timothy Pickering
TS	Thomas Spencer
VPD	Volkert P. Douw
WB	Walter Butler
WH	William Howe
WJ	Sir William Johnson

ARCHIVES AND JOURNALS

APS	American Philosophical Society, Philadelphia
CLP	Carnegie Library of Pittsburgh, Pennsylvania
HC	Hamilton College, Clinton, New York
HLHU	Houghton Library, Harvard University
HMPEC	*Historical Magazine of the Protestant Episcopal Church*
HSP	Historical Society of Pennsylvania, Philadelphia
JAF	*Journal of American Folklore*
LC	Library of Congress, Washington, D.C.
MHM	*Maryland Historical Magazine*
MHS	Massachusetts Historical Society, Boston
MNHP	Morristown National Historical Park, Morristown, New Jersey
NA	National Archives, Washington, D.C.
NEHGS	New England Historical and Genealogical Society
NL	Newberry Library, Chicago
NYH	*New York History*
N-YHS	New-York Historical Society, New York City
NYPL	New York Public Library, New York City
NYSL	New York State Library, Albany
PAC	Public Archives of Canada, Ottawa
PH	*Pennsylvania History*
PHS	Pennsylvania Historical Society, Philadelphia

PMHB *Pennsylvania Magazine of History and Biography*
RAC *Religion and American Culture*
RUL Rutgers University Library, New Brunswick, New Jersey
SHSW State Historical Society of Wisconsin, Madison
WMQ *William and Mary Quarterly*

SOURCES

AA *American Archives.* Ed. Peter Force. 4th ser., 6 vols. 5th ser., 3 vols. Washington, D.C., 1837–1853

CCHS *Collections of the Connecticut Historical Society*

CMHS *Collections of the Massachusetts Historical Society*

CN-YHS *Collections of the New-York Historical Society*

CO Colonial Office Papers, Public Record Office, London, England

DAR *Documents of the American Revolution, 1770–1783 (Colonial Office Series).* Ed. Kenneth G. Davies. 21 vols. Shannon, Ireland, 1972–1981

DHSNY *The Documentary History of the State of New-York.* Ed. Edmund B. O'Callaghan. 4 vols. Albany, N.Y., 1849–1851

DRCHSNY *Documents Relative to the Colonial History of the State of New-York.* Ed. Edmund B. O'Callaghan et al. 15 vols. Albany, N.Y., 1853–1887

IAP *Indian Affairs Papers: American Revolution.* Ed. Maryly B. Penrose. Franklin Park, N.J., 1981

JCC *Journals of the Continental Congress, 1774–1789.* Ed. Worthington C. Ford et al. 34 vols. Washington, D.C., 1904–1937 (CC in notes stands for Continental Congress)

JPC *Journals of the Provincial Congress, Provincial Convention, Committee of Safety and Council of Safety of the State of New-York, 1775–1777.* 2 vols. Albany, N.Y., 1842. (PC in notes stands for Provincial Congress)

LDC *Letters of Delegates to Congress, 1774–1789.* Ed. Paul H. Smith et al. 26 vols. Washington, D.C., 1976–2000

MHSP *Massachusetts Historical Society Proceedings*

PAPS *Proceedings of the American Philosophical Society*

PCC Papers of the Continental Congress, National Archives, Washington, D.C.

PNJHS *Proceedings of the New Jersey Historical Society*

PN-YHS *Proceedings of the New-York Historical Society*

PNYSHA *Proceedings of the New York State Historical Association*

PRIHS *Publications of the Rhode Island Historical Society*

NOTES

Full citations for primary sources, secondary sources, and dissertations and papers can be found in the bibliography.

PROLOGUE: THE REVOLUTION'S JUBILEE, THE MARQUIS DE LAFAYETTE, AND SELECTIVE HISTORICAL MEMORY

1. James Monroe to MDL, 24 Feb. 1824, quoted in Levasseur, *Lafayette in America*, 1:9–10.
2. *Complete History Marquis de Lafayette*, 328 and 333–34; Malone, *Jefferson and His Time*, 6:405. For the tour and its meaning, see Levasseur, *Lafayette in America*, passim; Roberts, *With Lafayette in America*, passim; and Purcell, *Sealed with Blood*, 171–209.
3. *Complete History Marquis de Lafayette*, 329; Loveland, *Emblem of Liberty*, passim.
4. For the visit to Utica, see Bagg, ed., *Memorial History of Utica*, 167–69; Levasseur, *Lafayette in America*, 2:195–99; *Oneida Observer*, 14 June 1825; and *Utica Sentinel and Gazette*, 14 June 1825, Brandon, ed., *A Pilgrimage of Liberty*, 419–25 and 479–81.
5. Bagg, ed., *Memorial History Utica*, 168.
6. Ibid.
7. On the construction of public memories, often shaped with little attention to historical reality, see Purcell, *Sealed with Blood*, 1–10 and 213–14n4. Purcell notes MDL's "democratic message" and its importance in relation to recognizing African Americans who fought with rebel forces. See ibid., 180, 191–92.

ONE: THE PEOPLE OF THE STANDING STONE

1. Hewitt, "Iroquois Family" and "Iroquois," Hodge, ed., *Handbook American Indians North of Mexico*, 1:615–20; Hewitt, "Oneida," ibid., 2:123–26; Campisi, "Oneida," Sturtevant, gen. ed., *Handbook North American Indians*, 15:481–82. The Dutch

probably adopted the term *Maquas* from the Algonquian word for "eater of human flesh." See Richter, *Ordeal Longhouse*, 1 and 282.

2. Richards, *Oneida People*, 1; and Shoemaker, *Strange Likeness*, 24–25. On the history of the Oneida stone, see Wonderley, *Oneida Iroquois Folklore*, 1–4, 25–31, 134, and 220.

3. Fenton, *Great Law*, 34–50; Converse, "Myths and Legends of the Iroquois," Parker, ed., *New York State Museum Bulletin*, 125 (1908): 10; JBL Journ., 23 July 1776, Lender and Martin, ed., *Citizen Soldier*, 86.

4. Many versions of the Creation, or cosmogonic, Narrative exist, with slight variations. See Fenton, *Great Law*, 34–50; Wonderley, *Oneida Iroquois Folklore*, 57–86; Klinck and Talman, ed., *Journal John Norton*, 88–97; Beauchamp, *Iroquois Trail*, 1–5; Anthony Day, "Cosmogonic Myth," Oneidatown, Ontario, Nov. 1912, Frederick Wilkerson Waugh Collection of Iroquois Folklore, Canadian Museum of Civilization, Typed copy in APS.

5. For versions of this narrative, see Fenton, *False Faces of the Iroquois*, 95–128. The John Arthur Gibson version is presented here.

6. Archeological information primarily from Lenig, "Oneida Indians and Predecessors," *History Oneida County*, 25–30.

7. Fenton, *Great Law*, 20; Richter, *Facing East*, 53–58; Lenig, "Oneida Indians and Predecessors," *History Oneida County*, 25–26; Francis A. Van der Kemp to Sir [?], 1 Aug. 1792, Francis A. Van Der Kemp Paps., N-YHS.

8. Richter, *Ordeal Longhouse*, 1. Some legends suggest that the Oneidas were originally of Onondaga stock, which seems unlikely, since the Mohawk and Oneida languages are quite similar, and the Onondaga tongue is markedly different.

9. Pratt, *Archaeology Oneida Iroquois*, 1: 150; Hunt, *Wars of the Iroquois*, 66–104; Richter, *Ordeal Longhouse*, 7 and 169–70; Fenton, *Great Law*, 4–5, 69, and 494; White, *Middle Ground*, 2–6, 14, 29–34.

10. JBR's version is in Boyce, "A Glimpse of Iroquois Culture," *PAPS* 117 (1973): 288–89. See also Woodbury, ed., *Concerning the League*, passim; Fenton, *Great Law*, 51–103.

11. Fenton provided the spelling for Hodinonhsyo:ni, also rendered Haudenosaunee in the Seneca language (Richter, *Ordeal Longhouse*, 1). See also Durant, *History Oneida County*, 19; Clark, *Onondaga*, 1:19–20; Beauchamp, *History New York Iroquois*, 41–42.

12. Speech of Kanaghwaes, 30 July 1772, *DRCHSNY*, 8:309. In the document, his names is spelled *Conoghquieson*.

13. Bogaert Journ., 30 Dec. 1634, Gehring and Starna, ed. and trans., *Journey Mohawk Country*, 12–13. See also Fenton, *Great Law*, 20. We calculated the size of the village using an estimate of 2.5 feet for each pace. If the shape was roughly square, it would have contained 30,720 square yards; if it was more rectangular, the total area would have been smaller. Sixty-six longhouses at 25 feet by 100 feet would have occupied 18,333 square yards. Space between the longhouses and from the palisades to the longhouses would account for additional areas within the compound. Pratt, *Archaeology Oneida Iroquois*, 1:134, indicates this site is around modern-day Thurston, New York.

14. Observations of Wentworth Greenhalgh, 20 May–14 July 1677, *DHSNY*, 1:12. See

also Fenton, "Agricultural Tribes of the Northeast," 6, William N. Fenton Paps., APS; Pratt, *Archaeology Oneida Iroquois*, 1:11–12 and 17.

15. Morgan, *League of the Ho-De-No-Sau-Nee*, 1:74–82; Morgan, *Ancient Society*, 64; Shimony, *Conservatism among Iroquois*, 18–40; Fenton, *Great Law*, 27–29.

16. The Iroquois symbolically reflected this bilateral arrangement (mother's family–father's family) in the league and later the confederacy. The expression for the father's kinspeople is *agadoni*, which "balances" the mother's family, or the female principle in nature, called *kheya?tawenh*. See Fenton, *Great Law*, 27–28; Shimony, *Conservatism among Iroquois*, 20–21 and 32.

17. JBR's version, Boyce, "A Glimpse of Iroquois Culture," *PAPS* 117 (1973): 288–89. See also Woodbury, ed., *Concerning the League*, passim; Fenton, *Great Law*, 51–103. In some creation narratives, Skyholder actually founded the clans to conduct and preserve ceremonies and to honor the spirits, practices that Deganawi:dah reinforced.

18. Fenton, *Great Law*, 27, states that clan lineages became a "legal fiction" over the centuries. See also Morgan, *Ancient Society*, 67–80.

19. Morgan, *Ancient Society*, 87–88. Generally, the Oneidas did not act out dreams. Rather, they interpreted the dreams to find some sensible way to appease the spirit world. On the importance of dreams in the Iroquois world, see Wallace, *Death and Rebirth Seneca*, 59–75.

20. Morgan, *Ancient Society*, 70–71; Fenton, "Iroquois Confederacy in the Twentieth Century," *Ethnology* 43 (1965): 71–85; Shimony, *Conservatism among Iroquois*, 28–34; "The Nine Iroquois Tribes, 1666," *DHSNY*, 1:4.

21. Morgan, *Ancient Society*, 67–69, 101, and 103–104; Fenton, "Toward Gradual Civilization of Indian Natives, *PAPS* 100 (1956):572.

22. Fenton, "Iroquois Confederacy in the Twentieth Century," *Ethnology* 43 (1965): 74–75; Fenton, *Great Law*, 29. On women in Iroquois society, see Randle, "Iroquois Women, Then and Now," Fenton, ed., *Bureau American Ethnology Bulletin*, 149 (1951): 169–80.

23. Morgan, *Ancient Society*, 68; Fenton, *Great Law*, 217–21.

24. *Bogaert Journ.*, 3 Jan. 1635, Gehring and Starna, ed. and trans., *Journey Mohawk Country*, 15–17; Fenton, *Great Law*, 24–28; Richter, *Ordeal Longhouse*, 42–46.

25. In their national council, the Oneidas had a kind of tripartite structure, based on their kinship network and clans. Representatives from the Wolf and Turtle clans sat on the western side of the fire and called each other brothers. To the east, across the fire, were Bear Clan members, cousins to the Wolf and Turtle. The seating arrangement reflected the reciprocal obligations from one side of the fire to the other. For administrative purposes, the Wolf Clan served as judges. See Hewitt and Fenton, "Some Mnemonic Pictographs," *Journal Washington Academy of Sciences* 35 (1945): 306; Fenton, *Great Law*, 29.

26. Wonderley, "A Sketch," 6; Speech of GP on Behalf of Oneida Matrons in Proceedings with Four Rebel Indians Who Came to Hold a Meeting with the Chiefs of the Six Nations, 12–18 Feb. 1780. Add. MS 21779, R54, Haldimand Paps., PAC.

27. Fenton, "Locality as Factor in Social Structure," Fenton, ed., *Bureau American Ethnology Bulletin*, 149 (1954): 51–52; Woodbury, ed., *Concerning the League*, xvi–xvii. Tuscaroras did have sachems, though; Beauchamp, *History New York Iro-*

quois, 33–34; Fenton, *Great Law*, 4–5 and 193–94; Fenton, "Toward the Gradual Civilization of Indian Natives," *PAPS* 100 (1956):572. Because one of the Oneidas' own, Odatshehdeh, played a pivotal role in the league's formation, his name became the first of nine hereditary titles for those Oneidas who sat on the council. According to a seventeenth-century Jesuit missionary, the title of Odatshehdeh was "regarded from all antiquity as having been one of the mainstays of the nations." A century later, an Oneida called it "the first name in our national council, long published throughout the Confederacy." See Wonderley, "A Sketch," 2–3. Fenton, ed., *Parker on the Iroquois*, 76–94, offers a detailed account of Odatshehdeh's role.

28. Fenton, *Great Law*, 224–39; Snow, *Iroquois*, 66–67, 111–14; Cronon, *Changes in the Land*, 95–104.

29. Wonderley, "A Sketch," 2–3; Thwaites, ed., *Jesuit Relations*, 50:128.

30. James Emlen Journ., 2 Oct. 1794, James Emlen Paps., NYSL. See also Van Doren and Boyd, ed., *Indian Treaties Printed by Benjamin Franklin, 1736–1762*, for numerous examples of Oneida chiefs serving as mediators or representatives for various tribes.

31. Beauchamp, *History New York Iroquois*, 43.

32. Randle, "Iroquois Women, Then and Now," 172. See also Francis Van der Kemp to Sir [?], 1 Aug. 1792, 40, Francis A. Van Der Kemp Paps., N-YHS; Fenton, ed., *Parker on the Iroquois*, 21–22.

33. Fenton, "Agricultural Tribes of the Northeast," 5, William N. Fenton Paps., APS.

34. Fenton, *Great Law*, 22 and 46.

35. Cronon, *Changes in the Land*, 51.

36. Francis A. Van der Kemp to Sir [?], 1 Aug. 1792, 34, Francis A. Van Der Kemp Paps., N-YHS. See also Bogaert Journ., 30 Dec. 1634, Gehring and Starna, ed. and trans., *Journey Mohawk Country*, 13 and 44fn95; Jones, *Annals and Recollections*, 872–73.

37. The Oneidas had ready access to salt springs near Oriska, but they lacked the knowledge to use salt on their catches for preservation.

38. Journal of Count Paolo Andreani, 1790, APS.

39. Richter, *Ordeal Longhouse*, 76–77; Axtell, "At the Water's Edge," *After Columbus*, 167–77.

40. James Emlen Journ., 2 Oct. 1794, James Emlen Paps., NYSL. See also Journal of Count Paolo Andreani, 1790, APS.

41. Wallace, *Death and Rebirth Seneca*, 25–26; Cronon, *Changes in the Land*, 61–62; Richter, *Ordeal Longhouse*, 19, 21–22; and Fenton, *Great Law*, 432.

42. Richter, *Ordeal Longhouse*, 18–23. Sharing was high among the numerous reciprocal obligations and relationships in Iroquois society.

43. Morgan, *Ancient Society*, 72–73. On the importance of condolence ceremonies and related mourning activities in Iroquois society, see Wallace, *Death and Rebirth of Seneca*, 93–107.

44. Richter, *Ordeal Longhouse*, 32–38; Fenton, *Great Law*, 180–90. On the centrality of the spirit world more generally in Indian culture, see Martin, *Keepers of the Game*, 34–65.

45. For a well-documented example, see Ceremony of Condolence for Sir William

Johnson, 14 July 1774, *DRCHSNY*, 8:480–81; and Fenton, *Great Law*, 570–77, for an interpretation of that event and the requickening into Guy Johnson.

46. Hewitt, "Requickening Address of the League of Iroquois," *Anthropological Essays*, 163–79. Requickening usually took place in the autumn or winter because people thought the spiritual power during such ceremonies was potent enough to destroy seeds and crops.

47. Richards, "Matriarchy or Mistake," Ray, ed., *Cultural Stability and Cultural Change*, 36–38, for an argument that women could seek retaliation only under certain circumstances.

48. Journal of Count Paolo Andreani, 1790, APS.

49. Jones, *Annals and Recollections*, 835, 841, and 843. A safe estimate is that the Oneida population in the mid-1770s was approximately 1,200 people. For a higher figure (1,500), based on an estimate made by New York's royal governor William Tryon in 1774, see Campisi, "Ethnic Identity and Boundary Maintenance," 35. For a lower figure (800 in 1770), see Snow, *Iroquois*, 109–11.

50. "The Nine Iroquois Tribes, 1666," *DHSNY*, 1:4–6; Lafitau, *Customs of American Indians*, Fenton and Moore, trans. and ed., 2:155; Richards, "Matriarchy or Mistake," in Ray, ed., *Cultural Stability*, 36–38.

51. Beauchamp, *History New York Iroquois*, 64; Thwaites, ed. *Jesuit Relations*, 28:281.

52. Thwaites, ed. *Jesuit Relations*, 51:123. See also Lafitau, *Customs of American Indians*, Fenton and Moore, trans. and ed., 2:148–58, on the treatment of captives. One exception was the Jesuit Pierre Millet, whom the Oneidas requickened in 1689 as Odatshehdeh to help prevent war with France. Millet failed to keep the peace, and the Oneidas stripped him of the sachemship and expelled him from the village.

53. Certainly warfare and disease played havoc with virtually all American Indian nations. Some were able to maintain their national identity while others were not. An added difficulty for the Oneidas was how to survive and even prosper as an identifiable nation, given their limited population base. Reckoning with that problem would help frame the history of the Oneida people from pre-contact to modern times.

TWO: EUROPEAN INTRUDERS AND CONSEQUENCES

1. Bogaert Journ., 26–30 Dec. 1634, Gehring and Starna, ed. and trans., *Journey Mohawk Country*, 10–12 and 41n75. Early Dutch and French explorers were the first Europeans to encounter members of the Five Nations. The initial contact between the French and Iroquois occurred in the combat arena, on opposing sides in 1609 near Ticonderoga, New York. In 1610, Henry Hudson sailed up the river named after him, and soon the Dutch, who coveted beaver pelts, were trading with the Mohawks at Fort Orange (the site of Albany). By the early 1630s, at least one French trading party had visited the Oneidas, swapping various goods for furs.

2. Bogaert Journ., 12 Jan. 1635, Gehring and Starna, ed. and trans., *Journey Mohawk Country*, 20.

3. Fausz, "Fighting 'Fire' with Firearms," *American Indian Culture and Research Jour-*

nal 4 (1979):33–50; Starkey, *European and Native American Warfare,* 20–25; Malone, *Skulking Way of War,* 37–46; Axtell, "English Colonial Impact," *European and Indian,* 256–57. Even before the arrival of the musket, the Iroquois had begun to phase out their body shields when neighboring Indians introduced iron- or brass-tipped arrows.

4. Pratt, *Archaeology Oneida Iroquois,* 1:39; Joseph Plumb Martin Memoir, Scheer, ed., *Private Yankee Doodle,* 118–19; Henry Melchior Muhlenberg Diary, 14 May 1778, Tappert and Doberstein, ed., *Journals,* 3:152.

5. Richter, *Ordeal Longhouse,* 85–86; Mancall, *Deadly Medicine,* esp. 29–100; Lender and Martin, *Drinking in America,* 21–26.

6. Pratt, *Archaeology Oneida Iroquois,* 1:143; Axtell, "First Consumer Revolution," *Beyond 1492,* 125–51; White, *Middle Ground,* 94–141; Richter, *Facing East,* 174–79.

7. Richter, *Ordeal Longhouse,* 268; Calloway, *Am. Rev. Indian Country,* 14; Beauchamp, *History Iroquois,* 56.

8. Wolf, *Europe and People Without History,* 94–96.

9. On Oneida preferences of deer and moose meat, see Thwaites, ed., *Jesuit Relations,* 51:129. Comments about their enjoyment of bear meat are commonplace. Archaeological evidence indicates heavy consumption of deer meat. See Pratt, *Archaeology Oneida Iroquois,* 1:149.

10. Bogaert Journ., 16 Dec. 1634, Gehring and Starna, ed. and trans., *Journey Mohawk Country,* 5–6. For European influences on the beaver trade, see Norton, *Fur Trade Colonial New York,* 3–26 and passim; Wolf, *Europe and People Without History,* 158–94.

11. Hough, ed., *Proceedings,* 1:101; Richter, *Ordeal Longhouse,* 77. See also Trelease, *Indian Affairs Colonial New York,* 216.

12. Campisi, "Fur Trade and Factionalism," Bonvillain, ed., *Studies Iroquoian Culture,* 37–46; Wolf, *Europe and People Without History,* 93–94. For an argument that beaver hunting did not initially have much effect on the time devoted to searching for game, see Richter, *Ordeal Longhouse,* 76 and 319n2. Once the Iroquois started launching raids to plunder pelts and gain prisoners, their campaigns often lasted longer than two months, which reduced the number of days devoted to traditional hunting.

13. As a cautious estimate, one in every four or five persons in a village was a hunter and warrior. Brandão, *"Your fyre shall burn no more,"* 153–67 (appendix C), offers a much higher average ratio of one warrior for every fourteen persons in the late seventeenth century. If this estimate is accurate, then Iroquois hunter/warriors had a much more daunting task in delivering adequate meat supplies to sustain the general population.

14. Norton, *Fur Trade Colonial New York,* 27–34; Snow, *Iroquois,* 92–93. See also Wolf, *Europe and People Without History,* 178, for a similar experience with the Pawnee Indians.

15. Wolf, *Europe and People Without History,* 94; Fenton, *Great Law,* 11, 201, 251.

16. B. H. Quain, "The Iroquois," Mead, ed., *Cooperation and Competition,* 245 and 267–68.

17. Fenton, *Great Law,* 199–202, 215–23, and 580–81.

18. Crosby, *Columbian Exchange*, passim; Richter, *Facing East*, 59–68; Axtell, "English Colonial Impact on Indian Culture," *European and Indian*, 248–54. See also Fenn, *Pox Americana*, passim, for the devastating spread of smallpox during the Revolutionary era.

19. Richter, *Ordeal Longhouse*, 57–60. Snow, *Iroquois*, 94–100, estimated that half the Oneida population of some two thousand people died in just a few months as a result of the devastating 1634 smallpox epidemic.

20. Pratt, *Archaeology Oneida Iroquois*, 1:39. See also Hunt, *Wars of the Iroquois*, 72–75; and comments by Richter, *Ordeal Longhouse*, 57 and 311n14, regarding what he calls a "beside the point" debate concerning when beaver supplies "became extinct in Iroquoia."

21. Jesuit Isaac Jogues, quoted in Richter, *Ordeal Longhouse*, 61. For the diversity of reasons for Iroquois warfare, see Hunt, *Wars of the Iroquois*, 66–86; Brandão, "Your fyre shall burn no more," 31–61.

22. Daniel Gookin, quoted in Richter, *Ordeal Longhouse*, 31. See also Jones, *Annals and Recollections*, 846; Beauchamp, *History Iroquois*, 56. Richter, *Ordeal Longhouse*, 57–74, and *Facing East*, 59–67, suggests that severe population losses caused by killer epidemics, as much as the search for fresh beaver supplies, could explain the expansionist warfare of the Five Nations during this period. He proposes that these contests might better be called the Mourning Wars instead of the Beaver Wars, their traditional name.

23. Thwaites, ed., *Jesuit Relations*, 51:128 and 28:281; Leder, ed., *Livingston Indian Records*, 88. See also Campisi, "Fur Trade and Factionalism," Bonvillain, ed. *Studies Iroquoian Culture*, 40; Wolf, *Europe and People Without History*, 94; WJ to AL, 28 Feb. 1771, DHSNY, 4:436.

24. WJ to AL, 28 Feb. 1771, DHSNY, 4:436.

25. Campisi, "Ethnic Identity and Boundary Maintenance," 61–62.

26. Evidence of this pattern appears in later chapters. A good example may be found in the case of Good Peter, a chief warrior who emerged as a principal spokesperson. See Fenton, *Great Law*, 494–95, for a discussion of the formation of the confederacy in relation to struggles over representation and power.

27. Thwaites, ed., *Jesuit Relations*, 53:241–42. Since other Indian nations and European American settlers seldom made distinctions among the Five Nations, an act of warrior violence often produced retributive attacks against any Iroquois—those whom the aggrieved could strike at most easily, not the culprits.

28. Leder, ed., *Livingston Indian Records*, 87. See also Campisi, "Fur Trade and Factionalism," Bonvillain, ed. *Studies Iroquoian Culture*, 40. For examples of this pattern during the Revolution, see White Skin and GR to Brother Chief Warrior Arahocktea [HG], 31 Oct. 1777; and [G]P and [Hendrick] Thagneghtoris, 31 Oct. 1777, *New Jersey Gazette*, 31 Dec. 1777; Speech of GR, 10 Mar. 1778; Speech of Tenhoghskweaghta [Tuhuasquachta], 10 Mar. 1778, Council at Johnstown, *IAP*, 114–17.

29. Gov. Dongan's Report on the State of the Province, 1687, DHSNY, 1:154.

30. Thwaites, ed., *Jesuit Relations*, 49:127; Richter, *Ordeal Longhouse*, 102–104.

31. Richter, *Ordeal Longhouse*, 119–21; Green, "New People in an Age of War," 25–28.

32. Jennings, *Ambiguous Iroquois Empire*, 113–42. For prices, see Trelease, *Indian Affairs Colonial New York*, 217–18.
33. Beauchamp, *History Iroquois*, 128; Aquila, *Iroquois Restoration*, 43–81; Richter, *Ordeal Longhouse*, 172–74.
34. Thwaites, ed., *Jesuit Relations*, 64:91. See also Richter, *Ordeal Longhouse*, 175–76.
35. Richter, *Ordeal Longhouse*, 185–86 and 351; Thwaites, ed., *Jesuit Relations*, 65:25–26; Green, "New People in an Age of War," 153–54.
36. Brandão and Starna, "Treaty of 1701," *Ethnohistory* 43 (1996):209–44; Aquila, *Iroquois Restoration*, 70–81; Jennings, *Ambiguous Iroquois Empire*, 208–12. See also White, *Middle Ground*, 48–49. For Iroquois treaty making more generally, see Jennings et al., *History and Culture Iroquois Diplomacy*, esp. 3–65.
37. Wallace, "Origins Iroquois Neutrality," *PH* 24 (1957):223–35; Haan, "Problem Iroquois Neutrality," *Ethnohistory* 27 (1980):317–30, which modifies Wallace by placing more emphasis on a policy of neutrality that "changed with altered circumstances" instead of just functioning "as barrier to intrusion by European powers." See also Richter, *Ordeal Longhouse*, 214–15.
38. Haan, "Problem Iroquois Neutrality," *Ethnohistory* 27 (1980):322; Richter, *Ordeal Longhouse*, 211–13.
39. Haan, "Problem Iroquois Neutrality," *Ethnohistory* 27 (1980):322–27.
40. Parmenter, "At the Wood's Edge," 6–8, 12–13, 15–16, 442–43, and 452.
41. Merrell, " 'Their Very Bones Shall Fight,' " Richter and Merrell, ed., *Beyond the Covenant Chain*, 115–33.
42. McIlwain, ed., *Abridgement of Indian Affairs by Peter Wraxall*, 177–78. See also Merrell, *Indians' New World*, 121; Capt. [X] Civility to Gov. Patrick Gordon, 10 June 1729; and Conrad Weiser to Richard Peters, 10 Feb. 1745, Hazard, ed., *Pennsylvania Archives*, 1 ser., 1:238–39 and 671–72.
43. Minutes of the Proceedings of the Commissioners of Indian Affairs, 2 May 1743; and Commissioners of Indian Affairs to Lieut. Gov. George Clarke, 30 May 1743, DRCHSNY, 6:238–40.
44. Aquila, *Iroquois Restoration*, 85–128, 233–45; Steele, *Warpaths*, 151–77. For the Seven Years' War, see Anderson, *Crucible of War*, passim; Jennings, *Empire of Fortune*, passim; White, *Middle Ground*, 223–68.
45. Parmenter, "At the Wood's Edge," 375. At least one eminent Oneida chief warrior, Gawehe, dabbled in French interests. Late in the war he fought for the British.
46. List of Indians, [Oct. 1760]; and Journ. Warren Johnson, [29 June 1760–3 July 1761], *W Johnson Paps.*, 13:176 and 181–83; Anderson, *Crucible of War*, 404–406.
47. Conference among Sir WJ and Sachems and Warriors of the Six Nations, 17–23 Nov. 1756, DRCHSNY, 7:239–40. See also WJ's Account of Indian Expenses, [Aug.–Sep. 1759]; and List of Indians, [Oct. 1760], *W Johnson Paps.*, 3:176 and 13:173–78; Parmenter, "At the Wood's Edge," 375.
48. Jennings, *Empire of Fortune*, 190–92; Campisi, "Ethnic Identity and Boundary Maintenance," 60–66.
49. *W Johnson Paps.*, esp. vols. 3 and 13, for evidence of disbursements to Iroquois warriors who aided the British.

THREE: CHANGES IN THE ONEIDA LANDSCAPE

1. Address of Samuel Earl, *Utica Daily Observer*, 6 Aug. 1877, 2; Campbell, *Annals Tryon County*, 3.

2. "List of Inhabitants in the Several Counties in the Province of New York, Taken in the Year 1771," *DHSNY*, 1:649; SKI Journ., 21 Mar. 1773, Pilkington, ed., *Journals Kirkland*, 82. In the Treaty of Fort Stanwix in 1768, the Mohawks yielded virtually all their remaining lands.

3. Richter, *Ordeal Longhouse*, 261–63.

4. Barbé de Marbois Journ., 23 Sep. 1784, *Lafayette Paps.*, 5:251; SKI Journ., 3 June 1773, Pilkington, ed., *Journals Kirkland*, 82–84. For commentary on the process of change when incipient capitalism begins transforming communal-oriented societies, see O'Brien, *Revolutionary Mission*, passim.

5. Luzader et al., *Fort Stanwix*, 3–6 and 17; Mereness, ed., *Travels American Colonies*, 418. See also Wonderley, "A Sketch," 7–8.

6. Quoted in Calloway, *Am. Rev. Indian Country*, 111, which also contains a valuable treatment of the Oquaga community (108–28); WJ to Lords of Trade, 28 Sep. 1757, *DRCHSNY*, 7:278–79. See also RS Diary, 4 June 1769, Halsey, ed., *Four Great Rivers*, 68.

7. Hinman, "Onaquaga," map between 4 and 5.

8. RS Diary, 3 June 1769, Halsey, ed., *Four Great Rivers*, 63–66. Each of these residences consisted of a large, windowless room, perhaps twenty feet wide and thirty to fifty feet long, with wooden flooring and stalls for individual families. The Oneidas at Oquaga owned little furniture, and they used old blankets for bedding. Bark, held in place by timbered rafters, composed the roof. Residents built a fire in the entryway to cook meals; on a beam above the fire they hung their cooking pots. To let smoke escape, builders cut an opening in the roof. Nonetheless, the sooty streams left a coating over everything, and the fragrance of burnt wood penetrated garments.

9. Quoted in Halsey, *Old New York Frontier*, 77. Documents often spell Isaac's last name as Dakayenensese. Fenton renders it Tekayenenscis.

10. On the maintenance of bears, see Bogaert Journ., 16–22 Dec. 1634, Gehring and Starna, ed. and trans., *Journey Mohawk Country*, 6 and 8–9.

11. RS Diary, 3 June 1769, Halsey, ed., *Four Great Rivers*, 67 and 87.

12. Quoted in Hinman, "Onaquaga," 9.

13. RS Diary, 4 June 1769, Halsey, ed., *Four Great Rivers*, 68; Hinman, "Onaquaga," 9. For GP's approximate age, see Draper MS, 11 U 164, (1980, R57), SHSW.

14. RS Diary, 4 June 1769, Halsey, ed., *Four Great Rivers*, 68. See also Calloway, *Am. Rev. Indian Country*, 112–14.

15. RS Diary, 4 June 1769, Halsey, ed., *Four Great Rivers*, 67. See also Hinman, "Onaquaga," 15.

16. RS Diary, 4 June 1769, Halsey, ed., *Four Great Rivers*, 68.

17. Richter, *Ordeal Longhouse*, 257. Old Oneida was located in what is now the town of Vernon, New York. By the mid-eighteenth century, the Oneidas had eliminated the palisade as unnecessary for their protection.

18. Beauchamp, "Aboriginal Place Names New York," *New York State Museum Bulletin*, 108 (1907):137.

19. European demand for beaver pelts was declining, and the Oneidas were having increasing difficulty obtaining these furs. Still, enough trading was possible to enable warriors to secure commodities coveted by their fellow Oneidas. WJ to Charles Inglis, 26 Apr. 1770, *W Johnson Paps.*, 7:597.

20. Halsey, ed. *Four Great Rivers*, p. 84. By this time, the Mohawks had endured such prolonged contact with whites that their economies were intertwined. On contact with European Americans and loss of traditional ways, see also WJ to AL, 28, Feb. 1771, *DHSNY*, 4:430–32. On differences between traditional and nontraditional Oneidas, see *Journal of Indian Affairs*, 10 (Aug. 1770), *W Johnson Paps.*, 12:836–37. Similar responses occurred among other Iroquois groups. See, for example, SKI's experiences with the Senecas in 1765, Pilkington, ed., *Journals Kirkland*, 7–29, esp. 24. On diminished hunting lands, see Hough, ed., *Proceedings*, 1:91; and SKI Journ., 6 Feb. 1771, Pilkington, ed., *Journals Kirkland*, 71, as representative examples.

21. Hough, ed., *Proceedings*, 2:381. See also Campisi, "Oneida," *Handbook of North American Indians*, 15:481; Proceedings of GJ at Onondaga, Dec. 1762, *DRCH-SNY*, 7:512; Wonderley, "A Sketch," 10–11 and appendix A. Kanonwalohale was located in what is now the town of Oneida Castle.

22. "Account of Losses," Nov.–Dec. 1794, R62, 157–66A, Timothy Pickering Paps., MHS, Wonderley, "A Sketch," appendix A.

23. Wonderley, "A Sketch," appendix A and 10.

24. Ibid., appendix A and 10–11.

25. "Account of Losses," R62, 157–66A, Timothy Pickering Paps., MHS, Wonderley, "A Sketch," appendix A. Although this document relates to ownership during the Revolutionary years, some Oneidas started accumulating material possessions well before the rebellion began. Observers testified to the differences in the quality of homes in the mid-1770s, and those dating back to the 1760s.

26. Patrick, "Life and Times Kirkland," 2–31. For a brief summary of SKI's life, see Ronda, "Reverend Samuel Kirkland," Campisi and Hauptman, ed., *Oneida Indian Experience*, 23–30. Ronda points out that some scholars have turned missionaries, including SKI, into "self-seeking agent[s] of western imperialism and aggression," in short wanton destroyers of Indian culture. A moderate representative of this position is Berkhofer, *Salvation and the Savage*, 3–15 and passim. Much more strident is Jennings, *Invasion of America*, 53–56, 242–43, which castigates all Christian missionary work in colonial New England—and by implication everywhere else—as a "racket." One unintended effect of this dismissive approach is to turn GP and other Oneidas who embraced Christianity into nothing more than the mindless dupes of the "imperialist" likes of SKI. More sophisticated recent scholarship has placed the emphasis on what the Indians themselves came to believe in adopting Christian doctrines—and why. For summaries, see Ronda and Axtell, ed., *Indian Missions*, passim; Axtell, *Invasion Within*, 271–86; Wheeler, "Women and Christian Practice in a Mahican Village," *RAC* 13 (2003): 27–67; Wyss, *Writing Indians*, 1–16; and Winiarski, "Native American Popular Religion," *RAC* 15 (2005): 147–86.

27. Patrick, "Life and Times Kirkland," 16–34. See also Axtell, *Invasion Within*, 179–217; Bowden, *American Indians and Christian Missions*, 139–47.

28. Patrick, "Life and Times Kirkland," 30–34 and 105–109; SKI Journ., 7 Feb.–15 Mar. and 2 May 1765, Pilkington, ed., *Journals Kirkland*, xv–xviii, 7–13, 38, and 40; WJ to EW, 8 Aug. 1765, *W Johnson Paps.*, 4:812–14; Extract of Letter of Samuel Kirkland, 22 Aug. 1768, Kirkland Paps., HC. On the importance of commonalities in Indian-European-American relations, see Shoemaker, *Strange Likeness*, 3–12, the concept of which can be applied to SKI and the Oneidas.
29. WJ to Arthur Lee, 28 Feb. 1771, *DHSNY*, 4:430–32. See also SKI to WJ, 21 Feb. 1766, *W Johnson Paps.*, 12:26–27.
30. WJ to Charles Inglis, 26 Apr. 1770, *W Johnson Paps.*, 7:599; Extract of a Letter from SKI, 22 Aug. 1768, Kirkland Paps., HC. See also Goodwin, "Christianity, Civilization, and the Savage," *HMPEC* 42 (1973):101.
31. Extract of a letter from SKI, 22 Aug. 1768, Kirkland Paps., HC.
32. Ibid.
33. SKI Journ., 9 Mar. 1772, Pilkington, ed., *Journals Kirkland*, 75.
34. SKI Journ., 23 Dec. 1770, Pilkington, ed., *Journals Kirkland*, 64. SKI cited Genesis 22.
35. SKI Journ., 28 Jan. 1771, Pilkington, ed., *Journals Kirkland*, 66–67. SKI cited only the first words of John 11:25–26 in his journal.
36. For the broader context, see Axtell, "Were Indian Conversions Bona Fide?" *After Columbus*, 101–21. For comparable experiences elsewhere, see Lafaye, *Quetzalcóatl and Guadalupe*; Todorov, *Conquest of America*; and Furniss, "Resistance, Coercion, and Revitalization," *Ethnohistory* 42 (1995):231–59.
37. See Fenton, "World on the Turtle's Back," *JAF* 75 (1965):283–300, for an exploration of the Iroquois Creation Narrative in relation to other religious explanations of the beginning of the world.
38. SKI to Andrew Eliot, 6 Feb. 1771, Pilkington, ed., *Journals Kirkland*, 71–72. See also Bowden, *American Indians and Christian Missions*, 146–48, for a positive assessment of SKI as a missionary whose success in gaining Christian converts lay in his generosity and willingness to accept native practices that did not impinge on the development of strong relationships with Christ. For a harsher assessment, see Taylor, *Divided Ground*, 56–58.
39. SKI Journ., 20 Dec. 1770, Pilkington, ed., *Journals Kirkland*, 63.
40. SKI Journ., 20–30 Dec. 1770, and SKI to Andrew Eliot, 6 Feb. 1771, Pilkington, ed., *Journals Kirkland*, 62–64 and 71. Early in his ministry, SKI did not adhere to exacting standards. "I considered you as children," he explained, "& by reason [of] your pagan blind[ness], & prejudices [against?] the Truth, I used the most mild & gentle methods with you." Because his flock was "easily captivated with those things that are Showy, wear external pomp & grandeur," he stated to his sponsors: "I[t] is doubtless prudent & necessary in many instances to condesind to the imperfect prejudices, [of] the Indians & infirmities in their present state, if the dictates [of] right reason are not violated, & the noble simplicity [of] religion can be maintained." Once SKI won converts, he treated them more firmly, and he refused to ease requirements for full admission into the church and communion. See SKI Journ., 9 Mar. 1772 and 20 June 1774, Pilkington, ed., *Journals Kirkland*, 76 and 94.
41. SKI Journ., 4 Feb. 1771; 2 Mar. 1772; and 25 Nov. 1770, Pilkington, ed., *Journals Kirkland*, 67, 73, and 61. See SKI's reference to Micah 6:8.

42. David Avery to Oneida Chiefs, 24 Feb. 1772; Oneidas to David Avery, 3 Mar. [1772], Kirkland Paps., HC.

43. SKI to Rev. Andrew Eliot, 30 Aug. 1773, Pilkington, ed. *Journals Kirkland*, 83; Patrick, "Life and Times Kirkland," 113; Fenton, *Great Law*, 551–52. As SKI preached in the Oneida tongue, his choice of words conjured up familiar concepts and images among the audience, building bridges to traditional Oneida customs and religion. Using Oneida words enabled SKI's listeners to absorb new theological concepts more easily while more readily relating them to their everyday activities. For similar experiences in a different cultural setting, see Burkhart, *Slippery Earth*.

44. Hinman, "Onaquaga," 9. See also Fenton, *Great Law*, 576. In Iroquois society, deacons had specific duties, including the administration of all longhouse functions, including ceremonies. See Shimony, *Conservatism Among Iroquois*, 70–87. Whether Thomas was the deacon before SKI arrived or was chosen to assist SKI is unclear.

45. Only during periods of extended absence did SKI's reputation seem to slip, but when he returned, he quickly regained his venerated status.

46. Patrick, "Life and Times Kirkland," 111–12. See also SKI to WJ, 17 June 1765, *DHSNY*, 4:358–59; Halsey, ed., *Four Great Rivers*, 84; SKI Journ., 15 Mar. 1765; and SKI to Andrew Eliot, 6 Feb. 1771, Pilkington, ed., *Journals Kirkland*, 14 and 71.

47. SKI to Andrew Eliot, 6 Feb. 1771, Pilkington, ed., *Journals Kirkland*, 71–72.

48. For example, SKI Journ., 3 June 1773, Pilkington, ed., *Journals Kirkland*, and 83–84; Patrick, "Life and Times Kirkland," 216–18.

49. Thwaites, ed., Jesuit Relations, 51:123 and 129; and 53:241–42. See also Patrick, "Life and Times Kirkland," 112–14; Mancall, *Deadly Medicine*, 79–80, 111–13, 117, and 142–43; Lender and Martin, *Drinking in America*, 21–26.

50. SKI Journ., 25–27 Oct. 1767, Pilkington, ed., *Journals Kirkland*, 53.

51. SKI Journ., 25–28 Oct. 1767, Pilkington, ed., *Journals Kirkland*, 53–58. See also Matthew 10:22, 26, which SKI "acquainted them" with but did not quote in his journal.

52. Quoted in Pilkington, ed., *Journals Kirkland*, 87–88n1 and n10. Deacon Thomas was SKI's closest assistant. After the Revolutionary War, Konwagocet, the daughter of Thomas, spoke of her late father in a statement to SKI. See SKI Journ., 20 Dec. 1786, Pilkington, ed., ibid., 127.

53. SKI to Levi Hart, 17 Jan. 1771; SKI to Revd & Hon d Sir [?], 25 Mar. 1771; and SKI to Andrew Eliot, 13 June 1774, Kirkland Paps., HC. SKI Journ., Pilkington, ed., *Journals Kirkland*, passim, mentions frequent trips to other communities, such as Oquaga, and the visits of many Indians, including Tuscaroras, at Kanonwalo-hale.

54. SKI to Levi Hart, 17 Jan. 1771; SKI to Samuel Occum, 18 June 1772; and SKI to Andrew Eliot, 13 June 1774, Kirkland Paps., HC.

55. Flexner, *Lord of the Mohawks*, 7–42; Henry Fox to WJ, 13 Mar. 1756, DRCHSNY, 7:76–77.

56. Grant, *Memoirs American Lady*, 194. See also Hamilton, *Sir William Johnson*, 19; O'Toole, *White Savage*, 66–69.

57. On the colonists' perception of an imperial conspiracy to destroy their liberties, see

Bailyn, *Ideological Origins*, passim. On provincial opposition growing out of the Seven Years' War and toughened imperial policies, see Anderson, *Crucible of War*, 503–656; Nash, *Unknown American Revolution*, 18–87.

58. SKI's financial support came first from his mentor, EW, and then, after their falling-out, from various New England churches, Harvard College, and the Boston Board of Commissioners for the Society in Scotland for the Propagation of Christian Knowledge.

59. WJ to Rev. Henry Barclay, 30 Mar. 1763, W *Johnson Paps.*, 4:72–73. WJ crossed out the words inside the brackets; however, they reflect his most candid sentiments. See also WJ, "Review of Trade and Affairs of the Indians in the Northern District," *DRCHSNY*, 7:969–70.

60. Samuel Johnson to WJ, 1 Nov. 1766; WJ to EW, 19 Sep. 1767; and Samuel Auchmuty to WJ, 14 Nov. 1768, W *Johnson Paps.*, 5:407–408, 435–41, and 683–84; and 6:455–56; Samuel Auchmuty to WJ, 11 June 1771, *DHSNY*, 4:450. See also SKI to Rev. Dr. [?] Rodgers, 22 Aug. 1771, Kirkland Paps., HC; Patrick, "Life and Times Kirkland," 173–74 and 237–38.

61. WJ to EW, 16 Oct. 1762; and EW to Jeffrey Amherst, 2 Apr. 1763, *DHSNY*, 4:321 and 328–29. EW allied himself with Connecticut land speculators who sought tracts in northern Pennsylvania. He envisioned the region filled with thrifty yeoman farmers who would work the soil and tame the wilderness. The sooner the Indians became civilized, EW thought, the sooner colonists could establish themselves there. See also Guzzardo, "Superintendent and Ministers," *NYH* 57 (1976):254–83; WJ to Thomas Penn, 15 Sep. 1769; and Summary of Indian Conference, 19–23 Jan. 1771, W *Johnson Paps.*, 7:177 and 12:887–89.

62. WJ to Charles Inglis, 26 Apr. 1770, W *Johnson Paps.*, 7:597–98. See also WJ to Arthur Lee, 28 Feb. 1771, *DHSNY*, 4:430–37.

63. WJ to Earl of Hillsborough, 18 Nov. 1768; and Proceedings of Sir WJ with the Indians at Fort Stanwix to Settle a Boundary Line, *DRCHSNY*, 8:110–26; Transcript of Indian Conference, 19–23 Jan. 1771, W *Johnson Paps.*, 12:887–88; Hough, ed., *Proceedings*, 1:91; Tiro, "People of the Standing Stone," 70–80; Patrick, "Life and Times Kirkland," 177–79.

64. WJ to Henry Moore, 10 Aug. 1769; WJ to Thomas Penn, 15 Sep. 1769; and EW to WJ, 14 Aug. 1769, W *Johnson Paps.*, 7:89 and 177, and 12:748–49; Patrick, "Life and Times Kirkland," 236; WJ to Thomas Gage, 24 Nov. 1768, *DHSNY*, 4:397–98; Guzzardo, "Superintendent and Ministers," *NYH* 57 (1976): 254–83; O'Toole, *White Savage*, 273–79.

65. Oneida Chiefs to Gov. Lord Dunmore, 31 Dec. 1770; and WJ to Henry Moore, 10 Aug. 1769, W *Johnson Paps.*, 13:498–501 and 7:89.

66. WJ to Earl of Dunmore, 16 Mar. 1771, W *Johnson Paps.*, 8:28–30.

67. Quoted in Guzzardo, "Superintendent and Ministers," *NYH* 57 (1976):274. These controversies with WJ took place during difficult times for SKI. Although SKI married EW's niece, Jerusha Bingham, in 1769, EW and SKI had squabbled over money and the alleged misconduct of EW's son at Kanonwalohale, as well as other matters. By the late 1760s, they could no longer work together. Such problems with EW forced SKI to find new sponsors back east, which he accomplished by October 1770, at which point he again had a steady source of income to sup-

port his mission. See also *Journal of Indian Affairs*, 10 Aug. 1770, *W Johnson Paps.*, 12:837.

68. Patrick, "Life and Times Kirkland," 244; SKI to Rev d & Hon d Sir [?], 25 Mar. 1771, Kirkland Paps., HC.

69. SKI Journ., 4 Feb. 1771, Pilkington, ed., *Journals Kirkland*, 67.

70. Ibid., 68.

71. SKI Journ., 21 Mar. and 3 June 1773, Pilkington, ed., *Journals Kirkland*, 82–83; SKI to Andrew Eliot, 13 June 1774, Kirkland Paps., HC.

72. WJ to John Blackburn, [1] June 1770; and Daniel Campbell to WJ, 6 June 1770, *W Johnson Paps.*, 7:707–708 and 714–15. The struggle between WJ and SKI continued. See also Thomas Hutchinson to WJ, 21 Aug. and 8 Oct. 1771, ibid., 8:229 and 12:928–29; Vote of Propagation Society, WJ to SKI, 22 Aug. 1771, DHSNY, 4:460–61; and Guzzardo, "Superintendent and Ministers," NYH 57 (1976): 276–78.

73. *Journal of Indian Affairs at Johnson Hall*, 9–25 Feb. 1767, *W Johnson Paps.*, 12:271; WJ to Earl of Hillsborough, 18 Nov. 1768, DRCHSNY, 8:110–11; Halsey, ed., *Four Great Rivers*, 84. For WJ's efforts to keep warriors at peace, see SKI Journ., 27 Oct. 1772 and 21 Mar. 1773; and SKI to Andrew Eliot, 19 Nov. 1773, Pilkington, ed., *Journals Kirkland*, 79, 83, and 84–85; WJ to Earl of Dartmouth, 22 Sep. 1773, *W Johnson Paps.*, 7:890; Congress at German Flatts, 18 July 1770, DRCHSNY, 8:228–42.

74. SKI Journ., 4 Feb. 1771, Pilkington, ed., *Journals Kirkland*, 68. See also WJ to Earl of Shelburne, 14 Aug. 1767, DRCHSNY, 6:946–48.

75. Quoted in Guzzardo, "Superintendent and the Ministers," NYH 57 (1976): 282; *Journal of Indian Affairs*, 10 Aug. 1770, *W Johnson Paps.*, 12:836–37. See also Wonderley, "A Sketch," 9.

76. *Journal of Indian Affairs*, 10 Aug. 1770, *W Johnson Paps.*, 12:837.

77. Ibid. For the authority of the matrons, see Fenton, *Great Law*, 207–208, 215–23, and 580–81.

78. Quoted in Flexner, *Lord of the Mohawks*, 347. See also Hamilton, *Sir William Johnson*, 38–40; O'Toole, *White Savage*, 314–24.

79. Ceremony of Condolence for Sir WJ, 14 July 1774, DRCHSNY, 8:480–81. For an explanation, see Fenton, *Great Law*, 570–75.

80. SKI Journ., 15 and 17 July 1774, Pilkington, ed., *Journals Kirkland*, 95. SKI based his oration on Jeremiah 9:23–24, as presented here.

FOUR: INTO THE VORTEX OF REBELLION

1. SKI Journ., Mar. 1773, Pilkington, ed., *Journals Kirkland*, 79–80.

2. RS Diary, 4 June 1769, Halsey, ed., *Four Great Rivers*, 68; WJ quoted in Hinman, "Onaquaga," 9.

3. RS Diary, 4 June 1769, Halsey, ed., *Four Great Rivers*, 68; Rev. Gideon Hawley, quoted in Hinman, "Onaquaga," 9.

4. Hinman, *Onaquaga*, p. 16; Calloway, *Am. Rev. Indian Country*, 110–11.

5. J. Hector St. John de Crèvecoeur passed through Oquaga in the mid-1770s and said that there were about fifty houses, "some built after the ancient Indian man-

ner, and the rest of good hew'd logs properly dove-tailed at each end." See Bourdin and Williams, ed., "Crèvecoeur on the Susquehanna," *Yale Review* 14 (1925):581. The actual number of Mohawks resident at Oquaga in the mid-1770s is unknown. Loyalist WB estimated the community's size at about forty houses. If so, the population there had doubled in the years immediately before 1775, including about 75 to 100 Oneidas and about 100 to 150 Mohawks living there at that time.

6. DC to Sir [?], 2 Dec. 1774, Daniel Claus Paps., LC. The proximity of the Mohawks to WJ's home in Johnstown was another reason for their close relationship. From WJ's position as the Crown's representative and the wealthiest man in the region, he tried to prevent or rectify the worst land-grabbing abuses, which also kept him in the Mohawks' good favor. See Hamilton, *Sir William Johnson*, 34–35.

7. Flexner, *Lord of the Mohawks*, 291; Hinman, *Onaquaga*, 14–16.

8. See Kelsay, *Joseph Brant*, for a comprehensive biography of JBR. For JBR's birth and early years, see 38–91.

9. Flexner, *Lord of the Mohawks*, 185–86. According to DC, JBR was WJ's best translator. Others translated the words literally, whereas JBR, with his knowledge of both languages, conveyed the full meaning and substance. See DC, "Anecdotes of the Mohawk Chief Capt. Joseph Brant alias Thayendanagea," Daniel Claus Paps., LC. For Pontiac's War, see Dowd, *War under Heaven*, passim; and White, *Middle Ground*, 269–314. For JBR's activities during the Seven Years' War and Pontiac's War, see Kelsay, *Joseph Brant*, 55–65 and 98–103.

10. Hinman, *Onaquaga*, 13. See also Kelsay, *Joseph Brant*, 109–10, 113–14, and 133–34.

11. SKI Journ., 2–6 Mar. 1773, Pilkington, ed., *Journals Kirkland*, 79–80.

12. SKI to Jerusha, 24 Mar. 1773, Kirkland Paps., HC; SKI Journ., 9 Mar. 1773, Pilkington, ed., *Journals Kirkland*, 80–81. See also Tiro, "People of the Standing Stone," 92–95.

13. SKI Journ., 9 Mar. 1773, Pilkington, ed., *Journals Kirkland*, 81.

14. SKI Journ., 14 Mar. 1773, also 10–13 Mar. 1773, Pilkington, ed., *Journals Kirkland*, 83–84. For a similar problem with the Tuscaroras, see Seth et al. to WJ, 27 [21] June 1774; and WJ to the Tuscaroras, [June 1774], *W Johnson Paps.*, 8:1173–75, and 12:1110.

15. Proceedings of Col. GJ with the Oneidas and Oquagas, 10–16 Feb. 1775; and Aaron Crosby to GJ, 25 Jan. 1775, DRCHSNY, 8:551–52. See also Halsey, *Old New York Frontier*, 163.

16. Proceedings of Col. GJ with the Oneidas and Oquagas, 10–16 Feb. 1775, DRCHSNY, 8:554–55.

17. Adam, Peter, Petrus, and Hendrick to Col. GJ, 7 Mar. 1775, Kirkland Paps., HC. Peter was most likely Beech Tree, also known as "Oneyanha" and Peter the Quartermaster.

18. Adam, Peter, Petrus, and Hendrick to Col. GJ, 7 Mar. 1775; and SKI to [?], 28 Mar. 1775, Kirkland Paps., HC.

19. Proceedings of GJ with the Six Nations, 20–28 Jan. 1775, DRCHSNY, 8:535–36. GJ spelled the accuser's name *Conogquisen*. Quotation in Mancall, *Deadly Medicine*, 117.

20. Proceedings of GJ with the Six Nations, 20–28 Jan. 1775, DRCHSNY, 8:535–36;

GJ to SKI, 14 Feb. 1775, Pilkington, ed., *Journals Kirkland*, 105. See also GJ to Earl of Dartmouth, 13 Feb. 1775, *DAR*, 9:46–47.

21. Summary of Conversation with GJ in SKI to GJ, 21 Feb. 1775, Pilkington, ed., *Journals Kirkland*, 107.

22. SKI to GJ, 21 Feb. 1775, Pilkington, ed., *Journals Kirkland*, 106–10. SKI did not say that GJ was JBR's co-conspirator, although he likely suspected him. No known evidence indicates that GJ knew about or helped construct the charges.

23. Proceedings of GJ with the Six Nations, 20–28 Jan. 1775, *DRCHSNY*, 8:538–39. See also Stevens, "His Majesty's 'Savage' Allies," 267–70.

24. SKI to [?], 28 Mar. 1775, Kirkland Paps., HC.

25. Ibid.

26. *Boston Gazette & Country Journal*, 26 Dec. 1774, 2: col. 2. See also GJ to Thomas Gage, 24 Nov. 1774, *W Johnson Paps.*, 13:695–95; GJ to Lord Dartmouth, 14 Dec. 1774; and Proceedings of GJ and the Six Nations, 1–8 Dec. 1774, with a Summary of their Council at Onondaga, *DRCHSNY*, 8:515–27.

27. See Venables, "Tryon County, 1775–1783," for information on the formation of these groups. More generally, see Ammerman, *In the Common Cause*, 73–124.

28. For a comprehensive analysis, see Fischer, *Paul Revere's Ride*, passim; for battle details, see Ward, *War of the Rev.*, 1:32–51; and for Lexington and Concord as a source of popular myths about the Revolutionary War, see Martin and Lender, *Respectable Army*, 1–28.

29. Journ. of GJ, May–November 1775, *DRCHSNY*, 8:658; Graymont, *Iroquois Am. Rev.*, 60–62; SKI to Comm. of Albany, 9 June 1775, AA, 4 ser., 2:1309–10; Patrick, "Life and Times Kirkland," 285–86.

30. Stone, *Brant*, 1:71–72 and 85–86; GJ to Magistrates of Schenectady and Albany, 20 May 1775; Mohawks to Schenectady and Albany, 20 May 1775, and Responses; Comm. of Tryon County to GJ, Undated [June 1775], and Response, 5 June 1775, AA, 4 ser., 2:661–62, 841–43, and 879–80.

31. Levinson, "Explanation for Oneida-Colonist Alliance," *Ethnohistory* 23 (1976): 265–89.

32. Massachusetts PC to Mohawks and Others of the Five Nations via SKI, 4 Apr. 1775, AA, 4 ser., 1:4349–50.

33. Statement of Jacob Reed, June 1775, Kirkland Paps., HC; William Sunoghsis et al. to the Four New England Provinces, 19 June 1775, AA, 4 ser., 2:1116–17. See also Massachusetts PC to SKI, 4 Apr. 1775, AA, 4 ser., 1:1349–50. Reed's comments may have served as the basis for those of SKI, since he could not attend the council at Kanonwalohale. William Sunoghsis ("His House is Long") was the sachem Shononhse:s. See Fenton, *Great Law*, 193.

34. Statement of Jacob Reed, June 1775, Kirkland Paps., HC; William Sunoghsis et al. to the Four New England Provinces, 19 June 1775, AA, 4 ser., 2:1116–17. Those who signed included Kanaghwaes from Old Oneida; Hendrick from Oriska; Good Peter and Adam Wavonwanoren from Oquaga; and SKE and Jimmy Tayaheure from Kanonwalohale.

35. Ibid. Tiro, "People of the Standing Stone," 107–109, proposes that the Oneidas were most worried about expansive New Englanders invading and seizing their territory if they did not commit to neutrality.

36. Speech of Oneynyoagat and Thuegweyndack, [July 1775?]; and Speech of Chiefs of the Oneidas to Comm. of Cherry Valley and Communicated to the Inhabitants of the Butternuts, [July 1775], *AA*, 4 ser., 2:1746–47 and 1766. See also PS to CC, 29 June 1775; and Abraham Yates to PS, 26 July 1775, *PCC*, M247, r172, i153, v1, 5 and 85; Council between the Oneidas and Tryon County and Kingsland District, 28 June and 1 July 1775, Stone, *Brant*, 1:80–83.

37. Some historians, such as Walter Pilkington and Paul Stevens, claim that TS had no Oneida blood. They base their conclusion on that of J. North Van Dycke, who long ago asserted in an undated paper in the possession of the Cherry Valley Historical Association, that "reporting him [TS] as a 'half breed' is in error and no doubt the result of his living among the Indians." Van Dycke's position, however, contradicts many contemporary accounts of TS, as well as his brother Edward, as half Oneida in parentage.

38. Declaration of Rights, *PNYSHA* 16 (1917):183; Campbell, *Annals Tryon County*, 20–21; Stone, *Brant*, 1:53–54; Statement on Thomas Spencer by J. North Van Dycke, undated, Cherry Valley Historical Association.

39. Speech to the Six Nations from the Twelve Colonies, 13 July 1775, *AA*, 4 ser., 2:1880–83. See also Graymont, *Iroquois Am. Rev.*, 65–69; PS to CC, 29 June 1775, *PCC*, M247, r172, v.1, 5.

40. Journ. Col. GJ, May to Nov. 1775, *DRCHSNY*, 8:659–60. See also Graymont, *Iroquois Am. Rev.*, 68; PS to JH, 14 Dec. 1775, *PCC*, M247, r172, i153, v1, 362.

41. Having lost the prospect of combat achievements in 1774 when the Iroquois did not join the Shawnees in the Ohio country during the contest known as Dunmore's War, some younger warriors hoped to push their elders into the rebellion by getting involved themselves. The British were enticing them with ready supplies of weapons and ammunition. According to SKI, the matrons were persuasive in helping to avoid Iroquois participation during 1774. See SKI Journ., 24 Oct.–21 Nov. 1774, Pilkington, ed., *Journals Kirkland*, 96–98; and Fenton, *Great Law*, 581. No doubt they tried to have the same moderating influence as the Revolutionary War commenced in 1775.

42. Proceedings of the Commissioners of the Twelve Colonies with the Six Nations, 15 Aug.–2 Sep. 1775, *DRCHSNY*, 8:605–31. From his refuge in Canada, GJ sent three Mohawks south to discourage other confederacy nations from participating in this conference. These three and the Mohawks more generally faced a scolding from Oneida and Cayuga leaders for breaking with the policy of neutrality. The Mohawks in the area apologized and agreed to attend. See also Graymont, *Iroquois Am. Rev.*, 69–70.

43. Journ. Tench Tilghman, 14, 27, and 31 Aug. 1775, Tilghman, ed., *Memoir*, 84–86, 94, and 99.

44. Journ. Tench Tilghman, 23 Aug. 1775, Tilghman, ed., *Memoir*, 91–92. Fenton indicated that this event was known as a Brag Dance.

45. Proceedings of the Commissioners of the Twelve Colonies with the Six Nations, 15 Aug.–2 Sep. 1775, *DRCHSNY*, 8:617–18.

46. Ibid., 8:614. Sughagearat also stated that the rebels, in seeking to reduce GJ's influence, had cut off supplies that the Indians desperately needed. He demanded that the commissioners restore the trade.

47. Speech of Commissioners and Speech of Abraham, Proceedings of the Commissioners of the Twelve Colonies with the Six Nations, 15 Aug.–2 Sep. 1775, *DRCH-SNY*, 8:616 and 621–22.
48. Journ. Tilghman, 31 Aug. 1775, Tilghman, ed., *Memoir*, 99. See also Proceedings of the Commissioners of the Twelve Colonies with the Six Nations, 15 Aug.–2 Sep. 1775, *DRCHSNY*, 8:610 and 620–27.
49. Quoted in Patrick, "Life and Times Kirkland," 298. SKE's first name was Johannus, which translates from German to John. In one treaty, SKE's name appeared as Johnks, or John for short.
50. Obituary of SKE, *Utica Patriot*, 19 Mar. 1816, Campbell, *Annals Tryon County*, 223–24. See also Lothrop, *Samuel Kirkland*, 243–44; and Draper MS, 11 U 143 (1980, R57), SHSW.
51. Lothrop, *Samuel Kirkland*, 243–44.
52. GW to Massachusetts General Court, 28 Sep. 1775, *Paps. GW, RWS*, 2:61.
53. GW to JH, 30 Sep. 1775, *Paps. GW, RWS*, 2:70.
54. VPD Indian Account, 25 Oct. 1775, Schuyler Paps., R7 and R14, NYPL; Patrick, "Life and Times Kirkland," 298–300. Taylor, in *Divided Ground*, 81–83, rates SKI as a poor frontier diplomat, despite SKI's success in working with the Oneidas.
55. Quedon et al., Report on Negotiations with the Kahnawakes, 24 Sep. 1775, PCC, M247, r172, i153, v1, 176. Hanyost is listed as Jan Jost and Jacob Reed as Jacobus.
56. Ibid., M247, r172, i153, v1, 176. See also Recapitulation by Saristtago (alias Peter), probably Quedon, 30 Sep. 1775, in VPD to Peter V. B. Livingston, 4 Oct. 1775, *AA*, 4 ser., 3:798, 827, and 1275–76.
57. Richard Montgomery to PS, 19 Sep. 1775, R12; and PS to VPD, PS to VPD, 24 Sep. 1775, R29, Schuyler Paps., NYPL; Richard Montgomery to PS, 24 Sep. 1775, PCC, M247, r172, i153, vi, 184. The Seven Nations of Canada included the Kahnawakes (also rendered Caughnawagas), located close to Montreal; Lake of Two Mountains Oka (Mohawks); Lake of Two Mountains (Algonquins and Nipissings); St. Francis (Abenakis); Lorette (Hurons); and Oswegatchie (Onondagas and Cayugas), who eventually moved to St. Regis (joining the Akwesasnes). See Graymont, *Iroquois Am. Rev.*, 199; and Calloway, *Am. Rev. Indian Country*, 35.
58. PS to GW, 15 Dec. 1775, *AA*, 4 ser., 4:282. JDE served as the rebels' representative at this council. See ibid., 4 ser., 3:496.
59. PS to GW, 15 Dec. 1775, *AA*, 4 ser., 4:282. See also PS to JH, 14 and 21 Dec. 1775, R29, Schuyler Paps., NYPL.
60. Stone, *Brant*, 1:113–14. See also Penrose, ed., *Mohawk Valley in the Rev.*, 50; Stevens, "His Majesty's 'Savage' Allies," 526–28.

FIVE: STRUGGLING TO PRESERVE NEUTRALITY

1. Tryon County Comm. of Safety to New York PC, 28 Oct. 1775, *JPC*, 2:96. See also Penrose, ed., *Mohawk Valley in the Rev.*, 50–51. GJ was WJ's nephew, and GJ married one of WJ's daughters. See Hamilton, *Sir William Johnson*, 34.
2. Affidavit of Jonathan French, Jr., 11 Jan. 1776, PCC, M247, r66, i53, 19; PS's Account of Expedition to Tryon County, 23 Jan. 1776; and PS to JH, 23 Jan. 1776, R29, Schuyler Paps., NYPL; and PCC, M247, r172, i153, v1, 414; Printed copy in *New York Journal, or the General Advertiser*, 15, 22, and 29 Feb. 1776.

3. PS Speech to Six Nations, 21 Jan. 1776, AA, 4 ser., 4:855–56.
4. PS's Account of Expedition to Tryon County, 23 Jan. 1776, New York Journal, or the General Advertiser, 15 Feb. 1776, 1:col. 4.
5. Ibid., 1:col. 2.
6. PS's Account of Expedition to Tryon County, 23 Jan. 1776, New York Journal, or the General Advertiser, 22 and 29 Feb. 1776; PS Speech to Six Nations, 21 Jan. 1776, AA, 4 ser., 4:855–56.
7. PS's Account of Expedition to Tryon County, 23 Jan. 1776, New York Journal, or the General Advertiser, 22 Feb. 1776, 1:col. 4; PS Speech to Six Nations, 21 Jan. 1776, AA, 4 ser., 4:855–56.
8. PS to JH, 13 Feb. 1776; and JDE Journ., Mar.–Apr. 1776, AA, 4 ser., 4:1131, and 5:1100–1104; SKI to JJ, 8 Apr. 1776, Kirkland Paps., HC; PS to JDE, 26 Mar. 1776, R14, Schuyler Paps., NYPL; Stevens, "His Majesty's 'Savage' Allies," 576–79. For the critical parts played by Fort Niagara during the Revolution, see Calloway, Am. Rev. Indian Country, 129–57.
9. GJ to GG, 26 Jan. 1776, DAR, 12:53. See also Stevens, "His Majesty's 'Savage' Allies," 548–60.
10. Speech of Thayendanegea [JBR] to GG, 14 Mar. 1776, DRCHSNY, 8:670–71; Graymont, Iroquois Am. Rev., 81, 104–106; Kelsay, Joseph Brant, 162–72; Stevens, "His Majesty's 'Savage' Allies," 562–63.
11. Answer of JBR to GG, 7 May 1776, DRCHSNY, 8:678; GG to WH, 28 Mar. 1776, DAR, 12:95; Stevens, "His Majesty's 'Savage' Allies," 556–60.
12. Draft letter to Iroquois, undated, JPC, 2:483–85; Massachusetts PC to Mohawks and other Iroquois, 4 Apr. 1775; CC to Six Nations, 13 July 1775; and Speech of Commissioners to Six Nations, 8 Aug. 1776, AA, 4 ser., 1:1349–50, 2:1880–83, and 5 ser., 1:1037; SKI et al. to GCL, 27 Jan. 1790; and John Jury [Han Yerry] et al. to GCL, 28 Oct. 1789, Hough, ed., Proceedings, 1:362 and 353–54; JBL Journ., 23 July 1776, Lender and Martin, ed., Citizen Soldier, 81; Morgan, Ancient Society, 64, 67, 69, 71, and 79.
13. When JBR visited King George III, he apparently refused to kneel, since he did not consider himself a British subject. See Stevens, "His Majesty's 'Savage' Allies," 562–63; and Kelsay, Joseph Brant, 164–65.
14. SKI et al. to GCL, 27 Jan. 1790, Hough, ed., Proceedings, 1:362; Adam, Peter, Petres, Hendrick, and Seth to Henry Wisner, 14 June 1776, JPC, 2:301. The Oneida chiefs were Adam Wavonwanoren, GP, Peter the Quartermaster or Beech Tree, and Hendrick. Seth was a Tuscarora.
15. John Jury [Han Yerry] et al. to GCL, 28 Oct. 1789, Hough, ed., Proceedings, 1:353–54; JBL Journ., 23 July 1776, Lender and Martin, ed., Citizen Soldier, 81.
16. See Message from the Chiefs of the Mohawks, Onondagas, Cayugas, Senecas, Tuscaroras, Mississaugas, and Chippewas to Virginians and Pennsylvanians, 2 Feb. 1777, at Niagara, George Morgan Paps., CLP; Examination of Col. John Harper on his Confrontation with JBR, 16 July 1777, JPC, 1:996; PS et al. to JH, 14 Dec. 1775, AA, 4 ser., 4:259–60. See also Mancall, Valley of Opportunity, 140–42.
17. JDE to PS, 24 Feb. 1776, PCC, M247, r172, i153, v2, 25.
18. JDE to PS, 10 Mar. 1776, AA, 4 ser., 5:768. JBU urged the Iroquois to demand the

opening of the trade route to Quebec, which would have forced the rebels to release their stranglehold on the city. JBU also warned about the dangers of a patriot victory with regard to territorial possessions.

19. JDE to PS, 10 Mar. 1776; SKI to PS, 12 Mar. 1776; and JDE Journ., 21–24 Mar. 1776, *AA*, 4 ser., 5:768, 772, and 1100–1101.

20. JDE to PS, 10 Mar. 1776, *AA*, 4 ser., 5:768. The council had agreed to turn the war belt over to Schuyler, and a delegation with a large number of Oneidas executed the directive.

21. JDE to PS, 10 Mar. 1776; SKI to PS, 12 Mar. 1776; and JDE Journ., 21–24 Mar. 1776, *AA*, 4 ser., 5:768, 772, and 1100–1101.

22. JDE Journ., 21–25 Mar. 1776, *AA*, 4 ser., 5:1100–1101; and JDE to SKI, 22 Mar. 1776, Kirkland Paps., HC. The Mohawk sachem Little Abraham, who was also at the village, interrogated one of his warriors and corroborated the tale.

23. JDE Journ., Mar.–Apr. 1776, *AA*, 4 ser., 5:1101.

24. Ibid., 5:1102.

25. Ibid., 5:1100–1104; and *IAP*, 42–48.

26. JDE Journ., Mar.–Apr. 1776, *AA*, 4 ser., 5:1102–1103.

27. Ibid., 5:1103.

28. JDE to PS, 10 Mar. 1776, *AA*, 4 ser., 5:768. See also Graymont, *Iroquois Am. Rev.*, 88–91.

29. JDE Journ., Mar.–Apr. 1776, *AA*, 4 ser., 5:1103.

30. JDE to PS, 10 Mar. 1776; and SKI to PS, 12 Mar. 1776, *AA*, 4 ser., 5:768 and 772–73. Stevens, "His Majesty's 'Savage' Allies," argues that JBU had failed to achieve much success up to this point, but the feelings of other Iroquois toward the Oneidas suggests otherwise.

31. EE Journ., 30 June 1776, "Journal Kept During 1776," *PNJHS*, 1 ser., 2 (1847):134.

32. PS to JH, 8 June 1776, *AA*, 4 ser., 6:763.

33. Sughnageorat [Sughagearat] et al. to PS, 22 May 1776. *DRCHSNY*, 8:689.

34. Quoted in Schaaf, *Wampum Belts & Peace Trees*, 107.

35. Quoted in ibid., 104. See also Sughnageorat [Sughagearat] et al. to PS, 22 May 1776, *DRCHSNY*, 8:690.

36. Speech of Kayashuta, quoted in Stevens, "His Majesty's 'Savage' Allies," 665. See also PS to JH, 17 July 1776, R14, Schuyler Paps., NYPL; JBL Journ., 18 July 1776, Lender and Martin, ed., *Citizen Soldier*, 77.

37. See Sughnageorat [Sughagearat] et al. to PS, 22 May 1776, *DRCHSNY*, 8:690; and PS to commissioners of CC, 28 May 1776, R14, Schuyler Paps., NYPL. The document calls Sinavis by the name Sewajis and Kanaghwaes as Kanaghwiaiga.

38. Meeting between Thirteen Oneidas and PS and VPD in Albany, 19 June 1776, *AA*, 4 ser., 6:977–78. See also Henry Livingston to PS, 16 June 1776, Box 2, Folder 17, Henry Livingston Paps., NYSL; and BA to PS, 10 June 1776, PCC, M247, r172, i153, v2, 206.

39. Meeting between Thirteen Oneidas and PS and VPD in Albany, 19 June 1776, *AA*, 4 ser., 6:978–79.

40. See PS et al. to JH, 14 Dec. 1775; and Resolutions of CC, 27 Jan. and 5 Feb. 1776, *AA*, 4 ser., 4:260, 1656–57, and 1662.

41. Report on the Conference, 26 Apr. 1776, R14, Schuyler Paps., NYPL.
42. JBL Journ., 9 May 1776, Lender and Martin, ed., *Citizen Soldier*, 44; PS to GW, 10 May 1776, R14, Schuyler Paps., NYPL; and GW to PS, 15 May 1776, *Paps. GW, RWS*, 4:308–309.
43. PS to Six Nations, [March 1776], AA, 4 ser., 5:772. See also Meeting between Six Nations and Indian Affairs Commissioners, 2–10 May, 1776, IAP, 54–5; Tooghsquawtee et al. to Commissioners, [c. mid-May 1776], AA, 4 ser., 6:502.
44. Tooghsquawtee et al. to Commissioners, [c. mid-May 1776], AA, 4 ser., 6:502–503; PS to GW, 26 May 1776, R14, Schuyler Paps., NYPL; GW to PS, 9 June 1776, *Paps. GW, RWS*, 4:475; *Connecticut Gazette, and the Universal Intelligencer*, 24 May 1776, 2:col. 3.
45. Proceedings CC, 11 June 1776, AA, 4 ser. 4, 6:1701. See also Stone, *Brant*, 1:158; and Graymont, *Iroquois Am. Rev.*, 100–103.
46. PS to GW, 11 June 1776, PCC, M247, r172, i153, 208; GW to PS, 13 June 1776; and GW to JH, 30 July 1776, *Paps. GW, RWS*, 4:517, and 5:517; Resolution of 14 June 1776, JCC, 5:442.
47. PS to VPD, 14 May 1776, AA, 4 ser., 6:641; GW to PS, 22 May 1776, *Paps. GW, RWS*, 4:372–73; GJ to DC, 9 Aug. 1777; and JJ to DC, 20 Jan. 1777, Daniel Claus Paps., LC.
48. SKI to PS, 8 June 1776, AA, 4 ser., 6:764; JBL Journ., 19–21 May 1776, Lender and Martin, ed., *Citizen Soldier*, 47–51; IAP, 56–60; Conference with the Six Nations, 8 Aug. 1776, AA, 5 ser., 1:1036 and 1040.
49. SKI to PS, 8 June 1776, AA, 4 ser., 6:764.
50. SKI to PS, 8 June 1776; and PS to Brothers, Sachems, and Warriors of the Six Nations, [11(?) June 1776], AA, 4 ser., 6:764 and 914–15; GW to PS, 13 June 1776, *Paps. GW, RWS*, 4:517. See also GW to JH, 11 June 1776, *Writings GW*, 5:131 and 127–28.
51. PS to JH, 8 June 1776; and PS to GW, 11 June 1776, AA, 4 ser., 6:762–63 and 819; JCC, 5:442; GW to JH, 14 June 1776; PS to GW, 19–[20] June 1776; and GW to PS, 28 June and 31 July 1776, *Paps. GW, RWS*, 4:524, and 5:45, 140, 531; PS to GW, 1 July 1776, R14, Schuyler Paps., NYPL.
52. See SKI to PS, 8 June 1776, AA, 4 ser., 6:764.
53. For information on the founding of Oriska, see chapter 3.
54. See Martin, *Benedict Arnold*, 199–245, for the collapse of the rebel campaign in Canada during 1776.
55. Quoted in Stevens, "His Majesty's 'Savage' Allies," 667.
56. Ibid.
57. Speech of Kayashuta at Fort Pitt Conference, 6 July 1776; and Advices from the Indians by GM, 15 Aug. 1776, AA, 5 ser., 1:36–37 and 137–38; Stevens, "His Majesty's 'Savage' Allies," 668–69.
58. PS to Gov. Jonathan Trumbull, 31 July 1776; and PS to JH, 8 Aug. 1776, AA, 5 ser., 1:697 and 856; PS to CC, 1 Aug. 1776; and PS to HG, 1 Aug. 1776, R14, Schuyler Paps., NYPL.
59. PS to CC, 1 Aug. 1776, and PS to GW, 6 Aug. 1776, R29, Schuyler Paps., NYPL; PS to JH, 8 Aug. 1776, AA, 5 ser., 1:856.
60. Speeches of PS, Onondaga Sachem Onwasgwinghte, and Cayuga Sachem

Ojaghat, Conference with Indians of the Six Nations, 8 Aug. 1776, AA, 5 ser., 1:1035 and 1047. Tayaheure is called Taychanu in the document.
61. Speech by Oneida Chief Warrior GP, Conference with Indians of the Six Nations, 8 Aug. 1776, AA, 5 ser., 1:1049.
62. Speeches by an Oquaga Sachem Adam and Commissioners, Conference with Indians of the Six Nations, 8 Aug. 1776, AA, 5 ser., 1:1049.
63. JBL Journ., 13 Aug. 1776, Lender and Martin, ed., *Citizen Soldier*, 99.
64. Speech by Sastaitze, 18 Sep. 1776, Box 18, Gansevoort-Lansing Coll., NYPL; Stevens, "His Majesty's 'Savage' Allies," 773–80.
65. PS to JH, 18 Aug. 1776, PCC M247, r172, i153, v2, 285; Conference with the Indians of the Six Nations, 12 Aug. 1776, AA, 5 ser., 1:1044; Message from the Chiefs of the Mohawks, Onondagas, Cayugas, Senecas, Tuscaroras, Mississaugas, and Chippewas to Virginians and Pennsylvanians, 2 Feb. 1777, at Niagara, George Morgan Paps., CLP.
66. WJ to Lords of Trade, 28 Sep. 1757, DRCHSNY, 7:276–77.
67. Speech by Sastaitze, 18 Sep. 1776, Box 18, Gansevoort-Lansing Coll., NYPL; Stevens, "His Majesty's 'Savage' Allies," 773–76.

SIX: TIGHTENING BONDS WITH THE REBELS

1. For PS and the Revolutionary War, see Gerlach, *Proud Patriot*. On political liberties and perceived tyranny, see Wood, *Radicalism American Revolution*; and Bailyn, *Ideological Origins*.
2. "Proceedings of a General Court Martial . . . for the Trial of Major General Schuyler, October 1, 1778," *CN-YHS* (1879):5–211.
3. PS to Samuel Chase, 1 Aug. 1776, R29, Schuyler Paps., NYPL; Stevens, "His Majesty's 'Savage' Allies," 722–23. For evidence of PS's sensitivity to criticism, see PS to New York PC, 9 Sep. 1776, *JPC*, 1:621–22, in which PS insists on a court martial to clear his name of charges of incompetence, particularly with regard to the loss of Fort Ticonderoga during the 1777 campaign.
4. For European American as compared to Indian attitudes toward land and its use, see Cronon, *Changes in the Land*, 54–81; Shoemaker, *Strange Likeness*, 15–23; Jennings, *Invasion of America*, 128–45; Richter, *Facing East*, 53–55.
5. JS to ED, 17 May 1776, Lender and Martin, ed., *Citizen Soldier*, 148.
6. EE Journ., 4 July 1776, "Journal Kept During 1776," *PNJHS*, 1 ser., 2 (1847):136.
7. JBL Journ., 18–19 July 1776, Lender and Martin, ed., *Citizen Soldier*, 77–79.
8. JBL Journ., 23 July 1776, Lender and Martin, ed., *Citizen Soldier*, 85–86; Speech of GP, 19 Sep. 1788, Hough, ed., *Proceedings*, 1:222.
9. JBL Journ., 28 June, 31 July, and 24 Sep. 1776, Lender and Martin, ed., *Citizen Soldier*, 66, 93, and 107. JBL did not give a translation of this name. At another point, some Oneidas offered to pronounce his last name in their language, which sounded like "Yo chee chiah raw raw gou" to JBL and meant "Field-in-Bloom." See 3 Aug. 1776, ibid., 95–96.
10. JBL Journ., 23 July and 2 Aug. 1776, Lender and Martin, ed., *Citizen Soldier*, 82–83 and 95; EE Journ., 20 July 1776, "Journal Kept During 1776," *PNJHS*, 1 ser., 2 (1847): 155.

11. JBL Journ., 28 July 1776, Lender and Martin, ed., *Citizen Soldier*, 90–91; EE Journ., 28 July 1776, "Journal Kept During 1776," *PNJHS*, 1 ser., 2 (1847):164–65. Observers do not mention any Tuscaroras, but it is hard to imagine that none attended.

12. JBL Journ., 28 July 1776, Lender and Martin, ed., *Citizen Soldier*, 90–91; EE Journ., 28 July, 4 Aug., and 15 Sep. 1776, "Journal Kept During 1776," *PNJHS*, 1 ser., 2 (1847):164–65 and 173, and 3:25.

13. JBL Journ., 28 June and 23 July 1776, Lender and Martin, ed., *Citizen Soldier*, 65–66, and 82, 84–85.

14. JBL Journ., 23 July 1776, Lender and Martin, ed., *Citizen Soldier*, 84.

15. Ibid., 83–84.

16. SKI to PS, 8 June 1776; and PS to GW, 17 July 1776, AA, 4 ser., 6:74, and 5 ser., 1:394.

17. See GG to GCA, 22 Aug. 1776; and Aaron Kanorraron to Brother David, 28 Oct. 1776, AA, 5 ser., 3:770–71, and 1:1105; Letter from Chambly, 12 July [1776], Almon, ed., *Remembrancer*, 3:305; JBL Journ., 19–20 Sep. 1776, Lender and Martin, ed., *Citizen Soldier*, 107.

18. Intelligence from Oneidas, 7 June 1776, *JPC*, 2:203; ED to PS, 4 Sep. 1776, AA, 5 ser., 2:247–48; ED to PS, 22 Sep. 1776, R14, Schuyler Paps., NYPL; JBL Journ., 24 Sep. 1776, Lender and Martin, ed., *Citizen Soldier*, 107; EE Journ., 30 Aug., and 5 and 22 Sep. 1776, "Journal Kept During 1776," *PNJHS*, 1 ser., 2 (1847):189 and 192–93, and 3:22.

19. ED to PS, 4 Sep. 1776; and TS to ED, 4 Sep. 1776 (two letters), AA, 5 ser., 2:247–48; EE Journ., 16 July, 8–13 Sep., and 21–22 Sep., 1776, "Journal Kept During 1776," *PNJHS*, 1 ser., 2 (1847):145–46, and 3:22–27; PS to [?], 9 Sep. 1776, *JPC*, 1:621; ED to PS, 22 Sep. 1776, R14, Schuyler Paps., NYPL; JBL Journ., 16 July, 4 Sep., and 21 Sep. 1776, Lender and Martin, ed., *Citizen Soldier*, 73–74, 104, and 107.

20. JBL Journ., 14 Oct. 1776, Lender and Martin, ed., *Citizen Soldier*, 110; Report on Oneidas and Tories, late Oct. 1776, *JPC*, 1:703.

21. Speech by Sastaritze, 18 Sep. 1776, Box 18, Gansevoort-Lansing Coll., NYPL; Report of 6 Nov. 1776, *JPC*, 1:701.

22. Speech of Ojistalale, GR, 18 Nov. 1776, AA, 5 ser., 3:755. The warrior's name was Karahkontes. There is no evidence that JBL knew about the plot to kidnap Kirkland.

23. PS to JH, 30 Oct. 1776, PCC, M247, r172, v2, 471.

24. Speech of Ojistalale, GR, 18 Nov. 1776, AA, 5 ser., 3:754–55.

25. Ibid., 3:755.

26. PS to JH, 30 Oct. 1776, PCC, M247, r172, v2, 471. The Mohawks also suffered from clothing shortages. See PS to Thomas Cushing; and PS to CC, 30 Dec. 1776, *CN-YHS* (1879): 53 and 55.

27. William Smith Journ., 9 Jan. 1777, Sabine, ed., *Historical Memoirs*, 2:62. See also PS to Thomas Cushing; and PS to CC, 30 Dec. 1776, *CN-YHS* (1879): 53 and 55; SKI to PS, 3 Jan. 1777; Sonughsis et al. to PS, 16 Jan. 1777; and SKI to PS, 25 Jan. 1777, *IAP*, 63, 68–69, and 72. For officers and trading, see John Hanson to PS, 28 Jan. 1777, R15, Schuyler Paps., NYPL.

28. PS to CC, 13 and 25 Jan. 1777, R29, Schuyler Paps., NYPL. See also PS to CC, 4 Feb. 1777, *CN-YHS* (1879):70–71; PS to Abraham Livingston, 13 Jan. 1777; PS to Gov. Jonathan Trumbull, 23. Jan. 1777; PS to Pres. of Massachusetts, 23 Jan. 1777; and PS to Pres. of New Hampshire, 23 Jan. 1777, R29, Schuyler Paps., NYPL.
29. PS to Brothers, Sachems, and Warriors of the Six Nations, Jan. 1777, Kirkland Paps., HC.
30. Sonughsis et al. to PS, 16 Jan. 1777; and SKI to PS, 25 Jan. 1777, *IAP*, 68–69 and 72. No available record suggests how the Tuscaroras reacted. Most likely, they gladly accepted the news. The Oneidas devoted part of their response to grieving over the death of a warrior who got drunk at Fort Schuyler and froze to death.
31. Speech of the Oneida Chiefs to SE, 19 Jan. 1777, PCC, M247, r173, i153, v3, 59. See also SKI to PS, 19 Jan. 1777, *IAP*, 70–71; Fenton, *Great Law*, 211.
32. SKI to PS, 19 Jan. 1777, *IAP*, 70–71.
33. GJ to GG, 25 Nov. 1776, *DRCHSNY*, 8:687–88; DC, "Observations of Joseph Brant," Claus Paps., vol. 2 (M.G. 19, F1), RC1478, PAC; Kelsay, *Joseph Brant*, 174–89; Graymont, *Iroquois Am. Rev.*, 104–11.
34. Adam, Peter, Petres, Hendrick, and Seth to Henry Wisner, 4 June 1776, AA, 4 ser., 6:710–11. See also *JPC*, 1:539.
35. Warriors and Hunters of Onaquaga and Tuscarora to the Captain and other Officers of the Company of Rangers at Otsego, 22 Oct. 1776, *JPC*, 2:340.
36. See Adam, Peter, Petres, Hendrick, and Seth to Henry Wisner, 4 June 1776; and Conference with Indians of the Six Nations, 12 Aug. 1776, AA, 4 ser., 6:710–11, and 5 ser., 1:1044; Message from the Chiefs of the Mohawks, Onondagas, Cayugas, Senecas, Tuscaroras, Mississaugas and Chippewas to Virginians and Pennsylvanians, 2 Feb. 1777, at Niagara, George Morgan Paps., CLP; Examination of Col. John Harper on his Confrontation with JBR, 16 July 1777, *JPC*, 1:996.
37. SKI to PS, 17 Jan. 1777, *IAP*, 66.
38. Kelsay, *Joseph Brant*, 174–89; Graymont, *Iroquois Am. Rev.*, 104–11. DC claimed they unanimously placed themselves under JBR's command, an overstatement. See DC, "Observations of Joseph Brant," 209, Claus Paps., PAC.
39. DC, "Observations of Joseph Brant," 210, Claus Paps., PAC.
40. Ibid., 210–11.
41. SKI to PS, 25 Jan. 1777, *IAP*, 71. This source identified the first two Oneidas as Shenanden and Thayendalongive. Further examination of the source, PCC, M247, r173, v3, 21, indicates the names are spelled *Skenonden* and *Kayendalongwea*.
42. DC, "Observations of Joseph Brant," 211, Claus Paps., PAC. See also PS to Pierre Van Cortlandt, 15 Feb. 1777, *JPC*, 2:357.
43. SKI to PS, 25 Jan. 1777, *IAP*, 71.
44. Ibid. See also Oneida Chiefs to Four New England Provinces, 19 June 1775, AA, 4 ser., 2:1116–17. The first Kanaghwaes signed this document.
45. See Speech of Tayeheure, 7 May 1776, *IAP*, 52, in which he mentions the death of Kanaghwaes sometime after the Albany Council of Aug. 1775. The Oneidas appointed a successor who took the same name. For the letter in defense of SKI, see Tayaheure et al. to GJ, 23 Feb. 1775, Pilkington, ed., *Journals Kirkland*, 111. On Niklasko, see Wonderley, "Oneidas and Battle of Oriskany," 2.

46. The Oneidas at Oriska, according to postwar commentary by GP, supported the rebels. See Hough, ed., *Proceedings*, 1:238.

47. On leadership and consensus among the peoples of the Six Nations, see Fenton, *Great Law*, 203–14. See also Graymont, "The Oneidas and the American Revolution," Campisi and Hauptman, ed., *Oneida Indian Experience*, 34–38.

48. On age and respect, see Fenton, *Great Law*, 29.

49. Quoted in Kelsay, *Joseph Brant*, 187. See also SKI to PS, 4, 17, and 25 Jan. 1777, *IAP*, 63, 66–67, and 71.

50. For an overview of British northern strategy, see Martin and Lender, *Respectable Army*, 47–52, 79–81, 83–85; and Luzader, *Decision on the Hudson*, 7–12.

51. GG to WH, 14 Jan. 1777, *DAR*, 14:31. See Martin, *Benedict Arnold*, 246–92, for information on the British effort and failure to break through to Albany under GCA during the autumn of 1776.

52. Burgoyne, "Thoughts for Conducting War from the Side of Canada," *DAR*, 14:41–46.

53. WH to GG, 30 Nov. and 20 Dec. 1776, *DAR*, 12:264–66 and 268–69. See also GG to WH, 14 Jan. and 3 Mar. 1777; and WH to GCA, 5 Apr. 1777, ibid., 14:31–32, 47, and 66. WH would move his force to eastern Pennsylvania by water, making the prospect of supporting the forces of JBU or BSL that much more problematic.

54. SKI to PS, 17 Jan. 1777, *IAP*, 67. See also SKI to PS, 3 Jan. 1777, ibid., 63; PS to Gov. Jonathan Trumbull, president of New Hampshire, and president of Massachusetts, 31 Jan. 1777, R29, Schuyler Paps., NYPL.

55. Ezra Stiles Diary, 10 Mar. 1777, Dexter, ed., *Literary Diary*, 2:142. See also SKI to PS, 17 Jan. 1777, *IAP*, 67.

56. PS to Artemas Ward, 7 Feb. 1777, R29, Schuyler Paps., NYPL. See also William Gordon to GW, 5 Mar. 1777, *MHSP* 68 (1921):335–36.

57. Ezra Stiles Diary, 10 Mar. 1777, Dexter, ed., *Literary Diary*, 2:142.

58. Ezra Stiles Diary, 7 and 10 Mar. 1777, Dexter, ed., *Literary Diary*, 2:139–42. See also *Providence Gazette*, 8 Mar. 1777.

59. SKI's Expenses, 7 Feb. through 2 Apr. 1777, R7, Schuyler Paps., NYPL; SKI to Jerusha, 17 Mar. 1777, Kirkland Paps., HC.

60. GW to JH, 29 Mar. 1777, *Paps. GW, RWS*, 9:10. See also Alexander Hamilton to New York Comm. of Correspondence, 5 Apr. 1777, Syrett et al., ed., *Paps. Alexander Hamilton*, 1:221–22.

61. SKI's expenses, 7 Feb. through 2 Apr. 1777, R7, Schuyler Paps., NYPL. Speech by [William] Kayendalongwea, 1 Apr. 1777, *JPC*, 1:858.

62. PS to JDE, 6 and 7 Feb. 1777, R29, Schuyler Paps., NYPL.

63. JDE to PS, 20 Apr. 1777, PCC, M247, r173, i153, v3, 128–30. See also PS to JDE, 6 and 7 Feb. 1777, R29, Schuyler Paps., NYPL; Stevens, "His Majesty's 'Savage' Allies," 929–30; Edward Foy to [Capt. Alexander] Fraser, 7 Apr. 1777, Add. MS 21699, R15, Haldimand Paps., PAC. From PS's 6 Feb. letter, it appears that TS was a participant, based on PS's orders about the distribution of rations. However, TS was most likely at Kanonwalohale and Fort Schuyler performing translation duty. See PS to SE, 7 Feb. 1777, *CN-YHS* (1879):75; and SE to PS, 20 Mar. 1777, *IAP*, 75.

64. Edward Foy to [Capt. Alexander] Fraser, 7 Apr. 1777, Add. MS 21699, R15, Haldimand Paps., PAC.

65. SE to PS, 20 Mar. 1777, *IAP*, 74–75. See also Resolution of 29 Apr. 1777, *JCC*, 7, 308.

66. SE to PS, 20 Mar. 1777, *IAP*, 74–75; JBU to GCA, 31 Mar. 1777, CO 42/36, f. 117, RB33, PAC. JDE to PS, 20 Apr. 1777; and SE to PS, 22 Apr. 1777, PCC, M247, r173, i153, 128–30 and 124–26. See also Stevens, "His Majesty's 'Savage' Allies," 958–59.

67. JDE to PS, 20 Apr. 1777; and SE to PS, 22 Apr. 1777, PCC, M247, r173, i153, 128–30 and 124–26. See also JBU to GCA, 31 Mar. 1777, CO 42/36, f. 117, RB33, PAC.

68. Indian Affairs Department Reply to the Indians Concerning Their Meeting with Butler, [27 May 1777], *IAP*, 75–76. See also *Pennsylvania Gazette*, 4 June 1777, 2:col. 3; HG Speech, 29 May 1777, R7, Schuyler Paps., NYPL.

69. HG Speech to Six Nations, [29 May 1777], *IAP*, 77–78. See also John Welles to James Milligan, 28 May 1777, John Welles Paps., N-YHS.

70. GG to GCA, 26 Mar. 1777, *DAR*, 14:51–53; Report of Abell Sprauge to Council of Safety, 17 June 1777, *JPC*, 1:968; DC, "Observations of Joseph Brant," Claus Paps., PAC; Kelsay, *Joseph Brant*, 187–88.

71. TS to PS, 26 June 1777, *IAP*, 80; JDE to PS, 25 June 1777, *CN-YHS* (1879): 118–19. At Onondaga, TS also extended an invitation to some Cherokees, who were then gathering to discuss concerns with the Six Nations.

72. Report of Tryon County Comm. of Safety, 17 July 1777, *JPC*, 1:1007. See also Orders to JDE, 10 June 1777, *CN-YHS* (1879):101–102.

73. Report of Tryon County Comm. of Safety, 17 July 1777, *JPC*, 1:1007.

74. Ibid. See also JDE to PS, 25 June 1777, *CN-YHS* (1879): 118–19.

75. Edward Spencer to PG, 6 July 1777; and TS to PS, 26 June 1777, *IAP*, 79–80 and 85–86. See also JBU to GCA, 15 June 1777, CO 42/36. f. 310, RB33, PAC.

76. The major sources contain unclear recollections. See JBU to GCA, 28 July 1777, CO 42/37, f. 97–98, RB33, PAC; DC to GCA, 28 Aug. 1777, CO 42/37, f. 101–102, RB34, PAC. See also Stevens, "His Majesty's 'Savage' Allies," 1092–1107.

77. TS to Officers of Fort Schuyler, 29 July 1777, *JPC*, 1:1026; Graymont, *Iroquois Am. Rev.*, 126–28. The JBU gathering was at Three Rivers, located at the junction of the Oneida, Seneca, and Oswego rivers.

78. Stevens, "His Majesty's 'Savage' Allies," 1085–86 and 1124–25; Campbell, *Annals Tryon County*, 64.

SEVEN: DEFENDING THE ONEIDA HOMELAND

1. Affidavit of Peter Doxtator, *IAP*, 350. See also John Hadcock to Lyman Draper, 6 Feb. 1878, Draper MS, 11 U 242–43 (1980, R57), SHSW.

2. Testimony of Mrs. Jacob Doxtader, Henry Powless, and Cornelius Doxtader, Draper MS, 11 U 191–94, 200 (1980, R57), SHSW.

3. Testimony of Theresa Swamp, Mrs. Jacob Doxtader, and Aunt Polly Doxtader, Draper MS, 11 U 216, 191–92, 195, and 210 (1980, R57), SHSW. *Tyonajanegen* could also mean "Between Two Kettles."

4. Testimony of Theresa Swamp, Mrs. Jacob Doxtader, and Cornelius Wheelock,

Draper MS, 11 U 211, 191, and 210 (1980, R57), SHSW; List of Indians, [Oct. 1760], *W Johnson Paps.*, 13:176.

5. "Account of Losses," R62, 157–166A, Timothy Pickering Paps., MHS, Wonderley, "A Sketch," appendix A.

6. Testimony of Cornelius Doxtader and Mrs. Jacob Doxtader, 11 U 200, 202, 192 (1980, R57), SHSW; Jones, *Annals and Recollections*, 97.

7. See HG to PG, 26 Apr. 1777; and PG to Brothers, Sachems, and Warriors of the Six Nations, 2 July 1777, Box 18, Gansevoort-Lansing Coll., NYPL.

8. Kenney, *Gansevoorts of Albany*, x–xi, 32–38, 71–72, and 88–92. PG's grandson, Herman Melville, became one of America's most accomplished authors.

9. Ibid., 90–94 and 103.

10. Quoted in Graymont, *Iroquois Am Rev.*, 115; PS to PG, 9 June 1777; and Leonard Gansevoort to PG, 17 May 1777, Box 18, Gansevoort-Lansing Coll., NYPL.

11. See Garrison Orders, Fort Schuyler, 7 May 1777; PG to GVS, 1 June 1777; PG to PS, 15 June 1777; and PG to [?] 7 Mar. and 21 June 1778, Box 18, Gansevoort-Lansing Coll., NYPL; PG to PS, 4 July 1777, *IAP*, 84.

12. See Luzader et al., *Fort Stanwix*, pp. 27–28; Stone, *Brant*, 1:27–28.

13. Logs partially buried are called pickets. The slope that most concerned PG was the escarpment, which was the incline from the ditch to the parapet. See Luzader, *Fort Stanwix*, 24–29; PG to PS, 15 June 1777; PS to SE, 19 Mar. 1777; and PS to PG, 9 June 1777, Box 18, Gansevoort-Lansing Coll., NYPL; MW to PS, 24 July 1777, R16, Schuyler Paps., NYPL; PS to Col. Morgan Lewis, 17 Mar. 1777; and PS to Capt. Bernard La Marquisie, 18 Mar. 1777, *CN-YHS* (1879):86–87.

14. PG to PS, 27 June 1777, Gansevoort-Lansing Coll., NYPL; Extract of a letter from Fort Stanwix, 27 June [1777], Pennsylvania Gazette, 30 July 1777, 3: col. 1–2; William Colbrath Journ., 25 June 1777, Reid, ed. *Story Fort Johnson*, 88. See also Watt, *Rebellion Mohawk Valley*, 184.

15. Quoted in Stone, *Brant*, 1:227–28.

16. Ibid.

17. See letter from Fort Stanwix, 4 July 1777, *Pennsylvania Gazette*, 16 July 1777, 2: col. 3; DC to William Knox, 16 Oct. 1777, DAR, 14:220; PG to PS, 4 July 1777, *IAP*, 84.

18. Letter from Fort Stanwix, 4 July 1777, *Pennsylvania Gazette*, 16 July 1777, 2: col. 3; Ann Eliza Bleecker to Lenny, 5 Aug. 1777, Leonard Bleecker Coll., RUL; Isaac Patchin to Council of Safety, 4 July 1777; William Harper to Council of Safety, 8 July 1777; and Johannes Ball to the Council of Safety, 17 July 1777, JPC, 2:507 and 509.

19. PS to Council of Safety, 18 July 1777, *CN-YHS* (1879):175; Council of Safety to Comm. of Tyron County, 25 July 1777, JPC, 1:1015. See also John Jay to Gouverneur Morris, 21 July 1777, Stone, *Brant*, 1:211–12.

20. NH to PS, [15 July 1777], *IAP*, 89–91. See also PS to NH, 8 July 1777, *CN-YHS* (1879):160. Although NH ordered two hundred militiamen to Fort Schuyler, only one hundred were actually there during the siege.

21. Catherine Van Schaick to PG, 31 July 1777, Box 18, Gansevoort-Lansing Coll., NYPL.

22. Extract of a letter from Fort Schuyler, 28 July 1777, *New York Journal*, 4 Aug. 1777.

See also Scott, *Fort Stanwix*, 234–35; Colbrath Journ., 27–28 July 1777, Reid, ed., *Story Fort Johnson*, 88–89. A pregnant woman remained behind and gave birth during the campaign, despite being wounded. Oneida women were also present in the fort during the siege.

23. TS to PG, 29 July 1777, Box 18, Gansevoort-Lansing Coll., NYPL. See also Speech of Kiashuta in Conference at Fort Pitt, 6 July 1776, AA, 5 ser., 1:36; Graymont, *Iroquois Am. Rev.*, 126–28.

24. TS to PG, 29 July 1777, Box 18, Gansevoort-Lansing Coll., NYPL.

25. Testimony of Cornelius Doxtader, Draper MS, 11 U 202 (1980, R57), SHSW.

26. See Henry Bird to BSL, 2 Aug. 1777; and BSL to Henry Bird, 3 Aug. 1777, Box 18, Gansevoort-Lansing Coll., NYPL; Testimony of Cornelius Doxtader, Draper MS, 11 U 202–204 (1980, R57), SHSW.

27. Testimony of Cornelius Doxtader, Draper MS, 11 U 202–204 (1980, R57), SHSW.

28. Ibid.

29. Colbrath Journ., 2 and 3 Aug. 1777, Reid, ed., *Story Fort Johnson*, 89–90; Scott, *Fort Stanwix*, 171–72; Testimony of Cornelius Doxtader, Draper MS, 11 U 204 (1980, R57), SHSW.

30. BSL to GCA, 27 Aug. 1777; and DC to William Knox, 16 Oct. 1777, *DAR*, 14:171–74, and 219–24; Testimony of Mrs. Jacob Doxtader and Cornelius Doxtader, Draper MS, 11 U 191–92 and 204 (1980, R57), SHSW.

31. Luzader, *Fort Stanwix*, 33; Scott, *Fort Stanwix*, 232–34; DC to William Knox, 16 Oct. 1777, *DAR*, 14:220–22. The Senecas with JBU did not reach the fort until August 5, the day before the Battle of Oriskany.

32. Proclamation of St. Leger, reprinted in Stone, *Brant*, 1:230–31; Colbrath Journ., 3 Aug. 1777, Reid, ed., *Story Fort Johnson*, 90. See also Willett, *Narrative Marinus Willett*, 50–51.

33. Testimony of Polly Doxtader, Draper MS, 11 U 196 (1980, R57), SHSW; Willett, *Narrative Marinus Willett*, 48–51; BSL to GCA, 27 Aug. 1777, CO 42/37, f. 89–90, RB34, PAC. Although the fort still needed repairs, PG's soldiers performed the most pressing work at night, when darkness shielded them from enemy marksmen.

34. See DC to William Knox, 16 Oct. 1777, *DAR*, 14:220–22; Luzader, *Fort Stanwix*, 34–37; BSL to GCA, 27 Aug. 1777, and 27 Aug. 1777, CO 42/37, f. 89–93, RB34, PAC.

35. Herkimer Proclamation, Campbell, *Annals Tryon County*, 61–62; NH to PG, 29 July 1777, Gansevoort-Lansing Coll., NYPL. See also Luzader, *Fort Stanwix*, 43, who accidentally dates the order 30 June.

36. Watt, *Rebellion Mohawk Valley*, 136–54; Roberts, *Battle of Oriskany*, 16–17 and 63–64.

37. Watt, *Rebellion Mohawk Valley*, 145–54; Scott, *Fort Stanwix*, 194. Few militiamen admitted to falling out on the march. See Application of Anna Oosterhout Myers, Dann, ed., *Revolution Remembered*, 270, for an example. Nevertheless, as many as 10 to 20 percent of NH's original eight hundred dropped out and never caught up. Some no doubt fell out because they were sick, the summer months representing the worst time for illness in military forces.

38. John Hadcock's father also fought in the battle. See John Hadcock to Lyman Draper, 6 Feb. 1878, Draper MS, 11 U 265 (1980, R57), SHSW. William L. Stone

conversed with Judge John Frank in September 1837. Frank was a resident of German Flatts and a rebel participant; he recalled Cornelius as engaged in the battle. See Stone, *Brant*, 1:367. According to Oneida oral tradition, about one hundred Oneidas fought in the battle. For corroboration, see Testimony of Aunt Polly Doxtader, Draper MS, 11 U 196 (1980, R57), SHSW.

39. See Examination of Adam Hellmer, 11 Aug. 1777, *JPC*, 1:1038; 11 Aug. 1777, Willett, Narrative Marinus Willett, 50–53 and 131; Colbrath Journ., 6 Aug. 1777, Reid, ed., *Story Fort Johnson*, 91; Scott, *Fort Stanwix*, 183–84; Graymont, *Iroquois Am. Rev.*, 132.

40. Scott, *Fort Stanwix*, 194; Roberts, *Battle of Oriskany*, 18; Watt, *Rebellion Mohawk Valley*, 148–52.

41. BSL to GCA, 27 Aug. 1777, DAR, 14:171.

42. Stone, *Brant*, 1:234–35. See also Watt, *Rebellion Mohawk Valley*, 152–54; and Mintz, *Seeds of Empire*, 31–32.

43. One need only consider the movement of BA's relief column later that month to realize how slow an army would advance when carefully scouting the woods. See Ward, *War of the Rev.*, 2:485–86.

44. DC to William Knox, 16 Oct. 1777, DAR, 14:222. See also Luzader, *Fort Stanwix*, 43; and Schoolcraft, "Historical Considerations Siege and Defence of Fort Stanwix," *PN-YHS* 3 (1845):142.

45. Scott, *Fort Stanwix*, 199–200; Roberts, *Battle of Oriskany*, 18–20.

46. Campbell, *Annals Tyron County*, 69. John Lewis deposition, 13 June 1778; and Garred Van Brocklin deposition, 13 June 1778, N-YHS. Transcribed by Joseph Robertaccio. Lewis said that the fighting began at about 11:00 a.m.

47. See BSL to GJB, 11 Aug. 1777, Almon, ed., *Remembrancer*, 5: 392; BSL to GCA, 27 Aug. 1777; and DC to William Knox, 16 Oct. 1777, DAR, 14:171–72 and 222; JBU to GCA, 15 Aug. 1777, CO 42/37, f. 103–104, RB34, PAC; Luzader, *Fort Stanwix*, 43; Stevens, "His Majesty's 'Savage' Allies," 2287n4. How many pro-British Indians wielded muskets is open to question; Blacksnake claimed few had them. See Abler, ed., *Chainbreaker Rev. War Memoirs*, 128–30; and DC, "Anecdotes of Joseph Brant," *IAP*, 321.

48. JBU to GCA, 15 Aug. 1777, and BSL to GCA, 27 Aug. 1777, CO 42/37, f. 103–104 and f. 91–93, RB34, PAC; Klinck and Talman, ed., *Journal John Norton*, 273. For the battle, see Watt, *Rebellion Mohawk Valley*, 155–89; and Stevens, "His Majesty's 'Savage' Allies," 1237–54. Stevens describes a fishhook-shaped position; and Norton, who was not there but talked about the battle many years later with Oriskany veterans, spoke of a similar formation. Others, who also conversed with participants, described a U formation. Assuming tactical proficiency among the Iroquois, we cannot conclude that they would leave the marshlands unattended. Garred Van Brocklin deposition, 13 June 1778, N-YHS, described an attack from the left and the right.

49. See JBU to GCA, 15 Aug. 1777, CO 42/37, f. 103–104, RB34, PAC. In attacks during the eighteenth and nineteenth centuries like that at Oriskany, a standard rule was about 50 percent of all casualties occurred during the first volley. See Capt. Hertel de Rouville, Jr. [?], "The Unsuccessful Expedition," trans. and reprinted in *Rome Sentinel*, 2 June 1978, 6, for a relevant contemporary poem. Garred Van

Brocklin deposition, 13 June 1778, N-YHS, described the bunching up of militia troops as they fled for the rear. According to JBU, NH's column traveled with fifteen wagons.

50. Jones, *Annals and Recollections*, 344–45. See also Watt, *Rebellion Mohawk Valley*, 160–62.

51. TS to Sir [?], 29 July 1777, Box 18, Gansevoort-Lansing Coll., NYPL. See also *One Hundred Fiftieth Anniversary of the Battle of Oriskany and the Siege and Relief of Fort Stanwix, Souvenir Program* (1927), 33, which lists Edward Spencer as Henry Spencer.

52. See PS to NH, 9 Aug. 1777; and PS to CC, 10 Aug. 1777, R29, Schuyler Paps., NYPL; Peter Dygert to Comm. of Albany, 9 Aug. 1777, JPC, 1:1037–38; Garred Van Brocklin deposition, 13 June 1778, N-YHS; DC, "Anecdotes of Joseph Brant," *IAP*, 321; BSL to GCA, 27 Aug. 1777; and JBU to GCA, 15 Aug. 1777, CO 42/37, f. 91–93 and 103–104, RB34, PAC.

53. Extract of a Letter from JBU to GCA, 15 Aug. 1777, *Providence Gazette*, 27 June 1778.

54. Testimony of Jacob Cornelius; and Testimony of Elijah Skenandoah, Draper MS, 11 U 213 and 243 (1980, R57), SHSW.

55. Quoted in Scott, *Fort Stanwix*, 223.

56. Campbell, *Annals Tryon County*, 72; Scott, *Fort Stanwix*, 211–13; Jones, *Annals and Recollections*, 345–46. MW wanted to attack at 1:00 p.m., but rain delayed his sortie until about 2:00 p.m.

57. *New York Journal*, 25 Aug. 1777; Testimony of Polly Doxtader, Draper MS, 11 U 196–97 (1980, R57), SHSW; Moore, comp., *Diary Am. Rev.*, 1:486. The sources do not mention which son of Han Yerry was present. Since Jacob was most likely in and around the fort, Han Yerry's next-oldest son, now reaching fighting age, must have been involved. This was Cornelius, who eventually, as his father before him, became a chief warrior. Judge Frank recalled that the sachem Cornelius and Han Yerry fought "valiantly in that murderous conflict." See Stone, *Brant*, 1:367.

58. Roberts, *Battle of Oriskany*, 21–22; Graymont, *Iroquois Am. Rev.*, 139.

59. Abler, ed., *Chainbreaker Rev. War Memoirs*, 128–30; Seaver, ed., *Narrative Mary Jemison*, 68. See also Peter J. Deggart to Comm. of Albany, 9 Aug. 1777, JPC, 1:1037–38. JBU claimed thirty-three Seneca casualties and sixty-two Indian casualties overall, with thirty-three dead. See JBU to GCA, 15 Aug. 1777, CO 42/37, f. 103–104, RB34, PAC. DC fixed the total casualties for British forces at seventy-three. Both figures seem low. DC, "Anecdotes of Joseph Brant," *IAP*, 321, wrote that seventeen Senecas were killed. Jemison, who lived with the Senecas at the time, tabulated thirty-six Senecas dead. Unknown to DC and JBU, some wounds likely resulted in deaths after the battle. PS reported to JH what NH had told him, that there were some fifty dead Indians on the Oriskany battlefield. See PS to JH, 10 Aug. 1777, R29, Schuyler Paps., NYPL. For a summary of the debate over numbers of casualties at Oriskany, see Watt, *Rebellion Mohawk Valley*, 315–21.

60. Testimony of John Cornelius, Draper MS, 11 U 216 (1980, R57), SHSW; Wonderley "Oneidas and Battle of Oriskany," 13n21; Schoolcraft, "Historical Considerations Siege and Defence of Fort Stanwix," *PN-YHS* 3 (1845):147; GCL to Van Cortlandt, 22 Aug. 1777, JPC, 1:1047–48. Campbell reported that the survivors

camped that night at Old Fort Schuyler, certainly a long way for exhausted troops who had marched early and then fought a good part of the day. See Campbell, *Annals Tryon County*, 72.

EIGHT: ALLIED WITH THE REBELS

1. Colbrath Journ., 6 Aug. 1777, Reid, ed., *Story Fort Johnson*, 91; 11 Aug. 1777, Willett, *Narrative Marinus Willett*, 131.
2. Colbrath Journ., 6 Aug. 1777, Reid, ed., *Story Fort Johnson*, 91. For Willett's life, see Thomas, *Marinus Willett*, passim.
3. 11 Aug. 1777, Willett, *Narrative Marinus Willett*, 131. See also Watt, *Rebellion Mohawk Valley*, 189–94.
4. See SKI to TP, n.d. [1795], quoted in Wonderley, "Oneidas and Battle of Oriskany," 9–10, "Account of Losses," R62, 157–66a, Timothy Pickering Paps., MHS; Wonderley, "A Sketch," appendix A; Testimony of John Cornelius, Draper MS, 11 U 215 (1980, R57), SHSW.
5. Scott, *Fort Stanwix*, 238–39; Watt, *Rebellion Mohawk Valley*, 197.
6. PG to BSL, 9 Aug. 1777; and BSL to PG, 9 Aug. 1777, Box 18, Gansevoort-Lansing Coll., NYPL; Colbrath Journ. 8–9 Aug. 1777, Reid, ed., *Story Fort Johnson*, 92–94.
7. Colbrath Journ., 7–20 Aug. 1777, Reid, ed., *Story Fort Johnson*, 92–97.
8. "Account of Losses," R62, 157–66a, Timothy Pickering Paps., MHS, Wonderley, "A Sketch," appendix A. John Barclay to President of Council of Safety, 11 Aug. 1777, JPC, I:1037. See also Testimony of Polly Doxtader, Draper MS, 11 U 196 (1980, R57), SHSW; PS to CC, 8 Aug. 1777, R29, Schuyler Paps., NYPL.
9. PS to GW, 13 Aug. 1777, R29, Schuyler Paps., NYPL; Gerlach, *Proud Patriot*, 298; Martin, *Benedict Arnold*, 362–63; PS to BA, 13 Aug. 1777, CN-YHS (1879):187.
10. PS to BA, 13 Aug. 1777, CN-YHS, 188. See also PS to GW, 20 Aug. 1777, R29, Schuyler Paps., NYPL.
11. Minutes of Council of War at Fort Dayton and BA to HG, 21 Aug. 1777, R5, Gates Paps., N-YHS.
12. Ibid.; Martin, *Benedict Arnold*, 364–65.
13. See JJ et al. to Inhabitants of Tryon County, 12 Aug. 1777, Almon, ed. *Remembrancer*, 5:451; Willett, *Narrative Marinus Willett*, 61–62; Extract of a letter from Albany, 18 Aug. 1777, *Pennsylvania Gazette*, 27 Aug. 1777, 3:col. 1; DC to William Knox, 16 Oct. 1777, DAR, 14:223; Samuel Armstrong Diary, 18 Aug. 1777, Typescript copy, NEHGS. WB and his party were apparently not in uniform.
14. Martin, *Benedict Arnold*, 365–66; Stone, *Brant*, 1:258–60; Samuel Armstrong Diary, 18–21 Aug. 1777, NEHGS. To ensure that Hon Yost acted as promised, BA incarcerated Hon Yost's brother as a hostage.
15. Account of Gansevoort, *New York Journal*, 15 Sep. 1777; Almon, ed., *Remembrancer*, 5:447–48; Watt, *Rebellion Mohawk Valley*, 243–50.
16. BSL to GCA, 27 Aug. 1777; and DC to William Knox, 16 Oct. 1777, DAR, 14:173 and 223.
17. BSL to GCA, 27 Aug. 1777; and DC to Knox, 16 Oct. 1777, DAR, 14:173 and 223.
18. SKI to TP, n.d. [1795], quoted in Wonderley, "Oneidas and Battle of Oriskany,"

9–10. See also BA to PG, 21 Aug. 1777, Box 18, Gansevoort-Lansing Coll., NYPL; PG to BA, 22 Aug. 1777; and BA to HG, 23 Aug. 1777, *New York Journal*, 8 Sep. 1777.

19. BA to HG, 24 Aug. 1777, PCC, M247, r174, i154, 246; BA to HG, 28 Aug. 1777, *New York Journal*, 8 Sep. 1777. For a list of captured equipment and goods, see Accounts of PG, ibid., 15 Sep. 1777.

20. BA to HG, 24 Aug. 1777, PCC, M247, r174, i154, 246. See also Scott, *Fort Stanwix*, 290.

21. DC to William Knox, 6 Nov. 1777, *DRCHSNY*, 8:725. See "Account of Losses," R62, 157–66A, Timothy Pickering Paps., MHS, Wonderley, "A Sketch," appendix A. See also Graymont, *Iroquois Am. Rev.*, 142–43, who marks the bloody Oriskany battle and the sacking of Oriska as representing the commencement of "a civil war" among the Six Nations. Tiro, "People of the Standing Stone," 117, calls Graymont's conclusion "overstated." He points out that no other large-scale battle occurred among the Iroquois during the rest of the war. Tiro claims the Iroquois still kept their focus on "fighting whites rather than one another." If the only true measure of civil war is formal battle, then Tiro has a point. However, the leveling of Oriska and a whole series of destructive counter responses indicate that, even while trying to avoid direct combat with one another, the Iroquois were now very divided among themselves, to the point of demolishing property and villages, as in the case of Oriska and Canajoharie in 1777 and Kanonwalohale in 1780. Certainly, too, the Oneidas would live in fear of a deadly assault at the hands of JBR and other Indians, all of which can be described as a less intense form of civil war. If nothing else, it is safe to say that Oriskany represented a critical moment in the history of the Six Nations, a point that signaled the loss of that unity and harmony of purpose to which the league and confederacy had so long aspired.

22. DC to William Knox, 6 Nov. 1777, *DRCHSNY*, 8:725–26.

23. Affidavits of Martin Dillenback, Elisabeth Haberman, Hendrick S. Moyer, Johannus G. House, Henry Apple, George Herkimer, Hanyost Herkimer, and Jacob Pickett, 20 Apr. 1778; Jellis Fonda to Gentlemen, 21 Apr. 1778, *IAP*, 125–34; DC to William Knox, 6 Nov. 1777, *DRCHSNY*, 8:725–26.

24. Extract of a letter from Albany, 13 Sep. 1777, *New York Journal*, 22 Sep. 1777.

25. Jellis Fonda to Gentlemen, 21 Apr. 1778, *IAP*, 134; DC to Knox, 6 Nov. 1777, *DRCHSNY*, 8:725–26; GJ to GG, 11 Nov. 1777, *DAR*, 14:254–55. These Mohawks settled around Lachine in Canada and were soon taking government relief. See Edward Foy to Mr. Goddard, 3 Nov. 1777, Add. MS, 21700, R15, Haldimand Paps., PAC.

26. *Boston Gazette*, 29 Sep. 1777, 2:col. 2; Mat. Visscher to HG, 15 Sep. 1777, R5, Gates Paps., N-YHS; Speech of Tuhuasquachta, an Onondaga chief, Minutes of a Council held at Niagara [Dec. 1777], Add. MS 21779, R54, Haldimand Paps., PAC.

27. HG to PS, 14 Sep. 1777, R5, Gates Paps., N-YHS.

28. Speech of Tuhuasquachta, an Onondaga chief, Minutes of a Council held at Niagara [Dec. 1777], Add. MS 21779, R54, Haldimand Paps., PAC. See also PS to CC, 27 Sep. 1777, *CN-YHS* (1879):190–91.

29. Ibid.

30. Speech of Tuhuasquachta, an Onondaga Chief, Minutes of a Council held at Niagara [Dec. 1777], Add. Mss., 21779, R54, Haldimand Paps., PAC. See also George Measam to HG, 19 Sep. 1777, R5, Gates Paps., N-YHS.

31. See PS to CC, 27 Sep. 1777, *CN-YHS* (1879):190–91; Jeduthan Baldwin Journ., 20 Sep. 1777, Baldwin, ed., *Rev. Journal*, 120; Samuel Armstrong Diary, 20 Aug. 1777, NEHGS; Graymont, *Iroquois Am. Rev.*, 149–50. For an overview of the 19 September 1777, battle at Freeman's Farm, see Martin, *Benedict Arnold*, 373–83; and Luzader, *Decision on the Hudson*, 40–46.

32. GJB, State of the Expedition from Canada (1780), 17, 99, 122, and 124; William Smith Journ., 28 Sep. 1777, Sabine, ed. *Historical Memoirs*, 2:218.

33. Boardman Journ., 21, 23, and 24 Sep. 1777, "Journal of Oliver Boardman," *CCHS* 7 (1899):225–26. See also Jeduthan Baldwin Journ., 21–22 Sep. 1777, Baldwin, ed. *Rev. Journal*, 121; Samuel Armstrong Diary, 21–22 Aug. 1777, NEGHS.

34. Timothy Edwards to HG, 22 Sep. 1777, R5, Gates Paps., N-YHS. See also Jeduthan Baldwin Journ., 22 Sep. 1777, Baldwin, ed. *Rev. Journal*, 121; Letter from Albany, 27 Sep. 1777, *New York Journal*, 6 Oct. 1777.

35. Boardman Journ., 21, 23, and 24 Sep. 1777, "Journal of Oliver Boardman," *CCHS* 7 (1899):225–26. See also Hitchcock Diary, 21 Sep. 1777, Weeden, ed., "Diary Enos Hitchcock," *PRIHS* 7 (1899):149–50.

36. Jonn. Potts to Brother, 28 July 1777, Society Coll., HSP. See also Samuel Armstrong Diary, 24–26 Sep. 1777, NEGHS; Henry Dearborn Journ., 24–26 Sep. 1777, Brown and Peckham, ed., *Rev. War Journals Dearborn*, 107; Napier Journ., 25 Sep. 1777, Bradford, ed. "Lord Francis Napier's Journal," *MHM* 57 (1962):318; Jeduthan Baldwin Journ., 23–26 Sep. 1777, Baldwin, ed. *Rev. Journal*, 121–22; Boardman Journ., 24 and 26 Sep. 1777, "Journal of Oliver Boardman," *CCHS* 7 (1899):226; Hitchcock Diary, 23–26 Sep. 1777, Weeden, ed., "Diary Enos Hitchcock," *PRIHS*, 7:150–51.

37. Henry Dearborn Journ., 23 Sep. 1777, Brown and Peckham, ed. *Rev. War Journals Dearborn*, 107. See also Extract of a Letter from Albany, 27 Sep. 1777, *New York Journal*, 6 Oct. 1777; Extract of a Letter from Albany, 28 Sep. 1777, *Connecticut Courant*, 7 Oct. 1777, 2:col. 2–3.

38. Speech of Tuhuasquachta, an Onondaga Chief, Minutes of a Council held at Niagara, [Dec. 1777], Add. MS 21779, R54, Haldimand Paps., PAC; PS to HG, 15 Sep. 1777, *CN-YHS* (1879):190; William Smith Journ., 2 Oct. 1777, Sabine, ed., *Historical Memoirs*, 1:221; Stevens, "His Majesty's 'Savage' Allies," 1412.

39. Speech of Tuhuasquachta, an Onondaga Chief, Minutes of a Council held at Niagara, [Dec. 1777], Add. MS 21779, R54, Haldimand Paps., PAC; William Smith Journ., 2 Oct. 1777, Sabine, ed., *Historical Memoirs*, 1:221; Stevens, "His Majesty's 'Savage' Allies," 1412.

40. Speech of Tuhuasquachta, an Onondaga Chief, Minutes of a Council held at Niagara, [Dec. 1777], Add. MS 21779, R54, Haldimand Paps., PAC.

41. Testimony of John Hadcock, Draper MS, 11 U 164 (1980, R57), SHSW. See also Jeduthan Baldwin Journ., 28 Sep. 1777, Baldwin, ed. *Rev. Journal*, 122; Boardman Journ., 28 Sep. 1777, "Journal of Oliver Boardman," *CCHS* 7 (1899):227; General Orders, 30 Sep. 1777, Stanley, ed. *For Want of a Horse*, 155–56.

42. HG to JH, 12 Oct. 1777, R5, Gates Paps., N-YHS; GJB, State of the Expedition

from Canada (1780), 124. Maj. Gen. Baron Friedrich Adolphus von Riedesel also warned his troops at the end of Sep. 1777 about the danger posed by Indians who had joined the rebel army. See Stanley, ed. *For Want of a Horse*, 155–56.

43. Isaac Pierce to PG, 26 Sep. 1777, Box 18, Gansevoort-Lansing Coll., NYPL. Also see John Hadcock to Lyman Draper, 6 May 1872, Draper MS, 11 U 264 (1980, R57), SHSW. It is impossible to determine precisely how many casualties Oneidas and Tuscaroras inflicted. The British reported at least five scalped troops during 21–28 September. On 26 September the Oneidas rescued two rebel prisoners (see Samuel Armstrong Diary, 26 Sep. 1777, NEHGS). A safe estimate would be about thirty enemy soldiers taken by them, and at least one source claimed forty prisoners. See Extract of a Letter, 27 Sep. 1777, *New York Journal*, 6 Oct. 1777.

44. John Hadcock to Lyman Draper, 6 Feb. 1878, Draper MS, 11 U 265 (1980, R57), SHSW. The records do not indicate when Bread received the honor. It may have been during one of GW's visits late in the war period.

45. White Skin and GR to Brother Chief Warrior Arahocktea [HG], 31 Oct. 1777, *New Jersey Gazette*, 31 Dec. 1777.

46. [Good] Peter and [Hendrick] Thagneghtoris to [HG], 31 Oct. 1777, *New Jersey Gazette*, 31 Dec. 1777. For this Hendrick's identity, see Hough, ed., *Proceedings*, 1:246.

47. Tehosgueahto to Brother Commissioners, n.d. [late Oct. 1777], R6, Gates Paps., N-YHS.

48. Tehurgweahten to Arahocktea [HG], n.d. [late Oct. 1777], *New Jersey Gazette*, 31 Dec. 1777.

49. Tehosgueahto to Brother Commissioners, n.d. [late Oct. 1777], R6, Gates Paps., N-YHS. See also Mason Bolton to GCA, 9 Sep. 1777, CO 42/37, f. 105, RB34, PAC.

50. JBU to GCA, 14 Dec. 1777, DAR, 14:274.

51. Speech of JBU, [Dec. 1777], Minutes of a Council held at Niagara, [Dec. 1777], Add. MS 21779, R54, Haldimand Paps., PAC.

52. Speech of Tuhuasquachta, an Onondaga Chief, [Dec. 1777], Minutes of a Council held at Niagara, [Dec. 1777], Add. MS 21779, R54, Haldimand Paps., PAC.

53. Speech of Unknown Tuscarora chief, [Dec. 1777], Minutes of a Council held at Niagara, [Dec. 1777], Add. MS 21779, R54, Haldimand Paps., PAC.

54. JBU to GCA, 14 Dec. 1777, DAR, 14:274. See also Speech of JBU or MB, [Dec. 1777], Minutes of a Council Held at Niagara, [Dec. 1777], Add. MS 21779, R54, Haldimand Paps., PAC.

55. PS to HL, 15 Mar. 1778, *IAP*, 119–20. Since they had to beg for food and clothing that winter, the former residents at Oriska apparently did not gain as much from the plundering of Canajoharie as some scholars have suggested.

56. Hinman, *Onaquaga*, 36–76.

57. Resolutions of Council of Safety, 3 Sep. 1777, *JPC*, 1:1054; GCL to Col. Jacob Hornbeck, [3 Sep. 1777], *Clinton Paps.*, 1:272–74. See also Calloway, *Am. Rev. Indian Country*, 123–25.

58. Timothy Edwards to HG, 22 Sep. 1777, R5, Gates Paps., N-YHS; PS to Col. John Greaton, 24 Jan. 1778; and PS to HL, 26 Jan. and 8 Feb. 1778, *IAP*, 107–108 and 111.

59. PS to HL, 8 Feb. 1778, *IAP*, 111–12.
60. CC to Oneida and Onondaga, 3 Dec. 1777, *JCC*, 14:996; Council of Safety Resolution, 3 Sep. 1777, *JPC*, 1:1054. See also PS to HL, 8 Feb. 1778, Penrose, ed, *IAP*, 111–12.
61. Shy, "American Military Experience," *People Numerous and Armed*, 236; Commissioners of Indian Affairs to HL, 12 Jan. 1778, *Paps. Henry Laurens*, 12:288–89; JDU to HL, 12 Jan. 1778, *LDC*, 8:566.
62. JDE to Commissioners, 5 Feb. 1778, *IAP*, 109–10; JBU to GCA, 2 Feb. and 10 Apr. 1778, CO 42/38, f. 106–107 and 112–13, RB34, PAC.
63. Speech of Commissioners, 10 Mar. 1778; and PS to HL, 15 Mar. 1778, *IAP*, 116–17 and 121; JDU to GCL, 13 Mar. 1778, *LDC*, 9:288–90. The council transcript is incomplete, with various speeches omitted.
64. GW to HL, 26[–27] Nov. 1777, *Paps. GW, RWS*, 12:420–21. For MDL in the Continental Army, see Gottschalk, *Lafayette Joins the American Army*, and Gottschalk, *Lafayette and the Close of the Revolution*. On the attempted campaign, see GCL to MDL, 8 Mar. 1778, *Clinton Paps.*, 3:3; JDU to GCL, 13 Mar. 1778, *LDC*, 9:287–88.
65. JDU to GCL, 13 Mar. 1778, LDC, 9:289; PS to HL, 15 Mar. 1778, *IAP*, 118. See also JBU to GCA, 10 Apr. 1778, CO 42/38, f. 112–13, RB34, PAC.
66. JDU to GCL, 13 Mar. 1778, *LDC*, 9:289.
67. Speech of Tenhoghskweaghta [Tuhuasquachta], 10 Mar. 1778, Council at Johnstown, *IAP*, 114–15.
68. JDU to GCL, 13 Mar. 1778, *LDC*, 9:289–90. See also PS to HL, 15 Mar. 1778, *IAP*, 118. According to JDU in his letter to GCL, some rebels thought the kinship ties between the Oneidas and Onondagas would help keep many Onondagas neutral.
69. PS to HL, 15 Mar. 1778, *IAP*, 119.
70. JDU to GCL, 13 Mar. 1778, *LDC*, 9:289. See also VPD's list of expenses submitted to PS, 10 June 1777, R7, Schuyler Paps., NYPL; Stevens, "His Majesty's 'Savage' Allies," 1068–69.
71. Speech of GR, 10 Mar. 1778; and Speech of Tenhoghskweaghta [Tuhuasquachta], 10 Mar. 1778, Council at Johnstown, *IAP*, 116.
72. Ibid.
73. Speech of GR, 10 Mar. 1778; and Speech of Tenhoghskweaghta [Tuhuasquachta], 10 Mar. 1778, Council at Johnstown, IAP, 116; JDU to GCL, 13 Mar. 1778, *LDC*, 9:289.
74. Speech of GR, 10 Mar. 1778, Council at Johnstown, *IAP*, 116.

NINE: ASSISTING CONTINENTAL FORCES AT VALLEY FORGE

1. JDE to PS, 20 Apr. 1777, PCC, M247, r173, i153, 128–30; Timothy Edwards to HG, 22 Sep. 1777, R5, Gates Paps., N-YHS.
2. GW to CC Committee at Camp, [29 Jan. 1778], *Paps. GW, RWS*, 13:402.
3. CC Committee at Camp to Pres. CC, 20 Feb. 1778, PCC, M247, r40, i33, 171. For the activities of the Committee at Camp, see Bodle, *Valley Forge Winter*, 143–61.

4. CC Committee at Camp to Pres. CC, 20 Feb. 1778, PCC, M247, r40, i33, 171. See also Resolution of 4 Mar. 1778, JCC, 10:221.

5. CC Commitee at Camp to Pres. of CC, 20 Feb. 1778, PCC, M247, r40, i33, 171. This proposal from the CC Committee was unworkable, if for no other reason than the Oneidas, at this juncture, had no serious thoughts about moving away from their homeland, regardless of their threatened circumstances.

6. GW to Commissioners of Indian Affairs, 13 Mar. 1778, *Paps. GW, RWS*, 14:76–77.

7. GW to MDL, 10 Mar. 1778; MDL to Pres. CC, 20 Mar. 1778; and MDL to GW, 22 Mar. 1778, *Lafayette Paps.*, 1:342–43, 364, and 375–76; HL to MDL, 13 Mar. 1777, *LDC*, 9:292–93.

8. PS to GW, 22 Mar. 1778, R29, Schuyler Paps., NYPL.

9. See PS's summary of a message from the Oneidas in PS to HL, 26 Jan. 1778, *IAP*, 108.

10. PS to HL, 8 Feb. 1778, IAP, 110–12.

11. On patterns of acculturation when alien peoples mingle together, see Axtell, "English Colonial Impact," *European and Indian*, 245–48; White, *Middle Ground*, 50–93.

12. MDL to GCL, 16 Mar. 1778; and MDL to GW, 20 Mar. 1778, *Lafayette Paps.*, 1:355 and 370. See also Timothy Edwards to HG, 22 Sep. 1777, R5, Gates Paps., N-YHS; PS to Col. John Greaton, 24 Jan. 1778; and PS to HL, 26 Jan. and 8 Feb. 1778, *IAP*, 107–108 and 111; JDU to GCL, 13 Mar. 1778, *LDC*, 9:289.

13. MDL to GW, 20 Mar. 1778; MDL to GCL, 16 Mar. 1778; and MDL to Commander at Fort Schuyler, 21 Mar. 1778, *Lafayette Paps.*, 1:370, 355, and 374.

14. MDL to GW, 20 Mar. 1778; MDL to GCL, 16 Mar. 1778; and MDL to Commander at Fort Schuyler, 21 Mar. 1778, *Lafayette Paps.*, 1:370, 355, and 374; William Smith Journ., 11 and 18 Mar. 1778, Sabine, ed., *Historical Memoirs*, 1:318 and 327. MDL said he dispatched three French officers, but PS to GW, 26 Apr. 1778, R29, Schuyler Paps., NYPL, indicates that only two—Tousard and Gouvion—arrived at Kanonwalohale. Tousard to MW, 2 Apr. 1778, Kirkland, ed., *Letters at 'Karolfred,'* 2:47, claims the brief presence of Celeron.

15. MDL to GW, 20 Mar. and 22 Mar. 1778, *Lafayette Paps.*, 1:370 and 375; PS to MW, 22 Mar. 1778, R29, Schuyler Paps., NYPL.

16. Oneida Speech to MW at Fort Schuyler, Undated [Apr. 1778], Marinus Willett Paps., N-YHS.

17. Tousard to MW, 7 Apr. 1778, Myers Coll., NYPL. See also Tousard to MW, 2 Apr. 1778, Kirkland, ed., *Letters at 'Karolfred,'* 2:47. PS advised the CC that the Oneidas needed corn and clothing. Tousard's letter indicates they had plenty of corn but very much needed clothing. See PS to HL, 15 Mar. 1778, *IAP*, 119.

18. Tousard to MW, 2 Apr. 1778, Kirkland, ed., *Letters at 'Karolfred,'* 2:47.

19. PG to Thomas Conway, 4 Apr. 1778; and Meeting of Commissioners of Indian Affairs, 15 Apr. 1778, *IAP*, 122–24; Col. Jacob Klock to GCL, 1 May 1778, *Clinton Paps.*, 3:125 and 251–52; MDL to HL, 5 May 1778, *Henry Laurens Paps.*, 13:260; PS to GW, 26 Apr. 1778, R29, Schuyler Paps., NYPL.

20. Col. Jacob Klock to GCL, 1 May 1778, *Clinton Paps.*, 3:251–52.

21. PS to GCL, 16 Mar. 1778, *Clinton Paps.*, 3:44–45.

22. JDU to GCL, 13 Mar. 1778, *LDC*, 9:289.

23. Meeting of the Commissioners of Indian Affairs, 15 Apr. 1778, *IAP*, 122–23.
24. Oneida Speech to MW at Fort Schuyler, Undated [Apr. 1778], Marinus Willett Paps., N-YHS.
25. Ibid.
26. Ibid.
27. Ibid. See also JDU to HL, 24 Apr. 1778, *LDC*, 9:475.
28. Speech of Kayendalongwea, and SKE to MW, 22 Apr. 1778, Marinus Willett Paps., N-YHS.
29. Ibid.
30. The commissioners had sent some goods to the Oneidas. See Speech of Kayendalongwea, and SKE to MW, 22 Apr. 1778, Marinus Willett Paps., N-YHS.
31. SKI to Tousard, 24 Apr. 1778, in Tousard to GW, 23 May 1778, PCC, M247, r95, i78, 157–60; PS, VPD, and the Other Commissioners of Indian Affairs, an Expense Report (first date, 13 June 1778), 1 and 7 July 1778, R7, Schuyler Paps., NYPL; Levasseur, *Lafayette in America*, 2:195; Wonderley, "A Sketch," 40; Halbritter, "Oral Traditions," Campisi and Hauptman, ed., *Oneida Indian Experience*, 145.
32. SKI to Tousard, 24 Apr. 1778, in Tousard to GW, 23 May 1778, PCC, M247, r95, i78, 157–60.
33. Speech by GR to a Party of Warriors, 24 Apr. 1778, PCC, M247, r95, i78, v9, 158–59.
34. Reply to Speech by GR to a Party of Warriors, 24 Apr. 1778, PCC, M247, r95, i78, v9, 159.
35. Halbritter, "Oral Traditions," Campisi and Hauptman, ed., *Oneida Indian Experience*, 145; Tousard to MW, 7 Apr. 1778, Myers Coll., NYPL. PS and VPD refer to them in their financial records specifically as Oneidas. See PS, VPD, and the Other Commissioners of Indian Affairs, an Expense Report (first date, 13 June 1778), July 1 and 7, 1778, R7, Schuyler Paps., NYPL.
36. On the advantages of the bow and arrow, see Malone, *Skulking Way of War*, 37–46; Starkey, *European and Native American Warfare*, 20–25. On the Oneidas using the same while traveling to Valley Forge, see Henry Melchior Muhlenberg Journ., 14 May 1778, Tappert and Doberstein, ed., *Journals*, 3:152.
37. Tousard to MW, 16 May 1778, Emmet Coll., NYPL; Tousard to GW, 23 May 1778, PCC, M247, r95, i78, 157–60.
38. Henry Melchior Muhlenberg Journ., 14 May 1778, Tappert and Doberstein, ed., *Journals*, 3:152.
39. Entry for 15 May 1778, Orderly Book 58, Malcolm's Regt., N-YHS. Trussell, *Birthplace of an Army*, 77, 111–13, and Fleming, *Washington's Secret War*, 291–93, note the presence of the Oneidas among the soldiery at Valley Forge and their participation in the Barren Hill engagement.
40. Extract of a letter from Camp, 13 May 1778, *New York Journal*, 1 June 1778.
41. Headquarters, Valley Forge, 15 May 1778, Wayne's Command, Unidentified Regt. at Valley Forge, HSP. See also General Orders, 4 June 1778, *Writings GW*, 12:16. Albigence Waldo, a surgeon with GW's army, had trouble with a drunken Indian, although the incident occurred in 1779 and did not involve an Oneida. See "Notes Written by Waldo on the Endpaper of a Medical Textbook," Trent Coll., Duke University Medical Center Library.

42. See Elijah Fisher Journ., 15 May 1778, *Fisher's Journal in the War for Indep.*, 8. No source specifically named Han Yerry, but as the ranking chief warrior, he was likely GW's supper guest.
43. Charles Moré, Chevalier de Pontgibaud, Douglas, ed. and trans., *A French Volunteer*, 69.
44. Halbritter, "Oral Traditions," Campisi and Hauptman, ed., *Oneida Indian Experience*, 145. Tiro, "People of the Standing Stone," does not discuss the Oneidas at Valley Forge and treats the Cooper story as a metaphor. For additional analysis, see Wonderley, *Oneida Iroquois Folklore*, 20, 193, 210–14.
45. Halbritter, "Oral Traditions," Campisi and Hauptman, ed. *Oneida Indian Experience*, 145.
46. GW's Instructions to MDL, [May 18, 1778], Sparks, ed., *Writings GW*, 5:368–70.
47. MDL Memoirs, *Lafayette Paps.*, 5:6.
48. Joseph Plumb Martin Memoir, Martin, ed., *Ordinary Courage*, 71–72; Martin Memoir, Scheer, ed., *Private Yankee Doodle*, 118–19.
49. MDL Memoirs, *Lafayette Paps.*, 5:6.
50. Ibid., 5:6–7; Tower, *Marquis de La Fayette*, 1:333; Garden, *Anecdotes Am. Rev.*, 3:73.
51. Accounts of the Barren Hill battle vary widely. A trustworthy overview may be found in Ward, *War of the Rev.*, 2:556–69. See also Tower, *Marquis de La Fayette*, 1:328–36; Willcox, "Comic Opera Battle," *PH* 13 (1946):265–73; Boyle, "Indians at Valley Forge," draft essay; Reed, "Indians at Valley Forge," *Valley Forge Journal* 3 (1986):26–32; Lossing, *Pictorial Field-Book Rev.*, 2:326–30; Gottschalk, *Lafayette Joins the Army*, 184–93; Fleming, *Washington's Secret War*, 292–98.
52. Willcox, "Comic Opera Battle," *PH* 13 (1946):269. Possibly the Pennsylvania militia scouted out too far beyond the White Marsh Road, allowing WH's forces to slip in behind them, with neither command aware of the presence of the other.
53. MDL Memoirs, *Lafayette Paps.*, 5:6–7; Tower, *Marquis de La Fayette*, 1:334–35.
54. Tower, *Marquis de La Fayette*, 1:334–35.
55. Elijah Fisher Journ., 20 May 1778, *Fisher's Journal in the War for Indep.*, 8. See also MDL Memoirs, *Lafayette Paps.*, 5:7.
56. See Tousard to Pres. CC, 23 May 1778, PCC, M247, r95, i78, 157–60; Henry Melchior Muhlenberg Journ., 23 May 1778, Tappert and Doberstein, ed., *Journals*, 3:156; Extract of a Letter from a Gentleman Who Was in Camp When Lafayette's Detachment Returned, *Pennsylvania Gazette*, 30 May 1778.
57. MDL Memoirs, *Lafayette Paps.*, 5:7. MDL made similar comments to the Marquis De Chastellux. See Rice, ed. and trans., *Travels by Chastellux*, 1:171. MDL said that the Oneidas had not seen cavalry before and were intimidated. He apparently was unaware that many Oneida families owned horses and that various Oneidas had served with and observed cavalry units before. Some have accepted Lafayette's comments and disregarded such contemporary sources as Tousard's letter.
58. Henry Melchior Muhlenberg Journ., 23 May 1778, Tappert and Doberstein, ed., *Journals*, 3:156; Extract of a Letter from a Gentleman Who Was in Camp When Lafayette's Detachment Returned, *Pennsylvania Gazette*, 30 May 1778; Anthony Wayne to Col. Sharp Delaney, 21 May 1778, *PMHB* 11 (1887):115–16; HL to Francis Hopkinson, 27 May 1778, *Henry Laurens Paps.*, 13:347. Such a retreat was

standard in Indian warfare. See also MDL to Allen McLane, 12 June 1778, Letter no. 58, Allen McLane Paps., N-YHS.

59. Tousard to Pres. CC, 23 May 1778, PCC, M247, r95, i78, 157–60.

60. Tower, *Marquis de La Fayette*, 1:336–37; Willcox, "Comic Opera Battle" *PH* 13 (1946):271.

61. Johann Ewald Diary, 19 May 1778, Tustin, ed. and trans., *Hessian Diary of the Am. War.*, 130. See also GW to HL, 24 May 1778, Sparks, ed., *Writings GW*, 5:377; MDL to Wife, 16 June 1778, *Lafayette Paps.*, 5:79; *The Royal Gazette*, 3 June 1778, 3:col. 3; 20 May 1778, Journ. Kept by the Distinguished Hessian Field Jäeger Corps, Hessian Docs. of the Am. Rev., Letter L, Microfiche no. 245, Lidgerwood Coll., MNHP; John Montresor Journ., 9 May 1778, "Journals of Capt. John Montresor," *CN-YHS* (1881):492–93; "Account of Losses," R62, 157–166A, (Wolf Clan no. 6), Timothy Pickering Paps., MHS, Wonderley, "A Sketch," appendix A. In the record, Jacob's name is spelled *Shy-yo-we-yooh*.

62. Doebler and Ludwig, *St. Peter's Lutheran Church, Barren Hill*, 167. See also "Account of Losses," R62, 157–166A, (Bear Clan no. 6), Timothy Pickering Paps., MHS, Wonderley, "A Sketch," appendix A.

63. See GW to Pres. CC, 3 May 1778, *Writings GW*, 11:343–44; PS to GW, 26 Apr. 1778, R29, Schuyler Paps., NYPL; Meeting of the Commissioners of Indian Affairs, 15 Apr. 1778, *IAP*, 122–23.

64. GW to PS, 15 May 1778, *Writings GW*, 11:390.

65. Ibid., 11:390–91. See also PS to JDE, 22 May 1778, R29, Schuyler Paps., NYPL.

66. GW to PS, 15 May 1778, *Writings GW*, 11:391.

67. Ibid.; and GW to Jacob Klock, 13 June 1778, *Writings GW*, 11:390–91, and 12:56; PS to GW and CC, 29 May 1778, R29, Schuyler Paps., NYPL; MDL to Allen McLane, 12 June 1778, Allen McLane Paps., N-YHS.

68. GW to Jacob Klock, 13 June 1778, *Writings GW*, 12:56.

TEN: THE ENEMY OF OLD FRIENDS

1. GW to JK, 13 June 1778, *Writings GW*, 12:56; PS, VPD, and the other Commissioners of Indian Affairs, an Expense Report (first date, 13 June 1778), 1 and 7 July 1778, R7, Schuyler Paps., NYPL. The document refers to Thomas, but since Thomas Sinavis was dead, Deacon Thomas was the likely person.

2. On trophy leggings, see Anthony Wayne to Col. Sharp Delaney, 21 May 1778, *PMHB* 11 (1887):115–16.

3. Not forgotten during this period of grieving were the two Oneidas taken prisoner during the Barren Hill battle. Eventually, an exchange occurred, but no record has been found. See "Account of Losses," R62, 157–166A, (Wolf Clan no. 6), Timothy Pickering Paps., MHS, Wonderley, "A Sketch," appendix A.

4. Louis began scouting for the rebels and serving as an emissary to Canada in 1777. See PS to HL, 15 Mar. 1778, *IAP*, 120.

5. VPD's Expenses, undated [1778], to "Condole the Death of an Oneida Chief," R7, Schuyler Paps., NYPL.

6. "Account of Losses," R62, 157–166A, (Bear Clan no. 6), Timothy Pickering Paps., MHS, Wonderley, "A Sketch," appendix A.

7. PS to Oneidas, 11 May 1778, in Response to the Oneidas [Oneida doc. missing]; and SKI to PS, 23 May 1778, *IAP*, 135 and 141; JDE to PS, 19 May 1778, Stark, ed., *Memoir John Stark*, 145; Stevens, "His Majesty's 'Savage' Allies," 1566–68.

8. PS to SKI, 11 May 1778, Kirkland Paps., HC. See also PS to Oneidas, 11 May 1778, *IAP*, 135–37; PS to JDE, 12 May 1778, *CN-YHS* (1879):204–205; PS to GW, 17 May 1778, PCC, M247, r189, i170, v2, 281; PS to GW, 22 May 1778, R29, Schuyler Paps., NYPL.

9. SKI to PS, 23 May 1778; and JDE to PS, 25 May 1778, *IAP*, 140–44; JDE to PS, 19 May 1778, Stark, ed., *Memoir John Stark*, 145.

10. Atskearax's name has received various spellings. See PS to CC, 11 May 1778, R29, Schuyler Paps., NYPL. Speeches by GR and GP are missing, but PS's response has survived. See PS Speech to the Oneidas, 11 May 1778; and SKI to PS, 23 May 1778, *IAP*, 135–37 and 140–42.

11. PS to HL, 29 May 1778, *IAP*, 144–45. Among those who went was a part-Oneida, part-French man named Stephannus, who served as the translator. Whether Stephannus counted as one of the Oneidas is unclear. See VPD's Expenses to Jellis Fonda (first date, 13 June 1778), 30 July 1778, R7, Schuyler Paps., NYPL; HL to PS, 28 May 1778; and HG to HL 11 June 1778, *Henry Laurens Paps.*, 13:356–57 and 476–77; GW to CC, 21 June 1778; and GW to BA, 21 June 1778, *Writings GW*, 12:98–99 and 101–102; Commissioners of Indian Affairs to GW, 9 June 1778, PCC, M247, r168, i152, v6, 131; Extract of a Letter from Albany, 10 June 1778, *Boston Gazette*, 22 June 1778, 3:col. 2, and Draper MS, 11 U 180 (1980, R57), SHSW.

12. GW to BA, 21 June 1778, *Writings GW*, 12:101–102. See also James McHenry Diary, 21 June 1778, Flynt and Flynt, ed., *Journal of a March*, 2.

13. GW to BA, 21 June 1778, *Writings GW*, 12:101–102; PS, VPD, and the other Commissioners of Indian Affairs Accounts to Jellis Fonda (first entry 13 June 1778), 22 and 30 July 1778, R7, Schuyler Paps., NYPL.

14. RC to PG, with JDE to RC, 10 Oct. 1778, Box 18, Gansevoort-Lansing Coll., NYPL; TP to PS, 16 June 1778; and JDE to PS, 10 Oct. 1778, *IAP*, 146 and 156–57; PS to TP, 27 June 1778, R29, Schuyler Paps., NYPL.

15. Col. JK to Brig. Gen. Abraham Ten Broeck, 31 May 1778, *Clinton Paps.*, 3:382.

16. JK to GCL, 5 June 1778 and GCL's reply; Jellis Fonda and Abraham Van Home to GCL, 5 June 1778; Maj. Samuel Campbell and Samuel Clyde to Gen. JST, 5 June 1778; Col. Abraham Wemple to Gen. Abraham Ten Broeck, 6 June 1778; Col. JK to Gen. Abraham Ten Broeck, 6 June 1778; JDU to GCL, 6 June 1778; J. Gregg to GCL, 11 June 1778; and JK to GCL, 22 June 1778, *Clinton Paps.*, 3:402–405, 407–10, 413–15, 418, 449–50, and 475–76; PS to GCL, 6 June 1778, R29, Schuyler Paps., NYPL; JJ to DC, 18 June 1778, Daniel Claus Paps., LC; Extract of a Letter from Albany, 8 June 1778, *New Jersey Gazette*, 24 June 1778.

17. See JBU to Capt. Francis Le Maistre, 28 Jan. 1778, Add. MS 21756-1, R39, Haldimand Paps., PAC; Deposition of Josiah Parks, 17 Apr. 1778, *Clinton Paps.*, 3:192.

18. See JBU to MB, 8 July 1778; and GJ to GG, 10 Sep. 1778, *DAR*, 15:165–66 and 199–200; Wyoming Valley Campaign, 20 July 1778, *New York Journal*, 20 July 1778; JBU to FH, 17 Sep. 1778, Add. MS 21756-1, R39, Haldimand Paps., PAC. Among the many summary accounts of the Wyoming Valley battle and "massacre"

are Graymont, *Iroquois Am. Rev.*, 167–72; Mintz, *Seeds of Empire*, 54–64; Williams, *Year of the Hangman*, 114–33. A few have insisted that no real massacre occurred, apparently because European Americans butchered numbers of Indians at other locations during the Revolutionary War. See Mann, *George Washington's War*, 15–20; Knouff, *Soldiers' Rev.*, 168–70.

19. JDE to PS, 25 May 1778, Stark, ed., *Memoir John Stark*, 153; JDE to GCL, 15 June 1778, *Clinton Paps.*, 3:458–59; Commissioners of Indian Affairs to GW, 9 June 1778, PCC, M247, r168, i152, v6, 131; JDE to HG, 15 June 1778, PCC, M247, r174, i154, v1, 449.

20. JDE to GCL, 15 June 1778, *Clinton Paps.*, 3:458–59. See also Resolution of 4 May 1778, *JCC*, 11:456; and JDE to HG, 15 June 1778, PCC, M247, r174, i154, v1, 449.

21. PS to HL, 19 July 1778, *IAP*, 148–49.

22. RC to PG, 8 Sep. 1778, Box 18, Gansevoort-Lansing Coll., NYPL.

23. Ibid.

24. Ibid.

25. Extract of Minutes of Council of Safety, 3 Sep. 1777, and Journal of the Council of Safety; William Dickson et al. to GCL, 23 Feb. 1778; Robert Jones Statement, 10 July 1778; GCL to Brig. Gen. Abraham Ten Broeck; and GCL to Gen. JST, 11 June 1778, *Clinton Paps.*, 2:271–72 and 821–22, and 3:447–48 and 542–43; Peter S. Dygert to Tryon County Comm., 14 Nov. 1777, *JPC*, 1:1054 and 1090–91; William Smith Journ., 13 Feb. 1778, Sabine, ed., *Historical Memoirs*, 2:303; JST to HG, 20 June and 1 July 1778, Stark, ed., *Memoir John Stark*, 167 and 174.

26. William Caldwell to JBU, 21 Sep. 1780, Add. MS 21765, R46, Haldimand Paps., PAC.

27. Graymont, *Iroquois Am. Rev.*, 178; Col. JK to Col. Frederick Fisher, 16 Sep. 1778; Col. Peter Bellinger to GCL, 19 Sep. 1778; and Abraham Wemple to Gen. Abraham Ten Broeck, 20 Sep. 1778, *Clinton Paps.*, 4: 39, 47–50, and 82–83; *Boston Gazette*, 12 Oct. 1778, 4: col. 1; Stone, *Brant*, 1:363–66; Taylor and Duffin to DC, 26 Oct. 1778, *IAP*, 167–68.

28. William Caldwell to JBU, 21 Sep. 1780, Add. MS 21765, R46, Haldimand Paps., PAC.

29. RC to Gentlemen, 28 Sep. 1778, enclosed in VPD to GCL, 2 Oct. 1778; and Deposition of Robert McGinnis, 27 Sep. 1778, *Clinton Paps.*, 4:115 and 131–32. See also RC to PG, 28 Sep. 1778, Box 18, Gansevoort-Lansing Coll., NYPL.

30. RC to Gentlemen, 28 Sep. 1778, enclosed in VPD to GCL, 2 Oct. 1778, *Clinton Paps.*, 4:131–32. The name of the Oneida spokesperson is not known, but it was not GR. Not long afterward, as part of Lt. Col. William Butler's raid on Oquaga, Butler's force demolished part of Unadilla.

31. RC to Gentlemen, 28 Sep. 1778, enclosed in VPD to GCL, 2 Oct. 1778, *Clinton Paps.*, 4:131–32.

32. GW to JST, 8 Oct. 1778, *Writings GW*, 13:50.

33. GW to Pres. of CC, 22 July 1778, *Writings GW*, 12:241; Return of the Dept. of Foot that was at Oquaga under William Butler, [Oct. 1778]; and William Butler Journ., 1–6 Oct. [1778], *Clinton Paps.*, 4:223–24 and 231. See also William Gray to Robert Erskine, 28 Oct. 1778, *Journals Expedition Sullivan 1779*, 288–90.

34. William Butler Journ., 9 Oct. [1778], *Clinton Paps.*, 4:225–27.

35. For examples, see JDU to GCL, 22 Sep. 1778, *Clinton Paps.*, 4:67–68; JST to GW, 24 July 1778, Stark, ed., *Memoir John Stark*, 182; Resolution of 11 June 1778, *JCC*, 11, 587–88; Calloway, *Am. Rev. Indian Country*, 124; PS to HL, 29 May 1778, *IAP*, 144–45.

36. Speech of GP, 21 Oct. 1778, *IAP*, 161. JC to GCL, 30 Dec. 1778, *Clinton Paps.*, 4:437–38, mentioned seventeen Oquagas receiving food rations from the government when they joined the Oneidas. It is not clear how many Oquaga Oneidas moved to Old Oneida and other settlements.

37. JDE to VPD, 15 Oct. 1778, *IAP*, 157–58, on this problem.

38. Meeting of the Commissioners of Indian Affairs, 15 Apr. 1778, *IAP*, 124. See also MW to PS, 23 Apr. 1778, Marinus Willett Paps., N-YHS; MW to PS, GCL, and John Jay, 29 Apr. 1778, Ayer MS 996, NL.

39. The quotation marks around *reasonable* have been added for emphasis. See Meeting of Commissioners of Indian Affairs, 15 Apr. 1778, *IAP*, 124.

40. Resolution of 4 May 1778, *JCC*, 11:456–57; John Hanson to Indian Commissioners, 16 Oct. 1778, PCC, M247, r173, i153, v3, 370; JDE to VPD, 15 Oct. 1778, *IAP*, 157–58. For payments to various Oneida traders, see expense reports in R7, Schuyler Paps., NYPL; Commissioners of Indian Affairs to HL, 12, Jan. 1778, *Henry Laurens Paps.*, 12:290; Draper MS, 11 U 182 (1980, R57), SHSW.

41. Speech of GP to VPD, 21 Oct. 1778, *IAP*, 161.

42. Ibid., 159–60.

43. Ibid., 160–61; Patrick, "Life and Times Kirkland," 320–24.

44. Patrick, "Life and Times Kirkland," 322–24.

45. Speech of GP to VPD, 21 Oct. 1778, *IAP*, 160–61.

46. Speech of VPD to Oneidas, 22 Oct. 1778; Paper of VPD, 22 Oct. 1778; and Speech of GP to VPD, 21 Oct. 1778, *IAP* 161–65.

47. Speech of VPD to Oneidas et al., 22 Oct. 1778, *IAP*, 162–63; Resolution of 30 Nov. 1778, *JCC*, 12:1177–78. See also HL to PS, 2 Dec. [1778], *LDC*, 11:276–77.

48. VPD's Reply to GP's Speech, 22 Oct. 1778, *IAP*, 164. See also Patrick, "Life and Times Kirkland," 322–23.

49. [PG to Ichabod Alden], 6 Nov. 1778; and Alden to PG, 8 Nov. 1778, Box 18, Gansevoort-Lansing Coll., NYPL; WB to MB, 17 Nov. 1778, DAR, 15:261–63; Tracy, *Notices of Men and Events*, 14.

50. Abraham Yates to GCL, 21 Apr. 1778, *Clinton Paps.*, 3:203–204; JJ to DC, 16 July 1778, Daniel Claus Paps., LC; [?] Taylor and [?] Duffin to DC, 15 Nov. 1778; and DC to FH, 17 Mar. 1779, *IAP*, 173 and 191–92; MB to FH, 11 Nov. 1778, Add. MS 21756-1, R39, Haldimand Paps., PAC.

51. JC to GCL, 28 Nov. 1778, with attachments; Abraham Ten Broeck to GCL, 13 Nov. 1778; Edward Hand to GCL, 15 Nov. 1778; and various other letters from participants, *Clinton Paps.*, 4:337–45, 266–67, 284–89; Extract of a Letter from Tryon County, 24 Nov. 1778, *New York Journal*, 28 Dec. 1778; Account from an Officer in the Fort at Cherry Valley on 11 Nov. 1778, *Boston Gazette*, 7 Dec. 1778, 3:col. 1–2; Draper MS, 4 F 5, 10, 12, 31, 178–84, 202 (1980, R14); 5 F, and 20 F 9–16, 18–20 (1980, R15), SHSW; WB to MB, 17 Nov. 1778, DAR, 15:261–63. For

overviews, see Graymont, *Iroquois Am. Rev.*, 183–91; Williams, *Year of the Hangman*, 173–87; and Campbell, *Annals Tryon County*, 100–115. For an attempt to rationalize the loss of life at Cherry Valley as something less than a "massacre," see Mann, *George Washington's War*, 22–26.

52. WB to PS, 12 Nov. 1778, Add. MS 21765-83, Item 74; and WB to GCL, 18 Feb. 1779, Add. MS 21765-95, Item 83, R46, Haldimand Paps., PAC. FH reacted negatively to the butchery at Cherry Valley. See FH to JBU, 25 Dec. 1778, Add. MS 217222. R23, Haldimand Paps., PAC.

53. Capt. William Johnson et al. to Col. John Cantine, 13 Dec. 1778, *Clinton Paps.*, 4:364.

54. CVD's Summary of Speech of GP, 23 Dec. 1778, enclosed in CVD to GCL, 23 Dec. 1778, *Clinton Paps.*, 4:418–19; Speech of Osenegechta, an Onondaga, 5 Mar. 1779, Add. MS 21779, R54, Haldimand Paps., PAC.

55. CVD's Summary of Speech of GP, 23 Dec. 1778, enclosed in CVD to GCL, 23 Dec. 1778, *Clinton Paps.*, 4:418–19; Speech of Osenegechta, an Onondaga, 5 Mar. 1779, Add. MS 21779, R54, Haldimand Paps., PAC.

56. CVD's Summary of Speech of GP, 23 Dec. 1778, enclosed in CVD to GCL, 23 Dec. 1778, *Clinton Paps.*, 4:418–19. See also Speech of Osenegechta, an Onondaga, 5 Mar. 1779, Add. MS 21779, R54, Haldimand Paps., PAC.

57. CVD's Summary of Speech of GP, 23 Dec. 1778, enclosed in CVD to GCL, 23 Dec. 1778, *Clinton Paps.*, 4:419; Fenton, *Great Law*, 310.

58. JD to PS, 18 Jan. 1779, *IAP*, 181. For the same text, see CVD to JC, 18 Jan. 1779, *Clinton Paps.*, 4:493–94.

59. JD to PS, 18 Jan. 1779, *IAP*, 181.

60. Return of Indians Who Received Clothing, Arms, Ammunition, Etc., at Niagara from Nov. 1778 to Mar. 1779, Add. MS 21769, R48; and Return of Indians at Niagara from 30 Dec. 1778 to 26 Jan. 1779, Add. MS 21765-90, Item 79, R46, Haldimand Paps., PAC. Some rebels were becoming suspicious about the allegiance of many Tuscaroras. See Extract of a Letter from a Gentleman in Albany, 9 Aug. 1778, *New York Journal*, 31 Aug. 1778. The "Present State of Officers, Men, and Indians of the Command of Col. Guy Johnson, 4 Nov. 1777," Add. MS 21769, R48, Haldimand Paps., PAC, lists 11 Oneidas, 154 Oquagas, and 240 Tuscaroras.

61. JBU to FH, 14 Feb. 1779, Add. MS 21756-1, R39, Haldimand Paps., PAC. See also MB to FH, 12 Feb. 1779, Add. MS, 21756-1, R39; JBU to FH, 1 June 1779, Add. MS 21765-138, Item 111, R46; and JBU to FH, 8 June 1779, Add. MS 21765-139, Item 113, R46, Haldimand Paps., PAC.

62. JC to GCL, 30 Dec. 1778, *Clinton Paps.*, 4:437–38; Letter from a Gentleman in Albany, 15 Aug. 1778, *New York Journal*, 24 Aug. 1778; VPD to JDU, 18 Aug. 1778, James Duane Paps., N-YHS; RC to PG with JDE to RC, 10 Oct. 1778, Box 18, Gansevoort-Lansing Coll., NYPL; JDE to PS, 10 Oct. 1778, *IAP*, 156–57.

63. JDE to PS, 18 Jan. 1779; and Commissioners' Meeting with Onondagas in Albany, 15 Aug. 1778, *IAP*, 149–53. See also Board of Commissioners to Onondagas, 15 Aug. 1778, James Duane Paps., N-YHS; Extract of a Letter from a Gentleman in Albany, 9 Aug. 1778, *New York Journal*, 31 Aug. 1778.

64. Louis Atayataghronghta to Indian Commissioners, 15 Aug. 1778, PCC, M247, r183, i166, 397.

65. See ibid., DC to FH, 19 Nov. 1778, Add. MS 21774-18, Item 13, R51, Haldimand Paps., PAC.
66. VPD to PG, 13 Nov. 1778, Box 18, Gansevoort-Lansing Coll., NYPL. See also Summary of Caughnawagas to Cayugas, 22 Mar. 1779, Brymer, *Report on Canadian Archives, 1887,* 187; JDE to PS, 29 Mar. 1779, *IAP,* 192–93.
67. PS to HL, 15 Mar. 1778, *IAP,* 120. See also Resolution of 3 Apr. 1779, *JCC,* 13:411; John Jay to GW, 7 Apr. 1779, *LDC,* 12:307.
68. See List of Oneidas and Tuscaroras Appointed Officers, undated, R7, Schuyler Paps., NYPL; Resolution of 15 June 1779, *JCC,* 14:733; SKI Journ., 25 Feb. 1799 and 9 Jan. 1800, Pilkington, ed., *Journals Kirkland,* 309 and 333; Conversation with Cornelius Doxtater, 11 U 200–02, Draper MS (1980, R57), SHSW; Henry Knox to House of Representatives, 26 Feb. 1791, *Am. State Paps.,* 4:123; Wonderley, "A Sketch," 44–45.
69. Henry Knox to House of Representatives, 26 Feb. 1791, *Am. State Paps.,* 4:123.
70. Petition of Jacob Reed to CC, [30 Aug. 1782], *IAP,* 281. See also RC to PG, 8 Sep. 1778, Box 18, Gansevoort-Lansing Coll., NYPL.
71. GW to JC, 19 Jan. 1779; and GW to JC, 25 Jan. 1779, *Writings GW,* 14:23–24 and 43; PS to [GW] and [John Jay], 5 Jan. 1779, cited in Comm. Conference Report by JDU, 16 Aug. 1779; and Jay to PS, 15 Jan. 1779, *LDC,* 13:374, and 11:469. The PS letter of 5 Jan. 1779, has not been found.
72. JC to GCL, 31 Jan. 1779, *Clinton Paps.,* 4:529; John Copp to CVD, 27 Jan. 1779, Willis T. Hanson Paps., NYSL.
73. John Copp to Captain [?], 16 Feb. 1779; and John Copp to Capt. [?], 15 Feb. 1779, Henry Glen Paps., NYPL; John Copp to CVD, 27 Jan. 1778, Willis T. Hanson Paps., NYSL.
74. John Copp to Capt. [?], 15 Feb. 1779; and John Copp to Capt. [?], 16 Feb. 1779, Henry Glen Paps., NYPL; John Copp to Capt. [?], 24 Feb. 1779, PCC, M247, r173, i153, v3, 424.

ELEVEN: WARFARE BY DEVASTATION

1. JDU to GCL, 6 June and 22 Sep. 1778, *Clinton Paps.,* 3:419, and 4:67–68. See also GW to GCL, 16 Mar. 1778, *Paps. GW, RWS,* 14:206–207.
2. GW to Pres. of CC, 16 Nov. 1778, *Writings GW,* 13:264. See also GCL to John Jay, 17 Nov. 1778; Abraham Yates to GCL, 9 Jan. 1779, *Clinton Paps.,* 4:289–90 and 479–80. In early August 1778, after the Wyoming Valley disaster, a campaign against the Iroquois was already "in contemplation." See GW to Col. Morgan Lewis, 5 Aug. 1778, *Writings GW,* 12:284. After Cherry Valley, such a plan became a pressing priority for GW and other rebel leaders.
3. GW and GCL, 5 Nov. 1778; GW to PS, 25 Jan. and 11 Feb. 1779; GW to Maj. Gen. Nathanael Greene, 24 Feb. 1779; GW to Col. William Patterson, 1 Mar. 1779; GW to Joseph Reed, 3 Mar. 1779; GW to JSU, 6 Mar. 1779; GW to Edward Hand, 16 Mar. 1779; GW to PS, 21 Mar. 1779; GW's Queries Concerning the Indian Country, [Mar. 1779]; GW to PS, 19 Apr. 1779; and GW's Instructions to JSU, 31 May. 1779, *Writings GW,* 13:203–204; 14:45–46, 94–98, 142, 168–69, 188, 201, 251–52, 268–73, 314–18, 407–408, and 15:189–96; PS to GW, 3 Apr.

1779; and Unknown Report Regarding Indians in the Susquehanna River Area, [Mar. or Apr.] 1779, PCC, M247, r183, i166, 155 and 302; GCL to New York Delegates in CC, 9 Feb. 1779; PS to GCL, 2 Mar. 1779; GCL to GW, 3 Mar. 1779; and GW to GCL, 4 Mar. 1779, *Clinton Paps.*, 4:555–56, 602–605, 612, and 615–17; PS to GW, 4 Feb. 1779, *IAP*, 183.

4. GW to JDU, 11 Jan. 1779, *Writings GW*, 13:500. See also GW's Instructions to JSU, 31 May 1779, ibid., 15:189–96; and GCL to JC, 16 May 1779, *Clinton Paps.*, 4:831. On the JSU-JC campaign, see Fischer, *Well-Executed Failure*, passim. Mann, *George Washington's War*, 51–110, employs terms such as *holocaust* and *genocide* to characterize the intent and outcome of the JSU-JC expedition.

5. GW to PS, 21 Mar. 1779, *Writings GW*, 13:271–72; PS to GW, 1 Mar. 1779, *IAP*, 189–90; JC to GCL, 8 Apr. 1779, *Clinton Paps.*, 4:702–704; GVS, Minutes and Proceedings of the Onondaga Expedition, 24 Apr. 1779, *Pennsylvania Gazette*, 12 May 1779, 3:col. 2.

6. JC to GCL, 8 Apr. 1779, *Clinton Paps.*, 4:702–704; Capt. Leonard Bleeker, Order Book, 1779, 22–23n1. PS explained the campaign plan to GW in PS to GW, 3 Apr. 1779. Apparently, this letter has been lost.

7. Thomas McClellan to PG, 14 Mar. 1779, Box 18, Gansevoort-Lansing Coll., NYPL. See also Extract of a Letter from PS to GCL, 7 Mar. 1779, *Clinton Paps.*, 4:620.

8. Erkuries Beatty Journ., 15 and 16 Apr. 1779, *Journals Military Expedition*, 16. GVS had specific instructions not to take any Indians with him. See Stone, *Brant*, 1:404–405.

9. Erkuries Beatty Journ., 15 and 16 Apr. 1779, Journals Military Expedition, 16; Thomas McClellan to JC, 30 Apr. 1779, *Clinton Paps.*, 4:804.

10. On the expedition against Oswegatchie, see Thomas McClellan to JC, 30 Apr. 1779, *Clinton Paps.*, 4:804–05; James Davis to FH, 27 Apr. 1779, Add. MS 21780, R54, Haldimand Paps., PAC. By coincidence, GW asked that an Oneida party scout the route to Oswegatchie. See GW to PS, 27 Apr. 1779, *Writings GW*, 14:447–48.

11. Thomas McClellan to JC, 30 Apr. 1779, *Clinton Paps.*, 4:804–805; Extract from a Letter from Fort Schuyler [McClellan], 30 Apr. 1779, *Pennsylvania Journal*, 19 May 1779; James Davis to FH, 27 Apr. 1779, Add. MS 21780, R54, Haldimand Paps., PAC; FH to GCL, 26 May 1779, DAR, 17:134–38.

12. GVS, Minutes and Proceedings of the Onondaga Expedition, 24 Apr. 1779, *Pennsylvania Gazette*, 12 May 1779, 3:col. 2; Poughkeepsie, 3 May 1779, *Providence American Journal*, 20 May 1779, 4:col. 1–2; GVS to Henry Glen, 11 May 1779, Box 18, Gansevoort-Lansing Coll., NYPL; GCL to Maj. Gen. Alexander McDougall, 29 Apr. 1779, *Clinton Paps.*, 4:777; Speech of Tioguanda, an Onondaga Chief, 11 Dec. 1782, Ontario Indian Office, 16, Brantford Paps., NYSL; Thomas Machin Journ., 21 Apr. 1779, *Journals Military Expedition*, 192–93; Clark, *Onondaga*, 1:329; Stone, *Brant*, 1:404. For very different interpretations of GVS's attack, see Williams, *Year of the Hangman*, 206–212; and Mann, *George Washington's War*, 27–36.

13. PS to John Jay, 27 Jan. 1779; and Extract from JDE to PS, 1 Apr. 1779, PCC, M247, r173, i153, v3, 416 and 440.

14. GW to Daniel Broadhead, 3 May 1779, *Writings GW*, 14:483.
15. FH to JBU, 8 Apr. 1779, Add. MS 21756-1, R39, Haldimand Paps., PAC. JBU to FH, 28 May 1779, *Sullivan-Clinton Campaign*, 89–90. See also Speech by Onondaga Chief to SKI, SKI Journ., 23 Apr. 1787, Pilkington, ed., *Journals Kirkland*, 134.
16. JDE to PS, 21 May 1779, PCC, M247, r94, i78, v7, 243; Extract of a Letter from Albany, 6 June 1779, *New York Journal*, 14 June 1779; JBU to FH, 8 Mar. 1779, *Sullivan-Clinton Campaign*, 74; JBU to FH, 2 Apr. 1779, Add. MS 21765-116, Item 91, R46; and JBU to MB, 28 May 1779, Add. MS 21760, R42, Haldimand Paps., PAC.
17. DC to FH, 17 May 1779, *IAP*, 219. See also Dederick Brehm to FH, 15 May 1779, Add. MS 21759, R41, Haldimand Paps., PAC.
18. Message from Caughnawagas to Cayugas, 22 Mar. 1779, Brymer, Report Canadian Archives, 1887, 187; JDE to PS, 1 and 10 Apr. 1779, PCC, M247, r173, i153, v.3, 440; PS to John Jay, 24 and 25 Apr. 1779, *IAP*, 211–13; GW to Pres. of CC, 3 May 1779; and GW to PS, 5 May 1779, *Writings GW*, 14:484–85 and 496–97.
19. Quoted in Stone, *Brant*, 1:407–409.
20. JBU to MB, 21 May 1779; and JBU to MB, 28 May 1779, Add. MS 21760, R42, Haldimand Paps., PAC; Stone, *Brant*, 1:407–409.
21. GW to PS and VPD, 28 May 1779; and GW to JC, 28 May 1779, *Writings GW*, 15:168–69 and 173; JC to GW, 19 June 1779, *IAP*, 223. Almost all of the Indians at Oquaga in 1778 were Mohawks and Tuscaroras, and nearly all of the refugees moved to Niagara. There were 44 Oneidas, 49 Tuscaroras, 276 Mohawks, and 367 Oquagas listed as "Present" and "Absent." See Return of the Indians at Niagara, from 30 Dec. 1778 to 26 Jan. 1779, Add. MS 21760, R42, Haldimand Paps., PAC.
22. Disbursement of 5 May 1779 to GR, for Subsistence for Him and His Party and Maintenance of Onondaga Prisoners; Draft Document on Release of Onondagas, undated; Speech by Commissioners to Oneidas, undated [Aug. 1779], R7, Schuyler Paps., NYPL; JBU to MB, 28 May 1779, Add. MS 21760, R42, Haldimand Paps., PAC; Oneidas' Meeting with Commissioners, 21 July 1779; and PS to VPD, 10 Aug. 1779, *IAP*, 224–29; GW to VPD, 29 July 1779, *Writings GW*, 16:13–14.
23. GVS to JC, 22 May 1779, *Clinton Paps.*, 4:843–44; JBU to MB, 21 May 1779, Add. MS 21760, R42, Haldimand Paps., PAC. Buck Island is now called Carleton Island.
24. John Campbell to FH, 22 July 1779, Add. MS 21771, R49, Haldimand Paps., PAC. See also FH to John Campbell, 26 July 1779, Add. MS 21773-49, Item 69, R50, Haldimand Paps., PAC.
25. FH to Oneidas, no date, MS 21880, Item 197, R113; and Add. MS 21779, R54, Haldimand Paps., PAC. For a different version, see MG19, F1, v24, Item 8–10, RC1485, Claus Paps., PAC.
26. John Campbell to FH, 18 Apr. 1779, 3 May 1779, and 21 June 1779, Add. MS 21771, R49; and JBU to FH, 8 June 1779, Add. MS 21765-139, Item 113, R46, Haldimand Paps., PAC; JSU to GW, 1 July 1779, PCC, M247, r183, i166, 291; and GW to PS, 23 July 1779, *Writings GW*, 15:469.
27. Back in March, the Oneidas had predicted an attack. See PS to GW, 8 Mar. 1779, *Clinton Paps.*, 4:624–25.

28. JBU to MB, 18 June 1779, Add. MS 21760, R42; JBU to FH, 21 June 1779, Add. MS 21765-143, R46, Item 115; and JBU to MB, 7 July 1779, Add. MS 21760, R42, Haldimand Paps., PAC. See also JBU to MB, 23 July 1779; and JBU to FH, 21 July 1779, Canadian Archives Folder, Sullivan's Indian Campaign 1779, NYSL; JBU to MB, 24 June 1779; and John McDonnell to JBU, 24 July 1779, Add. MS 21760, R42, Haldimand Paps., PAC; JBU to MB, 27 June 1779, *Sullivan-Clinton Campaign*, 101.

29. GVS to JC, 5 June 1779, *Clinton Paps.*, 5:35–36.

30. M.R. to the Printer, 9 July 1779, *New York Journal*, 16 Aug. 1779. See also Capt. Leonard Bleeker, Order Book, 1779, 66n1; Robert Parker Journ., 6 July 1779, *Sullivan-Clinton Campaign*, 191; JC to GCL, 10 Aug. 1779, *Clinton Paps.*, 5:189; Officer at Fort Sullivan, Tioga, to [?], 16 Aug. 1779, *New York Journal*, 27 Sep. 1779; Tiro, "People of the Standing Stone," 127–32.

31. Alexander Fraser to FH, 29 July 1779, Add. MS 21780, R54; and John Campbell to FH, 31 July 1779, Add. MS 21771, R49, Haldimand Paps., PAC.

32. JC to GCL, 10 Aug. 1779, *Clinton Paps.*, 5:189; Officer at Fort Sullivan, Tioga, to [?], 16 Aug. 1779, *New York Journal*, 27 Sep. 1779.

33. Jeremiah Fogg Diary, 25 Aug. 1779, *Journals Military Expedition*, 94. See also Obadiah Gore Diary, 25 Aug. 1779, *Sullivan-Clinton Campaign*, 182.

34. JBU to MB, 31 Aug. 1779, CO 42/39, f. 363–64, RB35, PAC; Fischer, *Well-Executed Failure*, 85–96; Williams, *Year of the Hangman*, 264–73; Graymont, *Iroquois Am. Rev.*, 211–13; and various primary accounts in *Journals Military Expedition*.

35. JSU to the Oneidas, 1 Sep. 1779, *Letters Sullivan*, 3:114–15.

36. Poughkeepsie, 13 Sep. 1779, *Pennsylvania Journal*, 29 Sep. 1779; CVD to Henry Glen, 17 Sep. 1779, Henry Glen Paps., NYPL; Jeremiah Fogg Journ., 2 Sep. 1779, *Journals Military Expedition*, 96; JSU to John Jay, 30 Sep. 1779, *Letters Sullivan*, 3:129. The Seneca village Chenussio was also known as Beard's Town and Genesee Castle.

37. Extract from Philip Van Cortlandt's Account of the War, Van Cortlandt-Van Wyck Paps., Bancroft Coll., NYPL. See also Elwood, *Episode Sullivan Campaign*, 6–7.

38. JSU to John Jay, 30 Sep. 1779, *Letters Sullivan*, 3:129. See also Fischer, *Well-Executed Failure*, 96–97; Mintz, *Seeds of Empire*, 140–45; Williams, *Year of the Hangman*, 279–84; Mann, *George Washington's War*, 96–100.

39. O'Reilly, *Notices Sullivan's Campaign*, 102; Henry Dearborn Journ., 13 Sep. 1779, *Journals Military Expedition*, 75; Fischer, *Well-Executed Failure*, 97.

40. JSU to John Jay, 30 Sep. 1779, *Letters Sullivan*, 3:129–31; JBU to MB, 14 Sep. 1779, CO 42/39, f. 380, RB35, PAC; O'Reilly, *Notices Sullivan's Campaign*, 102; Fischer, *Well-Executed Failure*, 97.

41. *Sullivan-Clinton Campaign*, 43–44.

42. Oneida [Bluebeck] to JSU, [18 Sep. 1779], *Letters Sullivan*, 3:115–16. See also Fogg Journ. 18 Sep. 1779, *Journal Major Jeremiah Fogg*, 19; Robert Parker Journ., 18 Sep. 1779, *Sullivan-Clinton Campaign*, 206.

43. Oneida [Bluebeck] to JSU, [18 Sep. 1779]; and JSU to John Jay, 30 Sep. 1779, *Letters Sullivan*, 3:115–16 and 132.

44. JSU to the Oneidas, [Sep. 1779], *Letters Sullivan*, 3:117–18; Lt. Col. Adam Hubley Journ., 20 Sep. 1779, *Journals Military Expedition*, 164.

45. JSU to the Oneidas, [Sep. 1779], *Letters Sullivan*, 3:117–19.
46. Henry Dearborn Journ., 20–26 Sep. 1779, *Journals Military Expedition*, 76–78. JSU also sent PG with troops to destroy the Lower Castle of the Mohawks. Peaceful Indians occupied this area and had earned the enmity of pro-British Mohawks for their neutral stance. PS and, ultimately, GW overruled JSU's order. See JSU to PG, 20 Sep. 1779; PS to PG, 7 Oct. 1779; and PG to GW, 8 Oct. 1779, Gansevoort-Lansing Coll., NYPL; JSU to John Jay, 30 Sep. 1779, *Sullivan-Clinton Campaign*, 166; GW to PS, 12 Oct. 1779, *Writings GW*, 16:460–61.
47. JSU to John Jay, 30 Sep. 1779, *Letters Sullivan*, 3:136 and 134.
48. JSU to the Oneidas, 1 Oct. 1779; and JSU to John Jay, 30 Sep. 1779, *Letters Sullivan*, 3:137–38 and 136.
49. Aghsarigowa (Big Knife), Tuscarora Indian, and Teheaniyoghtiwat, Oneida, to JSU, 1 Oct. 1779, *Letters Sullivan*, 3:138–40.
50. JBU to FH, 20 Sep. 1779, B1, F3, Sullivan's Indian Campaign, 1779, Coll., NYSL. See also MB to FH, 16 Aug. 1779; and FH to GG, 13 Sep. 1779, and 3 Oct. 1779, *DAR*, 17:187, 209–11, and 231–32; GJ to FH, 12 Nov. 1779, Add. MS 21767, R47; GJ to FH, 3 May 1780. Add MS 21766, R47, Haldimand Paps., PAC; Graymont, *Iroquois Am. Rev.*, 220–22. For differing interpretations of the long-term consequences of the JSU-JC expedition, see Fischer, *Well-Executed Failure*, 191–97, and Williams, *Year of the Hangman*, 290–96.
51. MB to FH, 2 Oct. 1779, Canadian Archives Folder, Sullivan's Indian Campaign, NYSL; FH to GJ, 6 Oct. 1779, Add. MS 21767, R47, Haldimand Paps., PAC.
52. GJ to FH, 22 Oct. 1779, Add. MS 21766, R47; FH to Maj. Christopher Carleton, 1 Nov. 1779, Add. MS 21792, R61; and FH to John Campbell, 8 Nov. 1779, Add. MS 21773-73, Item 101, R50, Haldimand Paps., PAC. See also FH to GG, 1 Nov. 1779, CO 42/40, f. 3, RB35, PAC.
53. FH to MB, 11 Nov. 1779, Add. MS 21756-2, R39; FH to GJ, 11 Nov. 1779, Add. MS 21767, R47; GJ to FH, 12 Nov. 1779, Add. MS 21767, R47; MB to FH, 4 Dec. 1779, Add. MS 21760, R42, Haldimand Paps., PAC.
54. Meeting of the Commissioners of Indian Affairs with the Oneida and Tuscarora Indians at Albany, 9 Feb. 1780, R7, Schuyler Paps., NYPL.
55. Answer of the Commissioners of Indian Affairs to the Oneidas and Tuscaroras, [10(?) Feb. 1780], R7, Schuyler Paps., NYPL.
56. PS to SH, 5 Feb. 1780, PCC, M247, r173, i153, v3, 503; JSU to PG, 20 Sep. 1779; PS to PG, 7 Oct. 1779; and PG to GW, 8 Oct. 1779, Gansevoort-Lansing Coll., NYPL; JSU to John Jay, 30 Sep. 1779, *Sullivan-Clinton Campaign*, 166; GW to PS, 12 Oct. 1779, *Writings GW*, 16:460–61. Little Abraham and Johannes Crine had performed "Secret Services to Niagara" for the rebels before. See VPD to PS, Expenses, 4 Mar. 1779, R7, Schuyler Paps., NYPL.
57. GJ to PS, 7 Dec. 1779; and PS to GJ, 7 Jan. 1780, *IAP*, 240–41 and 245–46; PS to SH, 14 Jan. 1780, PCC, M247, r173, i153, v3, 488–90; GW to GCL, 3 May 1779, *Writings GW*, 14:477–78; Resolution of 20 June 1779, *JCC*, 14:753; An Act to Appoint Commissioners to Represent the State in a Treaty of Pacification with the Indians, 23 Oct. 1779, *Clinton Paps.*, 5:334–36; A Meeting of the Indian Commissioners in Albany, 3 Feb. 1780, R7, Schuyler Paps., NYPL.
58. A Meeting of the Commissioners of Indian Affairs with the Oneidas and Tuscaroras, 9 Feb. 1780, R7, Schuyler Paps., NYPL.

59. Ibid.
60. Proceedings with Four Rebel Indians Who Came to Hold a Meeting with the Chiefs of the Six Nations, 12–18 Feb. 1780, Add. MS 21779, R54, Haldimand Paps., PAC. See also Conversation with Elijah Skenandoah, Draper MS, 11 U 240–41 (1980, R57), SHSW; Graymont, *Iroquois Am. Rev.*, 225–27; Mintz, *Seeds of Empire*, 157–59.
61. Proceedings with Four Rebel Indians Who Came to Hold a Meeting with the Chiefs of the Six Nations, 12–18 Feb. 1780, Add. MS 21779, R54, Haldimand Paps., PAC; GJ to Alexander McKee, 6 Apr. 1780, Daniel Claus Paps., LC; Graymont, *Iroquois Am. Rev.*, 225–27.
62. Proceedings with Four Rebel Indians Who Came to Hold a Meeting with the Chiefs of the Six Nations, 12–18 Feb. 1780, Add. MS 21779, R54, Haldimand Paps., PAC. For what seems like a more precise version of Aaron's speech, see MG19, F1, v24, Item 4–6, RC1485, Daniel Claus Paps., PAC.
63. Proceedings with Four Rebel Indians Who Came to Hold a Meeting with the Chiefs of the Six Nations, 12–18 Feb. 1780, Add. Mss. 21779, R54, Haldimand Paps., PAC. FH referred to them as "hostages." See FH to GJ, 1 Sep. 1780, Add. MS 21767, R47, Haldimand Paps., PAC.

TWELVE: VENGEANCE AND VICTORY

1. Speech of Good Peter, 23 June 1785, Hough, ed., *Proceedings*, 1:87–88; Comments by GP and Johannes Crine, Draper MS, 11 U 149–54 (1980, R57), SHSW.
2. JDE to PS, 4 Apr. 1780, R16, Schuyler Paps., NYPL.
3. William Patterson to Gen. Nathanael Greene, 22 Mar. 1780, PCC, M247, r100, i78, v18, 273. See also GCL to New York CC delegates, 25 Mar. 1780; GCL to GVS, 27 Mar. 1780; Christopher Yates to Abraham Yates, 17 Mar. 1780; and GVS to GCL, 17 May 1780, *Clinton Paps.*, 5:556–58, 567–68, 548–50, and 715–17; "Poughkeepsie," 17 Apr. 1780, *Connecticut Courant*, 25 Apr. 1780, 2:col. 3; Meshech Weare to Nathaniel Folsom or Nathaniel Peabody, 28 Apr. 1780, PCC, M247, r78, i64, 106; GCL to New York CC delegates, 27 Apr. 1780, James Duane Paps., N-YHS; DC to FH, 15 May 1780, *IAP*, 257; "Fishkill," 8 June 1780, *Pennsylvania Gazette*, 21 June 1780, 2:col. 2–3.
4. Alexander Fraser to FH, 1 June 1780, Add. MS 21787, R58; Robert Mathews to John Campbell, 29 June 1780, Add. MS 21773-94, Item 133, R50; and Robert Mathews to [?] Houghton, 24 Feb. 1780, Add. MS 21773-80, Item 109, R50, Haldimand Paps., PAC; FH to DC, 6 Apr. 1780, Daniel Claus Paps., LC.
5. Egly, *History First New York Regiment*, 154–55; John Taylor to PS, 19 June 1780, R16, Schuyler Paps., NYPL; Alexander Fraser to FH, 30 May 1780, Add. MS 21787, R58, Haldimand Paps., PAC.
6. SKI to VPD, 3 [July] 1780, *IAP*, 260; GJ to FH, 2 July 1780, Add. MS 21767, R47, Haldimand Paps., PAC; Speech of Oneidas to Lieut. Col. CVD, 18 June 1780, Indian Paps., N-YHS.
7. Return of Indians Hitherto Deemed in the Rebel Interest Who Joined Col. Johnson's Department on Sunday, 2 July 1780, Add. MS 21769, R48; and Proceedings at Two Meetings with the Indians of Ganaghsaragy, Oneidas, Etc., from the Rebel Frontier, with Guy Johnson, 3 and 6 July 1780, Add. MS 21779, R54, Haldimand

Paps., PAC; Speech of the Oneidas to Lieut. Col. CVD, 18 June 1780, Indian Paps., N-YHS; Morgan Lewis to GCL, 24 June 1780, *Clinton Paps.*, 5:883–84.

8. Proceedings at Two Meetings with the Indians of Ganaghsaragy, Oneidas, Etc., from the Rebel Frontier, with Guy Johnson, 3 and 6 July 1780, Add. MS 21779, R54, Haldimand Paps., PAC.

9. Speech of Oneidas to Lieut. Col. CVD, 18 June 1780, Indian Paps., N-YHS.

10. For a description of Kanonwalohale, see Wonderley, "Oneida Community in 1780," 25–29.

11. Speech of Oneidas to Lieut. Col. CVD, 18 June 1780, Indian Paps., N-YHS. The rendition of this speech in *Clinton Paps.*, 5:883–84, is slightly incorrect.

12. John McDonnell to MB, 1 July 1780, Add. MS 21760, R42, Haldimand Paps., PAC; SKI to VPD, 3 [July] 1780, *IAP*, 258–60; CVD to GVS, 3 July 1780, *Clinton Paps.*, 5:912–15.

13. John McDonnell to MB, 1 July 1780, Add. MS 21760, R42, Haldimand Paps., PAC.

14. SKI to VPD, 3 [July] 1780, *IAP*, 258–60. See also John McDonnell to MB, 1 July 1780, Add. MS 21760, R42, Haldimand Paps., PAC; CVD to GVS, 3 July 1780, *Clinton Paps.*, 5:912–15.

15. SKI to VPD, 3 [July] 1780, *IAP*, 258–60; John McDonnell to MB, 1 July 1780, Add. MS 21760, R42, Haldimand Paps., PAC.

16. Daniel Robertson to Frederick Brehm, 8 Aug. 1780, Add. MS 21780, R54; and FH to MB, 31 Aug. 1780, Add. MS 21764, R45, Haldimand Paps., PAC; SKI to VPD, 3 [July] 1780, *IAP*, 260; GVS to GCL, 24 June 1780, *Clinton Paps.*, 5:883; VPD to PS, 24 June 1780; [?] to PS, 25 June 1780; and John Lansing, Jr., to PS, 7 July 1780, R16, Schuyler Paps., NYPL.

17. They did not take horses and cattle because they could not feed them. For the quantity of losses, see "Account of Losses," R62, 157–66a, Timothy Pickering Paps., MHS, Wonderley, "A Sketch," appendix A; and Wonderley, "Oneida Community in 1780," tables C and D.

18. Maj. John Graham to GVS, 27 July 1780, *Clinton Paps.*, 6:59; Alexander Fraser to FH, 25 July 1780, Add. MS 21787, R58, Haldimand Paps., PAC. Rebel leaders anticipated a campaign against Fort Schuyler. See GCL to GW, 3 July 1780, *Clinton Paps.*, 5:909–11.

19. Proceedings of a Meeting with the Deputies of the Six Nations on Their Return from the Southward, 17 June 1780; and Proceedings at Two Meetings with the Indians of Ganaghsaragy, Oneidas, Etc., from the Rebel Frontier, with Guy Johnson, 3 and 6 July 1780, Add. MS 21779, R54, Haldimand Paps., PAC.

20. Wonderley, "Oneida Community in 1780," 25–26.

21. Maj. John Graham to GVS, 27 July 1780. *Clinton Paps.*, 6:59–60; GJ to FH, 11 Aug. 1780, Add. MS 21766, R47; Daniel Robertson to Frederick Brehm, 8 Aug. 1780, Add. MS 21780, R54; MB to FH, 8 Aug. 1780, Add. MS 21760, R42; Lieut. Joseph Clement to GJ, 14 Aug. 1780, Add. MS 21767, R47; and GJ to FH, 18 Sep. 1780, Add. MS 21766, R47, Haldimand Paps., PAC; Draper MS, 11 U 238 (1980, R57), SHSW.

22. Maj. John Graham to GVS, 27 July 1780, *Clinton Paps.*, 6:59–60; GJ to FH, 11 Aug. 1780, Add. MS 21766, R47, Haldimand Paps., PAC.

23. GJ to FH, 24 Aug. 1780, Add. MS 21766, R47, Haldimand Paps., PAC; PS to MDL, 18 Aug. 1780, Rice and Brown, ed. and trans., *American Campaigns Rochambeau's Army*, 1:121. See also GJ to FH, 3 Sep. 1780, Add. MS 21767, R47; and AM to FH, 18 May 1783, Add. MS 21763, R44, Haldimand Paps., PAC.

24. GJ to FH, 3 Sep. 1780, Add. MS 21767, R47; and GJ to FH, 18 Sep. 1780, Add. MS 21766, R47, Haldimand Paps., PAC.

25. GJ to FH, 24 Aug. 1780 and 18 Sep. 1780, Add. MS 21766, R47, Haldimand Paps., PAC. GJ's figure of 424 is derived from 294 listed in early July and 132 in August. GJ omitted the eleven who came in mid-July with Captain McDonnell, Spruce Carrier, and David. The Oneida numbers represent the 32 persons who arrived on July 2, the 10 to 12 who returned with the first British approach to Kanonwalohale, and 132 (most likely, not all of them were Oneidas, but they can be assumed to be so) who left with Skenandoah and reached Niagara around 20 August. Adding these numbers to Good Peter, Skenandoah, and the 50 Oneidas at Niagara in early 1779 (there is no evidence of Oneidas fleeing to Niagara during 1779, except for a small number who still resided at Oquaga), the approximate total was close to 250. In "General State of the Six Nations as They Were in 1781," which GJ completed on 28 December 1786, he listed the Oneida population at 403. This number is likely too high. Around 1770, there were perhaps 130 Oneidas at Oquaga. As tensions in the community mounted, more and more Oquaga Oneidas moved to Kanonwalohale. At most, sixty to seventy Oneidas at Oquaga relocated to Niagara. See Return of Indians Who Received Clothing, Arms, Ammunition, Etc., at Niagara from Nov. 1778 to Mar. 1779, Add. MS 21769, R48; Return of Indians at Niagara from 30 Dec. 1778 to 26 Jan. 1779, Add. MS 21765-90, Item 79, R46; and Return of Indians Hitherto Deemed in the Rebel Interest Who Joined Col. Johnson's Department on Sunday, July 2nd, 1780, Add. MS 21769, R48, Haldimand Paps., PAC.

26. Captain Dalton's Estimate of the Number of Warriors Annexed to Each Nation That Were Employed by the British, Superintendent of Indian Affairs for the United States, 12 Aug. 1783, Folder marked "List of Prisoners Retained by Indians," Indians Coll., Box 2, NYPL; SKI's Estimate to Dr. Ezra Stiles, *CMHS* 10 (1809):123; PS to MDL, 18 Aug. 1780, Rice and Brown, ed. and trans., *American Campaigns Rochambeau's Army*, 1:121. The "Present State of Officers, Men, and Indians of the Command of Col. Guy Johnson, 4 Nov. 1777," Add. MS 21769, R48, Haldimand Paps., PAC, listed 11 Oneidas, 240 Tuscaroras, and 154 Oquagas. A census document for 1778 claims that 787 Oneidas and Tuscaroras were in Canada. See Population Report of the Oneidas and Tuscaroras, 1778, Six Nations Coll., NYSL. This number also seems high, but if it is accurate, then nearly all these persons were likely Tuscaroras. All other evidence suggests a very small Oneida population living under the British and fighting for them.

27. Henry Knox to House of Representatives, 26 Feb. 1791, *Am. State Paps.*, Class II, 1:123. See also Col. Frederick Weissenfels to GCL, 9 Dec. 1780, *Clinton Paps.*, 6:480–83. The document lists one of the deserters as Joseph Banaghsatirhon, which likely was *Kanaghsatirhon*, as B sounds do not exist in Iroquois languages.

28. JDU to PS, 12 May 1780; and PS to Duane, 6 Mar. [May] 1780, *LDC*, 15:110–11 and 92; John Lansing, Jr., to VPD, 26 July 1780, R16, Schuyler Paps., NYPL. The

figure of six hundred is a reasonable estimate. According to PS, only a few were Tuscaroras. Seven were Kahnawakes, and the rest were Oneidas. See Meeting of the Commissioners with the Oneida Nation, 16 Aug. 1780, *IAP*, 262. A clothing count at Schenectady in early Oct. 1780 indicated 409 persons. Of the 409, 98 were men, 54 were women, and 254 were children. Many warriors were out hunting and scouting at that time, and some women accompanied them. By December 1780, rebel officials tallied 390 Oneidas living at Schenectady. At that time, a sizable number of Oneidas had established a community in the vicinity of Saratoga.

29. Meeting of the Commissioners with the Oneida Nation, 16 Aug. 1780, *IAP*, 261.

30. PS to Pres. CC, 10 Oct. 1780, PCC, M247, r173, i153, 541; List of Necessary Clothing for 406 Oneidas, included with PS to Pres. of CC, 10 Oct. 1780, PCC, M247, r173, i153, 545. This tabulation was incomplete. The Schenectady population estimate represents 24.4 percent men, 13.3 percent women, and 62.3 percent children. By comparison, according to the General State of the Corps of Indians and Department of Indian Affairs Under Col. Guy Johnson, Niagara, 1 Jan. 1781, Add. MS 21769, R48, Haldimand Paps., PAC, the breakdown there was 31.3 percent men, 40.2 percent women, and 28.5 percent children. The Oneidas at Schenectady had twice as many children, three times fewer women, and about one-third fewer men. These discrepancies suggest that the headcount of 409 excluded a large number of parents who were not present but rather out scouting and hunting for food. The ratio of men to children for Indians at Niagara was 1.096:1, and for women to children there the ratio was 1.409:1. Assuming roughly the same ratios among all the Six Nations, the number of men at Schenectady would have been 284 and the number of women 365, based on the headcount of children there. As such, the number of adult Oneida men still supporting the rebellion could easily have surpassed three hundred.

31. PS to Henry Glen, 6 Nov. 1780, Henry Glen Paps., NYPL. See also PS to Pres. of CC, 10 Oct. 1780, PCC, M247, r173, i153, 541; List of Necessary Clothing for 406 Oneidas, included with Schuyler to Pres. CC, 10 Oct. 1780, PCC, M247, r173, i153, 545; Meeting of the Commissioners with the Oneida Nation, 16 Aug. 1780, *IAP*, 261. For a description of the buildings, see Rice, ed. and trans., *Travels by Chastellux*, 1:208.

32. PS to SH, 2 Dec. 1780, *IAP*, 265–66. On the devastating effects of smallpox during the Revolutionary era, especially among native populations, see Fenn, *Pox Americana*, 135–277.

33. Meeting of the Commissioners with the Oneida Nation, 16 Aug. 1780, *IAP*, 262. See also MW to PS, 28 Sep. 1780, R17, Schuyler Paps., NYPL. Over a fifteen-month period, 286 gallons of rum were made available for Oneida consumption.

34. PS to SH, 2 Dec. 1780, *IAP*, 265–66.

35. On the harsh winter weather and its consequences, see GJ to FH, 19 Feb. 1781, Add. MS 21767, R47, Haldimand Paps., PAC.

36. PS to SH, 2 Dec. 1780, *IAP*, 265–66.

37. GCL to Maj. Gen. William Heath, 30 Oct. 1780, *Clinton Paps.*, 6:349–50. For an overview of the destruction along the New York frontier, see GCL to Pres. CC, 5 Feb. 1781, PCC, M247, r81, i67, v2, 344.

38. Pierre Van Cortlandt and Evert Bancker to New York Delegates, 17 Jan. 1781,

PCC, M247, r81, i67, v2, 340; GVS to GCL, 28 July 1780 and 5 Sep. 1780; GW
to GCL, 6 Nov. 1780; Col. Frederick Weissenfels to GCL, 6 Nov. 1780; and GCL
to SH, 6 Nov. 1780, *Clinton Paps.*, 6:62, 171–72, 384–86, and 388–90; GVS to
Henry Glen, 16 Feb. 1781, Henry Glen Paps., NYPL. Other groups, especially wid-
ows and orphans, also had a strong claim to scarce resources. See Mary Tenis et al.
to GCL, 18 Aug. 1780, *Clinton Paps.*, 6:123.

39. PS to Pres. CC, 10 Oct. 1780, PCC, M247, r173, i153, v3, 541.
40. PS to SH, 2 Dec. 1780, *IAP*, 265–66.
41. PS to Pres. of CC, 26 Dec. 1780, PCC, M247, r173, i153, v3, 589; PS to SH,
    18 Jan. 1781, *IAP*, 269; Resolution of State of New York, in Senate, 24 Feb. 1781,
    PCC, M247, r173, i153, v3, 563. The New York legislature eventually reimbursed
    PS for some of his outlay of funds.
42. New York Delegates to GCL, 11 Mar. 1781, *LDC*, 17:51. See also PS to GCL, 27
    Oct. 1780; GCL to New York Delegates in CC, 5 Feb. 1781; and GCL to Capt. [?]
    Lawrence, 5 Feb. 1781, *Clinton Paps.*, 6:343–44 and 634; Resolution of State of
    New York, in Senate, 24 Feb. 1781, PCC, M247, r173, i153, v3, 563; John Maylan
    to PS, 29 Jan. 1781, R17, Schuyler Paps., NYPL; D. Brooks to Maj. Platt, 23 Feb.
    1781, War Dept. Coll. of Rev. War Manuscripts, Item 24495, M859, R84, Record
    Group 93, NA; Resolution of 30 Apr. 1781, *JCC*, 20, 465; Richard Peters to JDU,
    20 Apr. 1781, PCC, M247, r173, i153, v3, 559.
43. Testimony of Brig. Gen. Robert Van Rensselaer in Court Martial of Brig. Gen.
    Robert Van Rensselaer, 12 Mar. 1781, *Clinton Paps.*, 6:692–703. See also John
    Lansing, Jr., to GCL, 18 Oct. 1780; GCL to GW, 18 Oct. 1780; John Driskill, Re-
    turn of Ordinance & Stores taken from British Army, 19 Oct. 1780; PS to GCL,
    20 Oct. 1780; Lewis Duboys to GCL, [21 or 22 Oct. 1780]; GCL to PS,
    26 Oct. 1780; and GCL to GW, 30 Oct. 1780, *Clinton Paps.*, 6:305–307, 322–26,
    and 351–55; Roof, *Colonel John Brown*, passim; Extract of a Letter from a Corre-
    spondent in Albany, 21 Oct. 1780, *Pennsylvania Gazette*, 1 Nov. 1780, 3: col. 1;
    Extract of a Letter from an Officer of Distinction, 20 Oct. 1780, *Boston Gazette*,
    6 Nov. 1780, supplement, 2:col. 1; "Poughkeepsie," 30 Oct. 1780, *Pennsylvania
    Gazette*, 8 Nov. 1780, 2:col. 2; Alexander Fraser to FH, 27 Oct. 1780, Add. MS
    21787, R58, Haldimand Paps., PAC.
44. PS to SH, 2 Dec. 1780, *IAP*, 265–66; GCL to Pres. CC, 5 Feb. 1781, PCC, M247,
    r81, i67, v2, 344.
45. GJ to FH, 30 Sep. 1780, Add. MS 21766, R47; and GJ to FH, 25 July 1780, Add.
    MS 21767, R47, Haldimand Paps., PAC.
46. FH to MB, 31 Aug. 1780, Add. MS 21764, R45; and GJ to FH, 12 Sep. 1780, Add.
    MS 21766, R47, Haldimand Paps., PAC.
47. FH to GJ, 24 July 1780, 1 Sep. 1780, and 9 Oct. 1780, Add. MS 21767, R47; and
    GJ to FH, 30 Sep. 1780, Add. MS 21766, R47, Haldimand Paps., PAC.
48. GJ to GG, 20 Nov. 1780, CO 42/41, f. 148–49, RB36, PAC. For other Oneida war-
    rior actions on behalf of the British, see GJ to FH, 24 Aug. 1780, Add. MS 21766,
    R47; GJ to FH, 3 Sep. 1780, Add. MS 21767, R47; and Capt. William Caldwell to
    H. Watson Powell, 19 Aug. 1781, Add. MS 21761, R43, Haldimand Paps., PAC.
49. FH to GG, 28 Nov. 1780, Add. MS 21715, R21; and GJ to FH, 30 Sep. 1780, Add.
    MS 21766, R47, Haldimand Paps., PAC; Col. Frederick Weissenfels to GCL,

9 Dec. 1780, *Clinton Paps.*, 6:480–83. See also FH to GG, 25 Oct. 1780, CO 42/40, f. 334–38, RB35, PAC.

50. DC to Robert Mathews, 26 Feb. 1781, John Campbell Paps., NYSL. See also FH to Maj. John Ross, 1 Mar. 1781, Add. MS 21784, R56; Robert Mathews to DC, 9 July 1781, Add. MS 21774-188, Item 202, R51; and FH to John Campbell, 16 July 1781, Add. MS 21773-143, Item 27, R50, Haldimand Paps., PAC.

51. Capt. William Caldwell to H. Watson Powell, 19 Aug. 1781, Add. MS 21761, R43, Haldimand Paps., PAC; Daniel Servos to DC, 12 Apr. 1781; and Aron to Isaac, 10 May 1781, *IAP*, 273–74.

52. PS to MDL, 18 Aug. 1780, 1:195–99, Sparks Coll., 66, HLHU; Verger Journ., 29 Aug. 1780, Rice and Brown, ed. and trans., *American Campaigns Rochambeau's Army*, 1:121–22, also n12–15; PS to Jonathan Trumbull, 18 Aug. 1780, *CMHS* 7 ser., 3 (1902):109–10; Meeting of the Commissioners with the Oneida Nation, 16 Aug. 1780, *IAP*, 262.

53. Col. Louis Atayataronghta to Pres. CC, 11 Sep. 1781, PCC, M247, r98, i78, v14, 489. See also Committee of Congress and Board of War Speech to Oneidas, Tuscaroras, and Kahnawakes, [13 Sep. 1781], *IAP*, 276; Barbé de Marbois Journ., 23 Sep. 1784, *Lafayette Paps.*, 5:249.

54. Committee of Congress and Board of War Speech to Oneidas, Tuscaroras, and Kahnawakes, [13 Sep. 1781], *IAP*, 276–77.

55. Ibid. See also William Heath to PS, 2 Sep. 1781, R17, Schuyler Paps., NYPL; Board of War to the Oneida Indians, 19 Nov. 1781 (draft), PCC, M247, r171, i152, v10, 387.

56. Board of War to the Oneida Indians, 19 Nov. 1781 (draft), PCC, M247, r171, i152, v10, 387. Two Kahnawakes were among those who visited GW's army. See JD to PS, 2 Feb. 1782, R17, Schuyler Paps., NYPL.

57. For a summary of the Yorktown campaign, see Martin and Lender, *Respectable Army*, 173–80. For greater detail, see Greene, *Guns of Independence, Yorktown*, passim.

58. MW to Lord Stirling, 2 Nov. 1781, PCC, M247, r177, i157, 401; MW's Summary of 1781–82 Service, n.d., Ayer MS, NL; Henry Glen to PS, 14 Oct. 1781, Henry Glen Paps., NYPL.

59. MW to GCL, 2 Nov. 1781; Henry Glen to Lord Stirling, 26 Oct. 1781; Lord Stirling to GCL, 27 Oct. 1781; MW to GCL, 4 and 16 Nov. 1781; and MW to Troops, 2 Nov. 1781, *Clinton Paps.*, 7:472–75, 443–44, 447–51, 481–84, and 504–505; MW to Lord Stirling, 2 Nov. 1781, PCC, M247, r177, i157, 401; Nelia Ann Angus to Lyman Draper, Aug. 1878, 3 F 66 (1980, R14); and Draper MS, 3 G 11 (1980, R20), SHSW; Address of Douglas Campbell, 15 Aug. 1878, *Utica Morning Herald*; John Ross to FH, 7 Oct. [Nov.] 1781, Add. MS 21784, R56; H. Watson Powell to FH, 13 Nov. 1781, Add. MS 21761, R43; and FH to GG, 23 Nov. 1781, Add. MS 21715, R21, Haldimand Paps., PAC; PS to John Hanson, 29 Oct. 1781, *IAP*, 278–79. Anthony was likely Anthony Shonoghleoh, a known rebel supporter who by the end of the war had become a chief warrior. See Hough, ed., *Proceedings*, 1:40.

60. FH to GG, 23 Nov. 1781, Add. MS 21715, R21, Haldimand Paps., PAC; MW to GCL, 4 Nov. 1781, *Clinton Paps.*, 7:482.

61. MW to Lord Stirling, 2 Nov. 1781, PCC, M247, r177, i157, 401. See also Extract of a Letter from a Gentleman in Albany, 3 Nov. 1781, *New York Journal*, 12 Nov. 1781.

62. PS to GCL, 15 May 1781, *Clinton Paps.*, 6:880–81; GJ to FH, 23 Apr. 1781, Add. MS 21767, R47; and FH to John Campbell, 16 July 1781, Add. MS 21773-141, Item 213, R50, Haldimand Paps., PAC; Orders to Col. Abraham Wemple, 16 Aug. 1781; Abraham Wemple to PG, 12 Oct. 1781; and Col. Anthony Van Bergen to PG, 14 Oct. 1781, Box 18, Gansevoort-Lansing Coll., NYPL.

63. MW to CCL, 9 Aug. and 7 Nov. 1781; GCL to William Heath, 9 Sep. 1781; and John Tayler to GCL, Sep. 1781, *Clinton Paps.*, 7:186–88, 487–88, 316, and 304.

64. FH to H. Watson Powell, 17 Sep. 1781, Add. MS 21756-2, R39; and John Campbell to FH, 19 July 1781, Add. MS 21772-64, Item 31, R50, Haldimand Paps., PAC.

65. Robert Mathews to DC, 22 Nov. 1781, *IAP*, 279–80; FH to GG, 23 Nov. 1781, Add. MS 21715, R21; and Robert Mathews to John Campbell, 17 Jan. 1782, Add. MS 21773-161, Item 246, R50, Haldimand Paps., PAC; JD to PS, 2 Feb., 12 Feb., 20 Feb., and 4 Mar. 1782, R17, Schuyler Paps., NYPL.

66. PS to Robert Morris, 30 Aug. 1781, Oversize Box, Willis T. Hanson Paps., NYSL. See also William Health to PS, 12 Oct. 1781, R17, Schuyler Paps., NYPL.

67. Quoted in Hanson, *Schenectady During the Revolution*, 112. See also PS to Inhabitants of Tryon County, 1 May 1782, Schuyler Paps., NYSL.

68. PS to Inhabitants of Tryon County, 1 May 1782, Schuyler Paps., NYSL.

69. Mayor to Washington and Washington's Reply, 27 June 1782, Extract of a Letter from Albany, 2 July 1782, *Pennsylvania Gazette*, 17 July 1782, 2–3.

70. Extract of a Letter from Albany, 2 July 1782, *Pennsylvania Gazette*, 17 July 1782, 2–3; Albany, 24 June 1782, *Boston Gazette*, 15 July 1782, 2:col. 1; Report of Adongots's Son, 31 Aug. 1782, Add. MS 21761, R43, Haldimand Paps., PAC; Baker, *Itinerary of Washington*, 296–97; Freeman, *George Washington*, 5:416–17.

71. Abraham Wemple to PG, 20 Apr. 1782, Box 18, Gansevoort-Lansing Coll., NYPL; Extract of a Letter from Fort Rensselaer, 15 July 1782, *Pennsylvania Gazette*, 7 Aug. 1782, 2: col. 3; Extract of a Letter from an Officer at Fort Rensselaer, 18 July 1782; *Connecticut Courant*, 13 Aug. 1782, 2:col. 3; Albany, 22 July 1782, *Boston Gazette*, 5 Aug. 1782, 2: col. 2; Extract of a Letter from an Officer at Fort Rensselaer, 28 July 1782, *Pennsylvania Gazette*, 14 Aug. 1782, 3:col. 1; FH to H. Watson Powell, 28 May 1782, Add. MS 21756-2, R39; and FH to Lord Shelburne, 17 Aug. 1782, Add. MS 21717, R21, Haldimand Paps., PAC.

72. FH to H. Watson Powell, 28 May 1782, Add. MS 21756-2, R39; John Ross to Robert Mathews, 7 July 1782, Add. MS 21784, R56; FH to Lord Shelburne, 17 July and 17 Aug. 1782, Add. MS 21717, R21; and Return of the Six Nations at Oswego, 26 June 1782, Add. MS 21765-323, R46, Haldimand Paps., PAC.

73. Excerpt of a Letter from Canada, 3 Sep. 1782, enclosed with PS to John Hanson, 21 Sep. 1782, *IAP*, 282–83. See also PS to GW, 20 Sep. 1782, R17, Schuyler Paps., NYPL; and Response by Brig. Gen. AM to Speech of Tioquando, 12 Dec. 1782, Add. MS 21756-2, R39, Haldimand Paps., PAC.

74. JJ to FH, 28 Nov. 1782, Add. MS 21775, R52; FH to JJ, 5 Dec. 1782, Add. MS 21775, R52; and AM to FH, 16 Dec. 1782, Add. MS 21756-2, R 39, Haldimand Paps., PAC; Kelsay, *Joseph Brant*, 336–37.

75. JDU to GCL, 20 Aug. 1782, *Clinton Paps.*, 8:34–35.
76. GW to MW, 2 Feb. 1783; and also GW to MW, 18 Dec. 1782, and 22 Jan. 1783, Willett, *Narrative Marinus Willett*, 142–48.
77. MW to Henry to Henry Glen, 19 Feb. 1783, Henry Glen Paps., NYPL. See also Stone, *Brant*, 2:233–34; Thomas, *Marinus Willett*, 146–50; John Ross to FH, 17 Feb. 1783, Add. MS 21784, R56, Haldimand Paps., PAC.
78. GW to MW, 5 Mar. 1783, Willett, *Narrative Marinus Willett*, 149.
79. On the Peace of Paris and its silence regarding any protection of Indian land titles, see Calloway, *Am. Rev. Indian Country*, 272–78; Graymont, *Iroquois Am. Rev.*, 259–66; Taylor, *Divided Ground*, 111–19; Campisi, "Oneida Treaty Period," Campisi and Hauptman, ed., *Oneida Indian Experience*, 48–64; Mintz, *Seeds of Empire*, 173–78. See also GW to GCL, 8 Apr. 1783; GW to GCA, 9 Apr. 1783; and GW to MW, 14 Apr. 1783, *Writings GW*, 26:306–307 and 316.

THIRTEEN: FORGOTTEN ALLIES

1. GW to Pres. CC, 16 July 1783; and GW to PS, 15 July 1783, *Writings GW*, 27:65–66 and 70. See also Thomas, *Marinus Willett*, 152; Freeman, *George Washington*, 5:450–51; Wonderley, "A Sketch," 56.
2. Garrison Order, Fort Schuyler, 2 Oct. 1783, Orderly Book Willett's Regt., NYSL.
3. AM to FH, 18 May 1783, *DAR*, 21:169–72. See also Speech of Sayenqueraghta, Proceedings with the Six Nations and Sir John Johnson, 22–31 July 1783, Add. MS 21779, R54, Haldimand Paps., PAC.
4. GW to MW; GW to GCL; and GW to AM, 14 Apr. 1783, *Writings GW*, 26:316–17 and 319–20; AM to FH, 5 May 1783, Add. MS 21756-2, R39, Haldimand Paps., PAC; and AM to FH, 18 May 1783, *DAR*, 21:169–72.
5. AM to FH, 10 July 1783, Add. MS 21763, R44; and Extract of a Council Held with the Chiefs and Warriors of the Six Nations, 2 July 1783, Add. MS 21779, R54, Haldimand Paps., PAC.
6. For SKE's presence, see A Meeting at Niagara of the Principal Chiefs and Warriors, 11 Dec. 1782; and A Council Held in Niagara, in Consequence of a Speech from Haldimand and Sir John Johnson, 1 Apr. 1783, Add. MS 21779, R54, Haldimand Paps., PAC.
7. Speech of GP and SKE, 21 July 1783, *IAP*, 294–95.
8. PS to Six Nations, [29 July 1783]; PS to JBR, [29 July 1783]; and PS to Pres. of CC, 29 July 1783, *IAP*, 291–93 and 295–97.
9. Speech of JJ, Proceedings with the Six Nations and Sir John Johnson, 22–31 July 1783, Add. MS 21779, R54, Haldimand Paps., PAC.
10. Six Nations to PS, [8 Sep. 1783], *IAP*, 297–98. See also FH to Lord North, 20 Aug. 1783 and 14 Oct. 1783, *DAR*, 21:209–211 and 222–25; Meeting Held at Niagara of the Chiefs and Warriors of the Six Nations with the Shawnees and Cherokees, 2–6 Oct. 1783, Add. MS 21779, R54, Haldimand Paps., PAC.
11. PS to Elias Boudinot, 11 Oct. 1783; and JBR to PS, [23 Oct. 1783], *IAP*, 299–303.
12. PS's Speech to the Deputation of the Six Nations, Jan. 1784, Add. MS 21779, R54, Haldimand Paps., PAC.

13. JBR to PS, [23 Oct. 1783], *IAP*, 300–303; PS's Speech to the Deputation of the Six Nations, Jan. 1784, Add. MS 21779, R54, Haldimand Paps., PAC.
14. PS's Speech to the Deputation of the Six Nations, Jan. 1784, Add. MS 21779, R54, Haldimand Paps., PAC.
15. JBU to JJ, 17 Mar. 1784, Add. MS 21779, R54, Haldimand Paps., PAC.
16. PS to Pres. of CC, 29 July 1783, *IAP*, 291–93.
17. GW to JDU, 7 Sep. 1783, *Writings GW*, 27:133 and 140.
18. Congress initially named five commissioners. See Thomas Mifflin to GCL, 22 Mar. 1784; and Mifflin to George Rogers Clarke, Oliver Wolcott, Nathanael Greene, RB, and Stephen Higginson, 22 Mar. 1784, PCC, M247, r24, i16, 295. Then the CC added PS. See Commission to PS as an Additional Indian Commissioner, 8 Apr. 1784, PCC, M247, r196, i182, 27. When PS turned down the appointment, the CC offered the appointment to AL, who accepted.
19. GCL to AL, RB, and Oliver Wolcott, 13 Aug. 1784; AL and RB to Six Nations, 18 Aug. 1784; and AL and RB to GCL, 19 Aug. 1784, *Clinton Paps.*, 8:323, 332–33, 337–38, and 339–40; AL and RB to Six Nations [July or Aug. 1784], Add. MS 21779, R54, Haldimand Paps., PAC. For the legal debate over authority, see James Monroe to James Madison, 15 Nov. 1784, *LDC*, 22:18–20; and Campisi, "From Stanwix to Canandaigua," Vecsey and Starna, ed., *Iroquois Land Claims*, 53.
20. Speech by JBR, 6 June 1784; JBR to Henry Glen, 21 July 1784; GCL to JBR, 14 Aug. 1784; GCL to Henry Glen, 25 Aug. 1784; GCL to JBR, 25 Aug. 1784; and Minutes of the Proceedings between the Commissioners of New York and the Six Nations, 31 Aug. 1784, *Clinton Paps.*, 8:323–25, 327–28, 334–35, 343–44, and 349.
21. Speech of GCL, 4 Sep. 1784, Minutes of the Proceedings Between the Commissioners of New York and the Six Nations; Jellis Fonda to GCL, 31 Aug. 1784; and Meeting of Commissioners of Indian Affairs, 1 Sep. 1784, *Clinton Paps.*, 8:348, 350–51 and 354–55. See also Campisi, "From Stanwix to Canandaigua," Vecsey and Starna, ed., *Iroquois Land Claims*, 53.
22. Speech of [GR], 4 Sep. 1784, Minutes of the Proceedings Between the Commissioners of New York and the Six Nations, *Clinton Paps.*, 8:355–60.
23. Speech of GCL, 10 Sep. 1784, Minutes of the Proceedings Between the Commissioners of New York and the Six Nations, *Clinton Paps.*, 8:374–75.
24. Speech of JBR, 10 Sep. 1784; Speech of GCL, 5 and 10 Sep. 1784; Speech of JBR, 7 Sep. 1784; and Minutes of the Proceedings Between the Commissioners of New York and the Six Nations, *Clinton Paps.*, 8:361–69 and 371–77. See also Taylor, *Divided Ground*, 154–57.
25. Barbé de Marbois Journ., after 23 Sep. 1784, *Lafayette Paps.*, 5:251.
26. James Madison to Thomas Jefferson, 17 Oct. 1784, *Lafayette Paps.*, 5:272–73.
27. Speech of MDL, 3 Oct. 1784, *New Jersey Gazette*, 28 Nov. 1784. See also G. Evans to Sir [?], 5 Oct. 1784, Box 1, Folder 6, John Nicholson Paps., NYSL; Account of MDL's Meeting with the Six Nations, 3–4 Oct. 1784; and MDL to Wife, 4 Oct. 1784, *Lafayette Paps.*, 5:255–62; Griffith Evans Journ., 3–26 October 1784, Raup, ed., "Journal of Griffith Evans, 1784–1785," *PMHB* 65 (1941):207–15.
28. Speeches of a Mohawk Chief and Towanoganda, 3–4 Oct. 1784, *New Jersey Gazette*, 29 Nov. 1784.

29. For Minutes of the Treaty Negotiations, see Craig, ed., *Olden Time*, 2:406–30. See also Taylor, *Divided Ground*, 157–59.
30. Treaty of Fort Stanwix, 22 Oct. 1784, *IAP*, 312–13; FH to JJ, 26 May 1783, Add. MS 21775, R52; and FH to Lord Sydney, 28 July 1784, Add. MS 21717, R21, Haldimand Paps., PAC.
31. Speech of the Oneida Indians to the Commissioners, 20 Oct. 1784; and Commissioners to President of Congress, Oct. 1784, PCC, M247, r69, i56, 309 and 137. See also *LDC*, 22:26n1.
32. JDU to PS, 16 Aug. 1782, R17, Schuyler Paps., NYPL; Treaty of Fort Stanwix, 22 Oct. 1784, *IAP*, 312–13; Minutes of the Treaty of Fort Stanwix Negotiations, 20 Oct. 1784. Craig, ed., *Olden Times*, 2:426.
33. David Howell to Thomas G. Hazard, 26 Aug. 1783, *LDC*, 20:594; Oneida Indians to CC, 14 Sep. 1785, PCC, M247, r37, i30, 479. See also Lehman, "End of Iroquois Mystique," *WMQ*, 3 ser., 47 (1990):523–26.
34. Summary of GP in CVD to JC, 23 Dec. 1778, *Clinton Paps.*, 4:418; JDE to PS, 18 Jan. 1779, *IAP*, 182; JDE to CC, 11 July 1785, PCC, M247, r37, i30, 479; Resolution of 8 Aug. 1785, *JCC*, 29:619.
35. These are reasonable estimates. In 1774, Royal Governor William Tryon of New York thought the Oneida population was about 1,500. Campisi, "Ethnic Identity and Boundary Maintenance," 34–35, states that this figure is high. Campisi presents a variety of estimates from various time periods. Population reduction by 20 percent meant that the Oneidas had to lose as many persons as were born, plus two hundred more. Although the death of a few dozen warriors does not seem that devastating in comparison with losses suffered by the rebels or the Crown, these warriors comprised an estimated 2 percent of all Oneidas, the same percentage in losses suffered by Union and Confederate forces combined during the Civil War. Union-Confederate losses had three major sources: illness, combat, and accidents. Focusing only on battlefield losses, the Oneida percentage would triple that of Civil War armies.
36. Oneida Claims for Losses, 11 Jan. 1784, "Introduction," 28, Ontario Indian Office, Brantford Paps., NYPL.
37. MDL to GW, 8 Oct. 1784, *Lafayette Paps.*, 5:265.
38. Speech of Wale in SKI Journ., 9 Feb. 1800, Pilkington, ed., *Journals Kirkland*, 351–52; Barbé de Marbois Journ., after 23 Sep. 1784, *Lafayette Paps.*, 5:250.
39. Testimony of John Cornelius, Draper MS, 11 U 217 (1980, R57), SHSW.
40. Testimony of Christine Skenandoah, Draper MS, 11 U 188; and Testimony of Moses Schuyler, Draper MS, 11 U 260–64 (1980, R57), SHSW.
41. Speech by GR to a Party of Warriors, 24 Apr. 1778, PCC, M247, r95, i78, v9, 158–59; and Reply to Speech by GR to a Party of Warriors, 24 Apr. 1778, PCC., M247, r95, i78, v9, 159, convey the wartime harmony between sachems and chief warriors.
42. James Emlen Journ., 13 Oct. 1794, James Emlen Paps., NYSL.
43. John Thornton Kirkland Answer to Queries, Feb. 1795, *CMHS* 4 (1795):71.
44. This state of confusion over values suggests the condition of anomie, as originally discussed by the French sociologist Emile Durkheim in various works, including *Suicide: A Study in Sociology*, trans. Spaulding and Simpson. For a specific histori-

cal application, see McLoughlin, "Cherokee Anomie, 1794–1809," Bushman et al., ed., *Uprooted Americans*, 127–60.

45. For feelings of despair, see John Thornton Kirkland Answer to Queries, Feb. 1795, *CMHS* 4 (1795):69. For the range of problems facing the Oneidas, see Hauptman, "Oneida Nation," Hauptman and McLester, ed., *Oneida Indian Journey*, 19–37. Lehman, "End of Iroquois Mystique," *WMQ* 47 (1990):546–47, suggests that the despondency and anger felt by so many Oneidas helped produce a revival of traditional religious ceremonies and practices, a point disputed by Tiro, "People of the Standing Stone," 149n3. Certainly, embittered feelings, arising from many sources, played a significant role in the renewed commitment to traditional ways among numbers of Oneidas, especially those associated with the "Pagan" faction.

46. John Thornton Kirkland Answer to Queries, Feb. 1795, *CMHS* 4 (1795):69. See also John Lansing, Jr., to PS, 9 May 1783, R17, Schuyler Paps., NYPL; PS to Pres. of CC, 29 July 1783, *IAP*, 293; Draper Mss., 11 U 252–54 (1980, R57), SHSW; SKI to Wife, 10 Sep. 1785, Kirkland Paps., HC. PS blamed the problem on a shortage of resources to help the Oneidas get started again. To provision them properly from early spring to November 1783, he estimated that they needed at least 250 pounds of gunpowder, 500 pounds of lead, 100 large kettles, 100 axes, 50 hatchets, and 100 hoes, which apparently were not available. See PS to Contractors, 11 May 1783, John N. Bleecker Paps., NYSL; Barbé de Marbois Journ., after 23 Sep. 1784, *Lafayette Paps.*, 5:248–50; and SKI to James Bowdoin, 14 Jan. 1785, Pilkington, ed., *Journals Kirkland*, 125.

47. JBR quoted in Graymont, *Iroquois Am. Rev.*, 286. See also Barbé de Marbois Journ., after 23 Sep. 1784, *Lafayette Paps.*, 5:248–50; James Emlen Journ., 15 Oct. 1794, James Emlen Paps., NYSL; MW to PS, 28 Sep. 1780, R17, Schuyler Paps. NYPL.

48. SKI to Wife, 10 Sep. 1785, Kirkland Paps., HC; SKI Journ., 11 Mar. 1787, 25 Nov. 1788, and other dates, Pilkington, ed., *Journals Kirkland*, 130 and 143; John Thornton Kirkland Answer to Queries, Feb. 1795, *CMHS* 4 (1795):69; Meeting of the Commissioners with the Oneida Nation, 16 Aug. 1780, *IAP*, 262.

49. Lehman, "End of Iroquois Mystique," *WMQ* 47 (1990): 531–34 and 538–39.

50. Speech of GP, Apr. 1791, f. 122, 3, R60, Timothy Pickering Paps., MHS; Speech of GP, 25 June 1785, Hough, ed., *Proceedings*, 1:91–92.

51. Speech of GP, 27 June 1785; and Speech of GCL, 26 June 1785, Hough, ed., *Proceedings*, 1:95–100, 102, and 104–105; Speech of GP, Apr. 1792, f. 122–23, 4–5, R60, Timothy Pickering Paps., MHS.

52. Speech of GP, 27 June 1785; and Speech of Peter the Quartermaster, 27 June 1785, Hough, ed., *Proceedings*, 1:102–103 and 104–105.

53. Speech of GP, 11 Apr. 1792, f. 128, 15, R60, Timothy Pickering Paps., MHS. See also Jones, *Annals and Recollections*, 167–68; Vecsey and Starna, ed., *Iroquois Land Claims*, passim, which covers the dispossession of Oneida lands; Hauptman, *Conspiracy of Interests*, 27–97.

54. SKI to James Bowdoin, 10 Mar. 1788; Speech of GCL, 22 Sep. 1788; and Proceedings of the Commissioners to Hold Treaties at Fort Schuyler, Kirkland Paps., HC.

55. Campisi, "Ethnic Identity and Boundary Maintenance," 93–94.

56. In their mercantilist frame of mind, the British granted a steady stream of gifts, es-

pecially gunpowder and lead, to retain the Iroquois' favor and enable them to hunt fur-bearing animals, especially beavers. The Iroquois then traded the pelts for British goods, and the skins promoted the hat industry in England. Once the Revolutionary War ended, victorious European American officials showed little interest in continuing a regular flow of gifts, especially gunpowder and lead, to the Indians. As such, the Oneidas had unwittingly ensnared themselves in a trap. Lacking ammunition, they could not hunt; without skins, they could not procure ammunition on a regular basis; and without hunting, they could neither feed themselves well nor obtain the necessities of life through trade. At treaties in which the Oneidas forfeited land, they usually received money for essentials, and some gifts, including gunpowder and lead. Too often, though, they had to agree to exchange land for necessities. For other reasons, see Hauptman, *Conspiracy of Interests*, 1–27, 53–57.

57. See John Jury [Han Yerry] et al. to GCL, 28 Oct. 1789, Hough, ed., *Proceedings*, 2:353–54; John Thornton Kirkland Answer to Queries, Feb. 1795, *CMHS* 4 (1795):69.

58. For a discussion of the religious revival and split, see Campisi, "Ethnic Identity and Boundary Maintenance," 77–88 and 100–101; Hauptman, "Oneida Nation," Hauptman and McLester, ed., *Oneida Indian Journey*, 19–37. See also Fenton, "Further Note Iroquois Suicide," *Ethnohistory* 33 (1986):451–53, for an informative case of a male suitor who committed suicide when he learned that his girlfriend's father would not permit their union because the young man was a "Pagan."

59. Oneidas to GW, 6 Aug. 1789; and GW to Oneidas, 12 Oct. 1789, *Paps. GW, PS*, 3:543–44; Campisi, "Ethnic Identity and Boundaries," 88–9; Campisi, "Oneida Treaty Period," Campisi and Hauptman, ed., *Oneida Indian Experience*, 48–64; Wonderley, "Oneida Community in 1780," 13.

60. "Account of Losses," R62, 157–166A, Timothy Pickering Paps., MHS, Wonderley, "A Sketch," appendix A; Wonderley, "An Oneida Community," passim.

61. "Account of Losses," R62, 157–166A (Bear Clan no. 6), Timothy Pickering Paps., MHS, Wonderley, "A Sketch," appendix A.

62. Henry Knox to House of Representatives, 26 Feb. 1791, *Am. State Paps.*, Class II, 1:123; Concurrent Resolution of Senate and Assembly of New York, 11 Feb. 1785, PCC, M247, r81, i67, v2, 481.

63. See, for example, Pension Application of John Kennada, NA; appendix D, Indian Rev. War Pension Applications, *IAP*, 349–66.

64. Resolution of 25 Aug. 1786, *JCC*, 31:564–65. See also Dateline New York, *Boston Gazette*, 4 Sep. 1786, 2:col. 3; Speech of GP, 19 Sep. 1788, Hough, ed., *Proceedings*, 1:222; SKI Journ., 30 Nov. 1788, Pilkington, ed., *Journals Kirkland*, 144.

65. SKI Journ., 11 Aug. to 9 Sep. 1794 and 9 Jan. 1800, Pilkington, ed., *Journals Kirkland*, 225–30 and 333; Albany, 18 Sep. 1795, Draper MS, 11 U 123 (1980, R57), SHSW.

66. Report of the Sec. of War Regarding the Oneidas, 4 July 1787, *JCC*, 32:347–48; SKI Journ., 23 Aug.–14 Nov. 1790, Pilkington, ed., *Journals Kirkland*, 201–207; Testimony of Theresa Swamp; and Testimony of Jacob Cornelius, Draper MS, 11 U 211 and 11 U 214 (1980, R57), SHSW.

67. SKI Journ., 25 Nov. 1788 and 24 Feb. 1800, Pilkington, ed., *Journals Kirkland*, 143 and 361; Speech of GP, Apr. 1792, f. 121, 1, R60, Timothy Pickering Paps., MHS.

68. Interview with Christine Skenandoah, E. A. Goodnough to Lyman Draper, 26 Mar. 1863; Moses Schuyler to Lyman Draper, 27 Jan. 1863; and Testimony of Elijah Skenandoah, Draper Mss., 11 U 188, 260–64, and 242 (1980, R57), SHSW. See also Speech of John Onondiyo, f. 220, R60, Timothy Pickering Paps., MHS.

69. Speech of SKE; and Interview with Christine Skenandoah, E. A. Goodnough to Lyman Draper, 26 Mar. 1863, Draper MS, 11 U 159 and 188 (1980, R57), SHSW.

70. Obituary of SKE, *Utica Patriot*, 19 Mar. 1816, Campbell, *Annals Tryon County*, 222–25.

71. Campisi, "From Stanwix to Canandaigua," Vecsey and Starna, ed., *Iroquois Land Claims*, 58–60; Taylor, *Divided Ground*, 182–85.

72. Campisi, "Ethnic Identity and Boundary Maintenance," 103–11; Horsman, "Wisconsin Oneidas Preallotment Years," Campisi and Hauptman, ed., *Oneida Indian Experience*, 65–71.

73. Campisi, "Ethnic Identity and Boundary Maintenance," 262–66.

74. Ibid., 405–407 and 437–39; Campisi, "Oneida Treaty Period," Campisi and Hauptman, ed., *Oneida Indian Experience*, 61.

75. Quoted in Halsey, *Old New York Frontier*, 84.

EPILOGUE: FROM JUBILEE TO CENTENNIAL CELEBRATIONS AND BEYOND: TOWARD THE RESTORATION OF HISTORICAL MEMORY

1. The Frenchman Levasseur recorded three of their names as Taniatakaya, Sangouxyonta, and Doxtator. Han Yerry Doxtator had three sons who fought in the Revolution. One, later a chief named Cornelius Doxtator, was killed in the War of 1812. Henry Cornelius's Oneida name was *Sug-go-yone-tau*, which is similar to Levasseur's version, and Blatcop was *Ton-yen-ta-goyen*, which is fairly close. Both were very active in the Revolution and were still alive in 1825. See Levasseur, *Lafayette in America*, 2:195–96; Hough, ed., *Proceedings*, 1:179; "Account of Losses," R62, 157–166A, Timothy Pickering Paps., MHS, Wonderley, "A Sketch," appendix A. One Oneida, Peter Otsequette, went to France after the Revolution and lived with MDL's family for several years. He returned to America but died before the time of MDL's visit to the Mohawk Valley. See MDL Memoirs, *Lafayette Paps.*, 1:247; and Hough, ed., *Proceedings*, 1:179.

2. For the many problems facing the Oneidas, see Campisi, "Oneida Treaty Period," Campisi and Hauptman, ed., *Oneida Indian Experience*, 48–64; Hauptman, "Oneida Nation"; and Horsman, "Origins Oneida Removal to Wisconsin," Hauptman and McLester, ed., *Oneida Indian Journey*, 19–37 and 53–69.

3. Ellis H. Roberts, "The Battle of Oriskany: Its Place in History," *Utica Morning Herald*, 7 Aug. 1877, 2.

4. Ibid; *Utica Daily Observer*, 6 Aug. 1877, 3; and 7 Aug. 1877, 3; *Rome Sentinel*, 7 Aug. 1877, 2.

5. *Rome Sentinel*, 31 July 1877, 2.
6. *Utica Daily Observer*, 6 Aug. 1877, 1; *Rome Sentinel*, 7 Aug. 1877, 2.
7. *Utica Daily Observer*, 7 Aug. 1877, 2.
8. Ibid.
9. PS to Oneidas, 11 May 1778, *IAP*, 135.

AFTERWORD: NEW BEGINNINGS AMID REVIVED MEMORIES

1. See Campisi, "From Stanwix to Canandaigua"; Hauptman, "Iroquois Land Issues"; and Locklear, "Oneida Land Claims," Vecsey and Starna, ed., *Iroquois Land Claims*, 49–65, 67–86, and 141–53, for background information.
2. *Oneida Indian Nation of New York State v. County of Oneida, New York*, 414 U.S. 661 (1974).
3. *Oneida Indian Nation of New York State v. County of Oneida, New York*, 434 F. Supp. 527 (N.D.N.Y. 1977).
4. *Oneida County New York v. Oneida Indian Nation of New York State*, 470 U.S. 226 (1985). The U.S. District Court judge ruled during 2002, in settling the test case, that the Oneidas should receive $15,994 from Oneida County and $18,970 from Madison County, along with prejudgment interest. See *Oneida Indian Nation of New York v. County of Oneida, New York*, 217 F. Supp. 2d 292, 310 (N.D.N.Y. 2002).
5. *New York Times*, 13 Jan. 1999, A1, and 22 Jan. 1999, B1. Desirous of settling the test case, the Oneidas held in suspension another legal action seeking trespass damages from Madison and Oneida counties that covered some two hundred years. In 2000, they decided to reactivate this case. See *Oneida Indian Nation of New York State v. County of Oneida, New York*, 199 F.R.D.61, 66–68 (N.D.N.Y. 2000).
6. Letters from Ray Halbritter to Nation Employees, [Jan. 1999], and to Our Neighbors in Madison and Oneida Counties, 26 Jan. 1999; *New York Times*, 13 Jan. 1999, A1.
7. *City of Sherrill, New York v. Oneida Indian Nation of New York*, 125 S.Ct. 1478 (2005).
8. *Oneida Indian Nation of New York v. County of Oneida, New York*, 199 F.R.D.61, 66–68 (N.D.N.Y. 2000). In *City of Sherrill, New York v. Oneida Indian Nation of New York*, the Supreme Court directed the Oneidas to follow a process outlined in federal statutes (25 U.S.C. section 465) that would have the Secretary of the Interior take title to the purchased parcels of land "in trust" for the Oneidas' benefit. Should this process succeed, the Oneidas could then claim the acquired land parcels as sovereign territory—not subject to taxes.
9. *Oneida Indian Nation of New York v. County of Oneida, New York*, 434 F. Supp. 527 (N.D.N.Y. 1977); *Oneida County, New York v. Oneida Indian Nation of New York*, 470 U.S. 226 (1985).
10. *Oneida County, New York v. Oneida Indian Nation of New York*, 470 U.S. 226 (1985).

11. Speech from CC to the Six Nations, 3 Dec. 1777, *JCC*, 9:996. The phrase "historical amnesia" may be found in Nash, *Unknown American Revolution*, xvi. See Oneida Indian Nation, Annual Report, 2004, 4 and 46, for information about the bronze statue placed by the Oneidas in the National Museum of the American Indian (Smithsonian Institution, Washington, D.C.), bearing the words, ALLIES IN WAR, PARTNERS IN PEACE.

BIBLIOGRAPHY

See specific notes for archival and contemporary newspaper source citations.

PUBLISHED PRIMARY SOURCES

Abler, Thomas S., ed. *Chainbreaker: The Revolutionary War Memoirs of Governor Blacksnake as Told to Benjamin Williams.* Lincoln, Neb., 1989.

Almon, John, ed. *The Remembrancer, or Impartial Repository of Public Events.* 17 vols. London, 1775–1784.

American State Papers. Class II. *Indian Affairs.* 2 vols. Washington, D.C., 1832–1834. (*Am. State Paps.*)

Baldwin, Thomas Williams, ed. *The Revolutionary Journal of Col. Jeduthan Baldwin, 1775–1778.* Bangor, Maine, 1906.

Boardman, Oliver. "Journals of Oliver Boardman of Middletown, 1777, Burgoyne's Surrender." *Collections of the Connecticut Historical Society.* Vol. 7. Hartford, Conn., 1899. (CCHS)

Bradford, S. Sydney, ed. "Lord Francis Napier's Journal of the Burgoyne Campaign." *Maryland Historical Magazine* 57 (1962): 285–333. (MHM)

Brandon, Edgar Ewing, ed. *A Pilgrimage of Liberty: A Contemporary Account of the Triumphal Tour of General Lafayette . . . in 1825. . . .* Athens, Ohio, 1944.

Brown, Lloyd A., and Howard H. Peckham, ed. *Revolutionary War Journals of Henry Dearborn, 1775–1783.* Chicago, 1939.

Brymer, Douglas. *Report on Canadian Archives, 1887.* Ottawa, Ontario, 1888.

Burgoyne, John. *A State of the Expedition from Canada, as Laid Before the House of Commons, . . . with a Collection of Authentic Documents. . . .* London, 1780.

Chase, Philander D., et al., ed. *The Papers of George Washington, Presidential Series.* 12 vols. to date. Charlottesville, Va., 1987–2005. (*Paps. GW, PS*)

———., et al., ed. *The Papers of George Washington, Revolutionary War Series.* 14 vols. to date. Charlottesville, Va., 1985–2004. (*Paps. GW, RWS*)

A Complete History of the Marquis de Lafayette, Major-General in the American

Army . . . Embracing an Account of His Late Tour Through the United States. . . . Hartford, Conn., 1851.

Craig, Neville B., ed. *The Olden Time, . . . Devoted to the Preservation of Documents. . . .* 2 vols. Cincinnati, Ohio, 1846–1847.

Dann, John C., ed. *The Revolution Remembered: Eyewitness Accounts of the War for Independence.* Chicago, 1980.

Dexter, Franklin Bowditch, ed. *The Literary Diary of Ezra Stiles, D.D., LL.D.* 3 vols. New York, 1901.

Douglas, Robert B., ed. and trans. *A French Volunteer of the War of Independence* (Charles Albert Moré, *The Chevalier de Pontgibaud*). New York, 1898.

Elijah Fisher's Journal While in the War for Independence and Continued Two Years After He Came to Maine, 1775–1784. Augusta, Maine, 1880.

Elmer, Ebenezer. "Journal Kept during an Expedition to Canada in 1776." *Proceedings of the New Jersey Historical Society.* Ser. 1. Newark, N.J., 1847–1848. (*PNJHS*)

Fenton, William N., ed. *Parker on the Iroquois: Iroquois Uses of Maize and Other Food Plants.* Syracuse, N.Y., 1968.

Fitzpatrick, John C., ed. *The Writings of George Washington from the Original Manuscript Sources, 1745–1799.* 39 vols. Washington, D.C., 1931–1944. (*Writings GW*)

Flynt, Henry, and Helen Flynt, ed. *Journal of a March, a Battle, and a Waterfall, Being the Version Elaborated by James McHenry from His Diary of the Year 1778. . . .* [Greenwich?], Conn., 1945.

Fogg, Jeremiah. *Journal of Major Jeremiah Fogg, During the Expedition of Gen. Sullivan in 1779, Against the Western Indians.* Exeter, N.H., 1879.

Garden, Alexander. *Anecdotes of the American Revolution, Illustrative of the Talents and Virtues of the Heroes of the Revolution. . . .* 3 vols. Brooklyn, N.Y., 1865.

Gehring, Charles T., and William A. Starna, ed. and trans. *A Journey into Mohawk and Oneida Country, 1634–1635: The Journal of Harmen Meyndertsz van den Bogaert.* Syracuse, N.Y., 1988.

Grant, Anne MacVicar. *Memoirs of an American Lady: With Sketches of Manners and Scenery in America, as They Existed Previous to the Revolution.* New York, 1809.

Halsey, Francis Whiting, ed. *A Tour of Four Great Rivers: The Hudson, Mohawk, Susquehanna and Delaware in 1769, Being the Journal of Richard Smith.* New York, 1906.

Hamer, Philip M., et al., ed. *The Papers of Henry Laurens.* 16 vols. Columbia, S.C., 1968–2003. (*Henry Laurens Paps.*)

Hammond, Otis G., ed. *The Letters and Papers of Major-General John Sullivan, Continental Army.* 3 vols. Concord, N.H., 1930–1939. (*Letters Sullivan*)

Hastings, Hugh, et al., ed. *Public Papers of George Clinton, First Governor of New York, 1777–1795, 1801–1804.* 10 vols. Albany, N.Y., 1899–1914. (*Clinton Paps.*)

Hazard, Samuel, ed. *Pennsylvania Archives.* Ser. 1. Vol. 1. Philadelphia, 1852.

Hough, Franklin B., ed. *Proceedings of the Commissioners of Indian Affairs, Appointed by Law for the Extinguishment of Indian Titles in the State of New York.* 2 vols. Albany, N.Y., 1861.

Idzerda, Stanley J., ed. *Lafayette in the Age of the American Revolution: Selected Letters and Papers, 1776–1790.* 5 vols. to date, Ithaca, N.Y., 1977–1983. (*Lafayette Paps.*)

Kirkland, Fredric R., ed. *Letters on the American Revolution in the Library at "Karolfred."* 2 vols. New York, 1941–1952.

Klinck, Carl F., and James J. Talman, ed. *The Journal of Major John Norton, 1809–1816.* Toronto, Ontario, 1970.

Lafitau, Joseph-François. *Customs of the American Indians Compared with the Customs of Primitive Times.* William N. Fenton and Elizabeth L. Moore, ed. and trans. 2 vols. Toronto, Ontario, 1974–1977. Orig. pub. Paris, France, 1724.

Leder, Lawrence H., ed. *The Livingston Indian Records, 1666–1723.* Stanfordville, N.Y., 1979.

Lender, Mark E., and James Kirby Martin, ed. *Citizen Soldier: The Revolutionary War Journal of Joseph Bloomfield.* Newark, N.J., 1982.

Levasseur, A. *Lafayette in America in 1824 and 1825, or, Journal of a Voyage to the United States.* John D. Godman, trans. 2 vols. Philadelphia, 1829.

McIlwain, Charles H., ed. *An Abridgement of the Indian Affairs Contained in Four Folio Volumes, Transacted in the Colony of New York, from the Year 1678 to the Year 1751, by Peter Wraxall.* Cambridge, Mass., 1915.

Martin, James Kirby, ed. *Ordinary Courage: The Revolutionary War Adventures of Joseph Plumb Martin.* 2d ed. St. James, N.Y., 1999.

Mereness, Newton D., ed. *Travels in the American Colonies.* New York, 1916.

Montresor, John. "Journals of Captain John Montresor." *Collections of the New-York Historical Society for the Year 1881.* New York, 1882. (CN-YHS)

Moore, Frank, comp. *Diary of the American Revolution, from Newspapers and Original Documents,* 2 vols. New York, 1860.

The Order Book of Capt. Leonard Bleeker, Major of Brigade, in the Early Part of the Expedition under Gen. James Clinton, . . . in the Campaign of 1779. New York, 1865.

O'Reilly, Henry. *Notices of Sullivan's Campaign, or, the Revolutionary Warfare in Western New-York: . . .* Rochester, N.Y., 1842

Penrose, Maryly B., ed. *Mohawk Valley in the Revolution: Committee of Safety Papers & Genealogical Compendium.* Franklin Park, N.J., 1978.

Pilkington, Walter, ed. *The Journals of Samuel Kirkland: Eighteenth-Century Missionary to the Iroquois, Government Agent, Father of Hamilton College.* Clinton, N.Y., 1980.

Raup, Hallock F., ed. "Journal of Griffith Evans, 1784–1785." *Pennsylvania Magazine of History and Biography* 65 (1941): 202–33. (PMHB)

Reid, W. Max, ed. *The Story of Old Fort Johnson.* New York, 1906. (William Colbrath Journ.)

Rice, Howard C., Jr., ed. and trans. *Travels in North America in the Years 1780, 1781, and 1782 by the Marquis de Chastellux.* 2 vols. Chapel Hill, N.C., 1963.

———., and Anne S. K. Brown, ed. and trans. *The American Campaigns of Rochambeau's Army, 1780, 1781, 1782, 1783.* 2 vols. Princeton, N.J., 1972.

Sabine, William H. W., ed. *Historical Memoirs of William Smith, . . .* 2 vols. New York, 1956–1958.

Scheer, George F., ed. *Private Yankee Doodle: A Narrative of Some of the Adventures, Dangers and Sufferings of a Revolutionary Soldier* [Joseph Plumb Martin]. Boston, 1962.

Seaver, James E., ed. *A Narrative of the Life of Mrs. Mary Jemison.* Canadaigua, N.Y., 1824.

Sparks, Jared, ed. *The Writings of George Washington. . . .* 12 vols. Boston, 1834–1837.

Stanley, George F. G., ed. *For Want of a Horse, Being a Journal of the Campaigns Against the Americans in 1776 and 1777 from Canada by an Officer Who Served with Lt. Gen. Burgoyne.* Sackville, New Brunswick, 1961.

Stark, Caleb, ed. *Memoir and Official Correspondence of Gen. John Stark, with Notices of Several Other Officers of the Revolution.* Concord, N.H., 1877.

The Sullivan-Clinton Campaign in 1779: Chronology and Selected Documents. Albany, N.Y., 1929.

Sullivan, James J., et al., ed. *The Papers of Sir William Johnson.* 14 vols. Albany, N.Y., 1921–1965. (*W Johnson Paps.*)

Sullivan, John. *Journals of the Military Expedition of Maj. General John Sullivan Against the Six Nations of Indians in 1779, with Records of Centennial Celebrations.* Auburn, N.Y. 1887.

Syrett, Harold C., et al., ed. *The Papers of Alexander Hamilton.* 27 vols. New York, 1961–1987.

Tappert, Theodore G., and John W. Doberstein, ed. and trans. *The Journals of Henry Melchior Muhlenberg.* 3 vols. Philadelphia, 1942–1958.

Thwaites, Reuben Gold, ed. *The Jesuit Relations and Allied Documents: Travels and Explorations of the Jesuit Missionaries in New France, 1610–1791.* 73 vols. Cleveland, Ohio, 1896–1901.

Tustin, Joseph P., ed. and trans. *Diary of the American War: A Hessian Journal (Captain Johann von Ewald).* New Haven, Conn., 1979.

Van Doren, Carl, and Julian P. Boyd., ed. *Indian Treaties Printed by Benjamin Franklin, 1736–1762.* Philadelphia, 1938.

Weeden, William B., ed. "Diary of Enos Hitchcock, D.D.: A Chaplain in the Revolutionary Army." *Publications of the Rhode Island Historical Society.* Vol. 7. Providence, R.I., 1899.

Willett, William M., ed. *A Narrative of the Military Actions of Colonel Marinus Willett, Taken Chiefly from his Own Manuscript.* New York, 1831.

Woodbury, Hanni, ed. *Concerning the League: The Iroquois Tradition as Dictated in Onondaga by John Arthur Gibson.* Algonquian and Iroquoian Linguistics Memoir 9. Winnipeg, Manitoba, 1992.

PUBLISHED SECONDARY SOURCES

Ammerman, David. *In the Common Cause: American Response to the Coercive Acts of 1775.* Charlottesville, Va., 1974.

Anderson, Fred. *Crucible of War: The Seven Years' War and the Fate of the Empire in British North America, 1754–1766.* New York, 2000.

Aquilla, Richard. *The Iroquois Restoration: Iroquois Diplomacy on the Colonial Frontier, 1701–1754.* Detroit, 1983.

Axtell, James, *After Columbus: Essays in the Ethnohistory of Colonial North America.* New York, 1988.

———. *Beyond 1492: Encounters in Colonial North America.* New York, 1992.

———. *The European and the Indian: Essays in the Ethnohistory of Colonial North America.* New York, 1981.

———. *The Invasion Within: The Contest of Cultures in Colonial North America.* New York, 1985.

Bagg, M. M., ed. *Memorial History of Utica, N.Y.* Syracuse, N.Y., 1892.

Bailyn, Bernard. *The Ideological Origins of the American Revolution.* Enlarged ed. Cambridge, Mass., 1992.

Baker, William S. *Itinerary of George Washington.* Philadelphia, 1892.

Beauchamp, William M. "Aboriginal Place Names of New York." *New York State Museum Bulletin,* no. 108. Albany, N.Y., 1907.

———. *A History of the New York Iroquois, Now Commonly Called the Six Nations.* Albany, N.Y., 1905.

———. *The Iroquois Trail, or, Foot-Prints of the Six Nations in Customs, Traditions, and History,* . . . Fayetteville, N.Y., 1892.

Berkhofer, Robert F., Jr. *Salvation and the Savage: An Analysis of Protestant Missions and American Indian Response, 1782–1862.* Lexington, Ky., 1965.

Bodle, Wayne. *The Valley Forge Winter: Civilians and Soldiers in War.* University Park, Pa., 2002.

Bourdin, H. L., and S. T. Williams, ed. "Crèvecoeur on the Susquehanna, 1774–1776." *Yale Review* 14 (1925): 552–84.

Bowden, Henry Warner. *American Indians and Christian Missions: Studies in Cultural Conflict.* Chicago, 1981.

Brandão, José António. *"Your fyre shall burn no more": Iroquois Policy Toward New France and Its Native Allies to 1701.* Lincoln, Neb., 1997.

———, and William A. Starna. "The Treaty of 1701: A Triumph of Iroquois Diplomacy." *Ethnohistory* 43 (1996): 209–44.

Burkhart, Louise M. *The Slippery Earth: Nahua-Christian Moral Dialogue in Sixteenth-Century Mexico.* Tucson, Ariz., 1989.

Calloway, Colin G. *The American Revolution in Indian Country: Crisis and Diversity in Native American Communities.* New York, 1995.

Campbell, William W. *Annals of Tryon County.* New York, 1924.

Campisi, Jack. "From Stanwix to Canandaigua: National Policy, States' Rights, and Indian Land." *Iroquois Land Claims.* Christopher Vecsey and William A. Starna, ed. Syracuse, N.Y., 1988.

———. "Fur Trade and Factionalism of the Eighteenth-Century Oneida Indian." *Studies on Iroquoian Culture.* Nancy Bonvillain, ed. Rindge, N.H., 1980.

———. "Oneida." *Handbook of North American Indians.* William C. Sturtevant, ed. Vol. 15. Washington, D.C., 1978.

———. "The Oneida Treaty Period, 1783–1838." *The Oneida Indian Experience: Two Perspectives.* Jack Campisi and Laurence M. Hauptman, ed. Syracuse, N.Y., 1988.

Clark, Joshua V. H. *Onondaga, or Reminiscences of Earlier and Later Times.* . . . Vol. 1. Syracuse, N.Y., 1849.

Converse, Harriett Maxwell. "Myths and Legends of the New York State Iroquois." *New York State Museum Bulletin,* no. 125. Arthur Caswell Parker, ed. Albany, N.Y., 1908.

Cronon, William. *Changes in the Land: Indians, Colonists, and the Ecology of New England.* New York, 1983.

Crosby, Alfred W., Jr. *The Columbian Exchange: Biological and Cultural Consequences of 1492.* Westport, Conn., 1972.

Doebler, Harold F., and George A. Ludwig. *St. Peter's Lutheran Church, Barren Hill, Pa.: Two Hundred Years of Christian Service, 1752–1952.* Philadelphia, 1952.

Dowd, Gregory Evans. *War Under Heaven: Pontiac, the Indian Nations, & the British Empire*. Baltimore, 2002.

Durant, Samuel W. *History of Oneida County, New York*, Philadelphia, 1878.

Egly, T. W., Jr. *History of the First New York Regiment, 1775–1783*. Hampton, N.H., 1981.

Elwood, Mary Cheney. *An Episode of the Sullivan Campaign and Its Sequel*. Rochester, N.Y., 1904.

Fausz, J. Frederick. "Fighting 'Fire' with Firearms: The Anglo-Powhatan Arms Race in Early Virginia." *American Indian Culture and Research Journal* 4 (1979): 33–50.

Fenn, Elizabeth A. *Pox Americana: The Great Smallpox Epidemic of 1775–82*. New York, 2001.

Fenton, William N. *The False Faces of the Iroquois*. Norman, Okla., 1987.

———. "A Further Note on Iroquois Suicide." *Ethnohistory* 33 (1986): 448–57.

———. *The Great Law and the Longhouse: A Political History of the Iroquois Confederacy*. Norman, Okla., 1988.

———. "The Iroquois Confederacy in the Twentieth Century: A Case Study in the Theory of Lewis H. Morgan in *Ancient Society*." *Ethnology* 43 (1965): 71–85.

———. "Locality as a Basic Factor in the Development of Iroquois Social Structure." *Bureau of American Ethnology Bulletin*, no. 149. William N. Fenton, ed. Washington, D.C., 1951.

———. "This Island, the World on Turtle's Back." *Journal of American Folklore* 75 (1962): 283–300. (*JAF*)

———. "Toward the Gradual Civilization of the Indian Natives: The Missionary and Linguistic Work of Asher Wright (1803–1875) Among the Senecas of Western New York." *Proceedings of the American Philosophical Society* 100 (1956): 567–81. (*PAPS*)

Fischer, David Hackett. *Paul Revere's Ride*, New York, 1994.

Fischer, Joseph R. *A Well-Executed Failure: The Sullivan Campaign Against the Iroquois, July–September 1779*. Columbia, S.C., 1997.

Fleming, Thomas. *Washington's Secret War: The Hidden History of Valley Forge*. New York, 2005.

Flexner, James T. *Lord of the Mohawks: A Biography of Sir William Johnson*. Boston, 1984.

Freeman, Douglas Southall. *George Washington, A Biography, Vol. 5: Victory with the Help of France, 1778–1783*. New York, 1952.

Furniss, Elizabeth. "Resistance, Coercion, and Revitalization: The Shuswap Encounter with Roman Catholic Missionaries, 1860–1900." *Ethnohistory* 42 (1995): 231–63.

Gerlach, Don R. *Proud Patriot: Philip Schuyler and the War of Independence, 1775–1783*. Syracuse, N.Y., 1987.

Goodwin, Gerald J. "Christianity, Civilization and the Savage: The Anglican Mission to the American Indian." *Historical Magazine of the Protestant Episcopal Church* 42 (1973): 93–110. (*HMPEC*)

Gottschalk, Louis R. *Lafayette and the Close of the American Revolution*. Chicago, 1942.

———. *Lafayette Joins the American Army*. Chicago, 1937.

Graymont, Barbara. *The Iroquois in the American Revolution.* Syracuse, N.Y., 1972.

———. "The Oneidas and the American Revolution." *The Oneida Experience: Two Perspectives.* Jack Campisi and Laurence M. Hauptman, ed. Syracuse, N.Y., 1988.

Greene, Jerome. *The Guns of Independence: The Siege of Yorktown, 1781.* New York, 2005.

Guzzardo, John C. "The Superintendent and the Ministers: The Battle for Oneida Allegiances, 1761–75." *New York History* 57 (1976): 254–83. (*NYH*)

Haan, Richard. "The Problem of Iroquois Neutrality: Suggestions for Revision." *Ethnohistory* 27 (1980): 317–30.

Halbritter, Gloria. "Oral Traditions." *The Oneida Indian Experience: Two Perspectives.* Jack Campisi and Laurence M. Hauptman, ed. Syracuse, N.Y., 1988.

Halsey, Francis W. *The Old New York Frontier: Its Wars with Indians and Tories, Its Missionary Schools, Pioneers, and Land Titles, 1614–1800.* New York, 1902.

Hamilton, Milton W. *Sir William Johnson and the Indians of New York.* Albany, N.Y., 1967.

Hanson, Willis T., Jr. *A History of Schenectady During the Revolution.* Interlaken, N.Y., 1988.

Hauptman, Laurence M. *Conspiracy of Interests: Iroquois Dispossession and the Rise of New York State.* Syracuse, N.Y., 1999.

———. "Iroquois Land Issues: At Odds with the 'Family of New York.' " *Iroquois Land Claims.* Christopher Vecsey and William A. Starna, ed. Syracuse, N.Y., 1988.

———. "The Oneida Nation: A Composite Portrait, 1784–1816." *The Oneida Indian Journey: From New York to Wisconsin, 1784–1860.* Laurence M. Hauptman and L. Gordon McLester, III, ed. Madison, Wisc., 1999.

Hewitt, J.N.B. "Iroquois" and "Iroquois Family." *Handbook of American Indians North of Mexico.* Frederick Webb Hodge, ed. Vol. 1. Washington, D.C., 1910.

———. "The Requickening Address of the League of the Iroquois." *Anthropological Essays Presented to William H. Holmes in Honor of His Seventieth Birthday.* Washington, D.C., 1916.

———., and William N. Fenton. "Some Mnemonic Pictographs Relating to the Iroquois Condolence Council." *Journal of the Washington Academy of Sciences* 35 (1945): 301–15.

Hinman, Marjory Barnum. *Onaquaga: Hub of the Border Wars of the American Revolution in New York.* Windsor, N.Y., 1975.

Horsman, Reginald. "The Origins of Oneida Removal to Wisconsin, 1815–1822." *The Oneida Indian Journey: From New York to Wisconsin, 1784–1860.* Laurence M. Hauptman and L. Gordon McLester, III, ed. Madison, Wisc., 1999.

———. "The Wisconsin Oneidas in the Preallotment Years." *The Oneida Indian Experience: Two Perspectives.* Jack Campisi and Laurence M. Hauptman, ed. Syracuse, N.Y., 1988.

Hunt, George T. *The Wars of the Iroquois: A Study in Intertribal Trade Relations.* Madison, Wisc., 1940.

Jennings, Francis. *The Ambiguous Iroquois Empire: The Covenant Chain of Indian Tribes with English Colonies from Its Beginnings to the Lancaster Treaty of 1744.* New York, 1984.

———. *Empire of Fortune: Crowns, Colonies, and Tribes in the Seven Years' War in America*. New York, 1988.

———, et al. *The History and Culture of Iroquois Diplomacy: An Interdisciplinary Guide to the Treaties of the Six Nations and Their League*. Syracuse, N.Y., 1985.

———. *The Invasion of America: Indians, Colonialism, and the Cant of Conquest*. Chapel Hill, N.C., 1975.

Jones, Pomroy. *Annals and Recollections of Oneida County*. Rome, N.Y., 1851.

Kelsay, Isabel Thompson. *Joseph Brant, 1743–1807: Man of Two Worlds*. Syracuse, N.Y., 1984.

Kenney, Alice P. *The Gansevoorts of Albany: Dutch Patricians in the Upper Hudson Valley*. Syracuse, N.Y., 1969.

Knouff, Gregory T. *The Soldiers' Revolution: Pennsylvanians in Arms and the Forging of Early American Identity*. University Park, Pa., 2004.

Lafaye, Jacques. *Quetzalcóatl and Guadalupe: The Formation of Mexican National Consciousness, 1531–1813*. Benjamin Keen, trans. Chicago, 1976.

Lehman, J. David. "The End of the Iroquois Mystique: The Oneida Land Cession Treaties of the 1780s." *William and Mary Quarterly* 3 ser., 47 (1990): 523–47. (WMQ)

Lender, Mark Edward, and James Kirby Martin. *Drinking in America: A History, 1620–1980*. Rev. ed. New York, 1987.

Lenig, Donald. "The Oneida Indians and Their Predecessors." *The History of Oneida County*. Utica, N.Y., 1977.

Levinson, David. "An Explanation for the Oneida-Colonist Alliance in the American Revolution." *Ethnohistory* 23 (1976) 265–89.

Locklear, Arlinda F. "The Oneida Land Claims: A Legal Overview." *Iroquois Land Claims*. Christopher Vecsey and William A. Starna, ed. Syracuse, N.Y., 1988.

Lossing, Benson J. *The Pictorial Field-Book of the Revolution, . . .* 2 vols. New York, 1852.

Lothrop, Samuel K. *Life of Samuel Kirkland*. Boston, 1847.

Loveland, Anne C. *Emblem of Liberty: The Image of Lafayette in the American Mind*. Baton Rouge, La., 1971.

Luzader, John, et al. *Decision on the Hudson: The Battles of Saratoga*. Rev. ed. Fort Washington, Pa., 2002.

———., et al. *Fort Stanwix*. Washington, D.C., 1976.

McLaughlin, William G. "Cherokee Anomie, 1794–1809: New Roles for Red Men, Red Women, and Black Slaves." *Uprooted Americans: Essays to Honor Oscar Handlin*. Richard L. Bushman et al., ed. Boston, 1979.

Malone, Dumas. *Jefferson and His Time, Vol. 6: The Sage of Monticello*. Boston, 1981.

Malone, Patrick M. *The Skulking Way of War: Technology and Tactics Among New England Indians*. Baltimore, 1991.

Mancall, Peter C. *Deadly Medicine: Indians and Alcohol in Early America*. Ithaca, N.Y., 1995.

———. *Valley of Opportunity: Economic Culture Along the Upper Susquehanna, 1700–1800*. Ithaca, N.Y., 1991.

Mann, Barbara Alice. *George Washington's War on Native America*. Westport, Conn., 2005.

Martin, Calvin. *Keepers of the Game: Indian-Animal Relationships and the Fur Trade.* Berkeley, Calif., 1978.

Martin, James Kirby. *Benedict Arnold, Revolutionary Hero: An American Warrior Reconsidered.* New York, 1997.

———, and Mark Edward Lender. *A Respectable Army: The Military Origins of the Republic, 1763–1789.* 2d ed. Wheeling, Ill., 2006.

Merrell, James H. *The Indians' New World: Catawbas and Their Neighbors from European Contact Through the Era of Removal.* Chapel Hill, N.C., 1989.

———. " 'Their Very Bones Shall Fight': The Catawba-Iroquois Wars." *Beyond the Covenant Chain: The Iroquois and Their Neighbors in Indian North America, 1600–1800.* Daniel K. Richter and James H. Merrell, ed. Syracuse, N.Y., 1987.

Mintz, Max M. *Seeds of Empire: The American Revolutionary Conquest of the Iroquois.* New York, 1999.

Morgan, Lewis H. *Ancient Society, or, Researches in the Lines of Human Progress from Savagery through Barbarism to Civilization.* New York, 1877.

———. *League of the Ho-De-No-Sau-Nee, or Iroquois.* Rochester, N.Y., 1851.

Nash, Gary B. *The Unknown American Revolution: The Unruly Birth of Democracy and the Struggle to Create America.* New York, 2005.

Norton, Thomas Eliot. *The Fur Trade in Colonial New York, 1686–1776.* Madison, Wisc., 1974.

O'Brien, Thomas F. *The Revolutionary Mission: American Enterprise in Latin America, 1900–1945.* New York, 1996.

O'Toole, Fintan. *White Savage: William Johnson and the Invention of America.* New York, 2005.

Pratt, Peter P. *Archaeology of the Oneida Iroquois.* Vol. 1. Rindge, N.H., 1976.

Purcell, Sarah J. *Sealed with Blood: War, Sacrifice, and Memory in Revolutionary America.* Philadelphia, 2002.

Quain, B. H. "The Iroquois." *Cooperation and Competition Among Primitive Peoples.* Margaret Mead, ed. New York, 1937.

Randle, Martha C. "Iroquois Women, Then and Now." *Bureau of American Ethnology Bulletin,* no. 149. William N. Fenton, ed. Washington, D.C., 1951.

Reed, John F. "Indians at Valley Forge." *The Valley Forge Journal* 3 (1986): 26–32.

Richards, Cara E. "Matriarchy or Mistake: The Role of Iroquois Women Through Time." *Cultural Stability and Cultural Change: Proceedings of the 1957 Annual Meeting of the American Ethnology Society.* Verne F. Ray, ed. Seattle, Wash., 1957.

———. *The Oneida People.* Phoenix, Ariz., 1974.

Richter, Daniel K. *Facing East from Indian Country: A Native History of Early America.* Cambridge, Mass., 2001.

———. *The Ordeal of the Longhouse: The Peoples of the Iroquois League in the Era of European Colonization.* Chapel Hill, N.C., 1992.

Roberts, Ellis Henry. *The Battle of Oriskany: Its Place in History.* Utica, N.Y., 1877.

Roberts, Octavia. *With Lafayette in America.* Boston, 1919.

Ronda, James P. "Reverend Samuel Kirkland and the Oneida Indians." *The Oneida Indian Experience: Two Perspectives.* Jack Campisi and Laurence M. Hauptman, ed. Syracuse, N.Y., 1988.

———., and James Axtell, ed. *Indian Missions: A Critical Bibliography*. Bloomington, Ind., 1978.

Roof, Garret L. *Colonel John Brown, His Services in the Revolutionary War, the Battle of Stone Arabia*. Utica, N.Y., 1884.

Schaaf, Gregory. *Wampum Belts & Peace Trees: George Morgan, Native Americans, and Revolutionary Diplomacy*. Golden, Colo., 1990.

Scott, John Albert. *Fort Stanwix (Fort Schuyler) and Oriskany*. . . . Rome, N.Y., 1927.

Shimony, Annemarie Anrod. *Conservatism Among the Iroquois at the Six Nations Reserve*. New Haven, Conn., 1961.

Shoemaker, Nancy. *A Strange Likeness: Becoming Red and White in Eighteenth-Century America*. New York, 2004.

Shy, John. *A People Numerous and Armed: Reflections on the Military Struggle for American Independence*. New York, 1976.

Snow, Dean R. *The Iroquois*. Malden, Mass., 1994.

Starkey, Armstrong. *European and Native American Warfare, 1675–1815*. Norman, Okla., 1998.

Steele, Ian K. *Warpaths: Invasions of North America*. New York, 1994.

Stone, William L. *Life of Joseph Brant—Thayendanegea, Including the Border Wars of the American Revolution*, . . . 2 vols. New York, 1838.

Taylor, Alan. *The Divided Ground: Indians, Settlers, and the Northern Borderland of the American Revolution*. New York, 2006.

Thomas, Howard. *Marinus Willett, Soldier-Patriot, 1740–1830*. Prospect, N.Y., 1954.

Todorov, Tzvetan. *The Conquest of America: The Question of the Other*. Richard Howard, trans. New York, 1984.

Tower, Charlemagne. *The Marquis de La Fayette in the American Revolution*, . . . 2 vols. Philadelphia, 1895.

Tracy, William. *Notices of Men and Events, Connected with the Early History of Oneida County*. Utica, N.Y., 1838.

Trelease, Allen W. *Indian Affairs in Colonial New York: The Seventeenth Century*. Ithaca, N.Y., 1960.

Trussell, John B. B., Jr. *Birthplace of an Army: A Study of the Valley Forge Encampment*. Harrisburg, Pa., 1976.

Wallace, Anthony F. C. *The Death and Rebirth of the Seneca*. New York, 1971.

———. "The Origins of Iroquois Neutrality: The Grand Settlement of 1701." *Pennsylvania History* 24 (1957): 223–35.

Ward, Christopher. *The War of the Revolution*. John Richard Alden, ed. 2 vols. New York, 1952.

Watt, Gavin K. *Rebellion in the Mohawk Valley: The St. Leger Expedition of 1777*. Toronto, Ontario, 2002.

Wheeler, Rachael. "Women and Christian Practice in a Mahican Village." *Religion and American Culture* 13 (2003): 27–67.

White, Richard. *The Middle Ground: Indians, Empires, and Republics in the Great Lakes Region, 1650–1815*. New York, 1991.

Willcox, William B. "The Comic Opera Battle that Made a General." *Pennsylvania History* 13 (1946): 265–73.

Williams, Glen F. *Year of the Hangman: George Washington's Campaign Against the Iroquois.* Yardley, Pa., 2005.

Winiarski, Douglas. "Native American Popular Religion in New England's Old Colony, 1670–1770." *Religion and American Culture* 15 (2005): 147–86.

Wolf, Eric R. *Europe and the People Without History.* Berkeley, Calif., 1982.

Wonderley, Anthony. *Oneida Iroquois Folklore, Myth, and History: New York Oral Narrative from the Notes of H. E. Allen and Others.* Syracuse, N.Y., 2004.

Wood, Gordon S. *The Radicalism of the American Revolution.* New York, 1992.

Wyss, Hilary E. *Writing Indians: Literacy, Christianity, and Native Community in Early America.* Amherst, Mass., 2000.

DISSERTATIONS AND PAPERS

Boyle, Joseph Lee. "Indians at Valley Forge." Draft paper, Feb. 1995.

Campisi, Jack. "Ethnic Identity and Boundary Maintenance in Three Oneida Communities." Ph.D. diss., State University of New York at Albany, 1974.

Green, Gretchen Lynn. "A New People in an Age of War: The Kahnawake Iroquois, 1667–1760." Ph.D. diss., College of William and Mary, 1991.

Hinman, Marjory B. "Onaquaga: An Early Missionary Outpost." Paper presented to the Old Onaquaga Historical Society, 1968.

Parmenter, Jon William. "At the Wood's Edge: Iroquois Foreign Relations, 1727–1768." Ph.D. diss., University of Michigan, 1999.

Patrick, Christine Sternberg. "The Life and Times of Samuel Kirkland, 1741–1808: Missionary to the Oneida Indians, American Patriot, and the Founder of Hamilton College." Ph.D. diss., State University of New York at Buffalo, 1993.

Stevens, Paul Lawrence. "His Majesty's 'Savage' Allies: British Policy and the Northern Indians During the Revolutionary War." Ph.D. diss., State University of New York at Buffalo, 1984.

Tiro, Karim Michel. "The People of the Standing Stone: The Oneida Indian Nation from Revolution through Removal, 1765–1840." Ph.D. diss., University of Pennsylvania, 1999.

Van Dycke, J. North. Draft Paper on Cherry Valley, New York, in the Revolution. Presented to the Cherry Valley Historical Association, undated.

Venables, Robert William. "Tryon County, 1775–1783: A Frontier in Revolution." Ph.D. diss., Vanderbilt University, 1967.

Wonderley, Anthony. "An Oneida Community in 1780: Study of an Inventory of Iroquois Property Losses During the Revolutionary War." Draft paper, March 1998.

——. "The Oneidas and the Battle of Oriskany." Draft paper, Aug. 1994.

——. "A Sketch of the Oneidas in the Revolutionary War (circa 1770–1783)." Draft paper, Jan. 1995.

ACKNOWLEDGMENTS

We came upon the story of the Oneida Indians in the American Revolution, as is sometimes the case, unintentionally. Niels Holch, an attorney in Washington, D.C., and Joe Glatthaar's close friend going back to their college days, was at the time the chief of staff for the Oneida Indian Nation of New York. The Oneidas wanted a history of their participation and experiences in the Revolution. Since Joe, a specialist in American military history, was the only historian Niels knew, he asked him to take on the work.

As the project developed, Joe asked another close friend, historian James Kirby Martin, well known for his scholarship on the Revolutionary era, to join him in producing this study. Jim has written about the life of Benedict Arnold, whose martial adventures included contact with the Mohawk Valley region and the Oneida Indians. He has also co-edited for publication the wartime journal of Joseph Bloomfield, a young Continental Army officer from New Jersey. Bloomfield made valuable observations about the Oneidas and other Iroquois Indians while stationed in the Mohawk Valley during the early years of the Revolutionary War.

What we uncovered in our research was an incredible saga of service and sacrifice that ended tragically for the Oneidas. Rather than trying to embellish the harsh realities with some sort of artificial theoretical analysis, we committed ourselves to preparing a swift-moving narrative. We wanted to involve readers at both an intellectual and an emotional level, and we felt that a strong narrative pulse would best accomplish that objective. We likewise sought to present the participants as the real people they were, who also deserved to have their story told as impartially as possible.

At the same time, we worked to present the much-neglected Indian side of historical reality, so long stripped from our national memory, while also investigating the constantly changing patterns of interaction among Indians and European Americans. The challenges faced by the Oneidas, as well as their chosen remedies, lie at the heart of this incredible story; and their relations with fellow Indians, the British, the rebels, and the Tories, and their struggle between neutrality and becoming involved in the war as patriot allies, heighten the grand drama of their experiences. In the end, our hope is that the likes of Good Peter, Han Yerry, Skenandoah, and Grasshopper, among many other Oneidas, will achieve their deserved place as significant historical figures, certainly as worthy of attention as their famous loyalist antagonist, the Mohawk Joseph Brant.

Over the course of completing this volume, we have incurred many debts, which we gladly acknowledge here with grateful thanks. At the Oneida Indian Nation of New York, Anthony Wonderley aided us in developing the project, providing research assistance and critiquing an early version of the manuscript. Cynthia Copeland, Pam Fahey, and Steve McSloy gave support of various kinds during the research phase. Steve also offered comments on the last section, which carries the story to contemporary times. Gloria Halbritter, an Oneida from the Wolf Clan, read an early version of the manuscript and supplied valuable remarks. Her son, Ray Halbritter, the Oneida Nation Representative, ensured that the Nation provided full support to our efforts. At no time, however, did anyone in the Nation try to influence the content of this book. The presentation, content, and conclusions are strictly those of the authors, for which we accept full responsibility.

Many archivists gave generously of their time along the way. Among them, several went above and beyond the call of duty. Frank K. Lorenz at Hamilton College was exceedingly hospitable in facilitating research on Samuel Kirkland. At the Cayuga Museum, William Merritt preserved a spirit of cooperation amid great summer heat and no air-conditioning. William Evans and James Folts at the New York State Archives in Albany shared their vast knowledge of sources, besides materials from the collections. At Fort Stanwix, Anthony Tommel gave a thorough tour and assisted with the examination of sources there. Lee Boyle, historian at the Valley Forge National Military Park, was exceedingly helpful with research and kept up with the project for years afterward.

Others provided ideas and various items of assistance. Paul Stevens, who wrote a mammoth dissertation on British-Indian allies during the Revolutionary War, helped obtain a typescript copy of a George Morgan Letterbook, which was missing from the Pennsylvania Museum and Archives. Marion J. Cornelia of the Cherry Valley Historical Society offered background information on Thomas Spencer, and Edward T. Addison alerted us to the Oneida graves at St. Peter's Lutheran Church near the Barren Hill Battlefield. Eric Bloomfield, the Assistant Curator for Education, confirmed our suspicions about the use of black holes at Old Fort Niagara and shared vivid details about the fort and its operation during colonial and Revolutionary times. Historian J. Frederick Fausz kindly shared information about patterns of fighting, weapons, and warfare. Jeffrey L. Ward did a masterful job in preparing the maps for this book, and Sarah A. Jones generously helped with photographic work. Attorneys Niels Holch, Michael R. Smith, and Joseph T. Gagnon provided essential commentary about modern litigation involving the Oneidas and other Native American groups.

Several individuals read the manuscript in various stages of its development. Historian Laurence M. Hauptman scrutinized an initial draft and generated extensive comments. Through his careful reading and correspondence as questions arose, the late anthropologist William N. Fenton, the dean of Iroquois studies, shared his massive knowledge as well as ideas, insights, and corrections. Our longtime friends John Shy and Edward M. "Mac" Coffman read the manuscript and provided incisive suggestions and priceless encouragement. At the University of Houston, three historians were particularly helpful. Thomas O'Brien read the manuscript and recommended readings that helped place our questions about Indians and their world in a broader context. Susan Kellogg directed us to comparative literature that enhanced our understanding of the Oneidas. Gerald J. Goodwin, now retired, willingly shared his extensive knowledge of early American religious issues.

Joe Glatthaar would particularly like to thank his parents, Joseph B. and Kathleen M. Glatthaar, who offered all sorts of support during this professional journey and who also housed him during research in New York. Joe's brother, Michael Glatthaar, also provided lodging during research trips to New York City. Danielle Rhoades, Joe's daughter, never grumbled when work on the project prevented him from giving her the quality time she deserved. The same is true for his wife, Jacqueline Hagan, who has an uncanny knack for injecting a healthy dose of thrill into everyday life. Over the course of many years, Joe's great friend John Moretta listened patiently to one-sided conversations about the Oneidas during their daily runs. James H. Jones, another valued friend, engaged in discussions and provided encouragement and support throughout the course of the project. Lastly, Joe would like to thank another esteemed friend, Niels Holch, who drew him into this project and has been an unyielding supporter throughout its lengthy course. During Joe's many visits to Washington, D.C., Niels and his wife, Barbara, along with Charlie, Ben, and Jack Goodman, offered lodging and made him feel like family. Anyone who knows Niels realizes what a special person he is. This dedication is a small acknowledgment for his help and friendship.

Jim Martin would like to recognize his good friend, Indian activist and Cherokee native Jonathan Hook, for sage advice; graduate students Phillip Sinitiere, Elizabeth Hoskins, and Jennifer Ellis for helpful comments about various portions of the manuscript; daughter Sarah-Marie Martin and her husband Nicholas Brophy for lodging and great historical conversations during his travels to New York City; and brother Frederick W. Martin for his generosity and especially for loaning him a stylish new Mercedes-Benz to motor through Oneida country in central New York. Jim remains grateful to his wife, Karen W. Martin, daughter Darcy Martin Gagnon and her husband Joe Gagnon, and daughter Joelle Martin Hussey and her husband Lloyd Hussey, for their patience, kindness, and love. Jim would also like to acknowledge the immensity of his debt to his undergraduate mentor, Wilson J. Hoffman, one of the persons to whom this book is dedicated. Throughout his career as a professor at Hiram College, Wil made history come alive for his students as only a truly talented teacher-scholar can. Wil continues to be an inspiration to this very day.

Finally, at Hill and Wang, we have received the absolute highest level of quality support and assistance. We especially would like to acknowledge the masterful work of Thomas LeBien, whose care and concern for this volume has been phenomenal. No publisher or editor is more capable of producing meaningful books. We are also grateful to assistant editor June Kim, who has helped in so many ways to bring this study to fruition, as well as to production editors Don McConnell and Jane Elias and book designers Aaron Artessa and Jonathan Lippincott. We consider ourselves the most fortunate of authors to have had the privilege of working with so many talented persons at Hill and Wang.

INDEX

Page numbers in *italics* refer to maps.